AF791692

Ṛta: The Cosmic Order

Ṛta: The Cosmic Order

Edited by
Madhu Khanna

D.K. Printworld (P) Ltd.
New Delhi

in association with

Indira Gandhi National Centre for the Arts
New Delhi

Cataloging in Publication Data — DK

Ṛta : the cosmic order /edited by Madhu Khanna.
Includes bibliographical references.
Includes index.

1. Cosmology. 2. Hindu cosmology. 3. Civilization, Hindu. 4. Cosmology in art. 5. Philosophy, Hindu. I. Khanna, Madhu.

ISBN 81-246-0252-2

First Published in India in 2004

© Indira Gandhi National Centre for the Arts, New Delhi.

All rights reserved. No part of this publication may be reproduced or transmitted in any form or by any means, electronic or mechanical, including photocopying, recording, or any information storage or retrieval system, without prior written permission of both the copyright owner, indicated above, and the publisher.

The views expressed in this volume are those of Participants, and are not necessarily those of Editor and Publishers.

First Published in India by:
D.K. Printworld (P) Ltd.
Regd. office : *'Sri Kunj'*, F-52, Bali Nagar, New Delhi - 110 015
Phones : (011) 545-3975; 546-6019; *Fax* : (011) 546-5926
E-mail: dkprintworld@vsnl.net *Web*: www.dkprintworld.com

in Association with:
Indira Gandhi National Centre for the Arts
Central Vista Mess, Janapath, New Delhi - 110 001

Printed in India by: D.K. Printworld (P) Ltd., New Delhi - 110 015

Respectfully dedicated to

Dr. Kapila Vatsyayan

who has been the spirit and guiding force
behind such inter-disciplinary explorations
in fundamental concepts of Indian Culture

Foreword

WE feel immensely pleased placing in the hands of the scholars of Indian culture, this unique collection of erudite papers on '*Ṛta*', the most fundamental and at the same time the most ancient concept of Indian thought. Present anthology is an outcome of an international seminar accompanied by an exhibition on the same subject, arranged by our Centre as far back as 1996. It is a matter of regret that due to certain unavoidable circumstances the papers could not have been published earlier.

The concept of *Ṛta* is the very basis of Indian philosophical tradition. No one can understand the basic spirit of Indian philosophy and its gradual development without comprehending the concept of *Ṛta*. It is a fundamental principle which lies not only behind the 'Being' of this universe but also the one which sustains the universe, governs and runs it. Yet, it is not a static and a blind principle but a principle with full kinetic force which has its own dynamics. Derived from the root *ṛ* = 'to go', 'to move', it originally means 'movement' or 'dynamism' necessary to run this universe which in itself is *jagat*, i.e. 'constantly moving' (from the root *gam*).

The Vedic concept of '*dharman*' (n.gender; used mostly in plural as *dharmāṇi*, cf. RVI. 22.18, X.90.16) i.e. the fundamental laws as the sustainer of the universe is well established in the Ṛgveda and they are conceived as originating from the *Ṛta*. Later (in the Smṛtis) the word *dharmaḥ* is brought into association with human society and is understood as those fundamental tenets which hold or sustain the human society in and organized manner (e.g. non-violence, truth etc.). *Dharma* is thus nothing else but this-worldly manisfestation of the all-pervading, universal *Ṛta*. Since Dharma corresponds to and is a part of *Ṛta,* its practice leads to the ultimate goal of human being, the *niḥśreyas* — a state which is final, permanent and unchangeable (*satyam*) and any activity against the principle of *Ṛta* is '*Anṛta*' and brings about spiritual fall. Therefore even the divine forces perpetually strive to uphold the tenets of *Ṛta* and if somebody acts blatently against *Ṛta* disturbing the harmony of the universe, a divine voice (*ākāśavāṇī*) emanating from higher heavens warns the humans on the earth.

The concept of *Saṁskāra* is also closely related to the concept of *Ṛta*. The word *Saṁskāra* basically and originally means 'to put together' 'to join' or 'to make compatible to'. With the help of the sixteen *Saṁskāras* performed on the body of a person one strives to make the actions, behaviour and thinking of a person correspond to the universal *Ṛta*, so that he may act according to this universal law and be faithful towards it.

The law of *Karman* is the nucleus of all Indian religious thought. The whole of Indian philosophy revolves around it. *Karmans* get matured in the form of good or bad results (*vipāka*) and ultimately lead to higher or lower births giving rise to an almost unending cycle of births and deaths (*saṁsāra*). This law is not enforced or executed by any divine force, or by God; it is subservient to the law of *Ṛta*, which takes care of it.

There are many more such aspects of the concept of *Ṛta* which are dealt with in the papers of this volume in a most scholarly and convincing manner which would help the reader to grasp this highly abstract idea of *Ṛta* in its multifaceted function. Dr. Madhu Khanna, the scholarly Editor of this volume, has beautifully summarized the principal theses of all these articles along with her expert and scholarly comments on them. It was not an easy task, as everybody would agree, to grasp the basic premises of some of the highly philosophical speculations and technical deliberations but she has been wonderfully successful in comprehending the quintessence of all such articles in a commendable manner. Further, she has embellished the work with a long and brilliant exposition of the concept of *Ṛta*. The energy and effort that she has invested in this work in giving it the present magnificent shape is highly laudable. I congratulate her for having been exceptionally successful in editing this volume in a most scholarly manner.

We also express our deep gratitude to all the scholars who participated in the above-noted seminar, made this academic venture an enormous success and who later also sent in their revised papers to be included in this volume.

The Division has decided to dedicate this volume to Dr. Kapila Vatsyayan who raised this Centre from a scratch, was its Member Secretary/Academic Director for 13 long years, prepared blue prints of its academic activities and guided these activities all through those years in a diligent and dignified manner winning international recognition for the Institution. It was she under whose regime this Conference was organized and it was again she who has always been very keen to see this volume out.

We express our heartfelt thanks to Dr. L.M. Singhvi, President of the IGNCA Trust for his generous support and guidance as well as to the present Member Secretary, Prof. I.N. Choudhury, who has all along taken keen interest in the publication of this volume and has enriched it with his valuable suggestions at every stage.

New Delhi
October 15, 2003

— Prof. G.C. Tripathi
Head of the Kalākośa Division

Contents

PART III

ṚTA: MANIFESTATION IN THE ARTS

Introduction

Madhu Khanna

THE anthology of seminar papers in this volume on the theme *Ṛta: Cosmic Order and Chaos* is a culmination of an interdisciplinary cross-cultural dialogue initiated by the Indira Gandhi National Centre for the Arts on the fundamental categories of civilization that cut across diverse cultures, faiths, disciplines, and social strata. The first seminar in the series in 1986 on the theme *Kham* explored the concept of "Space," ancient and modern, and its concrete manifestation in the arts, architecture, music and performance. This was followed by a seminar on *Kāla* or "Time" in 1990, centered on a multidisciplinary discourse on the notions of time-across cultures. In 1992-93, the centre explored the theme of the Five Elements/Prakṛti, in a series of seminars, through the perspective of modern science, textual and oral traditions and in the arts. These endeavours were followed by the seminar on Man, Mind and Mask in 1998 which focused on the ancient and contemporary notions of persona/ self, as reflected in the mask traditions of different cultures. The notion on Space, Time, the Five Elements, and Mask/Persona reflect the speculative thoughts and structures of imagination of ancient civilizations that cut across cultures and periods of history. One of the insights that emerged from these deliberations was that the more fundamental the concept the greater its possibility of diverse interpretation.

The seminar on Ṛta : Cosmic Order and Chaos brought together physicists, philosophers, social scientists, historians, anthropologists, scholars of religion architects, poets, and art historians. The multi-layeredness of meanings of *ṛta* were discussed at length and the invariable-variability of the concept of *ṛta* provided a fertile source for dialogue between disciplines. Like the previous years, the seminar was complemented by an exhibition on *Ṛta-Ṛtu*[1]; Cosmic Order and Cycle of Seasons which gave a cross-cultural interdisciplinary perspective on the manifestation of *ṛta* in nature, human life-cycle, in architecture, in the realm of moral order and its expression in the cycle of seasons, *ṛtu*.

---

1. See Exhibition Catalogue: Madhu Khanna, (ed.), *Rta-Ritu: An exhibition on Cosmic Order and Cycle of Seasons*, Delhi, IGNCA, 1996.

Ṛta : concept

The concept of *ṛta* is traceable to the earliest layers of human civilization. The polysemantic Sanskrit term *ṛta*, occurs for the first time in the *Ṛgveda* (10,98; 4,23,9-12; 10-190) and is found in nearly all its declensions and inflexions. *Ṛta* is a multifaceted concept linked to all the significant concepts in the Vedas. In its most basic sense, *ṛta* is the inflexible law or harmony underlying the natural phenomenon. *Ṛta*, universal order, is all-pervasive and same at all levels and the universe is the expression of this order. Parallel concepts of harmony and order are found in all the ancient civilizations of the world. Chinese culture describes it as the principle of Tao, or the mystical path of the union of the male and female principles; the Islamic world as the principle of Haqq, the merciful decree of divine; Greco-Roman culture as Logos, the universal form of reason, and the Tibetan tradition as Dharma, the law of righteousness. In all cultures, the concept is unanimously accepted as a blue-print of cosmic harmony. However, the concept is *ṛta* is unique to India in that an all-inclusive principle of cosmic and human order pervades all the aspects of life, the natural world, the human world, the social world of everyday community life, the moral world as also the realm of arts, creativity, architecture, and it is this principle which shapes the pattern of the cycle of life in traditional cosmocentric societies.

The sphere of *ṛta* is both physical, metaphysical and ethical. *Ṛta* is closely related to the dynamism of manifested universe. In the Vedic world-view the universe functions in accordance with the inflexible law, intrinsic to nature's processes. Nature, as we cognize it, is not based on a haphazard conglomeration of events, but functions on a well defined orderly principle — a law unto itself. The term *ṛta* signifies, at its most elemental level, the course of the natural world perceived through its rhythms, time sequences, seasons, and cyclic transformations and the orderly balance and harmony in nature. It refers to three basic elements; "activity, order, and law". *Ṛta* is the act whereby the transcendent principle, the unmanifest, becomes referential to the senses, as the manifested universe. Hence, "heaven and earth exist in close unison in the womb of *ṛta*" (*Ṛgveda*, X.65.8b). *Ṛta*, then is the one, single unitary law that undergirths the cosmos.

Ṛta in the Veda is closely aligned to the principle of *satya* or inherent beingness, or inner truth, that sustains *ṛta* like a hub of a wheel. *Satya* or truth is the foundation of *ṛta*. *Ṛta* is the structure and matrix of reality, *satya*, its truth or substance which characterizes the content of reality. It is on account of these two principles that the universe is not amorphous and inconsistent but a harmonious ordered whole. *Ṛta* and *satya* are two facets of the principle of order governing the outer cosmos and our inner reality. *Satya* is that which mirrors the truth which lies hidden but becomes visible through the functioning of *ṛta*. *Ṛta* and *satya* are therefore composite concepts that bridge the macrocosmic level of order to the human and social levels of life.

At the socio-ethical level, humans align themselves to this cosmic order on the human plane by adhering to a moral order expressed through norms of truth, equality and justice. At the socio-religious level, in the Vedic world-view humans recall the dynamics of *ṛta* through their participation in the performance of the sacrificial ritual (*yajña*) which is based on the law of give-and-take, of reciprocal balance, and harmony between the human and divine. The sacrificial rite is a human attempt to recapture and re-enact the macrocosmic drama of creation, held firm by the principle of *ṛta*. The rite of *yajña* translates in human terms the dynamics of cosmic order.

Ṛta is based on the fundamental unity of all spheres — the earthly and the transcendental. While *Ṛta* denotes cosmic order, its opposite manifestation is agitation, disorder or chaos (*anṛta/saṁkṣobha*). These two mutually dependent creative principles of manifestation form two sides of a cosmic process which is continuous and perpetual. The equilibrium between the two creates organizations, order and harmony in the universe, their imbalance, disorder and disharmony.

Emerging from this wide ranging concept of *ṛta* this seminar explored the theme of Cosmic Order and Chaos in different cultures through a multidisciplinary approach. The anthology reconstructs the diverse idea of *ṛta* according to which this singular principle or order pervades the working of the physical universe, the natural world and, in the social dimension, the realm of the arts, architecture, religion and everyday community life. The human being in ancient times lived in the intersection of this multiple axes of cosmic order. So much so, that in every ancient civilization, from ancient Greece in the West to China in South, the construction of sacred ritual practices and the celebratory occasions are ways to mirror a larger cosmic order as is understood by that people.

I

The twenty-four papers presented here analyse this multifaceted concept of *ṛta*. The multiple interpretations of the ancient concept of *ṛta*, cover as diverse disciplines as philosophy and ancient speculative thought, religious and theological discourse on the meaning of this multivalent term, the parallel between this ancient concept and the emerging new sciences, the social, cultural and anthropological dimensions, and the manifestations of this concept in aesthetics and art expression.

The seven essays in the first section explore the notion of order in ancient speculative thought — Hindu, Chinese and Islamic. The multidimensional concept of *ṛta* may not be looked upon as an antique relic of the past with no contemporary relevance. While discussing the multiple meanings given to the concept of *ṛta* in Vedic culture, such as *satya*, *dharma*, law, deity, beauty, *yajña*, *karma* and *dīkṣā*, Swami Jitatmananda argues that the concept needs to be looked upon more constructively as a parallel category, alongside those of the emergent views of modern science. His paper is inspired by a new orientation, a search for universality between the ancient ideas on *ṛta* and the new sciences. This new orientation looks upon religion and the newly emergent science as two mutually inclusive disciplines that has the potential to create a new order of civilization.

Vidya Niwas Mishra surveys the multiple meanings of *ṛta* beginning from the Vedas down to its modern interpretations in the writing of Aurobindo, Coomarswamy, K.C. Chattopadhyay and P.V. Kane. S. Mukhopadhyay traces the meanings of the cognate term *asa* from the Avesta, the ancient Aryans' basic text of the Zoroastrian faith and shows the similarity of its meaning with *ṛta*. His reading of the word further translates the spiritual import of the word to the living tradition of the Parsis who consider Asoi to mean bodily purity. These wide-ranging meanings allude to the concurrent perspectives that can be applied to this ancient concept.

According to the *Ṛgveda* the cosmic *ṛta* is maintained and upheld by the reinforcement of the *yajña*, or performance of sacrificial ritual. Humans and gods maintain the universe through perpetual *yajña*. This process of interconnectivity and correspondence is taken up by Ravi Ravindran who gives an interpretation on the relationship of *yajña* and *dharma* based on the principle of reciprocale exchange between the human and the divine in the microcosm.

The two papers by scientists convey that the ancient concept of *ṛta* may be read into the theories of order supported by modern science. Ancient cosmologies, in India, China, and the Greco-Roman world, conceive chaos and order as mutually defining polarities stretching between good and evil. However, both Mathematics and Physics in the twentieth century, made chaos as a synonym for the principle of order inherent in creation, demonstrating that chaotic systems veil an inner order. The term chaos, therefore, has assumed another well-defined meaning that certain chaotic systems are not so chaotic at all. If one were to trace the trajectory of a chaotic regime we get a fractal, that is, a set of points which constitute a pattern. When magnified, these points mirror the original pattern. This goes to show that what appears to be irregular actually has, some well defined regularities.

The theme of order has played a significant role in the evolution of the natural sciences. The supreme law that physical laws are a manifestation of order and are universal is a necessary presupposition of all sciences. It is known that large scale glaciers and super- clusters of galaxies are arise out of tiny fluctuations in the primal distribution of matter at the time of Big Bang several billion years ago. Gravity appears to be the fountainhead of generating the cosmic order. Ranging from the smallest atom to the largest galaxies nothing is ever at rest in the universe. Both the pattern and the organization of the structure of the universe is based on order. Varun Sahni's paper elaborates upon such levels of organization in the physical and galactic plane. The order of the world is procured through gravity which is the fountainhead of cosmic order. In nature and in human, order is "contained" through the clustering of system and sub-systems — the plants, the earth, the solar system, Milky Way Galaxy and a group of Galaxies. On the smaller scale, the most fundamental clustering is in the atom. They are connected to another as "super-clusters". Matter is recycled from generation to generation and this recycling of resources is an integral part of stellar life.

Order in our daily times and nature at large is easily recognized from the rhythms that govern our bodies and the natural world, the rhythm of time, the clock of life's evolution: evolving and growing extinct embracing incomprehensible sunspot cycles, the wandering volcanoes and ocean currents, expanding and contracting glaciers and melting of icicles. The most natural expression of rhythm is reflected in our daily experience of cyclical nature of time-diurnal, seasonal and bio-chemical. Modern research has proved that we have a complex system of 100 or more internal clocks clicking simultaneously that govern our heart beat, body temperature to reaction time and our memory. Each clock strikes its own cycle, creating its biological rhythms that help us adapt to our environment. The nuclear sub-system of microbiology is discussed by G.P. Talwar. Biorhythms and reproductive cycles in the human and animal life give a biologists view of order. By an analysis of molecular structure the author shows that order is the most fundamental requisite of molecular structure and proportion of hormones or enzymes. All our life processes are governed by rhythms. These rhythms are parallel to the rhythmic cycle of nature. These observations from modern science have close affinity to the way the concept of *ṛta* may be interpreted through the lens of modern science.

The vision of order in science of Islamic Culture Area is recaptured in A. Rehman's article. They are found at three levels — in cosmology, geography and biological system and in the correlation of natural order with the human system. The two orders the natural which is external and the spiritual, which is internal to man. Islamic culture used symbolism of numbers and the macro-micro correspondences, and order as being part of the hierarchies of the cosmos.

II

Essays in section II take the discourse further to embrace the social dimensions of order. The concept of *dharma* discussed so fervently in the narrative context in the *Mahābhārata* has its genesis in the Vedic *ṛta*. In Vedic times it is the notion of cosmic order that maintained the equilibrium between the psychic, social, moral and the cosmic. Later, the more comprehensive term *dharma* gained currency and absorbed the multiple shades of meaning given to the concept of *ṛta*. It is essentially the human search for order in the social, moral and ethical spheres that led to the consolidation of the notion of *dharma* in ancient India. The varieties of notion of *dharma* — *sva-dharma*, *varṇāśrama-dharma*, *loka-dharma, deśa-dharma* or *jāti-dharma* provided the strategies to equip, organize and control norms of social, ethical and moral order.

The word *dharma* gained popularity in the epics and served to retain the full meaning of *ṛta*, as also, acquired a new found significance in the *Mahābhārata* where *dharma* becomes the very foundation of morality. In the code of *dharma*-ethics, there is a balance between "fact" and "value" and *dharma* stands for both a virtue and a moral principle that is adhered to for the collective good. A moral principle that does not represent the collective good of all is to be dispensed with. The notion of *dharma* is relative to the situation. Even though the notion of *dharma* is absolute, and fixed in essence, its adherence in day-to-day life is relative to the given situation, and, therefore a wide varieties of *dharma*.

All the seven essays in this section explore the notion of moral order that sustain societal ethos, and political order that ensure equality, justice and harmony in society. These interdisciplinary essays span a variety of disciplines from religion, oral-narrative, anthropology to Gandhian perspectives. Arindam Chakrabarti discusses at length about the Vedic metaphysics of food and the moral principles that sustain the inseparable relationship of the eater and the eaten. The social ethos of food is drawn from the metaphysical principle: "The food as God preserves those who give food to the hungry but eats up those who eat without giving". This cosmology of eating must give way to the ethos of eating. It is our "duty" to give then eat. To eat without offering "amount to theft"! A food consumed must acknowledge the "give-and-take with nature". One who violates the moral order of eating does not maintain the natural order of food production and the value of sharing food with all the lessor creature of the earth as a daily duty. In sharp contrast to this philosophy of food, of sharing and sustaining environment, the author draws a parallel to contemporary consumerism. The comparative exercise is to show the unethical values of modern society with referene to food. Taking this reasoning further, the author celebrates the unity of the eater and the eaten as expressions of ecstatic consciousness.

Chaturvedi Badrinath takes us into an enquiry on order and disorder, truth and untruth as reflected in the *Mahābhārata*. Quoting fables and stories that invariably take the shape of long dialogues on *dharma* and truth from this great epic, that proves the significance as also the relative nature of *dharma*. The most significant lesson of the *Mahābhārata* is the necessity of relationship of abstract knowledge with a pronounced personal ethics "the process of reading the *Mahābhārata* is the process of reading the self". Social order is dependent on the order in the individual self. If one's relationship with one's self is right then one's relationship with the others will also be right as the two are "inseparable" as the "personal" and "universal" are one. Social order, intrinsically personal in nature, holds the social, the individual and the cosmic into a interlacing web of unity. It is said that in post-Vedic India, the focus of *dharma* ordained injunctions "shift from acts to relationship. The *Mahābhārata* radically changes the meaning of *yajña, tapas, karma* and *tīrtha* and, in making them relational, gives them a deeply ethical meaning". In the *Mahābhārata* the "Vedic idea of *ṛta* is replaced by the idea of *dharma*". The *Mahābhārata* gives prominence to the system of social relationships, and by implication, an enquiry into the nature of the self is a way of maintaining *dharma* or as a universal human order with the gamut of its social relationships at all levels of life.

The next three papers in this section are by anthropologists who take us into the domain of oral history and sacred narratives. Aditya Malik discusses the religious construction of order in two narratives — The Sanskrit Pushkara Mahatmya linked with the pilgrimage site, Pushkar in Rajasthan; and a oral epic, the Bagaravat Bharat, in the Marwari language. Malik examines these two texts and the manner in which the "social and cultural configurations" are reflected through the medium of texts. Societies create order by means of texts and literary devices and then these texts get "lived" and enters the domain of public discourse in cultural and social situations. The text itself gets organized and arranged in relation to values that are embedded, albeit, what Ricocur calls "chronological and non-chronological" events. The text, thus has the ability to transform our perceptions and influence the actions. New plots are introduced to reorder the myth to justify the creation of the *puṣkara tīrtha*, pilgrimage site. The ordering that goes beyond the episodic level of the text at the collective level of social organization ultimately serves to legitimize the community. The tribal vision of order as expressed through the myths, ceremonies, symbols and patterns of living is taken up by B.N. Saraswati who gives a description of the fivefold order of the myths of origin of creation. Tribal cultures are ordered "as the honeycomb cells in a beehive". All are interdependent nature and ritual both are repetitive. He portrays the conflict between the old order and the new order. Ramjee Singh reminds us that Gandhi's philosophy is held together on the "changeless Truth" that holds together all that changes with the flux of time. Truth as god is to be sought through righteous conduct which is propelled by the universal law of moral causation. Life is supported by a higher law and this law may be equated to the Vedic *ṛta*.

The Chinese vision of order, expounded in the works of Confucius, forms the subject of Tan Chung's essay. The Chinese vision stems from an indisputable recognition of order in nature, the four seasons, the daily and fortnightly cycles of the waxing and waning of the moon. The Chinese farmer lived in harmony with the natural economy until crass commercialization broke the natural cycle of life. The Chinese society has been inspired by the profound philosophy of Confucius which was coded as early as the fifth century BC. The Chinese were guided by the notion of *Ren*, contained in the adage, "If you want to make yourself prosper, you make others prosper". Human relations must be based on the concept of Ren. Society is like "a human body and individuals are its cells". Confucius world-view unites individual ambition with societal aspiration, and aspires for synthesis between individual aspiration and orderly function of the human race. S.C. Malik argues for the primal mythic domain which is the universal. It is the sacred world-view and in-depth understanding of the universal order which is the basis of social order of alternate world-views of indigenous-non-Western cultures. These are more relevant today as they give a perspective on interconnectedness, simultaneity and multilayeredness of reality, of a seamless whole. This domain is expressed through myths. Contrasting this with the single-dimension of scientific and rational discourse which is the basis of the foundation of Western knowledge systems, as well as the neurological findings, he questions the limitations of their views "what is the relationship between language and communication to cultures which use only the left half of their brain leaving the intuitive and the synergetic untouched?" The oppositional duality between the two halves of the brain, two kinds of knowledges, each with a specific well-defined function has taken us further away from the non-verbal, non-logical and fluid methods of Eastern thought.

III

Do the arts share common principles of aesthetic order? What kind of order is established in the plan and arrangement of ancient cities and sacred spaces and icons? Is there a unifying framework of viewing diverse arts, such as the attempts made by Bharata in his *Nāṭyaśāstra*. How and by what means do the principles of compositional organization, such as symmetry, balance, rhythm, recurrence, etc., create systems of aesthetic order. Such questions were explored in the third session on Art and Aesthetics. The composition and semantics of order in various art forms in particular, compositional structures that work primarily with temporal category, such as music, poetry and performing arts and those that work with spatial category, such as architecture and paintings; and those that combine both, such as dance. In the context of this broad framework, this session was devoted to the elements and relationships that create the cognition of order in various temporal and spatial expressions of the arts.

J. McKim Malville draws parallels between the creation of sacred sites — ancient sites and pilgrimage sites and the evolutionary process of the Big Bang Cosmology. Malville, like Sahni (ante) describes the successive stages of order from the vast galaxies to the solar system to the planets. Similarly a billion years of biologicaol system also undergoes similar process of ordering. Comparing this scientific basis of self-organizing system to the first cities, he says that "like a galaxy, a star or fertilized egg, the city (has) its now geometry, proper and ordering systems". Ancient cities like Harappa, embody the geometry of the macrocosm suggesting a complex astronomy. However, in comparison to the sacred pilgrimage site, "the cosmic cities are masterpieces of city planning but are closed systems whereas a pilgrimage site is inextricably a self-organizing system is open and flexible".

Kamlesh Dutta Tripathi's paper takes us into the domain of aesthetic theory propounded in the *Nāṭyaśāstra*. *Pūrṇatā* and *ṛta* or cosmic order emerging from metaphysics are the basis of Indian aesthetics. *Nāṭya* is equated with the Vedic ritual of *yajña*. Dramatic presentation is an active act, which is identified with the creative play of creation. The performer is the primeval creator and the performance is equated with both the divine art of *yajña*, and the creation itself. The author compares the notions of *ṛta* and *pūrṇa* in Vedas to the concept of *sāmarasya* in the Āgamas and traces the similarity between the conceptual framework on which these ideas are based.

M.C. Joshi traces the symbolism of order in the 3-D *stūpa* structure of pre-Buddhist origin or circular plan with peaked or hemispherical elevation. Aśoka constructed 84,000 *stūpa*s. Once the *dhātu*s of Buddha. The author traces the relation of the *vāstika*, in the *Mahācaitya* of Bharhut and Sane — with the *skhambha* and *yūpa* of symbolism in the Vedas. The architectural arrangement of various elements of *stūpa* is "not only harmonious but aesthetically rhythmic, as the part of an order . . . compared with the Cosmic Body (*dharmakāya*) of Tathāgata". They were intended to represent the sacred mountain, Sumeru; cosmic form of Buddha.

Lokesh Chandra in his article "Meditative Architectonics and Borobudur" makes a distinction between the biological art of seeing (*paśyati*) and the psychological act of seeing with the spiritual eye (*darśana*) visualized by divine intuition. *Darśana* brings enlightenment or realization of the divine. The sense of psychological order is interwoven not only in the exterior architecture or Borobudur but in the meditational architecture of Borobudur, which triggers off an interior process of meditation. Architectural structures enhance meditation. The Buddhist texts speak of complex structure or planes of meditation *dhyāna-bhūmi*s, evolving a stages of meditation along with the cosmology and theory of doctrines illustrated through deities. The Borobudur synthesizes three meditations, (i) symbolism of Sumeru; (2) the bas-reliefs; (3) and their relation to Abhidharma. Architecture must convey the apperception of inner enlightenment. The biological act of "seeing" and the psychological experience of "knowing/envisioning" are complementary. These he concludes are "living images for meaningful meditation".

In similar vein, Devangana Desai traces the iconic scheme of the medieval Khajuraho temple (tenth century AD) built by the Chandella kings. She shows that the theology governing the temple architecture of Khajuraho is based on the theory of emanation of the deities. The author asks the pertinent questions: are the images/ sculptures on the exterior and interior of temples "randomly arranged on the walls? What, if any, is the order of their arrangement"? Desai expounds the fourfold scheme or order in the iconic arrangement of Khajuraho temples. They are (a) hierarchical order of cardinal and the Mahadeva Temple; (b) pairing and balancing of polarities as seen in the Lakṣmaṇa temple by balancing the heroic and yogic aspects; pairing of incompatible animals — lion and deer — in the penance grove of Pāravatī; (c) beauty and symmetry of sculptural figures; and (d) circumambulatory order of *pradakṣiṇā* in the placement of *pātraka* figures. Likewise, the *garbha* the planting divinities also encircle the Lakṣmaṇa and Veikuṇṭha temples. In these varied expressions of order, heierarchical, supplementary, and finally celestial and political the abstract notion of *ṛta* is easily traceable. The *stūpa* structure of pre-Buddhist origin or of the architecture of the Borobudur, or the monumental Hindu temple or the plan of the *śrī-cakra* — they all share a common aesthetic of order.

Madhu Khanna's paper on the "Dienergic Order of the Śrī-cakra" reflects upon the dynamic centripetal and centrifocal movement of the symbolism of the *śrī-cakra* based on the tripartite cosmological acts; creation, preservation and withdrawal. This creative play of *śakti* is embodied in the complex and subtle symbolism of the *śrī-cakra*. This hermeneutics of the *śrī-cakra* shares a common principle of aesthetic order with the medieval Hindu temple at Khajuraho and the great Buddhist monument at Borobudur at Java. The parallel between sacred monuments and the holistic iconic *yantra*s employed in Tāntric worship show the means whereby art expression employ the symbolic systems of compositional order in unison with a sophisticated metaphysical symbolism that create systems of aesthetic order.

Chandra Rajan analyses literary metaphors from Sanskrit poetry. *Ṛta* works through an interwoven network of relationships in the natural world. Rajan seeks to employ the concept of *ṛta-dharma* to decode Kālidāsa's poem, *Meghadūtam* — a lyrical monologue. The story shows how the protagonist, *yakṣa* is banished by Kubera from his ordered world. This violation disrupts the flow of life. The *yakṣa* and his beloved Alkā are both rendered rootless and alone. On the other hand, Megha, the cloud-messenger is an elemental being invested with qualities of conduct and responsible for life-sustaining waters. Megha is full of beneficial powers — cooling scorched soil, extinguishing forest fires and filling up streams. The rain-cloud is a medium through which the protagonist learns about the cycles of the ordered universe. Nature represented as Megha is a profound teacher bringing home to people the blessings of the sustaining waters of life. Thus, Megha, following its natural course in one way, is the personification of the Vedic *ṛta*; he is to adore Lord Śiva. There he watches Śiva in the form of Mahākāla, dancing the cosmic dance and becomes part of Śiva's blazing aura. The author shows how the ecological motif of *ṛta* is subtly intervowen in the symbol of rain-cloud. His selfless pilgrimage is the basis of an environmental ethic, a model for the modern man to follow. Those who do not respect *ṛta*, do so at their peril.

Keshav Malik takes us on reflective journey on the ironical paradox of order and chaos in the day-to-day plan of life. Physical nature knows no chaos, only laws; men, on the other hand, know only chaos. But the human psyche, is a fine receptor equipped with memory, burdened with order-chaos. A full maturation of human potentiality is "order". Most of our highs are lows, joys and sorrows, emerge from the heart and the order that permeates the heart. The greatest enemies of man are the ego-envy, spite and jealousy. The battle between the ego and the heart continues.

Premlata Sharma and Sathyanarayan both undertake a reading on the concept of *ṛta*, as it is expressed in the rhythm and intrinsic melody of creation. Premlata Sharma speaks of *ṛta* in music, expressed through intervals, melodic organization, temporary element (*tāla*) compositional and improvizational forms, emotive content (*rasa* and *bhāva*). R. Sathyanarayan interprets the concept of *ṛta* in terms of the modern physical science theory, statistical mechanics and information theory. The varied meanings of *ṛta* can be applied to *saṅgīta-śāstra*. A good musical piece aims at balance of several elements — melody, rhythm, texture, tempo, timbre have be interrelated in a semblance of unity to create a fine piece of music. Style in presentation is again dependent on grammar, syntax, idiom and rhetoric. Patterns in musical modes are embodied in what the author terms as *saṅgīta*. In music, *ṛta* manifests through the dynamic of melodic configuration; in dance through kinematics to create complex body postures — articulated in movement and stillness in dance. Dance is visual *yajña*, music is *nāda-yajña*. The various artistic manifestations of order facilitate self-transformation and self-recognition of inner order of the individual and the collective psyche.

Many interpretations of *ṛta* have been generated through contemporary analysis in this volume to show that this ancient concept is as old as it is new. The present anthology is a fine example of integrated studies. The credit for initiating such integral explorations goes to Dr. Kapila Vatsyayan, who over a decade stressed the need to study the fundamental categories of civilizations from the interdisciplinary perspective. The diverse essays attempts to show that there can be a synergistic convergence of discipline that do not effect each other but enhance the all inclusiveness of the concept. It is this interconnectivity of ideas weaving through disciplines that gives contemporary validity to the perennial category of *ṛta*.

PART I

ṚTA: NOTIONS OF COSMIC ORDER

1

Ṛta-Satyam — Modern Relevance

Swami Jitatmananda

Dimensions of Ṛta in the Vedic culture

THE two basic foundations of the Vedic culture are *satya* or truth, and *ṛta* or the universal moral order of goodness and justice, based on truth. The pursuit of truth and *ṛta* in the Vedic culture stands supreme. *Satyameva jayate na anṛtam* (truth alone triumphs and not that is not *ṛta*) says the *Muṇḍaka Upaniṣad*. Both are inextricably bound together. *Ṛta* literally means, 'the course of things' or 'established way of the world'. It stands for law and justice. The concept of *ṛta* was probably born in the mind of Vedic seers from the regular movements of sun, moon and stars, the alternatives of day and night, and of the regular succession of seasons. *Ṛta*, thus, denotes the universal order or the unalterable laws behind the running of the universe.

The *Nāsadīya Sūkta* of *Ṛgveda* (X.129-1-2) describes the birth of this universe from a state which was neither existence nor non-existence.

> There was then neither existence nor non-existence. There was neither sky nor the heaven which is beyond. What covered all these? Where was it and in whose shelter?
>
> There was no light between night and day; neither was there death, nor immortality. That non-vibrating one began to vibrate, other than it there was nothing.
>
> He from whom this creation arose, one knows not whether he made it, or did not make it? The highest seer in the highest heaven may know the secret or does not even He know?
>
> *nāsadāsīn no sadāsīt tadānīṁ* ।
> *nāsīd rajo no vyomā paro yat* ।। *ṚV*, 10.129.1

na mṛtyur āsīd amṛtam na tarhi
na rātryā ahna āsīt praketaḥ ।
ānīdavātaṁ svadhayā tadekaṁ
tasmāddhānyanna paraḥ kiṁ canāsa ।। *ṚV,* 10.129.2

yo asyādhyakṣaḥ parame vyoman
tso aṅga veda yadi vā na veda । *ṚV*, 10.129.7

As the Vedic seers intuitively discovered that this creation came from an indescribable nothing, they also discovered that, *ṛta* or order is the end of chaos. With the discovery of *ṛta*, the world was no more a chaos representing the blind fury of chance elements, but emerged as the working of a harmony and order. The universal is prior to the particular, and so the Vedic seers think that the idea of *ṛta* is eternal and existed before the manifestation of all phenomena. The dawn (*uṣā*) follows the path of *ṛta* and appears always after noctural darkness. The sun follows the path of *ṛta* and so does the moon. The Vedic hymns, therefore, praise them for their orderly movement in the line of *ṛta*. *Anṛta* is disorder or violation of the cosmic order. Therefore, it stands for falsehood, the opposite of truth. The right conduct is called a *vrata*. The god Varuṇa, the perfect follower of *ṛta*, is *dhṛtavrata* who steers unalterable moral laws of the universe. Varuṇa's character resembles that of the divine supreme ruler in a monotheistic world. A god, in Vedas, is *ṛtavān*, one who follows *ṛta*; a goddess is *ṛtāvari*, one who follows *ṛta*.

Varuṇa, who was first the keeper god of the cosmic physical order, gradually appears as the custodian-god of the moral order (*ṛtasya gopā*) and the punisher of sin. The Vedic prayers to the gods are, in many cases, for keeping humanity in the right path. "O Indra, lead us on the path of *ṛta*, on the right path over all evils", says the Vedic prayer to the Supreme God, Indra.

Ṛta, in its moral aspects, in human life is more pervasive than a mere knowledge of truth; it includes justice and goodness, and is almost synonymous with *dharma* as an ethical concept. *Ṛta* is, therefore, opposed to evil or *a-dharma*. The Vedas speak of *ṛta* as 'stern and fierce' (*ugram*). The wicked tread not the path of 'Eternal Law', says the *ṚgVeda* (IX.73.6). The demon Vṛtra, whom Indra destroys is the power of evil, who obstructs the working of *ṛta*. The *dāsa* and *dasyu* are 'followers of evil laws, inhuman (*anyavrata*, *amānuṣa*)'. (*ṚV*, X.22.8, VIII.70.11) In the offering of the Soma-libation, the sage speaks of Soma as "declaring law (*ṛta*) and splendid by law (*ṛta*). We must praise the 'eternal order' (*ṛtam samantaḥ*) and think in a straight way" (*ṚV*, X.67.2). Gods, therefore, are identified with *ṛta*. Bṛhaspati, who rides the awe-inspiring car of *ṛta* and destroys evil, is, thus, described:

"Having chased the wicked ones and darkness, thou mountest the effulgent car of *ṛta*."

Indra, the Supreme Ruler among Vedic gods, identifies himself with *ṛta* and speaks to his worshippers:

> "I exist, O Singer, look at me here. All that exists I surpass in grandeur. The commandments of Eternal Law (*ṛta*) make me mighty. When I rend, I rend the worlds asunder."
>
> — *ṚV*, VIII.100.3-4

On the moral plane *ṛta* leads to the truimph of good over evil. On the cosmic plane *ṛta* stands for the triumph of light over darkness. The word *deva*, according to Max Müller, originally meant a shining being, one that sheds light.[1] Bṛhaspati, the protector of law (*ṛta*) "Subdues the foe, stays the worked, cleaves the strong, and brings the light". Indra is, thus, described:

> He, shining, caused to shine what shone out, by law (*ṛta*), he lightened up the dawns. He moved with steeds yoked by Eternal Order (*ṛta*). Making man happy by the chariot that finds the light.
>
> — *ṚV*, VI.39.4

Over the centuries *ṛta* developed an aesthetic dimension. In Vedas it stands out for splendour and beauty. For example, when in obedience to *ṛta* the rains break and the 'bubbling fountains' stream forward, "they are compared to young virgins skilled in order (*ṛta*)" (*ṚV*, IV.19.7). Nature becomes beautiful through conformity to law. The lovely dawn (Uṣā) 'true to eternal order', is 'sublime by law'. (*ṚV*, V.80.1)

> The youthful maiden (Uṣā) breaks not the laws of eternal order by coming day-to-day to her tryst.

Similarly, Varuṇa, the protector of *ṛta*, represents the beautiful form (*rūpa*) that lies behind the cosmic order:

> He the supporter of the world of life, who knows the secret names of the beams of the dawn, He, the poet (*kavi*) cherishes manifold forms (*rūpa*) by his poetic power (*kāvya*).
>
> — *ṚV*, VIII.41.5

The identification of *ṛta* with beauty in the cosmic life is a great leap forward. The Vedic sages uplifted the mind of men to mystical heights, through the aesthetic delight they perceived from the cosmic order. The monotheistic ruler standing for truth (*satyam*) and for punishing the breaker of *ṛta* or order, slowly emerged as the

1. Max Müller, *Heritage of India*, Cambridge India Lectures Compilation : Sushil Gupta, Calcutta, 1951, p. 54.

God who supports what is good and beneficial (*śivam*) and this beneficial aspect of godhead (*dakṣiṇam mukham*) over the centuries emerged in the Indian thinking as what is beautiful, elevating and sublime (*sundaram*).

Ṛta, again, is the central principle behind Vedic sacrificial rites. The deity of the ritual, *Soma* is invoked in the following words:

> O purifier, driving off the lawless, looking at the light, sit in the place of the sacred rite (*ṛta*). — *ṚV*, IX.13.9

A willing acceptance of *ṛta*, the cosmic moral order, brings joy to the follower of *ṛta*. *Ṛgveda* sings: *madhu vātā ṛtayate/madhu kṣaranti sindhavaḥ/madhumānno vanaspatiḥ*. To the man who lives by law (*ṛta*), the earth is sweet, the rivers shed sweetness, the trees and forests become nests of sweetness (*ṚV*, V.90:6-8). This new understanding brought confidence in the Vedic people that good *karma* will, of course, be rewarded. Whatever might happen, they felt that there was a law of righteousness in the moral order which will potect the right people. Through this new idea of *ṛta* the *Ṛgveda* anticipated the law of *karma*, which is the basic foundation of Indian religious thought on which Hinduism, Buddhism and Jainism stand. *Ṛta* stood for the irrevocable law of *karma* which all gods and men must obey.

With the evolution of higher culture bringing aesthetic delights and spiritual bliss, the Vedic seers felt the need of newer rituals. The *Ṛgveda* (1:105-15) says : "Let new rituals grow (*navyo jāyatām ṛta*)". A significant ritual which the Vedic seers developed in order to introduce the young initiates to a path of higher *ṛta*, a transition from darkness to light, from humanity to divinity, from untruth to truth, is the consecration ceremony or *dīkṣā*. The *Yajurvedic Vājasaneya Saṁhitā* (XIX.30) describes it thus:

> By self dedication (*vrata* or observance of *ṛta*)
> One gets fit for consecration (*dīkṣā*)
> By the grace of the teacher one attains faith in one's own self (*śraddhā*)
> By *śraddhā* is truth (*satya*) obtained.

The *Ṛgveda* speaks of the threefold culture of an ideal society. Brāhmaṇas (intellectuals) are the custodians of pure knowledge (*satya*), Kṣatriyas (rulers) uphold the rule of *ṛta,* and the Vaiśyas (merchants) follow the path of economic and commercial service to the society.

The *Ṛgveda* describes:

> Strengthen the power of knowledge (Brāhmaṇa)
> and strengthen the intellects;

and strengthen the ruling power (kṣatra)
and strengthen the heroes,
Give strength to the milch-cow and
strengthen the people (vaiśya)

— *ṚV*, VIII.35, 16-18

The *Yajurveda* declares: *brahma dṛṃha, kṣatram dṛṃha*

Strengthen the power of knowledge,
Strengthen the political power of rulers,

— *YVS*, VI.3

The Vedic seers realised that a social organisation would be perfect when the two powers, brāhmaṇa and kṣatriya, would work in harmony, where the military or administrative powers of kings would be guided by the intellectual-spiritual vision of sages and seers who realised the ultimate truth in their life.

The *Yajurveda* says:

Where brāhmaṇa and kṣatriya both move together in concern,
That world I shall know as one of bliss,
Where gods with Agni dwell.

— *YVS*, XX.25

From god and ruler of external order ṛta to God the infinite within all beings

In the midst of many Gods, finally the question arose in the mind of Vedic seers:

To which God shall we offer our oblations?
And the answer came: "It is He
Whose is the universe;
Who gives strength and vigour,
Whose law gods obey?
Whose shadow is in death and immortality?

Finally the answer came,

They speak of Indra, Mitra, Varuṇa, Agni and there are divine Suparṇa and Gurutman. The Supreme God (the Supreme Truth) is one, whom the wise calls by various names.
ekam sa viprā bahudhā vadanti

— *ṚV*, I.164.46

The One Being the sages contemplative in many ways
ekaṁ santaṁ bahudhā kalpayanti — *ṚV*, X.114.5

Over the centuries, the Vedic monotheism gradually matured into Upaniṣadic monism. The one supreme perfect (*ṛtavān*) God, who is also the law-giver, and dispenser of justice (*ṛta*) over erring mortals, was slowly found to be the One All-Pervading Reality, The Existence-Knowledge-Bliss Absolute, the *Brahman* uniting and interpenetrating all entities, living or non-living.

When rituals and sacrificial rites grew in importance, *ṛta* becomes a synonym for *yajña* or sacrificial ceremony. Slowly the old ritualistic ideas of *ṛta* matured into Upaniṣads where *ṛta* inextricably stood connected with Truth aspect of life. Prayers like *ṛtam vadiṣyāmaḥ* (we shall speak *ṛta*) or *ṛtañca svādhyāya pravacane ca* (one should also hold fast to the regular study of *ṛta*) was followed by *satyam vadiṣyāmaḥ* (we shall speak what is truth) or *satyañca svādhyāya pravacane ca* (one should always hold fast to the study of truths). The truth emerging out of order and law of the physical world, slowly pointed to the truth or the ultimate reality or *brahman* beyond the Physical World. And, thus, *ṛta* transcended to the highest Truth, the Absolute beyond relative truths. "The finite world is connected with the infinite background" (*saṁyuktam ṛtam dharam āśrama ca*) says the *Śvetāśavatara Upaniṣad* (I.8). *Brahman*, the infinite truth emerged as infinite knowledge (*satyam jñānam ānantam brahman*). The temporal truth transcended to infinite truth. Finally two basic truths emerged out of later Vedic literature known as Upaniṣads or the Vedānta: 1. The underlying unity of all existence. 2. The innate infinite Existence — Knowledge — Bliss hidden in finite realities, in all beings. And *anṛta* or violation of *ṛta* finally meant the violation of this holistic background of all existence. Ethics became the acceptance of the unity of all life, in action. Whenever *ṛta*, the fundamental unity of existence, whose basis is universal love, is violated by the overpowering greed and ambition of individuals, *anṛta* prevails.

The *Yajurveda* describes this cosmic diety as all-pervading

venas tat paśyan nihitam guhāsad
yatra viśvam bhavati eka nīdam
tasmin idaṁ saṁ ca vi caiti sarvam
sa otaḥ protaśca vibhuḥ prajāsu ||[2]

The loving sage beholds the one existence hidden

2. Abinaschandra Bose, *The Call of the Vedas*, Quotations compiled from the Vedic texts, Bharatiya Vidya Bhavan, Bombay, 1999 (rpt.)

wherein the universe comes to have one home
Therein unites, and therefrom issues the whole universe
That one reality has interpenetrated and
Interconnected all living beings.

— *YVS*, 32.8

The infinite reality later called *brahman* was in the end discovered, hidden with all its infinite potentialities in the minutest of finite entities — *aṇor aṇīyān mahato mahīyān*. The individual soul (*ātman*) was finally found inextricably connected and even identified with universal soul (*brahman*). The Vedic seer realising this infinite nature of finite man declared — *ahaṁ brahmāsmi* — (I am supreme *brahman*).

Vivekānanda, the prophet of modern India echoed this Vedic teaching in the West a century ago. (*Svāmī Vivekānanda's Complete Works*: Vol. 7) "Christs and Buddhas are but waves on the infinite ocean that I am." The individual consciousness sustaining the amoeba was found to be identified with the one all-pervading one consciousness behind everything (*cit*).

The individual particle-matter was seen to be floating on the one infinite ocean of existence (*sat*) which physicist John Wheeler calls, 'Quantam Foam', Man's temporal joys were found to be emanations of one supreme bliss (*ānanda*) covering, sustaining, and interpenetrating the universes. One subtle holistic foundation of all existence was, thus, discovered by the Upaniṣadic seers. (*sa eṣa aṇimā aitadātmyam — Chāndogya Upaniṣad*, 6:8:9)

From Chaos to order, infinite to finite

Infinite truth must have infinite dimension and infinite ways of expressing itself. This infinite hidden in the finite body-mind complex of human beings first of all expresses itself in the physical layer (*annamaya kośa*), then the mental layer (*manomaya kośa*), the vital layer (*prāṇamaya kośa*), finally in the spiritual layer (*ānandamaya kośa*) of infinite bliss. Finite leads to infinite. Man emerges as God. *ātman* (the individual soul) is equated to *brahman* (the universal soul). This is what Pierre Teilhard Chardin calls the process of Christogenesis, the evolution of 'thing within' from amoeba to Christ.

How could the Vedic seers come to know about the state of non-existence as described in the *nāsadīya sūkta*, the state of singularity where, according to Oxford physicist, Robert Penrose, time, space and causation cease to exist? The indescribable One then existed beyond time, space and causation. That non-vibrating one then vibrated, or projected itself in space-time and thus the creation began. This knowledge of state beyond space and time came to Vedic seers by pure mystic intuition. The *Vyāsa Bhāṣya* of Patañjali (*sūtra* 14 *pāda* III and *sūtra* 44 *pāda* I) says that an empirical intuition based on sense-data (*deśa-kāla nimitta-avicchinna savikalpa prajñā*) can intuitively grasp the truths about physical phenomena. But the non-empirical, pure, relationless intuition (*nirvicāra nirvikalpa prajñā*) can arrive at truths beyond the real world of space-time-causation by an 'intuitive leap' or mystical overview from the relative to the absolute.[3]

Modern science leads the way from order to Chaos to new order

The nineteenth-century science led by the discoveries of Newton, thoughts of Laplace, and Rene Descartes conceived of the world and the universe as a machine run by unfailing laws like Newton's laws of motion. The self-contained mechanistic view of science seemed to confirm the image of a mechanomorphic universe where God stood as the huge mighty mechanic running the world in an infaltering way. This was the machine-god painted by William Blake. By the early twentieth century, Einstein brought a newness by putting the observer in the system; the machine looked different but it was still the same deterministic machine. Mechanical determinism stood still as a paradigm for physics and the physical sciences in general. This order, certainty, and determinism of Newtonian science was suddenly thrown into choas with Heisenberg's discovery of *Uncertainty Principle* in 1927, which demolished the three foundations of old classical physics with three new findings:

1. The sure cause and effect relation of our ordinary world does not hold true in sub-atomic world. Non-local causes operate.
2. No one can know with certainty any individual sub-atomic particle, although we can know the aggregate of such particles, a motor, or a baseball.
3. There is no pure objective Reality outside. Realites emerge only when we observe them.

After the discovery of *Uncertainty Principle*, and *Schrödinger's Wave-Equation* along with the paradox of *Schrödinger's Cat* the world outside emerged as an *observer-created reality*. This is known since 1957 as the Everettee-Wheeler interpretation of quantum mechanics. The pure objective reality turned *omnijective*, a combination of the subjective and objective.[4]

Quantum physics threw the old classical physics into a world of chaos and brought what Heinz Pugels called, the 'Physics Revolution'. It shows that there must have always been an inherent, unavoidable sense of incompleteness in all mathematical

3. B.N. Seal, *The Positive Sciences of Ancient Hindus*, New Delhi, Motilal Banarsidass, 1983, p.18.
4. Micheal Talbot, *Mysticism New Physics*, New York, Bantam Books, 1881, pp. 33 & 34.

models to describe the sub-atomic world. An electron colliding with an atom has an equal probability that the electron will deflect to the left as to the right. This is quantum *stochasticity*, as physicist Prof. Paul David likes to call it.[5] Einstein refused to accept the idea of non-local cause, and disappearance of a pure objective reality in Uncertainty Principle and called it a 'false religion'. He believed in Spinoza's God of harmony who runs the universe in perfect order in a deterministic way. He often raised the objection against the Uncertainty Principle that '*God does not play dice*', and Neils Bohr, as a champion of Quantum Physics, gave him the celebrated reply, "Nor is it our business to prescribe to God how he should run the world."[6] Today even after nearly eighty years Quantum Physics have proved true, and with all its weirdness and uncertainty gives excellent results in experiments. Statistical character of atomic events and the unstability of many physical systems due to minute fluctuations and the presence of the observer, suggest that scientific investigations will remain undetermined and open for further future interpretations.

Yet there is, says Paul Davis, a difference between stochasticity and anarchy. The development of new forms and systems is subject to general principles or organisation that guide matter and energy to develop along certain predetermined pathways of evolution. To distinguish it from the old determinism of Laplace and Newton, Paul Davis uses the word pre-destination to refer to this tendency, which nevertheless works predictably and successfully in many experiments.[7] Physicist John Wheeler shows how law-like behaviour can emerge from the apparent lawlessness, unpredictability and random fluctuations of the quantum world. Even the Chaos of the sub-atomic world can possess statistical regularities. Quantum events form an ensemble that we can observe. From Chaos of quantum stochasticity, thus, emerges a new order which make quantum mechanics applicable to hundreds of successful experiments in new physics. How does Uncertainty Principle bring certainty in experiments? Eminent physicist Goeffrey Chew says that it is by a special mechanism called decoherence that failure of causality becomes miniscule and objective reality survives, despite quantum theory.[8] (P.B. Aug, 1996, p. 495)

"It is the combination of contingency (Uncertainty, non-equilibrium, and disorder) and intelligibility (Order)", writes philosopher Ian Barbour "Which prompts us to search for new and unexpected forms of rational order".[9]

---

5. Paul Davis, *Mind of God*, London, Penguin Books, 1991, p. 191.
6. Werner Heisenberg, *Physics and Beyond*, New York, Harper & Row, 1971, p. 81.
7. Paul Davis, *op. cit.*, p. 193.
8. G. Chew, Speech in *Prabuddha Bharat*, 1996, p. 495.
9. Paul Davis, *op. cit.*, p. 169.

Illya Prigogine, Nobel scientist in 1965, gave a still new idea of *Order Out of Chaos*. The big machine of the world, according to the second law of thermodynamics is running down, its energy continuously spreading out. It could not go on forever, and therefore, 'Must have a stop' as Shakespeare wrote. Time, thus, got a new meaning in physical sciences. Darwin's followers soon introduced a new contradictory thought. The world machine might be running down, losing energy and organisation, but biological systems were running up, evolving, and becoming more and more organised. Prigogine came forward and gave a still more new idea that even matter is evolving. Our universe has grown larger and larger since the moment of big bang through 13 billion years of expansion. Prigogine complains that science has neglected this 'Interiority' or the internal evolution going on even in the depth of our material universe. Unstability, change, and non-equilibrium are working inside every sub-atomic particle. Every new particle-seconds (one particle second is 10^{-23} sec.) sub-atomic or sub-nuclear particles are changing and evolving to newer particles, as Fritzof Capra has shown in his bestselling book, *Tao of Physics*. Śiva's continuous dance of construction and destruction, as Fritzof Capra likes to interpret, is going on inside every minute particle. Prigogine argues that the machine model of science offered by Ṇewton and others tended to emphasise stability, order, unformity and equilibrium, while in reality, every minute particle, even the empty space is in constant and violent fluctuation. Out of these constant fluctuations a new order and equilibrium eventually emerges which Prigogine calls, "Dissipative Structure". The old universal laws like the second law of thermodynamics, argues Prigogine, are not universal at all, but apply only to local regions of reality. It is everywhere a local time, as Einstein has earlier shown. Universal time is a misnomer. Uniformity exists mostly with closed systems. These closed systems, argues Prigogine, form only a small part of the physical universe. Most phenomena are, in fact, open systems, exchanging energy or matter and information with their environment. Biological and social systems are more open and they evolve with greater freedom. "These notions of time and evolution and creativity" says Prigogine, "are built inside everything. Classical and quantum physics ignored this."[10] Most of the Reality, instead of being orderly and stable is seething and bubbling with freedom to change, bring disorder, and undergo a process of evolution. "A huge rail engine", says Svāmī Vivekānanda, "will move gigantically only on rail tracks, while a worm crawling on the rail has got the resilience and freedom of moving out of it".

What is the way out of this Chaos and disorder to a new order?

According to Prigogine, all systems contain sub-systems which are continually

10. Rene Weber, *Dialogues with Scientists and Sages*, New York, Routelege & Kegan Paul, 1986, p. 191.

fluctuating. At times, a single fluctuation or a combination of a few of them may become so powerful as a result of positive feedback, that it shatters the pre-existing organisation. At this revolutionary singular moment or a Bifurcation Point, the systems might disintegrated into Chaos or leap to a new, more differentiated, and a higher level of Order which Prigogine calls "Dissipative Order". This is the Nobel Prize winning discovery of Prigogine. Human society thus, emerges as "organised complexity allowing human will to work".[11] Prigogine insists that, such a new order or organisation can actually arise 'spontaneously' out of disorder and chaos through a process of self-organisation.[12]

Prigogine's discovery has already drawn a wide attention from social thinkers like Alvin Toffler: "Words like 'Revolution', 'Economic Crash', 'Technological Upheaval', and 'Paradigm Shift' all take on a new shade of meaning when we begin to think of them in terms of fluctuation, feedback amplification, dissipative structures, bifurcation, and the rest of Prigoginean conceptual vocabulary."[13] Toffler thinks that the impending major power shift in the twenty-first century culture from machine to man, from capital to knowledge, from an industrial Mechanmorphic Society to a Super-industrial Spiritually-oriented Society, is a new leap forward towards a "Dissipative Structure" on a world scale.[14]

History gives evidence that in a disintegrated society a superhuman genius brings order out of a crumbling chaos. This is what exactly Vivekānanda did a hundred years earlier when he repeatedly pointed out both in East and West that the Monistic Vedānta philosophy with its two foundations of the essential divinity of man, and the essential unity of existence, would stand out as the only rational religion for modern humanity. This new religio-cultural change came at a 'bifurcation point' when materialism in the West threatened to wipe out all religio-spiritual culture after Darwin's discovery that man came not from Adam & Eve but from monkeys. At once the theological foundation of Judeo-Christian belief was found to be irrational. Physicists like Tyndaland Haxley in London threatened to replace Christianity with the new religion of science and the new philosophy of scientific materialism. At this moment, Svāmī Vivekānanda emerged in both Europe and America and brought the gospel of Advaita Vedānta as the only philosophy and religion acceptable to scientific community. Vivekānanda was inspired by the message of his master, Rāmakṛṣṇa, who appeared as a 'Spontaneuous' phenomenon

---

11. Illya Prigogine and Isabella Stengers, *Order Out of Chaos*, Flamingo, New York, 1985, p. xv.
12. *Ibid.*, p. xv.
13. *Order Out of Chaos*, p. xvii.
14. *Ibid.*, p. xxvi.

in a disintegrated and demoralised Indian society. His life and message exploded the old fundamentalism in the world of religions, and is leading humanity, as Arnold J. Toynbee had seen it, today to a more unitive and spiritual approach for its survival in this age of Thermo-nuclear warfare, and providing a rational basis for religion.

A holistic background of the universe has emerged in modern science

After the successful experiement of Bell's theorem in 1972 by Clauser, Freedman, David Böhm, and Alain Aspect in 1985, science discovered a synchronistic non-locality, where at the base of matter "non-local" causes operate and simlar particles at a space-like distance are somehow "instantaneously interconnected" without the connection of any signal like light or electromagenetic waves.

The discovery of a holistic background of our universe has brought the new 'Holistic Paradigm' in science replacing the old dualistic paradigm. David Böhm wrote on this great finding:

> The essential new quality implied by quantum theory is non-locality. This leads to the radically new notion of the unbroken wholeness of the universe.
>
> — *Foundations of Physics*, 5, 1975, p. 94

Fritzof Capra writes:

> Scientists will not need to be reluctant to adopt a holistic framework as they are often today, for fear of being unscientific. Modern physics will have shown them that such a framework would be not only scientific, it would be consistent with the most advanced scientific theories of physical reality.[15]

Einstein conceived of a grand unified theory (GUT) of all the five forces of nature. Today with the discovery of electro-weak force by Abdus Salam, Sheldon Glashaw and Steven Weinsberg, three of the five forces in nature (electricity, magnetism and weak-interaction force) have been unified. The fourth force, the strong interaction force that binds the nucleus inside the atom is expected to be unified, as it is claimed today by some scientists. The final stumbling block remains with gravity. For quantising gravity as Stephen Hawking puts it, the scientist has to reach a state of singularity beyond space and time when this one force existed without disintegration. There is no way, however, to reach that state except through the ways of highest intuition or *samādhi*. The One force or *prāṇa* according to Vedic language, existed in a condition when neither time nor space was created. Both time and space were

---

15. Satish Kumar (ed.), *The Schumacher Lectures*, London, Abacus, Sphera Books, 1982, p.135.

born after the One force began to disintegrate into five forces. At the instant of 10^{-33} sec. the electro Nuclear force broke into Electro-weak and strong interaction forces. Within the first second of creation after the Big Bang all the five forces are created.[16] Anything in space and time is finite. The state beyond space-time is the state of infinity which is the background of the five forces of the universe. And to reach that state one must take an intuititive leap beyond space and time.

Infinity and consciousness — The background of the finite

The fear of infinity lingered in Greek civilisation. In science the old belief that Infinity was paradoxical and self-contradictory persisted until the nineteenth century when mathematician George Cantor, while investigating problems of trignometry finally succeeded in proving a rigorous logical demonstration of the self-consistency of the actually infinite. Since then the rules for the consistent manipulation of infinite numbers, came to be accepted.[17] Much of the twentieth-century mathematics is, according to Paul Davis, founded on the concept of the Infinite or the infinitesimal. Today algorithmic information theory conceives of an uncomputable number known as *Omega*. Computer Scientists believe that *Omega* embodies an enormous amount of wisdom in a very small space, a wisdom which can "contain the answers to more mathematical questions than could be written in the entire universe". Since it is uncomputable, "Short of mystical revelation, *Omega*, can never be known", says Paul Davis.[18] Max-Born's discovery of electron as 'Probability wave' ultimately suggested, according to Richard Fynmann, that electron or subtomic particle may possess an 'organic conscioussness'. Scientists belonging to the Artificial Intelligence School, argue that if a cellular automation toy universe like a computer can serve as a replica of the real universe, then computers can also think like conscious beings.[19]

The Vedānta philosophy says that everything in this Universe from the minutest to the greatest, is permeated by the One All-Pervading consciousness. In stone, it is not expressed visibly, in vegetation world it is half expressed; in human beings it is most manifested. The idea of One All-pervading Cosmic Consciousness has been expressed in the Vedas as, 'I am the All-pervading Consciousness Brahman" or *aham brahmāsmi* or *prajñānm brahman* (consciousness itself is *Brahman*).

To a question, "Do you think that consciousness can be explained in terms of matter and its law?" Max Plank, the father of the Quantum Physics answered to an

---

16. The New York Times Magazine, 26 September, 1982, pp. 68-9 Magazine.
17. Paul Davis, *op. cit.*, p.130.
18. Paul Davis, *op. cit.*, p. 134.
19. *Ibid.*, p. 125.

interviewer in *Observer*, January 23, 1931, "I regard consciousness as fundamental, I regard matter as derivative from consciousness. We cannot get behind consciousness. Everything that we talk about, everything that we regard as existing postulates consciousness."[20]

Erwin Shrodinger, Nobel Physicist, wrote in 1924: "This life of yours which you are living is not merely a piece of this existence, but is in a certain sense the 'whole', only this whole is not so constituted that it can be surveyed in one single glance. This, as we know, is what the Brahmins express in that sacred, mystic formula which is yet really so simple and so clear: *tat tvam asi*, This is you. Or again, in such words as "I am in the East, and in the West. I am below and above. I Am This Whole World". (Jermy Benstein: I am this whole world) Erwin Schrödinger in *Project Physics Reader 5* (New York, Holt Reinbert & Weinston 1968-9, p. 178 (Quoted on p. 182, Fred Allan Wolf, *The Quantum Leap*, Perennial Library, 1989).

James Jeans echoed the same idea in the conclusion of his book, *The Background of New Science*:

> Our last impression of nature (as offered by the classical physics) was an Ocean of mechanism surrounding us on all sides. As we gradually discard old physics we see mechanical concepts continually giving place to mental. If from the nature of things we can never discard them entirely, we may yet conjecture that the effect of doing so would be total disappearance of matter and mechanism, mind reigning supreme and alone.[21]

Arthur Eddington feels that Newton's science sought to reduce God to 'system of different equations' in order to establish order in the physical scheme. But ultimate reality, says Eddington, is the 'Unknown Background'. "We can grasp the tune but not the player. This is the tune of our catch, played by the picture of nobody", says Eddington about the underlying relation of the finite with the infinite.[22] Stephen Hawking, the astrophysicist, genuinely wishes to have a godless universe, if only he could prove that there is no edge to the universe. But he admits: "It is very difficult to prove that there is not any edge."[23] He dreams of a genuine *Theory of Everything*,

---

20. CEM Joad, *Philosophical Aspects of Modern Science*, London : George Allen & Unwin, p. 12.
21. James Jeans, *The New Background of Science*, London, Cambridge University Press, 1933, pp. 297-8.
22. Arthur Eddington, *The Nature of the Physical World*, London, Cambridge University Press, 1929, p. 292.
23. Rene Weber, *Dialogues with Scientists and Sages, The Search for Universality*, New York, Routelege & Kegan Paul, 1986, pp. 209-11.

as he puts in *Brief History of Time*, which must explain not only the what of our Universe, but also why it is the only type of universe and the only set of physical laws.[24]

Svāmī Vivekānanda, the greatest exponent of Vedānta in modern times expresses it almost in the language of today's physics:

> Physics is bounded in both sides of metaphysics, so it is with reason — it starts from non-reason and ends with non-reason. If we push inquiry far enough in the world of perception, we must reach a plane beyond perception. Reason is really stored up and classified perception by memory.
>
> We can never imagine or reason beyond our perceptions. Religion is the science which learns the transcendental in nature through the transcendental in man. We know as yet little of man, consequently but little of the universe. When we know more of man we shall probably know more of the universe. Man is epitome of all things and all knowledge is in him. Only for the infinitesimal portion of the universe, which comes into some perception, are we able to find a reason: Never can we give the reason for any fundamental principle.[25]

Intuition — The way to perception of truths beyond space and time

Einstein, who began his scientific career with a firm belief in positivism, as taught by Ernest Mach, initially refused to accept anything not varifiable by immediate sense perception. That is why he measured time with a clock, and distance with a scale. But slowly by the pressure of new discoveries, Einstein turned to what he called the 'Intuitive Leap' for reaching out to Truths beyond the sensory perception.

Today intuition has formed the basis of the major bulk of discoveries especially in physics. James Jeans called mathematics an "independent world created out of pure intelligence." (*MG*, p. 151)[26] The 'Unreasonable Effectiveness' of mathematics, to use Nobel Physicist Engine Winger's phrase, as in the case of Indian Mathematician Ramanujan, Einstein or Heisenberg and others, was due to mystic intuition of super sensory perception of truths beyond ordinary sense perception[27]

---

24. Stephen Hawking, *A Brief History of Time*, Bentam Books, New York, 1988, p. 175.
25. Swami Vivekananda, *Complete Works*, Vol. 8. pp. 20-1.
26. Paul Davis, *op. cit.*, p. 151.
27. Paul Davis, *op. cit.*, pp. 150-1.

(p. 150). Ramanujan himself admitted that the British Mathematician G.H. Hardy thought of no useful application whatever for his own work. Yet years afterwards, the very same mathematical rules that Hardy had already formulated (P.N. 151) was found to be testified by nature. Heisenberg called his epoch-making discovery of Uncertainty Principle a *Gedanken-Experiment* (thought experiment), which he intuitively stumbled upon while contemplating on electron movements during a walk in Heine mountains. Einstein admitted that his own discovery of Relativity came in a vision when he himself in was in despair. (Einstein by Bouise De Broglie) Referring to the astonishing success of theories such as the general theory of relativity, or the uncertainty Principle, Oxford Physicist Penrose writes:

> It is hard for me to believe as some have tried to maintain, that such superb theories could have arisen merely by some random natural selection of ideas leaving only the good ones as survivors. There must, instead, be some deep underlying reason for accord between mathematics and physics, i.e., between Plato's world and the physical world.[28]

Pure thought can grasp reality as the ancient dream. Einstein, said in his Oxford lectures.[29] The Vedic seers say that the ultimate truth is revealed to the individual through purified intellect and purified mind (*hṛdā manīṣā*, *manasā abhikḷpto*). No one can know Cantor's absolute or the uncomputable Omega by rational means, for any absolute, being a Unity and hence complete within itself must include the knowledge and knower. The scientist going to conceive Infinity has realised that the Mindscape is one and he himself is included in infinity. Vedānta says that the finite has always the infinite as its background. To the seers of the Vedas and the Upaniṣads Infinity has been equated to fullness. Infinity has, to them become the foundation of consciousness, matter and human life. The universal self (*brahman*) has been merged with the individual self (*ātman*). Today this *ātman* = *brahman* equation has emerged, according to nobel physicist Erwin Schrödinger, as the final solution to the problem of consciousness in physics. 'Plurality of consciousness is Māyā' says Schrödinger.[30] Nothing can become full or complete (*pūrṇam*) unless it is Infinite, says the Vedic seer.

The Upaniṣads chant:

> *Oṁ* that ultimate reality is Infinite (*pūrṇam*)

---

28. Paul Davis, *op. cit.*, p. 152.
29. Pagels Aeinz, *The Cosmic Codes*, New York, Bentam Books, 1983, p. 24.
30. Erwin Schrodinger, *My View of the World*, Cambridge, *op. cit.*

This universe (physical) is Infinite.
That universe (spiritual-mental), is Infinite
When Infinity is extracted out of Infinity,
What remains is Infinity

Conclusion

The Vedic seers were insistent that *ṛta* or the order of this physical universe must be based on the truth behind the universe. Truth alone triumphs, not untruth, That is why the Vedic prayers ask us to keep hold of final Truth while observing *ṛta*.

In the *Taittirīya Upaniṣad*, the teacher teaches the student to chant:

ṛtam vadiṣyāmi (I will speak *ṛta* or what is moral and good).
satyam vadiṣyāmi (I will speak Truth) or

ṛtamca svādhyāya pravacane ca (one should study and listen to the talks on (*ṛta*)

satyam ca svādhyāya pravacane ca (one should study and listen to talks on truth).

What is the truth of which Vedic seers speak, through a hundred Upaniṣads? In the *Chāndogya Upaniṣad* (6:8.7) The seer Āruṇi teaches his son Śvetaketu about the final truth of existence.

> That ultimate reality, O Śvetaketu, is very subtle. That has interpenetrated and pervaded every single entity of this universe, living or non-living. That is the truth. That truth is known as *ātman*. And thou art that *ātman* (existence-knowledge-bliss absolute, hidden inside the tiny body-mind complex of every being).
>
> *sa ya eṣa aṇimā aitadātmyam idam sarvam tat satyam sa ātmā tat tvam asi śvetaketo!*

The new philosophy of modern science is the holistic paradigm based on the fundamental unity of all existence. The final *ṛta*, the socio-moral order, is, to Vedic vision, always based on the essential divinity and the underlying unity of all life. What is ethics but acceptence of the unity of existence? "The wife becomes dear to the husband not because of the wife, but because the husband sees his own self in the wife", says the *Bṛhadāraṇyaka Upaniṣad*. Similarly, the mother sees her own self in the child. In the same manner, the man of self-realisation, like Christ and

Buddha see their own self in all beings, and thus they stand out as symbols of the greatest moral force, universal love and total self-sacrifice for others. The *Kena Upaniṣad* says that this vision of the unity of Existence is the only way to immortality, when the individual begins to identify his own self with the self in all.

> Seeing his own self in all living beings, the wise one transcends the ordinary levels of consciousness and attains immortality.
>
> *bhūteṣu bhūteṣu vicitya dhīrāḥ*
> *pretya asmāt amṛtā bhavanti* ।

Sequence of history: Order to Chaos to order

Throughout history whether it is in human life or the world of the ideas and scientific experiments, always the old order has suddenly been threatened by new ideas, new situations or new discoveries, which has brought a temporary state of Chaos. Slowly out of this Chaos a totally new order of society, a new civilisation, new ideas in science have emerged. After Galeleo's or Copernicus' discovery the medieval science and culture were thrown into Chaos and out of this Chaos emerged the splendid and orderly machine universe of Newton. Similarly, the mechanistic universe of Newton was thrown into confusions by the new discoveries of quantum physics like Heisenberg's uncertainty Principle in 1927, or Schrödinger's wave equation in 1926, or David Böhm's successful experiments, or Bell's Theorem in 1972. From this Chaos has again emerged new paradigm of science popularly known as the Holistic paradigm or Holistic science. At the individual level, Siddhārtha's old order of life lived in complacency suddenly gave birth to the Chaos and dark night of the soul during his terrific spiritual struggle. Out of this Chaos emerged the new man — the enlightened one, the Buddha. St. Paul wrote in Corinthians, "The first man of earth, earthly, and second man was the son of God. . . . The seed is sown in dishonour. It was raised in glory."

At the socio-political level the chaos of Czarist Regime gave birth to the new order of Leninist Communism. Today when old Communism failed, the Communist world is slowly passing through a state of Chaos to a new democratic order fulfilling the democratic aspirations of the masses.

Periodic occurrence of the upheavals of chaos and the rise of new order, is the regular sequence of history. Yet history has its own lessons. The violation of the moral order of life based on the basic unity of mankind has brought not the vengeance of God, but the 'vengeance of history', as Svāmī Vivekānanda said. Konosuke Matshushita, the maker of modern technetronic Japan, admitted in his book, *Not for Bread alone*, that Japan's progress would be far more faster, if they had not been imperially aggressive on other nations in the past. The Japanese bombing of Pearl Harbour was returned by the atomic destruction of Hiroshima and Nagasaki. The Greek civilisation, despite perfection in all arts and science went down in history because it neglected this spiritual moral order or *ṛta* in its national life. Similarly, the Roman civilisation, despite its accomplishments in law, administration and warfare, violated the holistic paradigm, or the universal *ṛta* and brutalised over the non-Romans, thus, inviting the nemesis or vengeance of history and collapsed under the weight of a new Christian culture which succeeded with the gospel of "Charity never faileth", through the life-long sacrifice of Christ's apostles.

The need of the hour — A new ṛta for both science and society

Can science have this cosmic order *ṛta* as its foundation? Robert Oppenheimer the maker of world's first atom bomb said that physicists had known what is sin after the Hiroshima explosion. "There are cosmic laws. They cannot be bribed by prayer or incense" said Einstein. (*EP*, p. 63) Illya Prigogine writes: "We can no longer accept the old *a priori* distinction between scientific and ethical values. This was possible at a time when the external world and the internal world appeared to conflict to be nearly orthogonal. Today we know that time is a construction and, therefore, carries ethical responsibilities".[31] Prigogine's discovery of the dissipative order, has made it clear that "societies and religions are 'immensely complex systems' which are nevertheless, highly sensitive to fluctuations". 'Since even small fluctuations may grow and change the overall structure, "Individual activity is not doomed to insignificance," says Prigogine.[32] Einstein believed that scientists themselves will bring the new cosmic order in society. Perhaps that impulse must come from scientists in the tradition of Galileo, Capler and Newton. In spite of failures and persecutions, these man devoted their lives to proving that the universe is a single entity, (*EP*, p. 66), "Believe me", Einstein confided to a friend, "what religious leaders were never able to do — to tear down the barriers between religion and religion — the scientists of our age may do."

Exploring new avenues to holistic consciousness and universe

Modern science is exploring the ways to achieve this holistic vision. Dr. John C. Lily shows in his book, *The Human Biocomputer*, that our brain works as a biocomputer. Every learning is gained through a 'metaprogramming' of the biocomputer. 'consciousness' is the 'metaprogrammer'. And therefore, writes M. Telbot, it is important for us to feed the brain (bio-computer) with proper symbols. "Religion is a metaprogramme", says Talbot and "visualisation is a Yoga of the

31. Prigogine Illya, and Sabella Stengers, *Order out of Chaos*, p. 312.

32. *Ibid.*, p. 313.

33. William Hermanns, *Einstein The Poet in Search of Cosmic Man*, Branden Press, M.A. 1983, p. 68.

mind".[34] It produces quick results by utilising forces familiar to man only at the deeper levels of consciousness. That is why imagination, dwelling on higher thoughts, prayers, meditation and repeatation of holy words (*mantra*) are the processes for bringing the higher awareness. In fact, this is the way to reach the state of pure consciousness, the state of *samādhi*, which scientists call the state of *homeostatasis*. At this stage one sees, as Wordsworth says, into the life of things. A latest study in neurophysiology shows that 'bio-computer' is constructed to achieve what might be called a cognitive homeostasis; cybernetician Heinz von Forester points out: "The nervous system is orgainsed (or organises itself) so that it computes a stable reality".[35] In this state of *samādhi* or cognitive homeostasis the external reality no longer seems apart from the self. In this state of highest cognition, man sees vision of unity, and all his fears are gone. In the Chinese thinking the left half of brain (Yan) is meant for rational, logical, aggressive aspects of our thinking and the right half of the brain (Yin) is responsible for our mystical, supra rational, intuitive, holistic and spiritual modes of thinking. The Vedic seers realised the need of both modes of thinking.[36]

A time has come today when not only Yin should combine with Yan but Yin should lead the Yan. When Christ leads the murderous Soul, Soul is transformed into St. Paul. Today's civilisation is looking forward to such a new orientation of the scientific civilisation by a holistic and global outlook. While civilisations of Egypt, Maya, Greece and Rome are virtually extinct, the Vedic culture has survived five thousand years of history braving foreign invasions, cultural onslaughts and vicissitudes of history, only because of this foundation of *ṛta*, based on *satyam*, the truth of the essential divinity and unity of mankind. Our world today is trying to emerge out of a chaos where fundamentalist warfare is killing millions in the name of this God or that book, and statesmen are basking in the new power of thermo-nuclear weapons. We need a new order of civilisation based on this age-old Vedic concept of *ṛtam* and *satyam* where the entire world can become one home of mankind, as dreamt by the Vedic seers (*yatra viśvaṁ bhavati ekanīḍam*).

---

34. M. Talbot, *Mysticism and New Physics*, pp. 149-51.
35. *Ibid.*, p. 156.
36. *Muṇḍaka Upaniṣad* says: One must have two kinds of knowledge — the secular or the knowledge of external arts and sciences and the spiritual or the knowledge of the internal universe (*dve vidyā veditavye parā ca eva aparā ca*).

2

Ṛta in Veda

Vidya Niwas Misra

BEFORE we proceed to define what *ṛta* is and how it is so focal to the understanding of Indian world-view, a brief discussion about its etymology will be useful. *Ṛta* is derived from the verbal base √*ṛ* which means to move towards with the past particle *ta* added to it. Other related derivatives in Sanskrit are *ṛtu*: season (ordered sequence of time), *ṛti* and negation *niṛrti*, *ṛtavān*: keeping within the cosmic order, *ṛtavasu*: one who is wealthy is pretty and righteous; *ṛtajya*: one whose bow strung with propriety, *ṛtajāta*: truly born, *ṛtapāta*: sacrificial vessel, *ṛtapravīta*: invested with divine truth, *ṛtavāk*: true speech, *ṛtasadana*: the right seat, *ṛtambharā*: bearing the divine law in oneself, *ṛtāyu*: observing the divine law and *rīti*: style. The meaning of the verbal base *ṛ* has several connotations, namely, to move towards, to rise, to tend upwards, to reach, to obtain, to fall to one's share, to fix upon and to insert. We can also add *ara*, *arya*, *ārya*, *aram* (enough, plenty), *ari* which all denote 'excel', excelling' or to make something fruitful, to plough. Thus, the basic meaning is a creative or productive movement towards a defined, well-set aim.

This will be well borne out by its cognates in other Indo-European languages, viz., *aša* (*AV*: moral order), *ašāva* (Avesta, *AV*: righteous *airyo* (*AV*), *aristos* (Greek: the best), *arta*s (Latin), *arto*s (Greek) in the first series (Pokorny, pp. 24-6, pp. 55-7) and cognates of the series, in Sanskrit, *ṛṇoti* = moves forward, *arṇa*, *arṇava* (ocean) are *ornumi* (Greek) *erno*s (Greek), *horos* (Greek), runs (Gothic) (Pokorny, 327-31).

To sum up these correspondences bear out clearly that the word *ṛta* subsumes in itself a well purposive movement for betterment and has a potential to control a vast range of meanings starting from action to fruition and from fruition to a chain of open cycles.

This is further corroborated by the usages in the Vedic and the later literature. I shall take just a few passages to make this point.

1. प्राची अध्वरेव तस्थतुः सुमेके ऋतावरी ऋतजातस्य सत्ये।

— *ṚV*, III.6.10

These two, fair, true and holy (*ṛtāvarī*) and coming forward stand at the sacrifice which springs from divine order (*ṛtajāta*). Here sacrifice is said to have been born of *ṛta* (the cosmic or the divine order).

2. ऋतस्य दृळहा धरुणानि सन्ति पुरूषि चन्द्रा वपुंषे वपूंषि।
ऋतेन दीर्घमिषणन्त पृक्ष ऋतेन गाव ऋतमा विवेशुः।।
— *ṚV*, IV.23.9

Firmly rooted are *ṛta*s, the foundations of eternal law, in its form lie many lustrous beauties. By this eternal law they bring us lasting enjoyment. By this law cows, the sacred powers of the word have come to the seat of *ṛta*, namely the sacrifice. In this mantra the word *ṛta* gives two distinct meanings, one eternal law or cosmic order, secondly the seat of *ṛta*, sacrifice.

Thus, a bifurcation of meaning had taken place in the *ṚV* itself.

3. Coming to the third passage in *Śatapatha Brāhmaṇa* we find *ṛta* as a product of *yajña* (sacrifice).

यज्ञो वा ऋतस्य योनिः
— *ŚBr*, I.3.4.16

The sacrifice is indeed the source (*yoni*) of divine order or truth. In a way *yajña*, as translation of *ṛta* into action becomes the cause if furtherance of *ṛta* in due course.

4. In the later *Mahānārāyaṇa Upaniṣad, ṛta*, *satya* and *brahma* all bcomes one entity :

तदेवतं तदु सत्यमाहुस्तदेव ब्रह्म परमं कवीनाम्।

5. The last passage is from the tenth *maṇḍala* of *Ṛgveda*, which relates *ṛta* to the first act of creation. *Ṛta* and *satya* jointly are prime movers of all creative acts as one of the creation hymns in *ṚV* propounds: "*ṛta*, *satya*, cosmically ordered" truth was born of *tapa*s, the heated desire of creation, from them was born the dark night, the infinite time which in turn is transformed into the infinite space, spread out as a vast ocean. Then came into existence, the year, i.e., the finite time and along with the day-night pair in a wink of time. This was followed by the birth of the sun, the moon, the earth, the mid-region and the heaven, as had been the sequence in earlier creation-processes

ऋतं च सत्यं चाभीद्धात् तपसोऽध्यजायत। ततो रात्र्यजायत ततः समुद्रो अर्णवः।।
समुद्रावर्णवादधि संवत्सरो अजायत। अहोरात्रणि विदधद्विश्वस्य मिषतो वशी। सूर्याचन्द्रमसौ
यथापूर्वमकल्पयत्। दिवं च पृथिवीं चाऽन्तरिक्षमथो स्वः।
— *ṚV*, X.190

The use of singular after *ṛta* and *satya* indicates that they are juxtaposed as mutually dependent and complementary, so that one cannot operate without the other. This is why the opposition of *satya* is not *asatya* but *anṛta*. One has to speak truth which is pleasing to the other. Unpleasant truth is against *ṛta* (the driving force of life) and, therefore, is forbidden. Under no circumstance one should speak truth which goes against *ṛta*.

Nirukta (*Nir*, 2.25) has given another additional meaning of *ṛta*, namely the 'cosmic water' ऋतमित्युदकनाम. The creation hymn quoted above already speaks of the birth of the great night and the great ocean, both being unmanifest and immeasurable aspects of time and space. Water has been used in several passages as symbol of the unmanifest powers of creation and *vāk* (which subsumes both manifest and unmanifest speech, the latent as well as the articulate speech) is also described as born in the deep ocean and in later myth becomes equated with Sarasvatī, a great river. All the passages quoted above bring out clearly the dimensions of the concept of *ṛta* and lay down a foundation for seemingly diverse interpretation but in essence lead to a holistic view of *ṛta* as a focus of Indian thought.

I shall give a brief summary of three modern interpretations of *ṛta* expounded by Śrī Aurobindo, A.K. Coomaraswamy and Pt. K.C. Chattopadhyaya. Śrī Aurobindo, in his monumental work, *The Secret of Vedas*, has propounded that *ṛta* is the principle of *bṛhat*, the vast and is the truth of things and it leads upwards to *māyās*, bliss. He has rendered in another passage the translation of *satyam*, *ṛtam* and *bṛhat* as the truth, the right and the vast. He further elaborates that it is *satyam*, the truth of being, it is in action *ṛtam*, right — the truth of divine being regulating right activity both of mind and body; it is *bṛhat*, the Universal Truth proceeding direct and undeformed out of the Infinite (pp. 60-2). Thus, according to Śrī Aurobindo *ṛta* transforms the truth of being into a divine truth and in turn is transformed into a universal truth, in other words *ṛta* is an endless journey from truth to truth.

Ananda K. Coomaraswamy in his book, *The Vedas: Essays in Translation and Exegesis*, 1976, has equated *ṛta* with *sattva* when he says:

> In the *Ṛgveda* generally, *satya* = *ṛta*, the law or way of Heaven and hence also truth. In the same way in *Tai Up*, II.6 *sattva* is contrasted with *anṛta* (and not with *asatya*).

Thus, truth is truth only when it is surcharged with *ṛta*: a divine purpose. Anand K. Coomaraswamy in a similar context rendered *nirṛti* (the exclusion of *ṛta*) as 'mortality', suggesting thereby that *ṛta* leads to immortality. *Ṛta* drives away the fear of death. He has also discussed the word *sūnṛtā vāk* (as *su* + *ṛta*) meaning sweet speech. Sweetness helps in leading a dialogue to harmonious concord, and so the *ṛṣis* speak a well *ṛta*-formed speech. In another context, he has equated *ṛta* with *dharma*. This is well in agreement with the symbolisation of *dharma* by *vṛṣa* (bull, a procreator as well as a mover of a plough or a carrier) in Purāṇic lore, to sum up, *ṛta* is the life-principle which ensures harmonious dynamism and, therefore, it is an essential adjunct of 'truth', an essence of truth.

Pandit K.C. Chattopadhyaya explains the developement of *ṛta* in a different way. According to him, *ṛta* originally did not mean *satya* "My own reading of the texts reveals that the word meant 'the sacred rite'." He traces the development of the meaning of *ṛta* step by step as follows: *ṛta* as sacred rite became *yajña*. Later it became equated with the Sun God Viṣṇu and then with *puruṣa* (the Primordial Person). Ultimately this equation culminated in becoming the Cosmic Order itself. He further argues that '*satya* being the nature of gods, it became a *sine-qua-non* of *ṛta* (the worship of gods).*

His line of argument proceeds from gross to subtle, from manifest to unmanifest, from concrete to abstract and from act to ideation. This is in a way a reversal of the order of arguments put forward by Śrī Aurobindo and A.K. Coomaraswamy. But in essence all of them hold that *ṛta* is the nucleus, the navel or the hub of all movements, of the *Wheel* of *Life*. The Mīmāṁā definition of *dharma* 'as impeller' (*codanalakṣaṇa*) is an absorption of the earlier meaning of *ṛta*. P.V. Kane in his *History of Dharmaśāstra*, Vol. IV, has thus explained the development of meaning of *ṛta*. The primary meaning of *ṛta* is cosmic movement. The secondary meaning is a regulated cosmic order and its tertiary meaning is a proper layout of sacred rites leading to the pleasure of gods, the maintainers of the Cosmic Order and finally it comes to have a general meaning, moral conduct. Aśvaghoṣa while describing the wheel of *dharma* gives an appropriate adjective to it, *ṛta nābhi*. This wheel rotates around the hub of *ṛta*: moral conduct. Thus, *ṛta* has became an intrinsic component of the Indian world-view.

Though *ṛta* having been absorbed in the totality of *dharma*, is no longer in extensive use, its vide range of meaning is still the main driving force of a distinctive way of life. It is also reflected in all the creative arts and all the rites associated with cycle of seasons or cycle of life (both being mutually analogous), either as a frame of flowing lines or as recurrent motifs, such as twin birds, creepers, terraced structures, flying figures, dancers, hunt-chase and the like, or as depiction of the changing scenario in each season, or as weaving of a story within another story and leaving it open-ended, or as by *rāga* scales, giving full scope to improvisation within the traditionally inherited frames. At times, these elaborations of the principle of *ṛta* do not reveal themselves to a reader or an observer, or a listener, who has not had either an aptitude for looking for the whole or had sufficient exposure to the Indian susceptibility to the pulsating phenomenon around. *Ṛta* is like a wave pattern

* *Studies in Vedic and Indo-Iranian Religion and Literature*, Vol. I, pp. 113-14.

and *satya* is like a particle-pattern. Both of them are one reality, *ṛta* is the flow of time and *satya* is the expanse of space. Both are not only mutually transformable but they are also mutually dependent. Both together ensure a proper balance between change and continuity and both together go for eternity in a dynamic way. Even a slight imbalance leads to chaos (disorder) and disaster.

3

Aṣa (Ṛta) in the Avesta and the Iranian Society

Satkari Mukhopadhyaya

AṢA is one of the words which we come across in the Avesta, very often. It is derived from the Avestic word *aret*. The word *aṣa* is the cognate of Vedic *ṛta*.

Primarily, *aṣa* means righteous and just order or the immutable law. Its other connotations are rectitude, holiness, truth, and sanctity. Indo-Iranians had the conception of a great Cosmic Order regulating both the course of the heavenly bodies and of man's actions. Secondarily, the *aṣa* connotes virtues like purity, including that of the body, the mind and the soul, — rectitude of uprightness, truth and justice, all of which are essential for one who treads the path of *aṣa* in order to be in tune with the Cosmic Order which is also *aṣa*.

Zarathustra declared that the Supreme Lord first thought and then created *aṣa*.

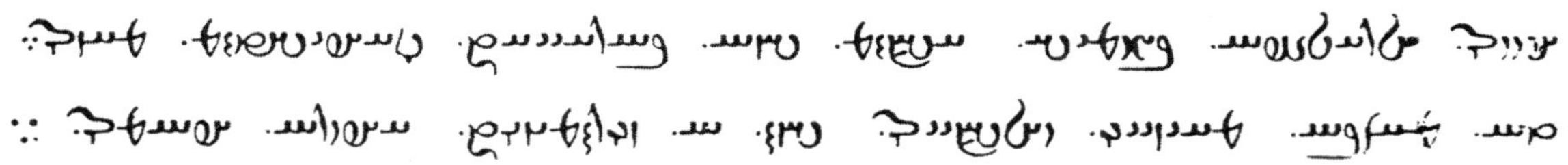

— *Yasna*, XXXI.7

> He is through His understanding the Creator of the Righteous Order (*aṣa*). And thus likewise He supports His beneficent mind (in his saints).

Ancient Aryans, i.e. Indo-Aryans and the Iranians were living in the bosom of nature. A careful observation of natural phenomena revealed to them that there was some regularity and order — the dawn, the day, and the night following each other in succession, the rising and falling of tides, the waxing and the waning of the moon, changes of season, birth, growth, maturity and disintegration of all living beings, — all these, in their view, was based on some immutable universal law, which is in the Avesta termed as *aṣa*, Therefore, *aṣa* is the Cosmic Order.

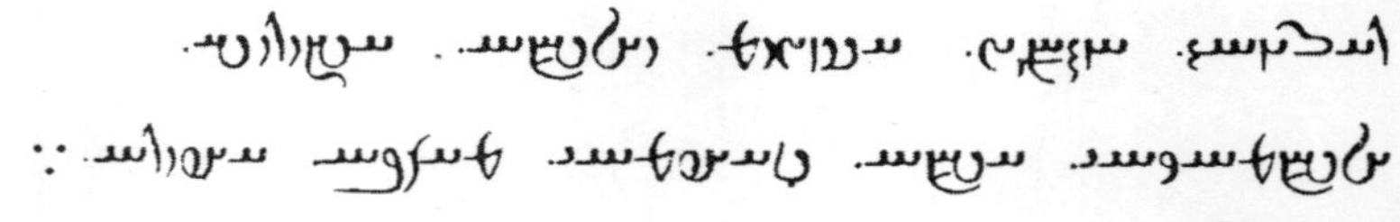

— *Yasna*, L.10

> The stars, the sun, the aurora which brings on the light of days, all through Righteous Order (*aṣa*), praise you, Ahura Mazda.

The law of *aṣa* is all-pervading. Natural phenomena proceed in accordance with the law of *aṣa*. As stated in the *Gāthās*, the luminaries, the day and the dawn are all in praise of Ahura Mazda through *aṣa*, to which they all conform.

Zoroastrian religion has laid down the path of *aṣa* for humanity. All the concepts and practices of this religion centre around the concept of *aṣa*, which embraces internal and external purity and all the principle values. The colophon of *Yasna* reads:

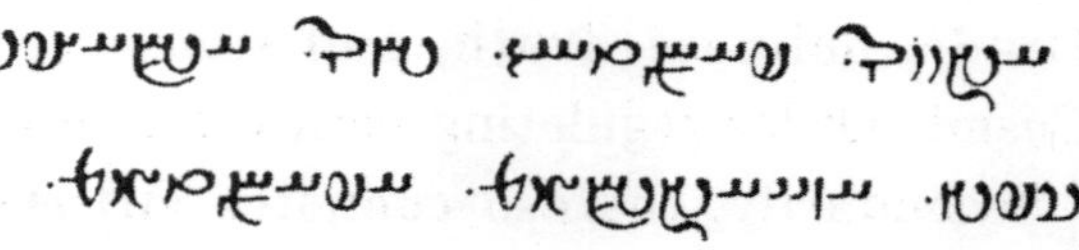

> There is but one Path, that is of *aṣa*, all other paths are false paths.
>
> — Tr. Taraporewala

Observing the basic principles of the religion is the beginning of moving into the right direction. This leads to external and internal purity, which in turn will discipline the mind and a disciplined mind is receptive of divine wisdom. Step by step one will be able to tune with the Cosmic Order, having gained complete mastery over one's thoughts, feelings and emotions. This, however, is not an easy task. It demands constant effort coupled with patience and perseverance. If mind is fully controlled, half the battle is won, for, there is a relation between the human mind and the Supreme Mind, the latter also being the progenitor of the immutable law which governs the universe. The highest ideal according to the Zoroastrian religion is to be in tune with *aṣa* and through it, with the Omniscient Lord, Ahura Mazda.

We read in *Yasna* (LX.12):

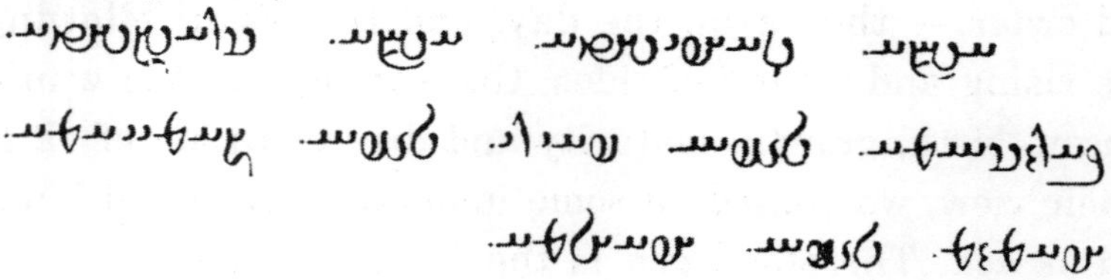

> Through the best righteousness, excellent righteousness, [oh Ahura Mazda] may we catch sight of Thee and may we come near Thee [and] attain to Thy eternal friendship.

The most sacred and oft repeated mantra of the Avesta reads:

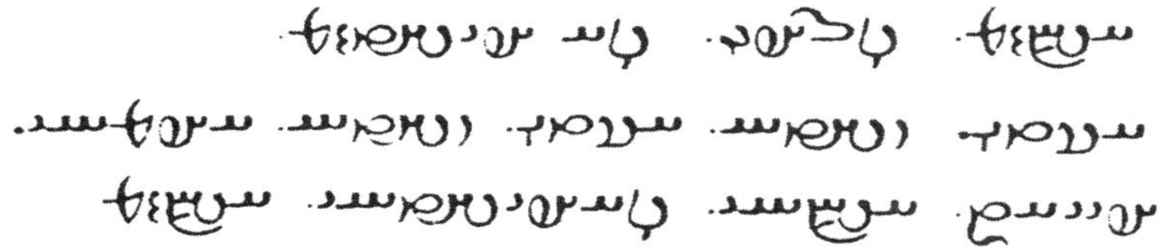

— *Yasna*, VIII.1

> Righteousness is the highest good: [and it] is happiness. Happiness [comes] to that (i.e. him) which (i.e. who) [is] righteous for the sake of the highest righteousness.

The word *aṣa* is rather loosely translated as 'purity' or 'righteousness'. Though near enough for all practical purposes, these renderings by no means give us an adequate idea of the original concept. It is true that the words 'purity' or 'righteousness' might be more or less accurate translations of the word *aṣa* as used in the later Avesta and in the Pahlavi texts. But if we go backwards to earlier and earlier ages we find the concept gradually getting fuller and fuller, until the *Gāthā*s — the sayings of the great master Zarathustra — we get the full breadth and depth of this concept exposed to our view. It would, therefore, be better if we trace this concept in gradually widening circles until we reach the thought of the teacher himself. But it is to be borne in mind that Zarathustra merely revived and elaborated the idea of the ancient wisdom which was the common heritage of the Indo-Aryans and the Iranians.

It will not be out of place if we look into the way in which the Parsis of today follow the path of *aṣa*. They name it *aṣoi*, a Pahlavi word, practically the same as Avestan *aṣa*. But to most of them this word means the bodily or earthly purity. This does not mean only bodily purity — baths, clean clothes, etc. — but also mental purity. Still it is confined to the earthly life, here down below. The implication of the higher degree of 'spiritual purity' is vague in this word *aṣoi* as understood by the modern Parsis.

The Parsi concept of *aṣoi* is, therefore, principally that if the righteous conduct upon earth — it will follow a clean body and fair and just dealing towards fellow human beings. What the Prophet of Iran understood by this was something far deeper and wider. Hence, we find that the nearer we approach his time, the clearer becomes the conception of *aṣa*, and the higher it rises in spiritual purport. Taking the first step backwards towards the Prophet we find that the Zoroastrian writers who wrote during the earlier centuries of the Christian era have had a clearer conception of *aṣa* than the Parsis of later times. They understood it in the light of their spiritual experience. Hence, we find in the books of Avesta compiled in this period that this concept of *aṣa* is distinctly at a higher level. In fact, to indicate the earthly purity, they used another word *Yaozhdao*. From the later Sassanian period onwards, the idea of spiritual purity as conveyed by the word *aṣa* receded slowly into background, at least with the masses.

At a yet earlier period, as is evidenced by later Avestan Hymns, the *Yasht* and *Vispered*, we get more and more spiritual import of the word *aṣa*. We get closer to the idea that the 'praiseworthy ones', the Yazatas, who correspond to the *deva*s of Indo-Aryans and the angels of Christianity have attained their high position in the spiritual world by dint of their *aṣa*. In this context, *aṣa* stands for a fundamental truth of the spiritual world, a truth which being understood and obeyed has led these great beings to what they are. As a matter of fact, Ahura Mazda himself is said to have reached the highest position through *aṣa*.

Finally we come to the concept of *aṣa* in the *Gāthās*. Here we find in the purest form the teacher's philosophy of life and his solution of the problems of existence. Here we find that *aṣa* is vaguely, though not as anthropomorphic as the Vedic gods, personified. *Aṣa* is there a great being, an aspect of god himself standing next to the place of Ahura Mazda. But most often, the meaning is that of a deep spiritual truth, or a spiritual law on which the governance of the universe is based. All that happens in the universe is through *aṣa*: we have to obey *aṣa* and it is *aṣa* which ultimately leads us to the presence of God.

4

Ṛta, Yajña and Dharma

Ravi Ravindra

A mastery am I

> *na vi jānāmi yadivedamasmi niṇyaḥ saṁnaddho manasā carāmi* ।
> *yadā māgan prathamajā ṛtasyādid vāco aśnuve bhāgamasyāḥ* ।।
> — *ṚV,* I.164.37
>
> I know not clearly whether I am the same as this cosmos: a mystery am I, yet conceived in mind I wander.
>
> When the first-born principle of *ṛta* entered in me, then of this *vāk* I obtained a portion.

Thus, speaks the great sage, Dīrghatamas, in one of the most striking verses of the *Asya Vāmiya* hymn of the *Ṛgveda* in his thousand-syllablled speech (*sahasram vācaḥ*), about the mystery of the relationship between the I (*aham*) and the cosmos (*idam*).

Both *aham* and *idam* are born of *ṛta* and are supported by it. The term *ṛta* in the *Ṛgveda* has many meanings — water, sacrifice, Āditya or truth. Its main meaning is Cosmic Law governing the universe. The very existence and expansion of the earth and heaven depend upon *ṛta*. *Ṛgveda* IV.23.9 records: "The whole universe is founded on *ṛta* and moves in it." *Ṛta* is both all-pervading and transcendent. The Vedic *ṛta* is much like the ancient Chinese *Tao*, the Mother of all things, and as *Tao te Ching* says: "The *Tao* that can be spoken of is not the *Tao.*" In the modern form of *vāk*, which is said to be the first-born of *ṛta* (*ṚV*, I.164.37), *ṛta* is the word, which was in the beginning, was with God and was God, and apart from whom nothing came to be (John 1:1-3).

Though in its original intrinsic sense *ṛta* transcends the power of space and time, the gods make it take the form of *satya* (truth) so that it can apply to the affairs of the universe. In some passages, *ṛta* and *satya* are used as synonymous; as are their opposites, *anṛta* and *asatya* — as in the well-known phrase, *satyameva jayate nānṛtam* (truth alone triumps, not untruth). Also, it is said that *ṛta* and *satya* were born from *tapas* (*ṚV*, X.190.1), and are, thus, twins, coexistent, coeternal.

Moral law and obligation, which in later literature was increasingly conveyed by *dharma*, is contained in the notion of more universal order of *ṛta* — even though in later Sanskrit, *ṛta* is described as a child of *dharma*. "Agni inflicts the severest punishment on those who commit transgressions against the law of *ṛta*" (*ṚV*, X.87.11). The gods are described as *ṛtvāns* (the possessors of *ṛta*), as well as *ṛta vradhas* (those who bear the burden of carrying out *ṛta*). The gods arise in order to carry out the purposes of *ṛta*, and are called *ṛtajaḥ* or *ṛtajātaḥ* (those who are born of *ṛta*). Gods are called *vratapas* because they carry out the *vrata* (vow) in obeying the law of *ṛta*.

Ṛta and yajña

As the gods do, so should the humans — follow the law of *ṛta*. The preservation and maintenance of *ṛta* depends on the proper relation between earth and heaven (*dyāvā-pṛthvī*). This proper relation is based entirely on *yajña* by which alone an act or the whole life can be made sacred. To sacrifice (derived from the Latin *sacer* + *facere*) is to make sacred. It is by *yajña* that one participates in the right order. *Yajña* is the 'abode of *ṛta*', 'the home of *ṛta*', 'the dwelling of *ṛta*', or 'the path of *ṛta*' (*ṚV*, I.43.9; I.84.4; III.55.14). *Yajña* becomes the cause, the origin and beginning of all righteous acts and prescribes obligations of the world (*ṚV*, I.164.50 ; X.90.16).

Yajña is the very navel of the universe (*viśva nābhi*); *'ahaṁ yajño bhuvanasya nābhiḥ'* (*ṚV*, I.164.35). *Yajña* is the central thread binding together the souls of men with the souls of the gods, for everywhere and in everything 'the all-pervading *Brahman* is ever established in *yajña* (*sarvagataṁ brahma nityaṁ yajñe pratiṣṭhitam*: *BG*, 3:15). Prajāpati first fashioned *yajña*, and through it he wove into one fabric the wrap and weft of the three worlds (*ṚV*, I.164.33-5). Prajāpati is also identified with *yajña*. The creation sustains itself through *yajña*.

It is important to emphasise that *yajña* is not only sacrifice in the sense that the lower levels must practice self-containment and obedience to what comes from above, but also it is the process of reciprocal exchange between levels. This is clearly brought out in the *BG* (3:9-16) where Kṛṣṇa says:

> Sustain the gods with *yajña* and let the gods sustain you, sustaining each other, you will reach the highest good. Fostered by *yajña*, the gods will bestow on you the joys you cherish.

As in the cosmos in the person

Following the well-nigh universally understood traditional principle, according to which *kṣudra brahmāṇḍa* (microcosmos) essentially mirrors the whole *brahmāṇḍa* (megalocosmos or macrocosmos), what is more cosmologically sung in the *Ṛgveda* concerning *yajña* is specified for human beings for spiritual practice in the *BG* and the *Yoga-sūtra* of Patañjali. The *nābhi* (navel) of the cosmos is the *hṛdaya* (heart) of the person. Kṛṣṇa, who is very essence of *yajña* (*adhiyajña*, *BG*, 8:4) in this body is seated in the heart of everyone (*hṛdi sarvasya dhiṣṭhitam*, *BG*, 13:17).

Kṛṣṇa is seated in the heart of everyone as *svabhāva* (essential calling; inner being), for it is only through being truly and deeply oneself that one can come to Kṛṣṇa's being (*madabhāva*). In order to carry out the actions and responsibilities corresponding to *svabhāva* (*svakarma* and *svadharma*) a person needs to engage in *yajña*, a sacrificing of those parts in one which do not wish to support the wishes of the deepest self. It is only *yajñakarma* which does not lead to the bondage of action. The way to be freed of the bondage — which is in fact the bondage of time and of causalty is not inaction, as Arjuna was tempted to think, but to engage in action as a sacrifice and a sacrament. As Kṛṣṇa says (*BG*, 3:30):

> *mayi sarvāṇi karmāṇi saṁnyasyādhyātmacetasā* ।
> *nirāśīrnirmamo bhūtvā yudhyasva vigatajvaraḥ* ।।
>
> Renouncing all action on Me, mindful of your inner self.
> Without expectation, and without acquisition, fight without agitation.

However, *yajña-karma* is not possible for a *prākṛta* (unformed, vulgar, uneducated) person who does what he wishes for himself and by himself. Only when a person has been made *saṁskṛta* (cultured, well-formed, cultivated) by the discipline of a spiritual path (generically, *yoga*), one is inclined to do and able to carry out the will of Kṛṣṇa. Such a person can come to an identity with the Highest — in himself and in the cosmos — which in the discourse of the *BG* is labelled Kṛṣṇa, and forget any other responsibilities arising from other levels of existence.

> *sarvadharmān parityajya māmekaṁ śaraṇaṁ vraja* ।
> *ahaṁ tvā sarvapāpebhyo mokṣayiṣyāmi mā ṣucaḥ* ।।
> — *BG*, 18:66
>
> Leave all responsibilities aside, turn only to Me as your sole refuge, I will deliver you from all evils; have no care.

Only at the very end of the transformation effected by the *yoga* of the *Bhagavad Gītā* can Arjuna say that:

> *naṣṭo mohaḥ smṛtirlabdhā tvatprasādānmayācyuta* ।
> *sthito'smi gatasandehaḥ kariṣye vacanaṁ tava* ।।
> — *BG*, 18:73
>
> Destroyed is the confusion, I have remembered myself through your

grace, O Unshakable One, with doubts dispelled I stand ready to do your bidding.

Yajña of the mind

The *YS* continues the Vedic sacrifice (*yajña*) by the sacrifice of the limited and limiting mind (*citta*) for the sake of *puruṣa* who is the only true seer. This *puruṣa* is not personally yours or mine; it is the pure power of seeing. One sacrifices the limitation for the unlimited power to see, a sacrifice of one's separated self — with all of one's fears and hopes, likes and dislikes, sorrows and pleasures, failures and ambitions — for the sake of the only one who truly sees. Then follows the sacrifice of the seen, for the sake of the only one who truly is. Then there is no separate object but the *puruṣa*, there is no separated subject but *puruṣa*, there is no knowing except *puruṣa*. The seer, the seen and the seeing are all one; there is no other. This is the state of *kaivalya* — of aloneness, not because there is an opposition or a separation by simply because there is no 'other'.

In this movement from *asmitā* ('I am this' or 'I am that') to *so'ham* (I AM), from a limited self to the Self, from the identification with *citta* to that with *puruṣa*, from the self-will of Arjuna to his willingness to carry out Kṛṣṇa's will, one places oneself in the right internal order. Thus, sacrifice permits order. *Yajña*, born of *ṛta*, is the ground for the re-establishment of *ṛta*. The resulting insight (see *YS*, 1:48-9; 2:15; 3:54) is naturally full of truth and order: *tatra prajñā ṛtambharā*.

Notes

In connection with the remarks on *yoga*, please see R. Ravindra, *Yoga: The Royal Path to Freedom*, in K. Sivaraman (ed.), *Hindu Spirituality: Vedas through Vedānta* (New York), Crossroad Publishers, 1989; Vol. 6 in the series *World Spirituality*), and R. Ravindra, *Yoga and Knowledge*, in R. Ravindra (ed.), *Science and Spirit* (New York, Paragon House Publishers, 1991).

In connection with the remarks on the *Bhagavad Gītā*, please see R. Ravindra, Teaching of Krishna, Master of Yoga, *The American Theosophist*, Vol. 72, 1984, pp. 55-61.

In connection with a discussion of some of the Christian parallels of the ideas presented above, please see R. Ravindra, *The Yoga of the Christ* (Shaftesbury, Element Books, 1992), especially chapters 6, 12 and 14.

5

The Organisation of Structure in the Universe

Varun Sahni

MAN is on the average, about a meter and a half tall. Our place in the cosmos is very central. We are roughly in the middle, size-wise, between the atoms and the stars. If we look down in scale, the atom is about 10^{-9} cm in size (a billionth of a cm) whereas typical stars have a circumference greater than a million km. This fact, that we are 'in-between', as much larger than an atom as smaller than a star, has defined for us the way we structure our sciences. Of the three fundamental forces in nature two operate on small scales (electro-magnetism and the strong nuclear force) whereas gravity, operates on the largest scale. Operationally, we use microscopes and particle accelerators to survey the world of the very small, and telescopes to study the very large.

It is essential to say something about the operation of gravity, because gravity is the fountainhead of much of the cosmic order perceived in the universe. If there were no gravity there would be no stars, in the absence of stars there would be no heavy elements because most of the atoms of which you and I are made were synthesised in first generation stars which existed long ago. So if there was no gravity no stars would exist nor would there be any planets, nothing would shine in space and the whole universe would be uniformly filled with hydrogen and helium and little else. So our very existence — our minds and bodies and everything else besides, arises because of gravity which forces matter to come together, grow more dense, and eventually begin to shine. Since gravity always attracts and never repels, it is also the only force that propagates on very large scales so that everything in the universe can influence almost everything else through gravity.

Now a little bit about the use of different length and time scales; to measure an atom the Angstrom is used as a unit, for conventional distances on earth the unit is a km, which is not of much use when very large distance are involved, such as those between two stars or two nearby galaxies. Instead we measure distance in terms of the light travel time between two astronomical objects. Light takes about eight minutes to travel from the sun to the earth, so we see the sun a little younger —

exactly as it was eight minutes ago. (Light takes only about a second to travel to the moon). However, as astronomical object such as our galaxy is really quite large — containing well over a billion stars, and it takes nearly a hundred thousand years for light to travel from one edge of the galaxy to the other. This means that light which arrives at the earth today left the outer reaches of the galaxy long before the time of the *Mahābhārata*. Now our nearest large galaxy — the Andromeda, is almost two million light years distant, light reaching us today left that galaxy two million years ago and we are seeing the Andromeda as it was in its distant past. Similarly, if there is intelligent life on Andromeda which could be viewing us today, it will see us the way we were two million years ago and will have no way of knowing that a certain species of ape has now become man! So looking into the distance we are actually looking into the past. There is no way we can know what the Andromeda galaxy looks like at this very moment because nothing can travel faster than the speed of light which is our only means of communication to distant parts of the cosmos.

Another important aspect of our universe is that matter likes to cluster or group together. On the smallest scales, the simplest level of clustering is revealed in an atom. The hydrogen atom presents a proton with an electron orbiting it. The electron orbits the proton essentially due to the attractive nature of the electromagnetic force. On much larger scales the gravitational force takes over, and on planetary scales we have the earth-moon system. The planet Jupiter has sixteen moons and Saturn has seventeen, which shows the clustering between planets and their moons. On a larger scale, the solar system is a beautiful example of clustering. Our sun has nine planets and there may be several million planetary systems in our own galaxy — the Milky Way. The Milky Way galaxy is made up of about a hundred billion stars clustered together. The clustering hierarchy does not stop here, galaxies cluster together to form groups and clusters, we belong to a group of about twenty galaxies which includes the Andromeda. These twenty galaxies move together in a common gravitational pool. On a still grander scale, clusters of galaxies consist of thousands of galaxies grouped together, and now it seems that we are seeing super-clusters of galaxies which could contain upwards of a hundred thousand galaxies each. That is tremendous amount of matter considering that each galaxy could have several billion stars in it! Now the big question which is being asked today is whether the clustering hierarchy stops there — do superclusters lie at the apex-point of this clustering hierarchy or do still larger size objects exist in the universe?

I shall substantiate the different levels in the astronomical hierarchy of structure through some illustrations.

At the beginning of the hierarchy we have our own planet the earth, as seen from space (*fig*. 5.1). As we know, the earth has a very complex eco-system, there is a lot of feedback from the environment which makes our planet a very non-linear system. The Gaia hypothesis in fact, describes the earth as a complex living system, sustained by the suns's energy and its very own mechanisms of bio-feedback.

In *figs*. 5.2 and 5.3, we see the planet Saturn and its rings. The rings of Saturn are an incredibly beautiful astronomical entity consisting of billions of frozen particles moving according to the laws of gravity and electromagnetism. Structurally, these rings are very complex and the laws they obey are very non-linear. Complex non-linear systems quite often show very simple and beautiful patterns which are stable for long periods of time as is the case with the rings of Saturn. We still do not know why these rings are structurally so stable when the orbits themselves can be quite complicated.

At the next higher level of clustering we have our planetary system consisting of the sun and nine planets. The earth in relation to some of the outer planets is quite small, as revealed in *fig*. 5.4, which shows the earth, together with the inner planets Mercury, Venus and Mars and the giant planets, Jupiter, Uranus and Neptune.

Our solar system may not be unique in the universe. Indeed, recent observations claim to have found evidence of large planets orbiting at least two other stars in the Milky Way galaxy. It is now widely believed that the sun and its planets originated from a primeval gas cloud many billions of years ago. Such gas clouds would have been fairly common in the distant past when the universe and galaxies, such as the Milky Way, were in their infancy. Star formation in such clouds would light them up making young galaxies spectacular objects, when the first stars began shining in them several billion years ago.

It is interesting that star formation is a continuous process with some stars being born and others dying, all the time. In *fig*. 5.5, we see newly born stars in a protostellar cloud. The death of stars like their birth, is not a quiet event! The death of very massive stars (more massive than the sun) is accompanied by violent ejection of matter from a star which becomes exceedingly bright for a very short interval of time. (A star having a mass 2-5 times that of the sun can become brighter than a billion suns in a spectacular supernova explosion.) The matter ejected from a star moves freely through interstellar space, and in due course becomes the source of gas for a future generation of stars. Meanwhile, the dying star rapidly cools and shrinks into a tiny white dwarf, neutron star, or sometimes, even a black hole. We, thus, see that the matter in stars is recycled from generation to generation, with new stars being born out of matter left behind from older ones which died after having exhausting their nuclear fuel. The recycling of resources, thus, seems to be as much as integral part of the stellar life-cycle, as it is of different biological life-cycles on our own planet — the earth.

Moving to the next higher level of organisation we come to *fig.* 5.7 which shows a galaxy viewed edge-on from space. Such a galaxy could be populated with over a billion stars, many with their own planetary systems, moving in orbits within a common gravitational pool. Although stellar orbits can themselves be quite complicated, the stellar system as a whole is usually quite stable and can exist in different morphological forms, the two most common being elliptical and spiral galaxies. The galaxy shown in *fig.* 5.8 is a spiral galaxy and resembles our own in many ways.

At the next (higher) level of organisation, we see a little group of galaxies consisting of four or five members vigorously interacting with each other (*fig.* 5.9). I would like to add that the mean intergalactic distance is actually much smaller than the interstellar distance, making it that much easier for galaxies to interact collide and merge with each other as they are seen doing in *fig.* 5.9. By contrast stars very rarely collide.

Fig. 5.10 shows the Universe on the largest scales. Each triangle shown is a galaxy, and there are several thousand galaxies in this figure. We see something

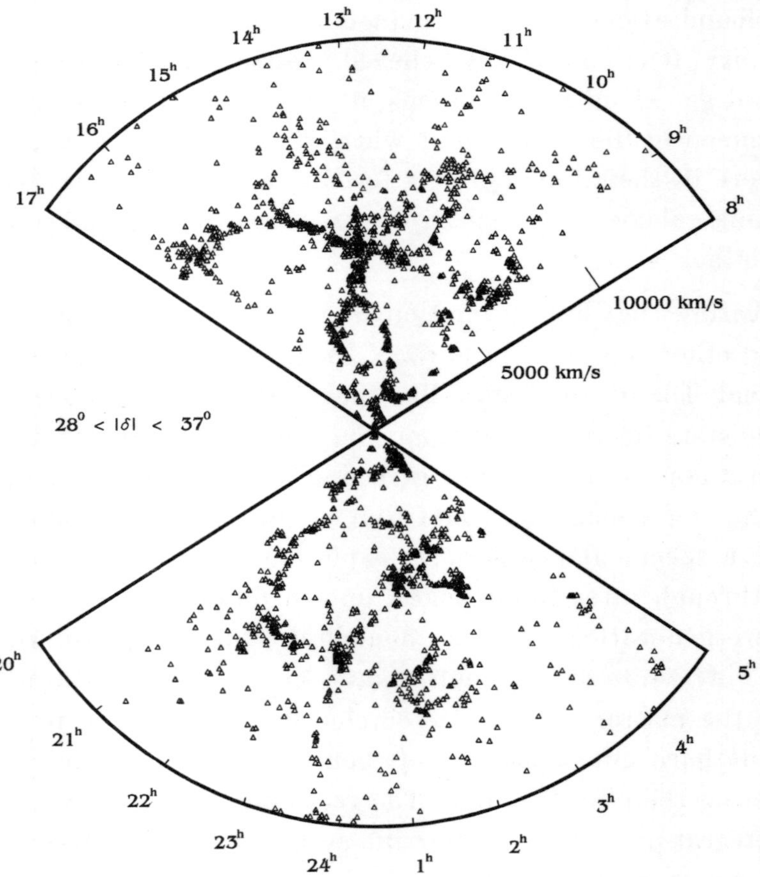

Fig. 5.10

quite extraordinary: galaxies are not distributed randomly in space but seem to connect-up to form dense clusters and super-clusters of galaxies.

Indeed, one clearly sees vast super-clusters of galaxies stretching from left to right in the northern galactic hemisphere, and from top to bottom in the southern galactic hemisphere. The frothy distribution of super-clusters that we see is complemented by giant 'Voids', regions virtually empty of any matter. The largest known super-cluster has been nicknamed the 'Great Wall', and extends to almost 300 million light years. The super-cluster — void network represents the highest level (and probably last) in the organisational hierarchy of the Universe. It has been demonstrated to have 'sponge-like' and 'bubble-like' features, and its quasi-cellular properties are being extensively explored today.

Our endeavour to chart the patterns formed by clusters and super-clusters of galaxies is in a sense a combination of a much older endeavour — to chart the patterns in the stars, our constellations — which our forefathers began many thousands of years ago. So, in a sense, cosmologists are very like the astronomers and geographers of previous millennia. Our present knowledge of the geography of the earth, the location of its continents and the extent of its oceans, is largely due to traibilasing voyages by explorers and travellers of the past who painstakingly noted the lands they journeyed through, and the diverse cultures they encountered. So, it is that we now have a fairly good idea of the texture and geographical location of most of the earths surface. Space travel was virtually non-existent till a few decades ago, and man has had to rely exclusively on rays of light — those unique messengers of information, to understand the layout of the heavens. Today travel to even nearby stars lies in the domain of science fiction, and we must instead rely on larger and more powerful telescopes to help us view the distant realms of the cosmos.

A central scientific question before us is to understand how matter manages to organise itself into galaxies and clusters and super-clusters of galaxies giving rise to the rich structure we have seen in the last few figures.

It is widely believed that galaxies did not always exist 'ready-made' but were formed out of small initial fluctuations present in the Universe billions of years ago. According to the currently popular Big Bang model, the Universe itself might have originated some ten or twenty billion years ago and galaxies cannot possibly be older than the Universe since they are a part of it. The mechanism which gave rise to galaxies is known as gravitational instability and its origin is the observation that all bodies in the universe exert an attractive force on each other. As a result, even tiny fluctuations in the distribution of matter get amplified and begin to grow as different particles of matter come closer and, according to the inverse-square law of gravity, attract each other more strongly. Although we cannot view galaxies directly at very large distances (they become very faint) wed can probe the Universe at early times (and the presence or absence in it of small perturbations) with the help of 'the Cosmic Microwave Background' — to fossil radiation left behind by the Big Bang. This radiation (sometimes called the afterglow of creation) is very cold; its omnipresent nature ensures that our galaxy and all other galaxies as well, are immersed in it. (The temperature of the Microwave Radiation is only about 3 degree K or –270 degree centigrade.) An important aspect of the radiation is that since the universe is expanding, radiation which is cold today was very hot in the past. (The reason for this is that light is made up of particles — photons, the energy E of a photon is given by the planck formula. $E = hc/\lambda$ where c is the velocity of light, and λ is its wavelength. As the universe expands, λ increases proportionally to the expansion which makes it very large now, consequently the photon energy E is very small today, and so is the temperature of the microwave background. However, since the universe was smaller in the past, so was λ, which makes the Microwave background (and hence the universe) very hot initially.

Going back to the origin of galaxies, a major scientific discovery of this decade has been the map of the Cosmic Microwave background made by the COBE satellite in 1992 (*fig.* 5.11). This temperature map clearly revealed that the Microwave background was not smooth but showed small distant fluctuations when viewed along different directions in space. After the discovery of initial fluctuations in the cosmic microwave background, scientists soon realised that similar tiny fluctuations (1 part in 1,00,000) must have existed in matter a few million years after the Big Bang. Later gravity in the course of billions of years, amplified those fluctuations and formed galaxies and super-clusters of galaxies out of them. Now a days the laws of gravity are encoded in a computer programme and an N-body simulation is conducted in which a 'virtual' universe is simulated with initial condition inferred from fluctuations seen in the Cosmic Microwave Background.

Viewing *fig.* 5.10, the following question naturally arises: how is it that gravity can arrange matter into such anisotropic structures as we see in that figure? The answer surprisingly comes to us from a sister field of science — optics.

All of us have seen swimming pools, rivers and lakes. When you look at the bottom of a pool of water you can see alternating very bright and dark regions (the former are called caustics) which form when light rays intersect (see *fig.* 5.12). Although this is an example from optics it is also a good description of how gravity works.

In *fig.* 5.13, shows a picture taken of particles moving by virtue of their mutual gravitational attraction, we see 'caustics' exactly like those seen earlier for light. (In this case 'caustics' form when nearby particle trajectories intersect.) It is very interesting that two apparently different disciplines in science give results that are

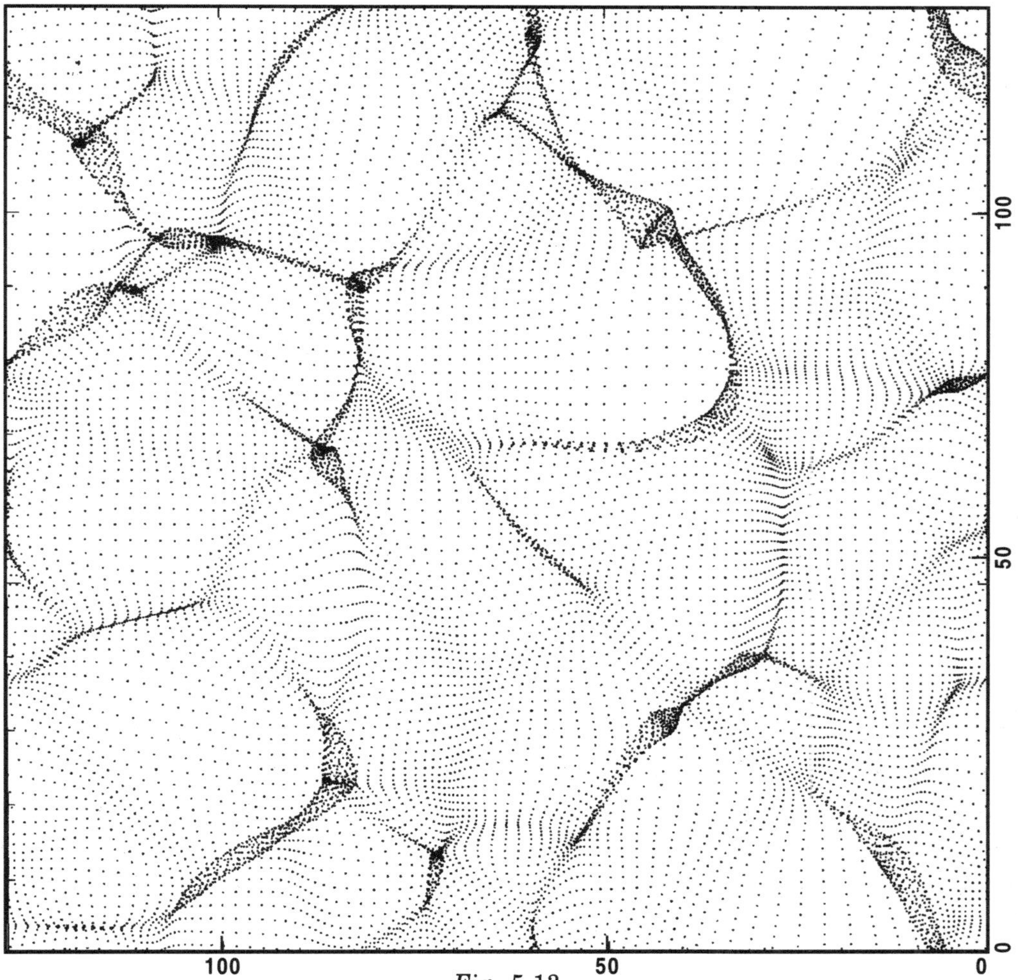

Fig. 5.13

so closely related! In some sense it shows the basic unity of the scientific endeavour.

As computers get more powerful, more realistic modelling of the universe can be attempted. Astrophysicists have accurately modelled collisions between galaxies and the subsequent galactic mergers. The largest scales which can be accurately modelled by moderate size comptures today are about 300 million light years across, roughly corresponding to the size of the Great Wall in *fig.* 5.10.

Finally, in cosmology too we have our very own 'hen and egg' problem. Stated simply it boils down to the question: Which originated first — super-clusters or galaxies? Complementary models provide different answers. The first, known as the bottom-up scenario of galaxy formation, describes the formation of large scale structure in the universe as a hierarchical process. The smallest objects form first, they cluster together under the laws of gravitation and form larger objects. In this scenario, dwarf galaxies and globular clusters are the first to form, merging with one another they form galaxies. Later galaxies group together to form clusters and super-clusters of galaxies, and so on.

According to this scenario the youngest objects in the Universe are also its largest, namely super-clusters.

In the rival top-down scenario, the largest objects — super-clusters, form first. After forming, super-clusters fragment into clusters which further fragment into galaxies. So the youngest objects in the universe are the smallest.

Current observations seem to favour the bottom-up scenario of structure formation. In fact, observations made by the Hubble space telescope reveal that galaxies may be present at very early times when the universe was only a small fraction of its present age. However, any theoretical model of the formation of large scale structure must also explain the existence of dark matter, matter which does not shine but does gravitate. It appears that most of the matter in the universe is dark, leading to the speculation that much of it may have a non-baryonic origin (i.e., dark matter is not made of protons, electrons and neutrons — the stuff are of which planets and stars are constituted).

A hypothesis, made in the early 1980s favoured dark matter to be made up of light massive neutrinos having a mass ten thousand times smaller than that of an electron. Galaxy formation with light neutrinos as the dark matter would lead to the top-down scenario for structure formation. Heavier dark matter particles, having masses between a thousand and a million times that of the electron have also been proposed by particle physicists. Such particles, if they exist as dark matter would lead to the rival bottom-up scenario.

An unambiguous determines of the nature of dark matter will undoubtedly be a big step forward in our understanding of the phenomenon of structure formation in the Universe. I am sure a breakthrough in this direction will come within the next decade.

Acknowledgement

It is a pleasure to thank Vidyulata Mahabal for her help in preparing this manuscript.

Figs 1-9 have been reproduced from the *Cambridge Atlas of Astronomy*. *Fig.* 10 is from L.N. da Costa, in: *Cosmic Velocity Fields*, Proceedings of the ninth IAP Astrophysics meeting; F.R. Bouchet and M. Lachieze-Rey (eds.) (Editions Frontieres 19994), p. 475. *Fig.* 11 is the four-year COBE map.

Fig. 5.1

Fig. 5.2

Fig. 5.3

Fig. 5.4

Fig. 5.5

Fig. 5.6

Fig. 5.7

Fig. 5.8

Fig. 5.9

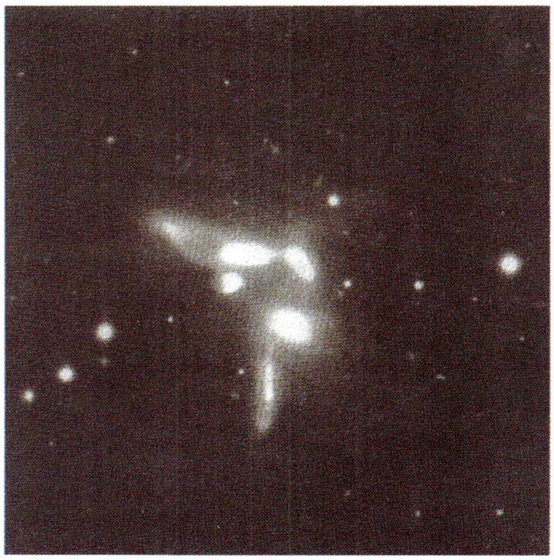

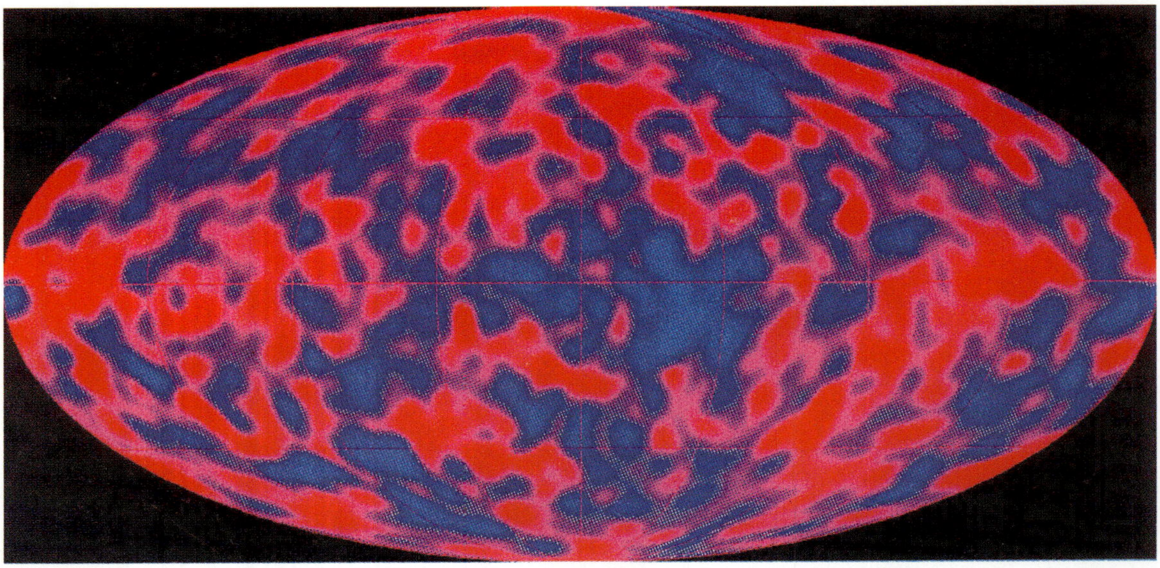

Fig. 5.11

Fig. 5.12

6

Order is Central to Life Processes and Biorythms to Reproduction

G.P. Talwar

जिंदगी क्या है अनासिर में ज़हूरे तरतीब।
मौत क्या है इन्ही अजज़ा का परेशां होना ।।

What is life? An organised state of some elements.
What is death? It is the disorder of these structures.

THE living state, is only attained when these elements get organised in an ordered fashion and in order to maintain these traits, it is important that they stay in that ordered state. Whenever there is dismemberment of the structure, there is a loss of functional properties. Of course, we see yet another reality in living systems, a constant breakdown of some molecules as a part of metabolism with the generation of energy which, in turn, is used to make new molecules, in ordered structures. These processes go on in a dynamic manner.

While discussing the phenomenon of creation, several views have been projected from various perspectives but as a biologist, I would say that the essential molecules which make possible the living state are the proteins and the nucleic acids. These have a landmark role in the transition of inert matter to a state where the properties of living matter are acquired. Proteins are important structural compounds of tissues, and are also the ones which make possible a myriad of reactions at the normal living temperatures under mild conditions. Proteins are macromolecules composed of 20 different types of amino acids, linked to each other in a defined sequence. A given protein differs from the other in the number and order of the amino acids, creating molecules of differing activity. Their functional traits emerged with the generation of the macromolecular state. The individual amino acids, the building blocks are devoid of such activity.

Fig. 6.1 is a schematic representation of a protein, the beta subunit of the pregnancy hormone, the human chorionic gonadotropin, abbreviated as hGG. It is a peptide of 145 amino acids linked to each other. The primary sequence of these amino acids generates a certain conformation, with loops formed by the amino acid cysteine and automatic folding in a way dependent on the spatial characteristics of the constituting amino acids.

Fig. 6.2 is a three-dimensional structure of this molecule, where the β hCG is represented in blue. Six cysteine-cysteine loops bring various points of this molecule proximal to each other. The pregnancy hormone is composed of 2 subunits, the beta and the alpha, another chain of 91 amino acids. The two subunits have intrinsic property of associating with each other in a 'hug' created by virtue of their complementary structures. Their combination endows the molecule with hormonal properties. hCG is important for the establishment of human pregnancy. It also stimulates the production of sex steroids, in females mainly progesterone, which is crucial to sustenance of pregnancy. hCG can also act on the male testes to generate the male sex hormone, testosterone. The effect can be demonstrated *in vitro*. *Fig.* 6.3 is an experiment illustrating the dose response of testosterone production as a function of the amount of hCG taken. While hCG (composed of both alpha and beta subunits) produces the effect, neither the alpha nor the beta subunits taken alone at the same concentration have this property. This brings me to yet another statement, namely the creation of new functional properties by aggregation of two complementary proteins generating a super structure.

Molecular evolution is illustrated by consideration of the structure of three hormones made by the pituitary, a gland located in the base of the skull, which makes master molecules regulating the endocrines in the body. These are the luteinising hormone (LH), the follicle stimulating hormone (FSH) and the thyroid stimulating hormone (TSH). LH and FSH influence the production of sperms (in males) and egg (in females). TSH stimulates the production of thyroid hormones. All of them are composed of two subunit proteins, alpha and beta in the same way as hCG. The alpha subunit is identical in all four hormones. The beta subunit confers in each case the hormonal specificity and thereby the variation in the biological activity. Thyroid stimulating property is very different from FSH and LH which stimulate the production of the egg or the sperm (Table 6.1).

Hormones or for that matter any molecule that influences another molecule or a process act by binding with a 'receptor'. The recognition operates by juxtaposition of two shapes or conformations unique to the interacting molecules. This *modus operandi* enables selective effect of a hormone on a given tissue, even though a number of hormones be circulating in the blood. For example, estradiol, a female sex hormone, would act on the uterus on which receptor molecules for this hormone are present and not on lungs lacking in similar molecules or receptors. *Fig.* 6.4 is a knowledge base computer graphic representation of the hCG interacting with its receptor. *Fig.* 6.5 is the way a master hormone regulating fertility in both males and females, the LHRH or GnRH hormone assumes a folded structure. The hormone is a short chain peptide composed of only ten amino acids. The two ends of the molecule are proximal to each other by the bend in the middle. The receptor for this hormone communicates with the three binding points adjacent to each other.

Table 6.1

Molecular evolution: Acquisitions of new functional properties by association of diverse proteins to a common subunit protein

Common Subunit	*In Association with*	*Properties*
alpha	beta hCG = HCG	Establishment and maintenance of human pregnancy
alpha	beta LH = LH	Ovulation induction production of sex steroid hormones
alpha	beta FSH = FSH	Development of egg in the female and spermatogenesis in male
alpha	beta TSH = TSH	Stimulation of Thyroid for production of thyroid hormones regulating energy metabolism in the body; also required for development

Fig. 6.6 is a three-dimensional structure of another hormone, insulin familiar to most. It is made by the pancreas and it promotes the uptake of glucose by tissues. Insulin is a protein of fifty-one amino acids, thirty-one on one chain and twenty on the other, the two chains linked by the S-S cysteine bonds. It exists as a hexamer, six units associated with each other stabilised by a metallic atom zinc.

Glucose is an important source of energy for several tissues. In particular, brain depends heavily on this sugar for deriving its energy needs. Once the sugar is internalised in cells, it is captivated and driven in the metabolic pathway by an enzyme hexokinase. *Fig.* 6.7 gives the structure of this enzyme and also shows the cleft in which the sugar fits into get phosphorylated.

The defence system (immune system) of the body operates by recognition of 'self' from 'non-self'. This discrimination operates through molecules (MHC) located on the surface of cells. There are two classes of such molecules: Type I are present on all somatic cells of the body and Type II on cells which transact the immune function. The former take part in rejection of 'foreign' or non-self grafts, whereas the latter category participate in elicitation of the immune response. A remarkable progress has been made in definition of the three-dimensional structure of the MHC molecules. *Fig.* 6.8 is a schematic representation of one of the MHC molecules, which also depicts the groove in which a portion of the antigen fits in to be presented to other immune cells.

Nucleic acids

As pointed out above, attributes of living state are acquired by aggregates composed of nucleic acids and proteins. Simple viruses are composed of just these two types of compounds. The combination of these two type of macromolecules through evolution created particles which possess the trait of replication, of giving rise to identical progeny. Reproduction is considered as a basic property of living entities.

Nucleic acids are of two types: the DNA and the RNA. DNA is the chemical repository of genetic traits in mammals. It is an enormous size molecule, where several genes are located next to each other with commas, full stops and sequences whose function is not fully understood. The language of DNA is written in four letters (A, T, G & C nucleotides), the order in which these occur defines one gene apart from the other. The human genome is currently being sequenced with a powerful battery of technical equipment in some countries and before long the full sequence of nucleotides in human chromosomes will be known. This knowledge can enable better understanding of the hereditary disorders and also lead to gene therapy or correction of a wrong gene responsible for some serious disabilities. Hopefully these tremendously important interventions will be employed ethically and not abused.

The property which enables faithful replication would be clear from the structure of DNA depicted in *fig*. 6.9. It consists of two helices coiled in a manner to have complementary bases (A-T; G-C) brought near to each other to form hydrogen bonds and hydrophobic interactions which stabilise the molecule in a given disposition. On heating, the two helics dissociate. However, on cooling, these again come together in the original form. Each helix can serve as a template for synthesis of a complementary strand. Thus, two strands of a given DNA give rise to four or two pairs. With the newly synthesised complementary strands, identity to the original DNA retained (*fig*. 6.10).

Fig. 6.11 gives the three-dimensional structure of polyoma virus which causes tumors in rats. This virus is closely related to another virus, papilloma virus, which causes cervical cancer in women. Polyoma virus has proved to be an ideal model for understanding the mechanism of self-regulated assembly through conformational switching of protein subunits incorporating the DNA inside an icosahedral coat virus, elucidated by one of my colleagues Dinkar Salunke, at the National Institute of Immunology.

An interesting aspect of some viruses is the ease with which they mutate to evade elimination by the host immune system. The virus causing AIDS has this hypervariability trait just as the virus causing influenza. Mutation occurs with one base changing to another causing an altered coat protein. This phenomenon which is taking place all the time leads to the projection that creation of new viruses has

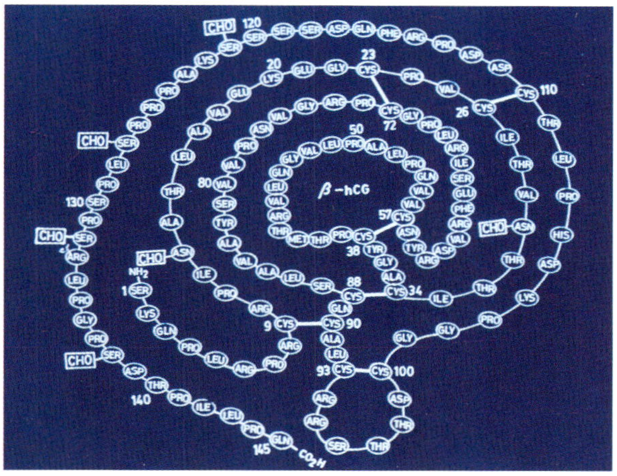

Fig. 6.1 : Beta subunit of the pregnancy hormone, hCG is a chain of 145 amino acids linked to each other. The chain assumes folds due to the formation of S-S bonds.

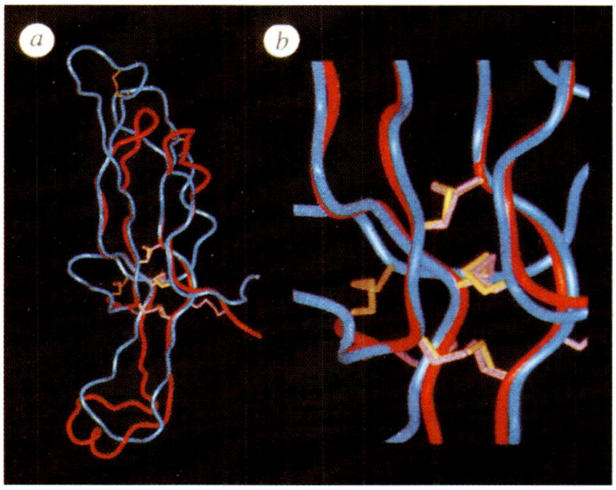

Fig. 6.2 : (a) Three-dimensional structure of hCG as published in Nature. The hormone is composed of two subunits, alpha (red) and beta (blue). The two subunits have complementary structure and associate with each other in an ordered way to generate a molecule with biological activity of the hormone, namely to establish and sustain human pregnancy.

(b) Is an enlarged view of the cysteine knot (S-S bonds) depicted in yellow, whereby the two subunits hug each other in a fairly tight manner.

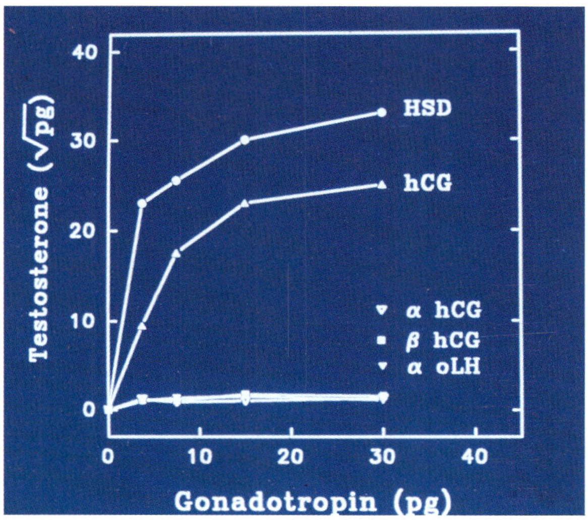

Fig. 6.3 : Neither the alpha subunit alone, nor the beta alone has any biological activity, biological activity (in this experiment measured by production of testosterone). However, the union of the two creates another ordered structure which has the hormonal activity.

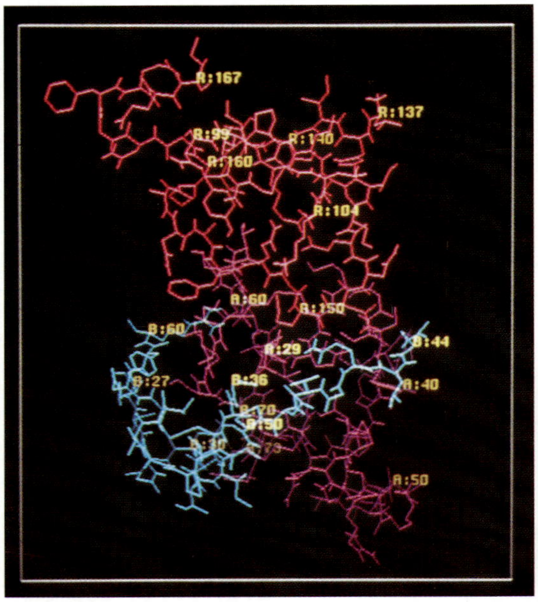

Fig. 6.4 : A hormone exercises its action on a target tissue by binding with and recognising a specific receptor with spatial fit. The interaction site of hCG with its receptor, the regions involved in the binding are shown, hCG *a* chain is in violet, b chain in cyan and receptor in pink.

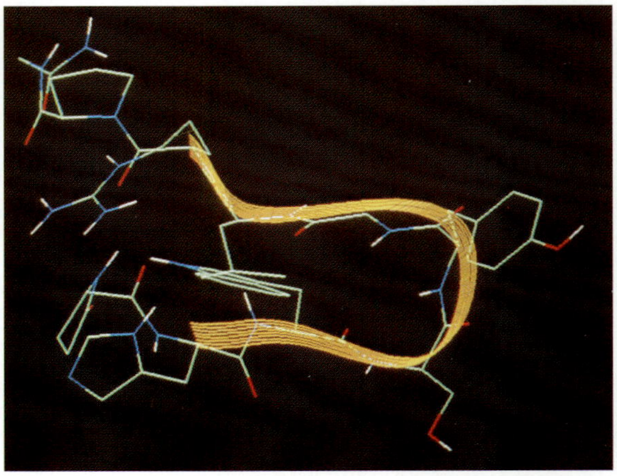

Fig. 6.5 : LHRH, a short peptide of ten amino acids, is released from hypothalamus located at the base of the brain. It is a master molecule regulating reproduction in both males and females. In spite of its short length, it has a distinct structure which enables communication to responding cells in the pituitary. It folds like an embryo with the two ends of the chain coming close to each other.

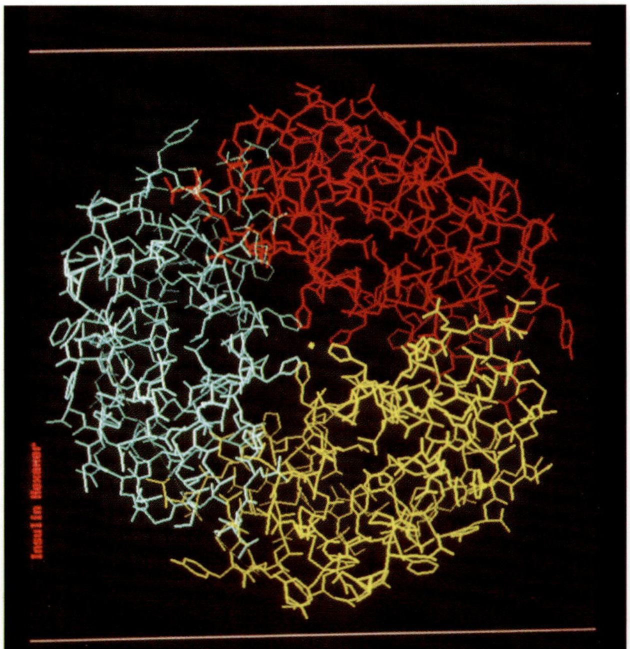

Fig. 6.6 : The structure of the hormone Insulin. It exists as a six molecule aggregate, a hexamer held together by at metal ion, zinc at the centre. When Zn is removed, the hexamer dissociates into three dimers. (The three dimers are shown in different colours in the figure.)

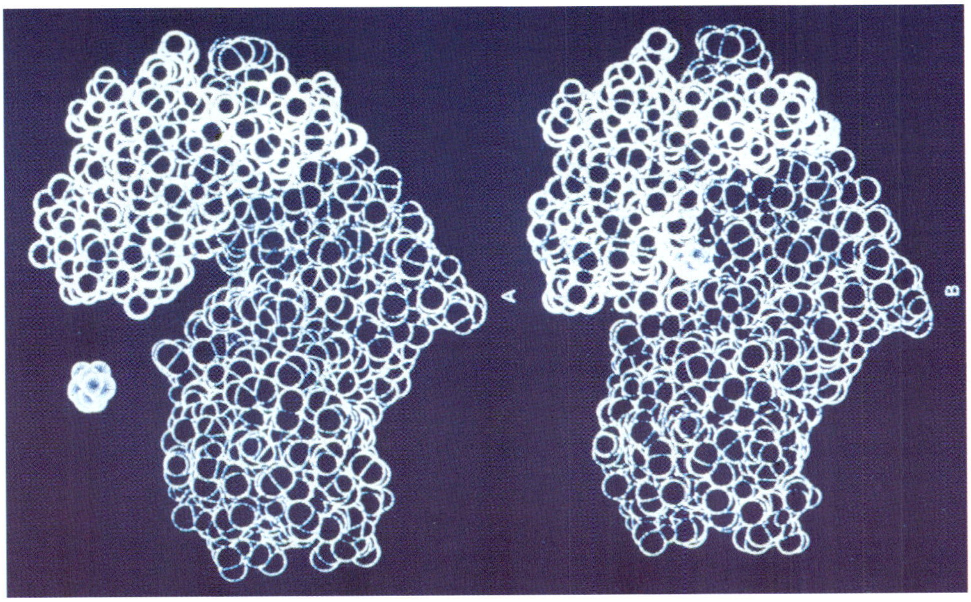

Fig. 6.7 : Space filling model of hexokinase, an enzyme metabolising glucose with the sugar bound (B) and without the sugar (A).

Fig. 6.8 : The recognition of 'self' in the immune systems operates through molecules located on the membrane of cells. The figure shows MHC class I molecule bound to a peptide antigen. The complex is viewed in the orientation in which T-cell receptor binds to it. The peptide is shown in white.

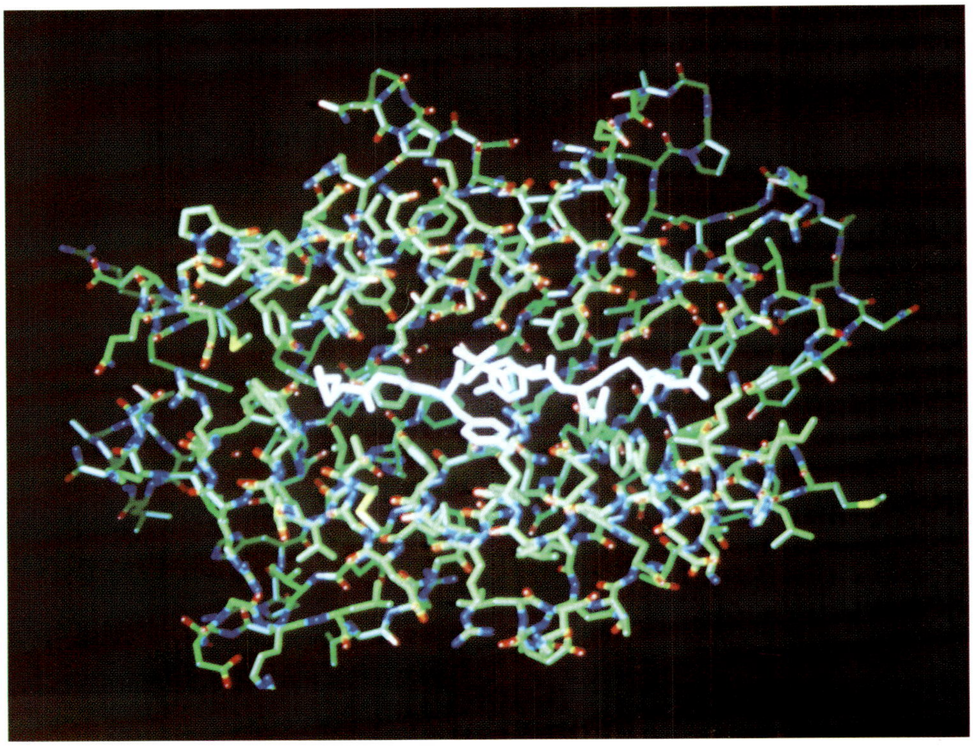

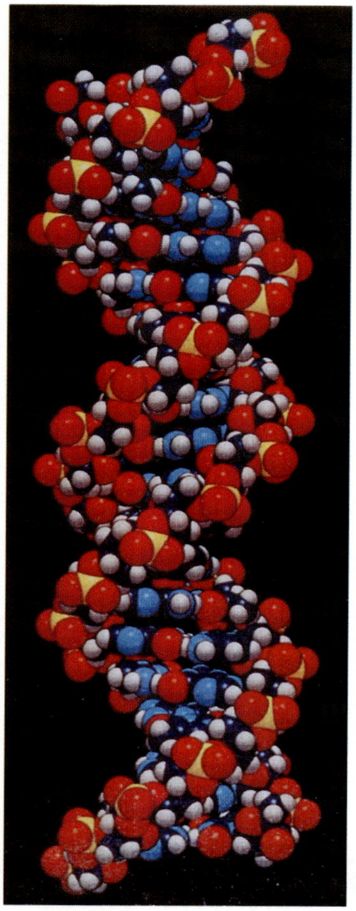

Fig. 6.9 : DNA, the material bearing hereditary (genetic) information is a double helix, the two helices stabilised by bonds between complementary bases. The space filling model given in this figure is colour coded as follows: Carbon atoms: Black; Nitrogen: blue; Oxygen: red; hydrogen: white; and phosphorous: yellow.

Fig. 6.11 : Viruses composed of nucleic acids and proteins organised in a framework assumes properties of living matter. The figure shows the morphological features of the polyoma virus. Red indicates the interior of the virus. The icosahedral structure of the virus is organised in pentameric units.

Parent strands

(A) ---A - T - G - C - C - G - T - A - G - C---

(B) ---T - A - C - G - G - C - A - T - C - G---

At the time of replication, each strand serves as a template to code for the complementary base (depicted in blue)

(A) ---A - T - G - C - C - G - T - A - G - C---
(B) ---T - A - C - G - G - C - A - T - C - G---

(A) ---T - A - C - G - G - C - A - T - C - G---
(B) ---A - T - G - C - C - G - T - A - G - C---

The two progenies are exactly identical to the parent DNA.

Fig. 6.10 : Illustrative sequence of bases in a strand of DNA. The two helices are stabilised by juxtaposition of complementary bases; A-T; G-C.

not stopped and is continuing. We perceive a new virus only when it causes an effect, useful or nefarious. The emergence of the AIDS virus is a manifestation of this continuum. It is erroneous to say this virus was created for biological warfare, as has been alleged by some ill-informed prophets of gloom.

To sum up then, I have endeavoured to demonstrate that order is a basic requisite of molecular structure, which endows these with functional traits, be it the remarkable regulatory properties of hormones or of enzymes capable of bringing about complex reactions at ordinary temperatures or of structures according shapes with ability to recognise specifically with discrimination an effector molecule or a drug. The basic property of replication — of giving rise to an identical molecule is inherent in the nucleic acids. I would now turn to the other theme of this enlightening symposium, the rhythms.

Biorhythms

Life processes have rhythms. It is best illustrated by reproductive process. Birds breed at a certain time of the year. It is linked to sun and light. Signals are sent to the brain through optic pathway, which cause the production of a master hormone that stimulates via another gland, the production of sperm (in the male) and eggs in the female. Along with the generation of the gametes, sex hormones are produced that motivate the copulation behaviour and prepare the reproductive tract organs to receive the fertilised eggs and rear the embryos. Dogs breed twice a year. When a female dog is in heat, she secretes a pheromone, which can be sensed by male dogs at long distances by the olfactory channels. It is an extremely sensitive mode of social communication.

Rhythms and cyclicity is evident in functioning of the reproductive system in humans also. Women normally ovulate once a month at an average span of 28 days which is roughly equal to the cycle of the moon. Derangement in these cycles occurs due to stress or other factors disturbing regular way of living.

Besides menstrual, biannual or annual rhythms, one can perceive also diurnal rhythms. Some hormones, such as the growth hormone is secreted at night during sleep. The male sex hormone testosterone is present at different concentration in the early morning and late evening. The same is true of gluco-corticoids. The composition of hormones and growth factors is not constant in blood throughout the day. A part of these variations are associated with diurnal rhythms, others prompted by stimuli and changes in the environment. A new discipline 'chronobiology' has emerged which recognises the daily rhythms. It is proposed that medication given at a certain time is more effective than that given at random.

7

Concept of Order in Science of Islamic Culture Area

A. Rahman

CONCEPT of order, as inferred from the writings of scientists in the Islamic Culture area in the medieval period was used to cover three features of natural phenomena, and has a slightly different connotation in the field of social phenomena.

Firstly in cosmology it used to describe the regulatory movement of planets as a part of astronomical observation. It is also used to describe the harmony. This was not described purely as a part of internal dynamics of the system but as a part of the display of God's wisdom and reflection of his omnipotence.

Secondly in the field of geographical and biological system, the concept was used to denote levels of development and as part of interlinking of non-living with the living on the one hand and on the other the degree or level of development of the living.

Thirdly, as a part of natural order, it is used to correlate the cosmic with human system. This is evident in the concept of macrocosm and microcosom. All the three orders have been ordained by God, as a manifestation of his Will.

In the case of knowledge and functioning of society, the position of the king and the nobility was accepted. The social order or disorder depended on the morality and virtuousness of the king. However, one also discerns the role of knowledge as a cutting edge for change as well as creating order.

Framework of social order

The teachings of Islam emphasise the concept of social order, built around man as the central feature. The three dimensions of which are:

(i) A prescription for self-discipline around a code and a set of practices.

(ii) A code of conduct in dealing with others.

(iii) A code of conduct for the use of materials and resources.

It may be worthwhile to briefly dilate on these features:

In the case of self-discipline apart from worship and prayer, it was advocated that a person should have self-control, particularly with regard to his needs and requirements, humility, capacity to sacrifice, honesty and personal integrity. In the case of dealing with others he should show kindness, be forgiving and have capacity for giving to others, should have compassion and show courtesy. In the area of material and resources, frugality was advocated for self and sharing with others was considered a virtue.

The belief was that if each individual practised these codes and followed the disciplines the social order would be harmonius. The emphasis on man is the most significant feature.

The social feature of Islamic teaching was the emphasis on acquisition of knowledge. The Islamic revolution was based on the twin features of morality, ethics and knowledge. It was a knowledge revolution against *jahiliya*, i.e., ignorance and superstition. Therefore, seeking of knowledge and its teaching and dissemination was considered a major responsibility of every individual. The emphasis of acquiring knowledge would be evident from what is written in *Quran*:

> "Say are they equal — those who know and those who know not".
> "Verily the men of knowledge are the inheritors of the prophets".
> "Seek knowledge from cradle to grave".
> "Go to China in search of knowledge".
> "The quest of knowledge is obligatory on every Muslim man and woman".

It was this emphasis on seeking of knowledge which motivated Muslims[1] from Spain to China to acquire knowledge from different countries and incorporate it in their own contribution to the promotion and development of knowledge. It is, therefore, not surprising to find reflections in the writings of Muslim scholars modification or adoption of ideas, concept and theories from earlier contemporary civilisations. This is stated in the *Resaile-e-Ikhwan us Safa* (Epistles of Brethren of Purity).

> It is true, we obtained most of sciences from the preceding philosophers as others now receive them from us. Such is the way of this world — for one people to derive benefit from another. Thus it is the Persian sages obtained their astrology and the sciences of observation (of the heavenly bodies) from the sages of India. Similarly, the Israelites got their knowledge of magic and talisman from Solomon, the son of David.

However, as the growth of knowledge raises basic questions and formulates concepts and theories, based on the knowledge, it comes into conflict with established ideas,

1. Nasr Seyyad Hussain, *Introduction to Islamic Cosmological Doctrine*, London, 1964, pp. 36-8.

concepts and theories, raising the question as to what is true. The earlier or the latter? How the conflict should be resolved? In the Islamic culture are this was the central feature, like other societies, of disorder. The one feature of removing the disorder was suggested that knowledge should be tempered with what *Quran* says. This was suggested by Al-Ghazali in Islamic culture Area. In the same manner in which Śaṅkarācārya, in India, emphasised the correlation of knowledge with Vedas for its validity. Knowledge has a dual role in society, both as a creator of order and harmony as well as creator of disorder and disharmony. This is reflected in different societies of Islamic culture area. Suppression of knowledge, in terms of new ideas and theories as well as the persecution of scholars was prevalent in different phases of the growth of the Islamic societies. In the early phase growth and promotion of knowledge is encouraged followed by its suppression. From Baghdad to Spain and from Iran to Central Asia, India and Chinese Turkistan we see these phases of order and disorder.

Having briefly discussed the concept of order, harmony and disorder and disharmony in social order and the role of knowledge in creating both, it may be worthwhile to discuss the ideas of order and harmony as is evident from the ideas and theories of scholar dealing with natural phenomena.

Natural phenomena

In the field of Astronomy the regularity of seasons, motions of planets was taken as an extreme example of perfect motion and perfection of cosmic order. Many scholars though considered it as a part of divine order, while the explanation of the functioning of it was in terms of the astronomical system developed by Ptolemy. According to the latter, the movement of the planets was in perfect circles, i.e., reflecting perfect orderly movements. Any observed deviation from it was explained by adding a number of spheres. Later on the basis of accumulation of data on the basis of continued observation, the concept of elliptical orbits appear. In India we find Mulla Mahmud Jaunpuri, a Court astronomer of Shah Jehan indicating the possibility of elliptical orbits, which was fully developed by Ghulam Hussain.

The concept of time was developed to order the social as well as the natural phenomena. Al-beruni developed the concept of time in a more explicit manner. According to him time precedes the creation of the world, it has both a beginning and an end. His concept of time is physical, in so far as it is based on the revolution of the sun. Further, according to him it is the revolution of the sun which creates order.

There are many dimensions in the treatment of time by Al-beruni. Firstly, he clearly distinguishes and describes the concept and reckoning of time in different cultures. Secondly, apart from night and day and seasons created by the revolution of the sun, there are other cyclic movements of the heavens producing geological and historical times. Thirdly, Al-beruni was much influenced by Hindu cosmological doctrine in developing his theory of qualitative nature of time. Fourthly, the cyclic nature of time covers both the historical as well as the natural phenomena. Lastly he also covers the interpretation of the past both in the context of civilisations as well as in natural phenomena.

The concept of time was deduced from the astronomical phenomena, both as a regular feature and also providing for plotting of successive events. The regulatory processes was compared to the motion of the wheel. This is evident in the poetry of Omar Khayyam. He was an astronomer, mathematician, poet and philosopher. Three dimensions of order are evident in his poetry, which may reflect the general outlook of the period.

Firstly, the concept of wheel, i.e., the motion and order it represents as independent phenomena, which may be used to explain natural phenomena in different ways. For instance, he says: "Since the wheel (of Heaven) did not revolve to the wishes of any wise men, you count the sphere seven, if you wish; if you wish eight."[2] Referring perhaps to astrology and astrological forecasts made about the future events and lives of people he again uses the concept of wheel. However, what is interesting in his usage is what could be termed as preordained nature of the movement which cannot be changed. As he says:

> The good and the bad which are in man's nature, the joys and sorrows which are in man's fate — leave not your efforts to the care of the wheel, for in the ways of the wisdom this wheel is thousand times more helpless than you are.

Secondly, he also makes the concept of wheel to describe cyclic order, of movement in time and space. In doing so his concern, which appears to be central to his philosophy for human life and its order is evident. He says:

> In the cycle of our coming and going neither a beginning nor an end is visible, no one can utter a single word on this subject — whence is this coming, and whither is this going.[4]

While in this couplet reflects the concept of onward movement, it also implies that there is no beginning and no end as much of time as of human life. Finally, according to him, whatever order one may construct or reconstruct, it is a construction of human imagination. For instance:

> This sea of existence has come out of the unknown. There is no one who can

2. *Rubaiyat Omar Khayyam*, tr. Paricher Kasra, New York, 1975.

3. *Rubai* 26.

4. *Ibid.*, 48.

> pierce this pearl of knowledge. Everyone has said something on (vain) imagination. No one can tell as it is.[5]

This order of existence is further divided by him in two orders, the spiritual and the natural:

> O thou hast come from the spiritual world with zeal and haste bewildered by five, four, six and seven.[6]

The two orders — the spiritual order which is internal to man and the natural order which is external are implicit. In this couplet four represents the theory of matter (hot, cold, moist, dry, fire, water, earth and air). Five represents five senses (sight, hearing, feeling, smell, taste), i.e., biological system. Six represents six directions (East, West, North, South, Up and Down), i.e., geography; and seven represents seven planets, i.e., astronomical system. In this, two implicit references are worth indicating. Firstly, in referring to the human order and the natural order, was Khayyam also implying a reference to the theory of macrocosm and microcosm to link the two systems? Or was he segregating the two as independent orders unrelated to each other? Secondly, the use of numbers, a common feature of Islamic culture ethos, probably derived from Babylonian and Pythagorean and probably Indian systems to denote order is most significant.

Framework of concept of matter

Matter was divided in various categories. In this first group was the matter found in nature and comprised fire, air, earth and water. Each one of them had a quality of hot, cold, dry and moist. In the second group was the celestial matter of stars and finally the ideal substance — the original matter, having no determination other than existence. In other words, matter exists at different levels of existence and their qualities and properties are part of the level of existence. The order, harmony and organisation of matter depend on their position in an hierarchical order — the lowest being minerals followed by plants, followed by animals and finally Man. According to *Rasail*:

> Plants come before animals in the series of beings and serve them as materials for the forms of animals and food for nutrition of their bodies. . . . Plants occupy an intermediate position — necessary and salutary — between the four elements and the animals. All the parts of the vegetables which the animals consume, such as seeds, leaves, fruits and so on, come from four elements digested and transformed by the Plants.[7]

5. *Rubai* 34.
6. *Ibid.*, 14.
7. *Ibid.*, vide Nasr, p. 72.

This concept is well described by Jalaluddin Rumi in his couplet:

I died from mineral and plant became
Died from plant and took a Sentient frame
Died from the beast and dressed a human dress
When by my dying did I ever grow less

One can discern besides an element of transformation of one form to another, indicating evolutionary process. Besides these broad hierarchies each group has its sub-hierarchies. In both the cases of plants as well as animals, one finds the division on the basis of organisation levels such as marine and land plants and animals, as, for example, those laying eggs or those reproducing young ones. One of the interesting features, which brings out the order based on the organisation structure and the functions based on the latter is brought out in the Dispute between man and animals. According to Nasr, as mentioned in the Dispute, the only point which justifies the domination of man over animal kingdom is that "among men there are a few who became angels on earth".[8]

As would be evident, and implied in the above quoted remark, man becomes a link between the earth and the heavens.

In the organisation of matter two more features of the thinking of Islamic culture are need be mentioned. Firstly, the use of numbers in creating an order of four elements and their linkage with the biological system. Secondly, the concept of microcosm and macrocosm, linking of human system with the cosmic.

The use of numbers to describe the order, in all probability, was taken over from the Babylonian and Pythagorean traditions. We find the first clear use of number is Jabir Ibn Haiyyan in his concept of Magic Square.

Hot		*Fire*		*Dry*
	4	9	2	
Air	3	5	7	*Earth*
	8	1	6	
Moist		*Water*		*Cold*

In developing this concept the four elements are linked with two of their qualities, and each of these have a sum of 15. Further, whichever way the numbers are added the sum is 15, whether two elements or two quantities are linked up or two qualities and an element is linked up.

8. *Rasail*, vide Nasr, p. 73.

Jabir further developed the system by linking the four elements and the four qualities with the human system.[9]

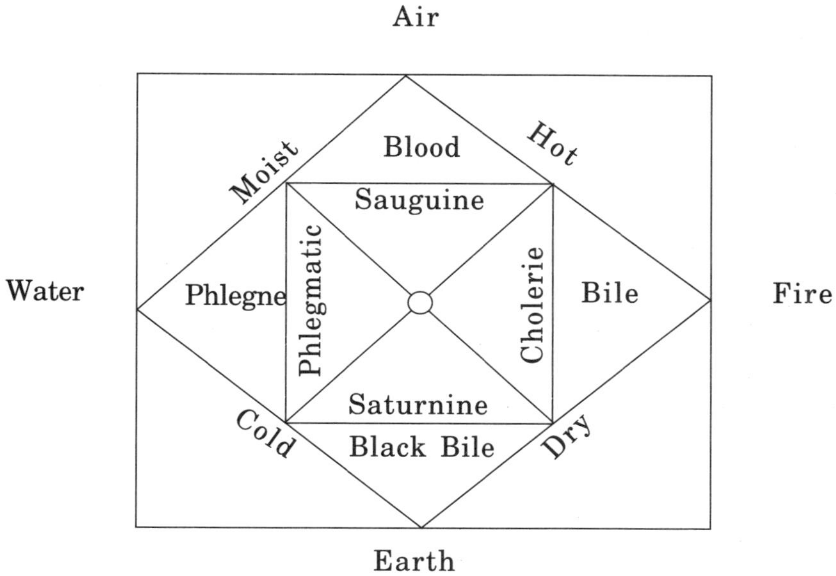

Jabir confines himself to organising elements with their qualities with number and also with these with human system. Another alchemist — Sufi Ibn Bishrun brings in the concept of being. According to Ibn Bishrun:

> What exists, what brings into being and how into being.[10]

The theory of being, according to Nasr was developed by Ibn Sina as a concept of sequence as a four-stage order.

Mahiya, i.e., essence of brings things, brings things into being, i.e., *wujūd*, i.e., existence which is *wājib*, i.e., necessary and finally as a result of what is possible or not possible. In this concept,

> necessary being (*Wajibul Wujud*) or God are essence and existence inseparably united, while for all other beings unity and existence are accidents added to their essence or quidity.[11]

The whole framework and philosophy dealing with matter and phenomena develops the concept of order as a part of hierarchies of the cosmos in which the multiplicity of phenomena reach harmoniously towards unity. However, in the understanding

---

9. For the development of Jubinian order of Matter, see Dr. S. Mehdi Hasan: *Islamic Culture*, April-July 1990, pp. 185-91.
10. Dr. S. Mehdi Hasan, *Part I Alchemy, Studies in History of Science*, June 1983, pp. 30-138.
11. Nasr, *op. cit.*, p. 198.

of the process, numbers play an important role.[12]

In the context of the concept of the relation between man the cosmos, the theory of microcosm and macrocosm was developed. The concept represented the unity of creations, and the power of God to bring together all elements of the world in man as well. While on one hand, different parts of the human body are linked up with the Zodiac signs, on the other some planets are called male, female or hermaphrodite, Al-beruni has dealt with these references:

> The following are various parts of the body which are related to several signs. The head and the face to Aries, the neck and windpipe to Taurus, the arms and hands to Gemini, the chest, breast, sides, stomach and lungs to Cancer, the heart to Leo, the womb and its contents to Virgo, the back and buttocks to Libra, the genitals to Scorpio, the thighs to Sagittarius, the knee to Capricorn, the shanks to Aquarius and the feet and heels to Pisces.[13]

In addition to the above linkages, the Zodiac sign was also linked to seasons and human life:

> Aries, Taurus and Gemini are vernal, changeable and govern childhood, the east and the east winds, the first watch of the day and night. Cancer, Leo and Virgo are acstivel, restful and govern youth, the south and the south wind and the second watch. Libra, Sagittarius and Scorpio are autumnal, changeable, govern adult life, the west and its wind, and the third watch. While Scorpio, Aquarius and Pisces are hibernal, peaceful and govern old age, the north and the north wind and the fourth watch.[14]

As would be evident, the way human systems, natural phenomena, matter and its qualities and astronomical phenomena are linked up and correlated with each other, the effort appears to bring the multiplicity and diversity within the framework of an order and to seek ultimate unity. The divine plan ordained this multiplicity, diversity and the ultimate unity and its order. Any disorder which may be noticed by humans was beyond human comprehension. This appearance of diversity and its unity was reflected in the Sūfī doctrines of *Wahdat ul Wujud*, i.e., unity of existence and *Wahadut ul shabud*, i.e., unity of appearance or observation.

A cursory look at the work of scholars, their ideas, conceptual theories reveals certain common problems to which they addressed themselves a common framework,

---

12. Nasr, *op. cit.*, p. 45.
13. Vide Nasr, *op. cit.*, p. 158.
14. Vide Nasr.

within which they tried to find answers to the problems. Their different points of view were also in this framework. Firstly, in developing their outlook and ideas they drew upon the different knowledge systems developed in different culture areas — the Babylonian, Chaldean, Zoroastrian, Indian, Persian and Greek. Secondly, Time occupies a significant place in order of things, which brings order out of chaos. They attempted to use time to provide an understanding of natural and social phenomena. A concept of cycle occupied a significant place in historical as well as natural phenomena. Thirdly, their treatment of nature, covers the theory of matter, treatment on the nature of minerals, plants, animals and man, and their distinctive features and their relation with astronomical and cosmic phenomena, as a part of one order, organised and regulated by divine plan. Lastly, the order as ordained, designed and functioned according to God's will, who is omnipotent and omnipresent.

It is interesting to note that all the scholars who discuss order and design as a divine attribute, and as a manifestation of God's Will, lived in a period of perpetual wars, social unrest and uncertainty about future and personal lives and were persecuted. They did have a theory of rise and fall of dynasties, depending upon the virtues or otherwise of rulers. Their thinking in this direction would be evident from Ibn Khaldum who quoted *Nausherwan*:

> Royal authority exists through the army, the army through money, money through taxes, taxes through cultivation, cultivation through justice, justice through the improvement of officials, the improvement of officials through forthrightness of wazirs, and the whole thing in the first place through the ruler's personal supervision of his subjects, conditions, and his ability to educate them, so that he may rule them and not they him.[15]

Finally, the scholars in Islamic Culture Area covered a wide ranging subjects — philosophy, science, religion, poetry, literature and commented on social and cultural life. Despite the controversies and the turmoil they found themselves in, they endeavoured to find some semblance of order and harmony in the multiplicity and diversity of life and nature.

---

15. *Ibn Khaldum Muqaddina*, tr. Franz Rozenthal, London, Routledge & Kegan Paul, 1958, pp. 80-1.

PART II

SOCIAL AND CULTURAL DIMENSIONS

8

The Cosmic and Social Order of Eating
The Vedic Metaphysics and Ethics of Food

Arindam Chakrabarti

He did not eat for fifteen days and came to his father.

> *"What should I say, Sir?"*
> *"Tell me all the Ṛks, the Yajus and the Sāmans you know."*
> *"Nothing is coming to my mind, Sir!"*
>
> (Hence the mind is made of food, life-breath is made of water and speech is made of fire.)

Chāndogya Upaniṣad VI.7.2-6

> *He said, "I am egoless, spiritual, free"*
>
> Then swore because his dinner was not ready.

Sri Aurobindo, Collected Poems, Page 162

> My song shall be of Food, producer of strength . . .
>
> O savory Food . . .
>
> Those who share your sweetness with others are truly your friends/
>
> Those who keep your fine taste to themselves are stiff-necked wretches.
>
> *Sadhamāda*, *Ṛgveda* I, 187 (tr. Panikar)

The cosmos as a kitchen

By the side of a lethal lake where all four of his brothers have lost their lives trying to show their human muscle against natural ecological justice, an awe-inspiring crane guarding the waters asked prince Yudhiṣṭhira a mysterious question, among hundreds of other tough questions and riddles: "What is the news?" asked the bird. The lives of all four of his brothers depended upon the right answer. Yudhiṣṭhira — firm in all battles, as his name indicated, replied calmly:

> In this cauldron filled with the grease of great delusion with the fire of the sun and the fuel of day and night, stirring with the ladles of months and seasons, Time the great cook is cooking all of us living beings. That, verily, is the news.

The Universe is an enormous kitchen. We are Time's food. Arjuna had a glimpse of this truth, when on the eve of the great war he saw Kṛṣṇa as Time incarnate chewing away and devouring all the past, present and future warriors, kings and heroes. All 'paths of glory' as it were could be seen as leading to that blazing fiery mouth of Kṛṣṇa, like rivers rushing towards the ocean. In wise amazement — the only befitting attitude that accompanies such a vision of the real cosmic order (*āścarayavat paśyati kaścid enam*, *Gītā* II/29), Arjuna had said:

> You are all because you consumed all.

If the Great spider who sets up his world-web (to use the language of the *Muṇḍaka Upaniṣad*, I/7) itself is so literally omnivorous, it is not at all surprising that each of us tiny simulators of that Self-multiplier should also live through cooking and consuming.

The present paper will try to sketch out the ancient Vedic metaphysics and ethics of food and eating. Contrary to some popular accounts of it, mainstream Indian spirituality never negates or berates bodily nourishment. In these days of concentrated over-consumption and greed glorified as the urge to develop, surrounded by large-scale hunger, we still have a lot to learn from the basic Vedic ideas of virtuous eating.

For a quick preview, the paper will be divided into the following six sections: (I) The Cosmos as a Kitchen, (II) Eater and Eaten — The Seven Pairs, (III) From Metaphysical Law to Moral Law — the two faces of Dharma, (IV) The Fate of the Lonely Eater, (V) Baudelaire and Śaṅkarācārya, (VI) I am Food — the *Taittirīya* Ecstasy.

To come back to the culinary ontology of life as Time's cooking of us through the seasons, this idea is older than the *Mahābhārata* from which the above story of the bird quizzing Yudhiṣṭhira is taken. "Time cooks all living things", is a statement found in *Maitrāyaṇī Upaniṣad*. Sooner or later we are all devoured by death. But apart from that, this premise of universal edibility should not be only taken as a grim reminder of universal mortality. When we are fed we flourish. Similarly, our being eaten may bring nourishment to our eater whoever that may be. Not all eating is violence or killing. When a baby suckles at its mother's breast it does not devour or destroy the mother, although it, in a sense, eats her or eats out of her. Sanskrit uses the same word for 'cooked' and 'ripe'. Not only that, a spiritually perfected person is called *siddha* which in common parlance means 'boiled'. Hence,

Ramakrishna's pun: "What is the mark of bring perfect (*siddha*)? Being tender, like vegetables which are boiled." So cooking is also a metaphor for desirable maturation. In English, 'I am cooked', may sound like bad news. We don't like the idea of being inside the cauldron getting fried or boiled because we are used to thinking of ourselves as being in control. We think we are the eaters and cooks. And we comfort ourselves with the idiom of 'time-management', 'time-saving', 'time-spending' and even 'buying time'. But the simple fact of irreversible ageing should incline us to rethink the matter. When we start thinking in these 'gastrometaphysical' (this term is adapted from 'gastrosemantics' used by Khare 1992) terms, we notice, to start with, that there is a sense in which our life-world is a perpetual preoccupation with eating (even without extending 'eating' metaphorically to cover consumption of oxygen). Every hour of the day is spent in directly or indirectly procuring, preparing, sharing, consuming, digesting, ejecting out, wanting, inventing or resisting food. Of course, like digestion, much of which happens beyond our conscious awareness and during sleep, much of this preoccupation is unacknowledged and unconscious. It is this phenomenological absence or hiddenness (see Leder 1990) that makes the felt body's relationship with food so intriguing. Just as we are growing older every moment, we are consuming and being consumed every moment, whether we feel it or not. Such a central activity must be capable of providing a comprehensive model for understanding the true order (*ṛta*) of the world, if mathematics, sport or rhythmic movement can do so.

The eater and the eaten — seven pairs

Dividing the world into the categories of the eater and the food is as old in Indian thought as its division into manifest and unmanifest, the consuming *agni* and the replenishing *soma*, subjective consciousness and objective matter. But the eater-food dichotomy itself covers at least seven distinct layers of meanings.

First, in any experience, action or mode of existence, the knower, actor or enjoyer is the eater and the object or accusative of knowledge, action or enjoyment is food. In the typical epistemic situation, for example in perception, a bit of the object, namely its form, enters the cognitive system where it is processed according to various appropriate recipes. An experienced person is thus well-nourished with memories and ideas. Thus, the mind grows by being fed by the environment. In classical Indian Aesthetics, a connoisseur or sensitive audience is called the 'relisher' (*rasika*) and the work of art, poetry or music is called the food to be relished. Just as the essence of good cuisine is the emergent total effect of a variety of ingredients and spices passing through a trained palate, the *rasa* or aesthetic essence — literally the juice — of the act of literary or dramatic appreciation arises out of a combination of several external and intenal emotional, performatory and preparatory factors. The tasting is called 'chewing' (*carvaṇā*). Notice that this conception of knowing or enjoying or savouring requires an active appetite or hunger. Experience gets coloured by expectation, thought by desire, knowledge by imagination.

Second, since the body is born of parts of the effects of food in one's parents' bodies and grows by ingestion of more food, food is the seed-cause (*vījam bhojyam* — *Maitrāyaṇī Upaniṣad*, V.10) and the eater an effect. At this level no distinction is made between the eater and her body. It is the body-mind complex which needs and digests food, not any immutable soul. So the eater is an effect, and food its material cause. One of the Upaniṣad (*garbhopaniṣad*) says:

> The food essence is of six kinds. From food blood is formed, from blood flesh, from flesh fat, from fat bone, from bone marrow, from marrow semen. From a combination of the man's semen and the woman's blood the fetus is formed.

It is not only the gross body which is a transformation of food. Most crucially it is the mind. The psyche of the person is a direct effect of what he eats. *Chāndogya* divides consumed victuals into three parts: the grossest is processed out as excrement, the middle part becomes flesh and the finest part becomes mind. That is why most of the food restrictions of a religious Hindu have to do with the temperamental and spiritual effects of eating rather than with the morality of the causal story behind the procurement of food. Your thoughts, desires and dispositions are supposed to be shaped by what you eat, just as if you do not eat anything the first casualty would be your mind. "From pure food comes pure nature", is an oft-quoted dictum. Thus, eaters including their mental and physical make-ups are effects and food the material cause.

Third, the eater is supposed to be remaining the same or unchanged while the food is changing and ceasing to exist. The eater is not a completely unmoved mover but he does not change his identity as a person while eating (except in myths or fables where eating or drinking something makes a human or non-human being turned into something else!! Did not Adam turn into a mortal by eating the apple?). When I eat a carrot, the carrot gets transformed immediately into many successive forms but I do not become something or somebody else. If, especially, we regard the decision-making self or *puruṣa* as the eater, it has to be the relatively unchanging thing compared to the food we grind, chew and digest. But this contrast misled Aristotle into holding that "food is acted upon by what is nourished by it, not the other way around". For, to be nourished, as we noted above is surely to be acted upon. So the eater also changes, but his transformation is *sarūpa pariṇāma*.

It remains interesting, however, that the conscious subject has a normative pull towards immutability so that for him to be changed beyond recognition is usually bad news, whereas for the food, after it is eaten, the faster it changes the better. In

Sanskrit we have the same word *jīrṇa* which means age-worn when applied to men or houses but well-digested when applied to food.

Fourth, the eater as a body lies outside while what is inside enveloped by that body is the food. Śaṅkarācārya interprets the *Taittirīya* texts: "Body is the eater, breath is food, Space is the eater, the earth its food" by enunciating principle: "If *x* finds a place inside *y* then *x* is the food of *y*" (*yat yasya antaḥ pratiṣṭhitam bhavati tat tasya annam bhavati iti*). There is also the implication that the eater is more spread out in space than the food because the former has to make room for the latter in itself.

From this, the *fifth* conceptual duality also follows. The more independent locus is the later while the relatively dependent located object is the food. Yet, between life-breath and food — the vitality which enables food to be digested and the food which enable vitality to sustain itself and grow — which one is the more independent? According to *Bṛhadāraṇyaka*, there is no one-way answer to this question. They are dependent upon each other. Without life food cannot be eaten, a weak or lifeless body cannot make use of food, and without food life withers. Together supporting each other, food and vitality, *anna* and *prāṇa*, constitute *brahman* that all-pervasive Divinity of which the human person is a miniature image.

The *sixth* dichotomy is thus the reverse of the fifth. Whatever is nourished and dependent is the eater and whatever is nourishing is the food. Edible plants and grains in pre-historic rain-forests would live without human intervention, but humans would not live without edibles.

Finally, in the *seventh* pair we see the interplay of those two senses of 'being for the sake of something or someone' which Aristotle distinguishes in *De Anima* in the context of nutrition.

"for the sake of which" can mean either:

(a) the end to achieve which, or

(b) the being in whose interest.

Now, the seventh pair, according to the Upaniṣads, goes like this: That for the sake of which something exists is the eater (the meaning-giver). That which exists for the sake of something else is the eaten (the meaning-carrier). It would seem obvious, at the first blush, that sentient creatures should be eaters by this criterion because all the earth's food exist for the sake of them. Surely insentient things cannot be meaning-givers! Apart from the fact that sentient beings eat each other, this simple equation ruptures at many points. If we take Aristotle's first sense — the end to achieve which — then sentient creatures themselves exist for the sake of food. We live to eat. This is not just some hedonists' view of life. The *Aitareya Upaniṣad*

(I.3.1-10) tells the story of life as a constant pursuit after food which plays the role of a fugitive, "having been so created (out of water, food) wished to flee away. He tried to grasp it by speech but failed. Hence, just by talking about food, people are not going to be satisfied. Similary He failed to capture food by the eyes, ears, touch, mind, and the genital organ and failed. This failure is evidenced in the fact that seeing, hearing and touching or thinking food are not enough to satisfy us. Finally the downward breath or the digestive-evacuative *vāyu* called *apāna* was able to bring food back to the body." To the extent we exist for the sake of food we should be the eaten and our food the eater. Our food indeed makes our life meaningful. Thus, we are our food's food. The word *anna* is derived therefore in two ways simultaneously as the accusative and nominative of the verb *ad* (to eat). That which is consumed by us and that which consumes us is food. Eaters are eaten because they are dependent upon, enveloped by and physically as well as psychologically situated in what they eat.

From metaphysical law to moral law

The *Ṛgveda* celebrates eating just as much as *Taittirīya Upaniṣad* praises food as *Brahman* and prohibits speaking ill of food. The seasonal or round-the-clock food festivals that go on in Hindu temples (like Purī Jagannāth or Nāthadwārā or Annapūrṇā Temple at Vārāṇasī or Govardhan temple at Braj, *cf.*, Toomey 1992) are sanctioned by the Śruti passage *annam bahu kurvīta* । *tad vratam* (*Taittirīya* III.9). But the joy of eating and feeding must not lead to any sense of domination or power over food. What is consumed is to be respected. Bakhtin, writing about Robelais, says,

> man's encounter with the world in the act of eating is joyful, triumphant; he triumphs over the world, devours it without being devoured himself.
>
> — Bakhtin 1965, p. 281

The Vedic philosopher will agree with everything except the last bit. As we have seen in the seventh pair of relationship between the eater and the eaten, nothing can devour without being devoured itself. What the *Mahābhārata* says by using the break-up "MĀṀ+SAḤ" (me-he) about meat can be said about any food which we consume covetously with a sense of power and aggression. The feeling of the food or the slain creature that it is ME that HE is eating, gets reflected back in the eater's justified fear that through dependence and decay this food or flesh is going to eat me (the Sanskrit pun works with the English 'Me-Eats' as well!). But Śaṅkara's comments on the *Taittirīya* passage about food leaves a very laconic hint of a way out of this reciprocal devouring. As embodied beings we have to eat. We are not free to go without food, especially because the Upaniṣad recommends clearly that one ought to wish to live for a hundred years. To go on eating and thereby be eaten (since literally, as Bhrtṛhari warns us, *bhogā na bhuktā vayam eva bhuktāḥ* — objects are not consumed, we are) for a hundred years does not sound like a good idea. But we are free to choose the manner of eating. We can sharingly or unsharingly. Food as God preserves those who give food to the hungry but eats up those who eat without giving. It is only the unsharing eater who should be afraid of becoming devoured. Just as one who knows that he is ignorant transcends ignorance, one who knows that he does not unconditionally own what he eats, that his relationship to food is reciprocal and, therefore, does not try to dominate or hog it all can escape the jaws of his own food. Food given protects the eater from itself. To be saved from food's devouring mouth, one has to give a share of one's food to other creatures who are fellow-eaters.

By giving away part of what I 'own' to others I give myself. Just as freedom consists in active acknowledgement of necessity, my freedom from the consumption-rut can come through a willing self-offering as a life-sustaining nourishment to others from whom I derive my nourishment in the first place. There is no release from the world without paying back our debts in this way. Hence, *Bṛhadāraṇyaka* (I.4.16) tells us that by giving food and shelter to the hungry and the homeless and feeding birds, beasts and insects, we perform sacrifices as much as by offering oblations to gods and ancestors. We make ourselves their *lokaḥ* or *upajīvya* object of enjoyment or life-support. By feeding ourselves thus, willingly, back to those that we live off, we escape becoming unwilling and unwilling *prey*s to our own food.

The idea of sacrifice or *yajña* provides us that bridge from the mere theory of the order in cosmic consumption to a practical order (in the sense of *command*) of ethical eating. In any sphere of human existence, just discovering the truth or reality of order or natural law (in the form of symmetry or regularity of pattern) is not enough. The concept of *ṛta* requires that somehow that order or law, when recognised, make a certain kind of ethos or practice obligatory for us. Logical or scientific law must be linked up with moral law. *Satya* must lead to *dharma*. Fire burns, wind blows and the sun rises everyday because *dharma* in the form of trurthful, non-injurious, non-covetous living leading to perpetual joy still holds sway. A full defence of this equation of moral and natural necessity (the 'must' in rain must come from 'clouds' and the 'must' in 'you must enjoy through renunciation') is beyond the scope of this paper. But the passage from a cosmology of eating to an ethics of eating, here, is supposed to illustrate the central idea behind this equation. In the *Gītā* (3.10-14) for instace, the rule of obligatory sharing of food is derived from the causal picture of the sacrifice-rainfall cycle. The first step is: *annād bhavanti bhūtāni*. From food, all living beings arise. Then, *parjanyād anna sambhavaḥ*. Without rainfall, grains and vegetables would not grow, so there would be no food. The third step may seem tied to an archaic metereology that the smoke rising from the sacrificial fire creates rain-clouds. But it is actually a deeper ecology which is based on the principle that a community gets the environment that it deserves. Through, the unseen merits (called *apūrva*) earned by ritual observances of sacrifices, life-enhancing weather-conditions are causally brought about. We can easily interpret *yajña* more widely. Any act of renunciation of giving up greed can be called 'sacrifice'. Unless humans give up desire to use every tree for building and burning and other greedy projects which deplete nature, normal rainfull cannot continue. And this rain-fall again produces the food which sustains life on earth. Culture and civilization, built up on the basis of normative laws, have a role to play in maintaining the ecological balance which, but for their intervention, may look purely natural and value-neutral. This is the crucial role of Sacrifice, or *yajña*. Personalising the forces of nature into principles of illumination, namely: *devatā*s, the Vedic seers rationalise the process of seasonal regeneration of earth and its resources as 'gifts from the gods who are dependent upon the human offering of clarified butter to the fire' (*havirbhujaḥ*). When humans dedicate to the gods the first share of food which they owe to the gods and consume only the leftover *yajña-śiṣṭāśinaḥ santaḥ*, then they free themselves of the usual blemishes attending eating. If, on the other hand, they eat without offering to those to whom they owe the food, their consumption amounts to theft (*tair dattān apradāya ebhyaḥ yo bhuñkte stena eva saḥ*). This opens up the possibility of a new interpretation of the oft-quoted *tena tyaktena bhuñjīthāḥ* from the *Īśopaniṣad*. It can be taken to mean 'one should consume only what has been left over by That Lord (*īśa*) by whom everything is pervaded'. Even if we do not buy the sacrifice-theory of rainfall, one thing seems obvious. Any consumption which fails to ackonowledge the give-and-take with nature through which food is produced is an instance of environmental misappropriation. One of the obligatory daily sacrifices enjoined by the Vedic code is *nṛ-yajña* where the guest is the god to be worshipped. Hence, the basic dictum, uttered in the same breath as 'Speak the truth': *atithi-devo bhava*. It is in this way that the mindful eater can enjoy eating without sinning against nature or without getting consumed by his own food. Hospitality, *unlike charity*, becomes a duty rather than a creditable super-arrogatory act. You do not eat first and then give whatever remains to charity as a laudable option. You first give a token amount and then eat whatever is left over and this is a duty with no special credit. This ancient distinction between *nitya karma* which is creditless but the omission of which is wrong and *kāmya karma* the omission of which is permissible but which brings added merit has been recently rediscovered, in the context of giving away money to aid the anonymnous starving (not just one's neighbour) by Peter Singer:

> Because giving money is regarded as an act of charity, it is not thought that there is any thing wrong with not giving. . . . This way of looking

> at the matter cannot be justified . . . we ought to give money away, rather than spend it on clothes which we do not need to keep us warm. To do so is not charitable or generous. Nor is it the kind of act . . . which it would be good to do but not wrong not to do. On the contrary, we ought to give the money away, and it is wrong not do so.
>
> — Singer, 1972

Such obligatory hospitality makes even eating (*bhojana*) a form of worship (*bhajana*). All food is then sacred *prasāda*.

The fate of the lonely eater

One who violates this order and fails to perform the obligatory sacrifices before eating, according to the *Gītā* 'lives in vain'. The word used here is *mogha* which is *Gītā*'s favourite word to describe the *āsurika* way of living without self-sacrifice. This latter demonic way of life has been vividly described by the sixteenth chapter of the *Gītā*:

> They say that the world has no basis in truth and no God behind it, that it has not come about through any reciprocal dependence . . . they are fiercely aggressive in action by which they deplete the world . . . they drive themselves to destruction with unending anxieties. They stop with satisfying their desires and cannot see anything beyond that. Fettered with a hundred hopes, they accumulate wealth in immoral ways thinking thus: this commodity I acquired today, tomorrow I shall get those other coveted objects. . . . I finished off that enemy, all the others I shall kill one by one. I am the boss, the enjoyer, the accomplished, the powerful and happy and rich. Who else can compete with me? . . .

Doesn't this sound like the diary of an average successful businessman or politician in the modern world who is atheistic, enterprising, competitive and ambitious?

The *Gītā* says that such a person's hopes are futile, actions are futile and even his knowledge (data-bank?) is futile (*moghāśā moghakarmāṇo moghjñānāḥ*). It is with this word *mogha* that *Ṛgveda*, X.117 rebukes the ungiving ignorant consumer who tries to keep it all for himself: *mogham annam vindate apracetaḥ*. Hunger has been called death. But this hymn in praise of giving starts dramatically by remarking that hunger is not the only way to die. "But deaths catch up with the well-fed too". This line can be interpreted in two ways. First it could be the massage of universal mortality being used to warn the miserly amasser of wealth. But a more pointed explanation of the plural *mṛtyavaḥ* here would be that the inhospitable scrooge, however, well-fed he may be, dies many deaths before his physical demise. Death here stands for loneliness and ignorance. The inhospitable eater is friendless because he cannot be a friend himself: *na sa sakhā yo na dadāti sakhye*. He is short-sighted because had he looked at the longer path (*drāghīaṁsam anupaśyet panthām*) he would have realised that ricehs are like chariot-wheels (going up and down as well as going round from person to person) such that he might find himself at the receiving end and have to beg from the very person he is refusing today. That this second interpretation taking unsharing consumption itself to be a kind of spiritual death is more plausible is confirmed by the sixth verse (quoted above) which uses the word *mogha*. "I am telling you the truth" the verse goes, "it is death for this unknowing, ungiving person. By his act of eating he nourishing neither the sun nor his friends. The lonely eater only incurs sin." What is this allusion towards nourishis the sun? This takes us back to the mystical/poetic/moral/metaphysical idea of the relation between sacrifice and the cosmic order. The Universal Self or *Brahman* made or become the world by means of sacrifice. So we maintain the world by our acts of sacrifice. It is because we are ready to nurture the needy, pass on our knowledge to our posterity, preserve our environment and support our friends and above all to give before we consume that the sun rises and sheds light on our plants and the cloud-god showers rain. This may sound absurd to us because we make a sharp distinction between the causal-natural laws and the moral-spiritual laws. But for the Vedic vision both of these are two aspects of the same *ṛtam satyam*. One who violates the moral order of eating also fails to do his share for maintaining the natural order of food-production. That is the sense in which the lonely eater 'does not nourish the sun'.

In the second verse of this hymn there is a description of over-eating *in front of* the hungry which deserves special attention:

> He who possessing food, hardens his heart towards the dependent poor asking for food, and *eats in front of him* can never make himself happy.

In the next section we shall see the negative impact of this idea of shamelessly conspicuous consumption in a world where famine and starvation is beamed into every affluent person's living-room TV screen.

The eyes of the poor: Baudelaire and Śaṅkarācārya

Charles Baudelaire's prose-poem (from the collection *Paris Spleen* 1931) called 'The Eyes of the poor' describes the interactions between a cynical lover and his capricious upper class fiance during a meal at a fashionable paris cafe. Let me quote fragments of the English translation:

> The cafe was dazzling . . . lighted with all its might, the blinding whiteness of the walls . . . fat-cheeked pages dragged along by hounds on leash, laughing ladies with falcons on their wrists, nymphs and goddesses

> bearing on their heads piles of fruits, *pates* and game . . . all history and all mythology pandering to gluttony.

But this scene of concentrated over-consumption was being silently witnessed by a starving family of street-beggars in rags. There was a father with two children. This is what their eloquent eyes said in a noiseless speech:

> The eyes of the father said: "How beautiful it is! How beautiful it is! All the gold of the poor world must have found its way onto those walls." The eyes of the little boy: "How beautiful it is! But it is a house where only people who are not like us can go." As for the baby, he was much too fascinated to express anything but joy. . . .

This family of eyes makes the man (the narrator) who is out to enjoy the evening with his beloved lady feel "a little ashamed of our glasses and decanters, too big for our thirst". Finally the lady, unable to take the shame any more says:

> Those people are insufferable with their great saucer eyes. Can't you tell the proprietor to send them away?

What is uncanny is that this very sense of visual torture is used by Śaṅkara in his commentary to the *Bṛhadāraṇyaka* passage about the seven kinds of food:

> One (the first) part of this food is 'common' says the mantra-text . . . 'of this' here means, of all the eaters. How is that? That which is eaten by all living beings everyday was meant for everyone's consumption. . . . Why is there a possibility of unavoidable sin in eating that common food? It is a mixed property of all. Because it is everyone's share, the handful of food as it is being thrown into the mouth is seen as tormenting others. Since every creature's yearning is fixed on that food in the form of the desire, "That morsel could have been mine", it is not possible to even swallow without causing pain to others.

The text after this goes on to prescribe obligatory offerings to insects, birds and dogs, etc., as a daily duty of the householder so that he is rescued from this sin. The same idea is expressed by the early Christian Saints Basil and Ambrose. The former comments:

> The bread you are hoarding belongs to the hungry, the clothes you keep in your wardrobe belongs to the naked, the shoes you hide away belong to the poor. In other words, you are committing as many injustices as there are things you could give away.
>
> — Quoted in Acquinas' *Summa Teologiae* 2a2. On Almsgiving 32, 5

Ambrose almost echoes the Upaniṣads by his remark: "Let no one say that what is common is his own". We must, remember that Śaṅkara's interpretation of *kasya svid dhanam* in *Īśa Upaniṣad* was that it is a rhetorical question challenging the idea of individual ownership of wealth: Whose, after all, is wealth? Nobody's!

No doubt, all of this will sound too sentimental and idealistic to be of any practical value in the present society where having redundant clothes, shoes and food is considered part of good standard of living for a few who do not feel morally obliged to sink their privileged life-boat by taking on 'undeserving' increasing populations of starving third-worlders abroad. The point of the above comparative exercise was to bring out the reason behind the dictum: "You must give with shame" (*hriyā deyam*). Of course, we cannot give enough to slake the need that surrounds us.

That is why, even the biggest donor should be ashamed of the inadequacy of the gift. The actual of imagined eyes of the underprivileged make us aware of the snatching involved in each redundant unsharing consumption that we indulge in. To give a little before we eat is to take away a bit of the shamelessness of our usual power-exuding act of munching the world. With the media revolution of the late twentieth century, vivid knowledge of hunger in the remotest corners of the earth reaches the affluent eaters as easily as knowledge of opulence and gluttony of the glamourous 'first world' strikes the eyes of the underfed dwellers of slums and shanty-towns where television precedes literacy. So the claim of the 'saucer-like eyes' is present more than ever before upon the lives of the feasting few. The production-history of the food purchased at an average Western supermarket is also much more enmeshed in global interdependence, such that the mutual idebtedness of nations is more palpable than ever. Inequality becomes much more jarring in such a close-knit world. A poem by Nazim Hikmet quoted by Ann Buchannan in *Cooking, Eating, Thinking* speaks for itself:

What a bewildering world!
While the fish are drinking coffee in Brazil
Babies go without milk here.
They feed people with words,
The pigs with choice potatoes.

I am food: The Taittirīya ecstasy

There is no point celebrating the cosmic and spiritual aspects of food as *Brahman* without recognising one's moral obligation to do whatever one can to remedy the *āsurika* inequality of consumption which is now openly welcomed, even in India, in the name of free market economy. Yet, the ultimate aim of *Taittirīya Upaniṣad*'s metaphysics of the Self engulfed in five sheaths and of its ethics of the basic duties from which one should not deviate (*na pramaditavyam*) is a spiritual overcoming of all dualities. The messages of the reciprocal interchangeability of the roles of the eater and the food is just a preliminary to that ultimate unification. A virtuous eater who prepares food in abundant amount so that he can feed others lives to enjoy fame and family and the special lustre of life called *brahma-varcas*. But at the end, he realises that he is not only a joiner (*śloka-kṛt*) between food and eater but he and his food are one. The seven pairs merge into one ecstatic consciousness which sings blissfully:

> *I am food, I am food, I am food!*
> *I am an eater, I am an eater, I am an eater!*
> *I am a connecter (or a poet, because* ślokakṛt *means that too), I am a connector, I am a connector.*
> *I am the Firstborn of the Cosmic Order. . . .*

One who knows the *ṛta* through sacrifice of one-sided dominance really overcomes the world, not in the sense of subjugating the object, but in the sense of melting away the eater-eaten dichotomy.

For such a universal eater-food — who being Time's food can dare to say to Time herself: "Now Kālī, I shall eat you up!" (*ebār kālī tomāy khābo* — Bengali devotional song) — the alimentary is not merely the elementary first sheath. *Annam* is *aham*. The cosmic kitchen is thus turned into the music-hall of Self-celebration!!

References

Bakhtin, Mikhail, *Rabelais and his World*, tr. Helen Iswolsky, Cambridge, MIT Press, 1965.

Baudelaire, Charles, *Paris Spleen*, tr. Louise Varise, New Direction Book, New York, 1947.

Curtin, Deane W. & Heldke (ed.), *Cooking, Eating, Thinking Transformative Philosophies of Food*, Indiana University Press, 1992.

Khare, R.S. (ed.), *The Eternal Food*, State University of New York Press, 1992.

Leder, Drew, *The Absent Body*, (ch. 2: Digestion), University of Chicago Press, 1990.

Singer, Peter, Famine, Affluence and Morality, paper in *Philosophy & Public Affairs*, Spring, 1972.

Telfer, Elizabeth, *Food for Thought: Philosophy and Food*, London, Routledge, 1996.

Toomey, Paul M., *Mountain of Food, Mountain of Love*, in Khare, 1992, pp. 117-46.

9

Dharma and Truth in the Mahābhārata

Chaturvedi Badrinath

I maintain that, of all the philosophical schools, it is in the *Mahābhārata* that we have a most systematic enquiry into the nature of order and disorder, truth and untruth. A great many philosophic discussions in the *Mahābhārata* begin with a question and a story. So, let me begin in the same order with the story of a young, arrogant brāhmaṇa who is humbled and taught what *dharma* is, and what truth is, first by a woman, a housewife, and then by a meat-seller.

Kauśika, an ascetic, had mastered the Veda with their six accessories; and since Veda means 'knowledge', he had the notion that he has mastered knowledge. One day, while he was sitting under a tree and studying, his clothes were soiled by the droppings of a bird on that tree. He looked up in anger, and so great was the power in his eyes, that the offending bird drops dead and is reduced to ashes. Somewhat remorseful, he set out on his daily round of begging for food, and called out in front of a house. A woman answered from inside: 'please wait', which he did. But she was long in coming, and Kauśika's anger mounted, for he felt insulted at being made to wait. Even at that time it was known, I suppose, that if you wanted to belittle someone, make him wait, even if for a few moments only, on principle. Eventually, when the woman came out with a tray of food for the waiting brāhmaṇa, he was by then exceedingly angry, and reproached her in words of great anger for having insulted him by making him wait indefinitely. "If you did not want to give me food, why did you say 'please wait'? You have insulted an ascetic. Don't you know, you ignorant woman, the power of a brāhmaṇa? When angry, he can burn the whole world."

The woman siad:

> I did not mean to insult you. But, reverend sir, nor am I that little bird that could be burnt to ashes by your anger

Kauśika is astonished by the woman's foreknowledge of that event. She noticed it, and continued to speak:

> If I took so long to attentd to you, it was because my husband had

> returned home a long journey, was tried and hungry, and I was attending upon him, which I regarded as my first duty.

On that point, too, there was an exchange between Kauśika and her.

The woman continued:

> You may have mastered the Veda, but you have not yet mastered your Self. There is one great enemy of man, which resides in his heart, and its name is 'anger'. Moreover, the woman said, she did not regard him as a brāhmaṇa either. Then, in clear and crisp six or seven verses, she proceeded to tell Kauśika what a true brāhmaṇa is like.

Finally, she said:

> I am an ordinary housewife, unlearned, and if I said to you something that was offensive, forgive me. But I believe, you do not yet know the meaning of *dharma*. I suggest that you travel to Mithilā, and seek Dharmavyādha there, who would teach you what *dharma* truly means.

Shocked at the very idea that he, a master of the Veda, was to learn the meaning of *dharma* from a meat-seller. a butcher, he is most curious nevertheless, and travels to Mithilā. There he is directed to the shop of Dharmavyādha, who was chopping meat and serving his customers. Seeking Kauśika, he said:

> I know who you are and why you have come, but please wait until I finish attending to my customers. Then we will go to my home. This is no place for a conversation.

Kauśika is astonished a second time, now by the foreknowledge on the part of the meat-seller. And, a second time, there is another 'please wait'.

After he has finished his work, the meat-seller takes Kauśika to his home; and the very first thing that he does is to attend to his old parents. That duty done, he respectfully turns to the ascetic, offers him some fruits, and says: "Now, let us have a conversation." What follows in the *Mahābhārata* is a long dialogue between the two. It explores in many concrete details the idea of *dharma* and truth, which Kauśika listens with greatest attention and increasing respect for Dharmavyādha.

Since the *Mahābhārata* is a monumental work, if someone were to ask me which one story he, or she, should read that would convey the essence of *dharma,* I would suggest the story of Kauśika and the housewife and the meat-seller, to begin with. It is to be found in the Vana-parva.

Like the other stories in the *Mahābhārata*, this story has several levels of meaning. First of all, the name of the woman is not mentioned, suggesting that in that context it was sufficient that she was a woman, and was a good woman. Neither is her *varṇa* mentioned. Secondly, the fact that a brāhmaṇa is made to learn further the meaning of *dharma* from a meat-seller, the lowest in the social hierarchy, is significant in that, after stating the preeminent position which the brāhmaṇas had given to themselves regardless of character, the *Mahābhārata* rejects that attitude. The 'please wait' part of the story is significant, too.

But what is important, above all, is the *Mahābhārata*'s view that it is not until knowledge is integrated with character, that knowledge has any meaning. That is one aspect of *dharma*. Detached from character, knowledge is not only *meaningless* but can also turn into a source of disorder, *adharma,* and its violence. The truth of this was demonstrated then; and it has repeatedly been demonstrated in modern times, both in personal and social relationships. Modern science, with its emphasis exclusively on knowledge and control, is one example of it.

In order to understand the *Mahābhārata*, we have to ask three questions, the answers which can provide us with a key to that large work. *One*, what is the direction in which the *Mahābhārata* takes us? *Two*, what is the method that it adopts in exploring the human condition? With these two, we may then ask the question as to the relevance of the *Mahābhārata* to our times when, more than ever before, there is an anguished search for human freedom.

So far as the first question is concerned, that of direction, the process of reading the *Mahābhārata,* is the process of reading one's Self. And both can be read wrongly. The direction which the *Mahābhārata* takes is a continuation of the direction which the Upaniṣads had taken. The latter had broken away from Vedic ritualism and its belief in the magical efficacy of 'acts', and had turned human attention to the *inwardness* of Self, instead. The Vedic idea of *ṛta*, the cosmic order out there, is replaced with the idea of *dharma*, which is a constituent part of every living being. Sacrificial act, or *yajña*, is replaced with Self-understanding. Gaining merit, or *puṇya,* is replaced with giving, sharing. Austerity, or *tapas*, is given an inward, ethical meaning. The focus shifts from 'acts' to relationships. If you read the text carefully, you will see that the *Mahābhārata* radically changes the meaning of *yajña*, *tapas*, *karma* and *tīrtha*, and, in making them relational, gives them a deeply ethical meaning. The word *ṛta* is heard only rarely, and *dharma* becomes the dominant sound. The chanting of *mantra* is replaced with the sound of enquiry. The Upaniṣads had moved the human mind away from the fearful worship of the many 'gods'. The focus of their enquiry was, instead, that one reality, *Brahman*, which pervades the universe and is alone one's self, the *ātman*. The *Mahābhārata* takes another leap forward; it becomes an enquiry into the nature of Self with the vastly varied, and infinitely complex, human living as its material. Since life is indisputably a system of relationships, personal and social, it becomes an enquiry into their order, or *dharma*, as universal human order, and into its negation, disorder, or *adharma*.

The enquiry revolves around the self and the other, or *anya*; that is, around the structure of human personality. It begins with the evident fact that, in the first place, one has a relation with one's Self, with one's physical body, desires, hopes, fears, searh for meaning; and one has a relation with the other. The two constitute the indivisible unity of life. The enquiry moves towards showing that it is not until one's relationship with one's self is right that one's relationship with the other can be right. Disturbed in my relationship with myself, I am bound to be disturbed in my relation with everyone else. Therefore, self-understanding is an essential condition of understanding the other, and the two become inseparable.

Concerning the *method* in the *Mahābhārata*, it will suffice to mention here, briefly, only a few of its many characteristics. They are manifest throughout that work.

(a) Every philosophical school that developed in India, developed its distinct ethical and spiritual discipline, which was derived from its particular view of Self, or the *ātman*, or from the denial, as in Buddhism, that any such entity exists. But their philosophical positions hardly related to everyday life and its puzzling complexities. Neither did they throw any great light on who one is, in his, or her, specific individuality; placed in his, or her, specific situation; with specific relationships; each having his, or her, specific temperament, inclinations, desires, fears, and joys. The big Self of Indian philosophy swallowed the small Self of the individual. The understanding of the Self did not necessarily lead to self-understanding. Therefore, the *Mahābhārata* takes up self-understanding, or self-knowledge, in relation to the contexts through which man lives. It cuts across philosophical opinions, or *sampradāya*s, and enables man to seek, not just Meaning with a capital 'M', but small little meaning of one's own life first of all. It lights up the inner recesses of the individual as 'I' and its particularity. That is what distinguishes the *Mahābhārata* from the other philosophical schools.

(b) However, while the small Self must not be swallowed by the big Self; the particularity of the former can be understood only in terms that are universal. There is, in the *Mahābhārata*, no dichotomy between the particular and the universal. It demonstrates the inherent paradox of human living: that the personal can be understood only by understanding the human issues that go beyond the personal. Even a moment's reflection will show us the truth of this.

(c) But what criteria will determine what 'right relationship' is?, and what *dharma* and 'truth' are upon which it is based? And who will decide what those criteria are? The *Mahābhārata* asks these very questions. Far from being a collection of moralistic statements, or *a priori* propositions, about order and disorder, the *Mahābhārata* is an enquiry as regards man and the world. If it is to have a universal meaning, then any view of life and relationships, or any view of order, must be derived from life itself, from the rhythms of life, and not be something in which the proof of what you want to prove is already provided. That is the case with rationalism, as it is the case with political ideology. They begin with *a priori* propositions in a way which is either manifest or concealed. That method fragments life because life is then seen only in a particular framework which breaks up its evident unity, leading to untruth, *anṛta*.

The *Mahābhārata* begins with the attributes of human personality and their natural order. As I said, in that it carries further the method in the Upaniṣads by exploring the workings of the body and the mind and of desire that permeates them. It demostrates that human attributes constitute a natural wholeness in which lie their order. Perceiving them wrongly, when we break up their natural wholeness in ourselves and in the others, we invite disorder, *adharma*. We do so by placing upon any one of them either too great a value or too little. The *Mahābhārata* demonstrates this in a most systematic manner by showing the place of material prosperity and sexual happiness in human life. It shows how one does violence to one's Self and to the *other* either by perceiving wealth to be of no value whatsoever, or by regarding it as the only reality of life that matters. Similarly, with sexual desire.

The *Mahābhārata* remains, moreover, independent of the views of the philosophical schools that had arisen in India before the *Mahābhārata* came to be written. Buddhism came later. This explains how that work recounts, with perfect honesty, the philosophy of each of those schools, without caricaturing it, something that happens frequently in philosophical and political discourse. However, that has created in modern times an impression that the *Mahābhārata*, apart from being a story of two sets of the warring cousins, is only a compendium of conflicting philosophical opinions, without a system of its own. Servapalli Radhakrishnan is among those historians of Indian philosophy who advance that view, which, on the fact of the text itself, is as astonishing as it is wrong. For example, it can be demonstrated, quite easily, that most of the Buddhist ethics, with compassion as its central part, is a paraphrase, word for word, of the ethical foundations of human relationships that were secured already in the *Mahābhārata*, in its analysis of *dharma* as that life-force which holds things together as a coherent unity of life.

Similarly, the Jaina view of 'the many-sidedness of truth', or the famous *anekānta-vāda*, was an elaboration of the relativistic temper of the

Mahābhārata. The latter maintained throughout, as Jainism would, that truth is relative to the point from where it is preceived; that is, it is relative to *deśa* and *kāla*, place and time. In other words, truth is related to the contexts in which our lives come to be: it is not context-independent.

The cardinal value in Jainism is *ahiṁsā paramo dharma*, or non-violence is the highest *dharma*. This very phrase, *ahiṁsā paramo dharma*, is to be found in scores of places in the *Mahābhārata*. Also, the Jaina analysis of the passsions, or *kaṣāya*, is the same as the *Mahābhārata* had worked out.

(d) Another aspect of this method in the *Mahābhārata* is to concern itself with the evident fact that all forms of relationships, personal and social, are rooted in history. *Deśa* and *kāla*, place and time, are its two co-ordinates. These keep changing with the flow of time. Self-understanding and the knowledge of the *other* are thus linked with history, *deśa* and *kāla*. This is emphasised at every turn. The *Mahābhārata* then takes another step. It is to show that undoubtedly while every person is located within history; he, or she, is not his, or her, history alone. In every act of relating, it is given to man to transcend history — not as any ethical 'ought', but as a spiritual necessity, indeed as an emotional necessity of living. People achieve it all the time; they go beyond their given contexts, their histories; and that is how the sanity of life is possible. Hence, you find in the *Mahābhārata*, the simultaneous presence of two languages: the language of experience, and the language of transcendence. They flow into each other. There is neither the idolatry of *history*, nor the empty abstraction of *transcendence*. Each when separated from the other, would lead to untruth, *anṛta*, and to its violence, as it always has in the lives of the individuals and societies.

(e) The *Mahābhārata* does not seek the definitions of order and disorder, of truth and untruth, but their attributes, *lakṣaṇa*, by which they can be seen, recognised. To define a thing is to set its boundary; that is the definition of 'definition'. But that is done arbitrarily; which explains how facts often upset definitions completely. Besides, life is so varied and complex that it cannot be limited to predetermined definitions of things without leading to untruth. This subject itself is open to examination in the *Mahābhārata*. It does not remain just a theory.

Hence, *dharma* and 'truth' are described by their *lakṣaṇa*s and not by their arbitrary definitions. *Dharma* is said to have ten attributes. They are: *ahiṁsā*, non-violence; *satya*, truth; *akrodha*, no-anger; *tapas*, austerity of the mind; *dāna*, sharing, giving; *dama*, self-control; *mati*, right perception; *anasūya*, not to seek fault in the *other*; *amātsarya*, not to be devious; *anarīrṣya*, not to be jealous and envious of others. *Śīla*, the combination of the previous attributes, is yet another attribute. All these are relational, in relation to one's Self and in relation to the *other*. They clearly form the basis, the foundation, of all relationships, personal and collective. And *dharma* literally means 'foundation'.

In more general terms:

प्रभवार्धाय भूतानां धर्मप्रवचनं कृतम्।
यत्स्यादहिंसासंयुक्तं ससंयुर्म इति निश्चयः।।१२/११०/१०।।

धारणाद् धर्म इत्याहुर्धर्मेण विधृताः प्रजाः।
यत्स्याद् धारणसंयुक्तं स धर्म इति निश्चयः।।१२/११०/११।।

अहिंसार्थाय भूतानां धर्मप्रवचनं कृतम्।
यः स्यादहिंसासम्पृतः स धर्म दति निश्चयः।।१२/२५१/१।।

Dharma is propounded with the aim of securing the good of all living beings; hence whatever fulfils that aim, is *dharma* — this is certain.

Because it sustains and holds the people, *dharma* is called so; hence whatever sustains, is *dharma* — this is certain.

Dharma is propounded so that there is no violence to living beings; hence whatever is free of violence, is *Dharma* — this is certain.

Truth is likewise known by its thirteen attributes, which, like the attributes of *dharma*, are relational. Including itself as a predicate, they are: *samatā*, an attitude of equality; *dama*, self-control; *amātsarya*, absence of envy; *kṣama*, reconciliation, forgiveness; *hṛ*, modesty; *titikṣā*, endurance; *anasūya*, not to find fault with others; *tyāga*, renunciation; *dhyāna*, concentration of the mind; *āryatā*, nobility of conduct; *dhṛti*, forbearance; and *ahiṁsā*, non-violence. Each of these in turn is shown to be as follows:

सत्यं नामाव्ययं नित्यमविकारि तथैव च।
सर्वधर्नाविरुद्धं च योगेनैतदवाप्यते।।१२/१५६/१०।।

आत्मनीष्टे तथानिष्टे रिपौ च समता तथा।
इच्छाद्वेषक्षयं प्राप्य कामक्रोधक्षयं तथा।।११।।

दमो नान्यस्पृहा नित्यं धैर्यं गाम्भीर्यमेव च।
अमयं क्रोधशमनं ज्ञानेन तदवाप्यते।।१२।।

अमात्सर्यं बुधाः प्राहुर्दानं धर्मे च संयमम्ः।
अवस्थितेन नित्य च सत्येनामत्सरी भवेत्।।१३।।

अक्षमायाः क्षमायाश्च प्रियाणीहाप्रियाणि च।
क्षमते सर्वतः साधुः साध्वाप्नोति च सत्यवान्।।१४।।

कल्याणं कुरुते गाढं ह्रीमान् न श्लाघते क्वचित्।
प्रशान्तवाङ्मना नित्यं ह्रीस्तु धर्मादवाप्यते।।१५।।

धर्मार्थहेतोः क्षमते तितिक्षा क्षान्तिरुच्यते।
लोकसंग्रहणार्थं तु सा तु धैर्येण लभ्यते।।१६।।

त्यागः स्नेहस्य यस्त्यागो विषयाणां तथैव च।
रागद्वेष प्रहीणस्य त्यागो भवति नान्यथा।।१७।।

आर्यता नाम भूतानां यः करोति प्रयत्नतः।
शुभं कर्म निराकारो वीतराग त्वमेव च।।१८।।

धृतिर्नाम सुखे दुःखे यथा नाप्नोति विक्रियाम्।
तां भजेत सदा प्राज्ञो य इच्छेद् भूतिमात्मनः।।१९।।

सर्वथा क्षमिणा भाव्यं तथा सत्यपरेण च।
वीतहर्षभयक्रोधो धृतिमाप्नोति पण्डितः।।२०।।

अद्रोहः सर्वभूतेषु कर्मणा मनसा गिरा।
अनुग्रहश्च दानं च सतां धर्मः सनातनः।।२१।।

एते त्रयोदशाकाराः पृथक् सत्यैकलक्षणाः।
भजन्ते सत्यमेवेह बृंहयन्ते च भारत।।२२।।

— १२.१५६.१०-२२

Truth is that which is undifferentiated, abiding, and without any defect: it is obtained through the discipline of not doing anything against any *dharma*.

Equality lies in displaying the same attitude towards friends and foes: it is achieved by destroying the feelings of attachment, antipathy, desire and anger.

Self-control consists in not desiring things that belong to others; in the seriousness and steadfastness of purpose; in the absence of deviousness; and in the conquest of anger: it is obtained by knowledge.

Absence of Envy consists in mental restraint while giving gifts, and in doing one's appointed duty: it is achieved through truthfulness.

Forgiveness consists in being able to bear the behaviour that is intolerable and the speech that is unpleasant: it is achieved through truthfulness.

Modesty consists in securing for others, without regret and always with peace within, what is good: it is acheived by following *dharma*.

Endurance is the capacity to bear difficulties in pursuing *dharma* and one's desired object.

Not to find fault with others consists in seriousness: it is achieved by generosity.

Renunciation consists in giving up partiality to things as well as sense-gratification: it is achieved by rising above attraction and repulsion.

Concentration of the mind is achieved through silence.

Nobility of conduct consists in working constantly for the good of others: it is achieved through giving up attachment to things for oneself.

Forbearance consists in rising above happiness and suffering: it is achieved through constant forgiveness, by sticking to truth, and by conquering fear and anger.

Non-violence consists in malice towards none, in act or in thought or in speech, and in kindness and generosity to others.

The above thirteen attributes of truth, although each mentioned as distinct, were regarded as aspects of one indivisible whole. That is the reason why each one of them is related to the rest, and each is spoken as the 'highest *dharma*'. Each invariably includes the rest. Truth is indivisible. And, in its essence, so is *dharma*.

(f) The woman in the story with which I began, also said to the arrogant ascetic: 'Truth and sincerity are the two *dharmas* that abide forever; but mostly *dharma* is subtle.' And so is truth. It is, therefore, a part of the method in the *Mahābhārata* that no sooner is a statement made concerning the human condition than it is put to test by stating, in opposition to it, the other evident truths concerning it. The ideas concerning *dharma* and truth most of all. For example, while the spirit of reconciliation is spoken of as one of the attributes of truth, a question is raised whether it can be so in *all* circumstances, regardless of place and time and the person concerned. And this question is examined in detail, always with reference to the complexities of human motive and character.

As regards truth-telling, the truth is that whoever, without due regard to *deśa* and *kāla*, place and time, always speaks the truth, often injures others, thus turning truth into untruth. The *Mahābhārata* has a long discussion on this. The conclusion was: 'To save others from being killed is a most superior *dharma*; if by speaking a lie, a life is protected, then speak the lie." "What is truth? Only formally in speech, it is not necessarily truth; one should discriminate between truth and untruth with regard to their effect." With the *Mahābhārata*, the *Tirukkuraḷ* says: "Even falsehood has the nature of truth, *if* it confers a benefit that is free from fault.

The *Mahābhārata* then takes up the agonising question that relativism can very easily degenerate, as it very often does, into cynical opportunism; and what is palpably wrong and untruthful, is sought to be justified, *in bad faith*, on one ground or another. It is for this reason that the *Mahābhārata*, recognising the conditionality of ethical norms, subjects them firmly at the same time to *dharma* as the force which sustains the people and secures the good of all beings. Beside the conception of truth as correspondence with facts as one knows them, there is the wider view of truth which, in relation to human life and its peotentialities, consists in self-control as its main attribute. In other words, the *Mahābhārata* views truth not merely as correspondence with facts but as the actual living of truth in relation with one's Self and with the *other*. For that relation to be creative, one has first to conquer oneself. And that is what the woman had said to the ascetic.

(g) As another part of its method, the *Mahābhārata*, like the Upaniṣads earlier, shows life to be both paradoxical and ironical. That method is manifest in it throughout, though it does not have, as far as I know, any word either for paradox or for irony. What it shows is that reality is composed of opposites, and they are related in a way that to assert the one is to assert the other. Thus, to take a few examples, intimacy requires distance: the most intense form of energy arises from inner stillness, of the mind and emotions: all the factors which create sexual pleasure and happiness are non-sexual in nature: self-control is the very first condition of pleasure. Similarly, the irony is that I can know my limits only after I have transgressed them. Irony shows the truth in a way that neither philosophy nor history can ever do. Irony is the mocking laughter of truth.

(h) The *Mahābhārata* demonstrates that order and truth, as well as their negation, revolve around *vāṇī*, or 'speech'. The Upaniṣads had done likewise, in showing the interrelation between the mind and speech. What the *Mahābhārata* does, unlike the Upaniṣad, is to show in a concrete way, with reference always to concrete situations, how in all human relationships, *vāc*, speech, is central. More than any other school of philosophy, it shows in concrete terms how the ordering of language is an essential part of the language of order.

The disorder of language, of speech, arises at two levels. It takes place, firstly, when I suppress the truth as I know it. Secondly, it arises when, by using concepts that are limited to arbitrary definitions, I fragment reality and break up its natural unity.

Of the first kind, suppressing the truth, the most disturbing example is provided by Śaṅkara. There is in the *Chāndogya Upaniṣad*, the deeply moving story of a woman, Jābāla, and her son, Satyakāma. When it was time for him to begin his studies, he asks his mother: What is my *gotra*? She replies by saying:

I do not know what your *gotra* is. When I worked in several households in my youth as a maid, I conceived you. I know only this, that my name is Jābāla, and yours Satyakāma. Call yourself Jābāla-Satyakāma.

The woman says this with dignity, that which comes from truth. The boy approaches Haridrumata Gautama, whom he had chosen as his teacher, and asks him to accept him as his student. Gautama asks him in turn what his *gotra* is. In other words, he asks him what his lineage is. Satyakāma tells him he does not know, and truthfully repeats the answer that his mother had truthfully given as to the question who his father is. Gautama says, "I will initiate you into you studies, for you have spoken the truth". In saying that, Gautama, the great teacher, was saying that truth is infinitely more important than lineage. In the years that followed, Satyakāma himself emerges as a teacher.

In his commentary on the *Chāndogya*, Śaṅkara, while narrating the story, left out deliberately that part of Jābāla's answer to her son which stated that she had conceived him when in her youth she had worked as a maid in several households, suppressing thereby *her* truth and its dignity. If he could do this once, one can legitimately doubt whether he would not have twisted the truth on other occasions as well, if it went against his prejudices.

Regardless of the fact that the boy had not known father, in his acceptance of Satyakāma (because he and his mother had spoken the truth). Gautama had also said that 'only a brāhmaṇa could speak truth'. In the context of his own conduct towards the aspiring student, it is perfectly clear that Gautama was not making an obviously indefensible statement. He was saying that concern with truth is a characteristic of one who would be a true brāhmaṇa, not by birth into a caste, but by conduct. Again, that is what the woman in the earlier story would tell Kauśika.

The other disorder of speech is illustrated by many philosophies and political ideologies; and one has to go into that, for only then can we understand the violence that flows from them.

Let me end by saying that, after the *Mahābhārata* had explored the disorder and untruth, *adharma* and *anṛta*, of speech in historical experience, both personal and collective, it took an immense leap in saying:

त्यज धर्ममधर्मं च उभे सत्यानृते त्यज।
उसे सत्यानृते त्यक्त्वा येन त्यजसि तं त्यज।।

त्यज धर्ममसंकल्पादधर्मं चाप्य हिंसया।
उम सत्यानृते बुद्धया बुद्धिं परमनिश्चयात्।।
— १२.३१६.४०-४१

Transcend *dharma*, transcend *adharma*; transcend 'truth', transcend 'untruth'. That achieved, transcend the faculties of the mind which you transcended them. Then take one last step: transcend the notion that you have transcended anything at all.

10

Religious Narratives and the Construction of Order

Aditya Malik

Introduction

The urge to distunguish between Order and Chaos is interwoven with the human quest for meaning in the cosmos, in society, and in individual lives. Cultures the world over — through the agency of their bearers — have developed numerous means and mechanisms for placing disparity and discontinuity in framework of continuity and coherence. Invariably though fundamental ideas concerning Order and Chaos are expressed through the medium of narratives, in India, 'myths' concerning the creation, sustenance, and dissolution of the cosmos are found in a variety of linguistic, social, and cultural contexts, ranging from the 'Sanskritic' to the 'folk' and the 'tribal'. One of the earliest expressions of cosmic and social order is found, for example, in the Ṛgvedic hymn, the *Puruṣasūkta* in which both the creation of the Universe and the establishment of social classes is described. Later, Sanskrit texts, such as the Purāṇas contain narratives that not only concern the creation of cosmic and social order, but also its breakdown and subsequent reestablishment. The condition of Order is thus not conceived of as a stable state, but rather as an incessant rearrangement of disrupture into system and pattern. Order must, therefore, be understood of as an oscillating modality that arises in perpetual tandem with the recurrent manifestation or chaos.[1]

---

* I would like to thank Ulrich Demmer and Claus Peter Zoller of the South Asia Institute. Heidelberg, for their valuable comments and suggestions on an earlier draft of this paper.

1. This process is especially borne out in myths of the manifold *avatār*s of Viṣṇu who incarnates himself on earth in successive *yugas* so as to restore the world order. The same idea is also found in cosmic myths regarding cyclical dissolution and creation.

In this paper, I examine two narratives by asking the question how Order[2] — by which I mean a response to what is perceived of as its *lack* — is constructed within and through these texts. The narratives are part of contemporary culture in India in the sense that they belong to the living religious culture of the region of Rajasthan. In addition, the narratives also transcend regional specificity by drawing on ideas and concepts that are part of the much wider context of Indian culture. Thus, although the focus of the paper is specific in nature, it is hoped that some points raised will serve for both an inter- and intra-cultural comparison. Of the two narratives, the first is a written text in Sanskrit called the *Puṣkara-Māhātmya*. The *Puṣkara-Māhātmya* is the main text associated with the well-known pilgrimage centre of Puṣkar. The second narrative is an oral 'epic' recited in Mārvāṛī called the *Bagaḍāvat Bhārat*, which is a central component of the religous cult of Devnārāyaṇa, a deity worshipped mainly in southern and eastern Rajasthan.

Given the emphasis I place on the role of narratives in the construction of Order and Chaos, this paper is primarily an exercise in textual exegesis. Beyond that, however, it is also an attempt to unfold the particular quality of literature that allows human beings to engage in *interpretations* of the world through the mediality of texts. It is with the quality of literature not only to describe the world, but, as Ricocur states it,[3] also to *redescribe* the world that this paper is chiefly concerned. As a consequence, my analysis will not be confined to symbolic meanings contained within the texts I discuss, but also to the force of those texts to constitute discourses about the world that in turn generate social and culturral configurations. In the context of the symposium's theme, the focus here will be on discourses of order, by which I generally mean such discourses that deal with the encompassment of disjuncture. However, given the multivalency of meaning attached to the term Order. I distinguish between 'spatial' and 'temporal' order on the one hand, and 'hegemonic' and 'existential' order on the other. Although the use of these categorisations are admittedly more 'etic' than 'emic',[4] I introduce them to be able to both particularise the notion of Order as well as to simultaneously gain access to its ideational and socio-political dimensions. As mentioned above, these attempts at creating Order

2. Of course it needs to be kept in mind that Order and Chaos are not absolute categories. They are dependent on one's perspective: order for one person may mean Chaos or Disorder for another and vice versa. This is specially true for narratives that embody a statement of the religious, social and historical identity of a particular group, region or nation. Such narratives define. Self in terms of an Other who exists as a counterpart beyond the edges of one's own idea of a moral and social Order. In the narratives dealt with in this paper, the construction of Order thus at once also entails a statement about Chaos.
3. See Valdés 1991 : 26ff.
4. For a recent discussion of these terms, see, for example, Melas 1989: 137-42.

through texts need finally to be understood in the general context of the cultural and social response to the experience of disjucture and disconnectedness.

Meaning and plot

The approach I take up to analyse the construction of Order in these two religious narratives is initially rooted in an understanding of the *plot* as a textual arrangement of meaning. Thus, is his essay entitled, *The Human Experience of Time and Narrative.* Ricocur distinguished between chronological and non-chronological dimensions of a narrative:

> A story is *made out* of events, to the extent that plot makes events *into* a story. . . . All narratives combine in various proportions, two dimensions — one chronological and the other non-chronological. The first may be called the episodic dimension. This dimension characterises the story as made out of events. The second is the configurational diemension, according to which the plot construes significant wholes out of scattered events. (1991:106).

It is, thus, the non-chronological dimension of the *plot* that binds the essentially unrelated constituents of a narrative into a meaningful pattern. However, in addition to an understanding of the plot as a literary devices, I am equally concerned with its double status, namely that of a constitutive element in the realm of 'public discourse'. Briefly, by this I mean the ability of the text to transform our perceptions and influence our actions in the world.

The Puṣkara-Māhātmya

The first text I discuss is the *Puṣkara-Māhātmya* (*PM*).[5] The *PM* can broadly be described as the 'origin myth' of Puṣkar. Most probably composed during the latter half of the eighteenth century, the *PM* contains twenty chapters written in Sanskrit *śloka*s. On the basis of their contents, the chapters can be divided into two approximately equal halves. Although all the chapters deal with the 'mythic' establishment of holy sites within the *Puṣkara-kṣetra*, one set of chapters is a relatively loose conglomeration of origin stories. The other set of chapters, in contrast, deals exclusively with Brahmā's — who is the 'residing' deity of Puṣkar — performance of an *agniṣṭoma yajña*[6] in Puṣkar. Thus, the plot of these chapters is provided by Brahmā's *yajña*. Each chapter is 'held together' or made whole by the ritual, consecratory, and creative act of the *yajña*. This 'holding together' of seemingly disparate events contained in each chapter, operates at two levels. The first level,

---

5. For a complete analysis, edition, and translation of this work, see Malik 1993a.

6. The *agniṣṭoma yajña* or 'Praise of fire' *yajña* is a particular type of Vedic cosmogonic ritual which is conducted over a period of five or more days.

is, of course, the purely episodic. In other words, the events described in the text follow a temporal and thematic succession bound together by the larger plan of the *yajña*. The second level of 'holding together' functions at a parallel plane of disconnectedness, in which the episodes themselves refer to a series of individual 'ruptures' or hindrances in the way of the orderly completion of the *yajña*.

Dealing with disjuncture

In the following section, I relate four examples from chapters of the *PM* that illustrate the manner in which lapses and interruptions are dealt with.

In chapter four of the *PM*, Brahmā is 'forced' to abandon his lawful wife Sāvitrī, and marry a cowherdess, who is subsequently named Gāyatrī. The cause for this being that Sāvitrī does not not appear in time for the commencement of the ritual, for which reason Brahmā must marry another woman to fill the gap created by the absence of the *yajamāna patnī* (the institutor's wife). Indra, who is sent on a mission to bring Brahmā a suitable wife, can only find a simple Abhīra cowherdess on her way to sell buttermilk. After abducting the cowherdess, Indra 'purifies' her by having her swallowed by a cow and pulled out of its anus. This 'second birth' through a cow (cows and brāhmaṇas being identical) raises her ritual and social status to that of a 'twice born'. The cowherdess is named Gāyatrī, emphasising her affiliations not only to the Veda but also to the nomadic, pastoralist background of her original clan, the Abhīras or Gurjars through a folk etymology (Hindi *gāya* — cow).

The next interruption occurs in chapter six when a naked ascetic carrying a skull as a begging bowl enters the sarificial awning. While being driven away by the brāhmaṇa priests, he drops the skull onto the consecrated floor and disappears. Removing the skull proves to be disastrous, since it multiplies exponentially, covering the entire sacrificial arena with skulls when Brahmā realises that Śiva is the cause of this calamity, he requests him to free the sacrificial awning of the skulls. Śiva agrees to this on the condition that Brahmā uses a skull (*kapāla*) as a ritual utensil. Brahmā promises to use potsherds (also called *kapāla*) and to chant the *śatarudrīya-stotra* during the *yajña*. Moreover, Brahmā requests Śiva to stay in Puṣkar, whereupon a *liṅga*, which is later named Śrī Aṭmaṭeśvara, splits open the earth and arises out of the ground.

In the following chapter, the Muni Maṅkaṇaka unknowingly disturbs the *yajña* by dancing ecstatically. His dance causes the entire world, with the exception of Brahmā, Viṣṇu and Śiva, to dance vigorously. Brahmā sends Śiva to halt the *muni* from performing his ecstatic, but, in this case, destructive dance. Not only is Śiva successful in doing this, he also promises to be present in the *muni*'s *āśrama*, especially during the last five days of the bright half of the month of *kārttika* during which the *puṣkara-melā* is held. The *muni*'s *āśrama*, now at the site of the shrine of

Baijnāth, forms the eastern tip of the *puṣkara-kṣetra*.

In chapter nine, the *yajña* is disturbed by a water serpent which a young brāhmaṇa has caught from the lake and thrown amongst the gathering of priests. As a punishment for his misdeed, Cyavana, son of the sage Bhṛgu, curses the boy to become a serpent himself. Later, Brahmā reveals that this has been a plan of his all along. He instructs the boy (now turned serpent) to go to the foot of the Serpent Mountain (*Nāg Pahāḍ*) and perform *tapas* whereafter he should marry the daughter of a Nāga king, and procreate the ninth lineage of serpents. The place where he performs *tapas* is called Nāga Tīrtha. Like the *āśrama* of muni Maṅkaṇaka, this too is one of the sacred spots within the *puṣkara-kṣetra*.

Beyond plot

In the examples provided above we see that second level of 'holding together' operates at a level distinct to the pattern of individual episodes created through the plot. In order to understand the operation of this second level, we need to thus move beyond the particular plot of the narrative, to what the plot *refers* to, namely the *yajña*. In other words, the text is not only structured by a plot that is determined by the performance of *a yajña*, it also refers to *the yajña*. By introducing *the yajña* — an abstract body of knowledge manifest in concrete performances — into the text, the plot succeeds in 'managing' disjuncture and transforming it into a meaningful whole. This 'meaningful whole' is the pilgrimage centre itself. But before expanding on this we need to understand (a) *how* the introduction of the *yajña* succeeds in creaing a whole out of that which is discontinuous, and (b) *why* the application of the *yajña* is so successful as a model of transformation for the discontinuous.

To answer the 'how' question, it is necessary to keep in mind that the *yajña* is a body of knowledge which within itself already contains procedures for dealing with lapses which occur when knowledge is *applied*. In other words, it takes into account the unpredictability that arises when *rules for action* are translated into actual action. Thus, however, precise rules and regulations may be at the level of prescription, in practice, discrepancies are bound to arise. It is interesting in this connection, therefore, that within the *Śrauta* complex, it was the role of the brāhmaṇa officiant to 'oversee' the *yajña* and to 'protect' it form breaks in ritual performance. The brāhmaṇa was supposed to protect the *yajña* both through a set of rules as well as through *improvisation*. The brāhmaṇa was the *bhiṣaj* or the 'healer':

> Attentive, he is the guardian who protects the sacrifice and is always ready to repair any error which could creep into the ritual order. Like a chief of the orchestra he directs the entire ceremony. (Silburn, 1955: 90; cited in Bailey 1983:6)

This specific function of brāhmaṇa is, on the cosmic level, furthermore reflected in the function of Brahmā, who commences and regulates creation, acting as a 'go-between' and advisor in times when the world order is threatened. (Bailey 1983:7) Thus, it is throrugh the implicit 'elasticity' of the *yajña* as well as both Brahmā's and the brāhmaṇa's roles as 'overseer' on the dual cosmic and ritual levels that the obstacles which arise in the course of the *yajña* are transformed. The crucial distinction between the performance of actual *yajña*s and the one narrated in the *PM*, lies in the fact that in the latter the 'interruptions' are not confined to ritual terms and procedures, but have been transferred onto 'other' social and religious traditions.

To answer the 'why' question, we may take recourse to the operation of what Ortner (1990) has termed 'cultural schemas', which refer to such 'key scenarios' or 'root paradigms' that structure cultural choices and social action in a persistant manner through time. These schemas are

> . . . preorganised schemes of action, symbolic programmes for the staging and playing out of standard social interactions in a particular culture . . . every culture contains not just bundles of symbols, and not even just bundles of larger propositions about the Universe (ideologies), but also organised schemas for enacting (culturally typical) relations and situation. (1990:60)[7]

Although Ortner uses the idea specially in the context of social and ritual action, I introduce it to understand the structure of the texts discussed here. Moreover, I use the concept as a possible alternative to notions such as 'Great', 'Classical', or 'Folk Tradition', which imply a hierarchical ordering of culture. The advantage in using the notion of 'cultural schemas' would lie in viewing certain concepts such as that of the *yajña* or that of *yugu*s[8] (in the case of the narrative of Devnārāyaṇa below), as historically recurring backdrop frames for ordering experience that are continuously rearticulated and reworked in distinct cultural and social contexts. An understanding of concepts such as *yajña* or *yuga* in such a framework thus avoids the issue of 'cultural ownership', which terms like 'Great', 'High', 'Little', 'Folk', and 'Low' tend to evoke. Thus, *yajña* and *yuga* need not be viewed as 'borrowings' from the 'Great Tradition' or assimilations of 'High' culture into 'Low' or 'Folk' culture,

7. This is not to deny the fact that cultural symbols are pervasively used to create power relations and hierarchies in society. The critique implicit in the idea of 'cultural schemas' is directed against a particular *academic* conceptualisation of culture.

8. The *yajña* appears as a creative base in numerous narratives pertaining to the origin of the pilgrimage sites, sacred rivers, temples, etc. Equally pervasive is the idea of the *yuga* that appears in varied contexts, in particular those relating to the history and genealogy of social groups, claims, lineages, etc.

but as key concepts that belong to the shared 'cultural field' of South Asia.[9]

Making public

The historical and social dimensions of the manifestation and application of 'cultural schemas' brings us to a level of 'holding together' or ordering that goes beyond the episodic and non-episodic aspects of the text outlined above. This brings us to a third, socio-politically significant level of order that transforms the plot as a textual feature by placing it in the arena of 'public discourse'. The *PM*, unlike other texts, is not confined to the boundaries of private readership. It is an agent in the dispersion and formation of public knowledge. Thus, the third level, therefore, is the level at which the text engages its readers and listeners in a 'redescription' of the world both in terms of cognition and authority — Outwardly unconnected physical, religious, and social components of the pilgrimage centre, which find expression in the individual chapters of the *PM*, are meaningfully ordered through the mediality of the text. The plot ceases to be a literary device and becomes an object of ideological instrumentation which lays authoritative claim on what pilgrims and scholars alike are to perceive as *real*. In other words, Order, by which I mean in this case both a definition of Self and an enclosure of the Other, begins to be defined in a quasi-uniform manner.[10] By virtue of repeated transmission through pilgrim priests to pilgrims, the narrative becomes part of a 'public discourse' that other literary genres may never enter or attain.

Moreover, by emerging as a dominant, entrenched position, the *PM* marginalises other narratives about the pilgrimage centre. This is not to say it completely suppresses 'other' perspectives into non-existence. Thus, for example, there is an oral story related by a Gujar *Bhopā* (singer-priest) about Brahmā's marriage with the cowherdess Gāyatrī that reorganises the power relationships prevailing in the *PM*.[11] In the oral telling, for example, Gāyatrī is neither abducted by Indra nor ritually purified by a second 'birth' through a cow. She is willing to marry Brahmā only after her father gives consent. And her father, for his part, lays down certain conditions for the marriage which aim at altering fundamental features of the *yajña*.[12]

9. In a similar vein, Sells while discussing apophasis in the work of five mystical writers from "separate religious traditions . . . of the West . . . ", suggest that it is " . . . profitable to see these traditions as competing within a partially shared intellectual and symbolic world, defining themselves in conversation with one another and against one another." (1994: 4f)

10. The transformation of the Other is evident in the fact that the so-called 'ritual breaks' in the *PM* represent distinct and coherent social and religious traditions within themselves. It is only against the ideological background of the *PM* that they manifest as 'irregularities'. Once altered, they cease to be 'disturbances', and become part of the world-view expressed in the *PM*. In other words, they become part of the sacred geographical territory of the *puṣkara-kṣetra*.

The voice of the oral telling is thus the voice of resistance and reflection. One may, therefore, envision the tradition of the pilgrimage centre as consisting of contesting perspectives. None the less, the contestation at work here cannont be understood to occur in a completely egalitarian climate. Thus, the *PM* not only transforms disjuncture, it also results in a hegemonic representation of reality.[13]

The Bhgaḍāvat Bhārat

The *Bagaḍāvat Bhārat* (*BB*) is one of the most popular oral narratives in Rajasthan. Performances of the narratives are an essential feature of the worship of Lord Devnārāyaṇa whose devotees mainly consists of the pastoral and farming community of the Gūjars, as well as members of other communities, such as the Bā̃bhī and the Kumahār. The *BB* is recited by pairs of itinerant singers most often from the Gūjar community, in front of an approximately 8 mt long scroll called *paṛ* on which various characters and scenes from the epic are elaborately depicted. In addition to reciting episodes from the epic, the singers also dance while playing a stringed instrument (*bīṇ*, *jantar*) and pointing to sections of the scroll that pictorially correspond to parts of the narrative being told.[14] The scroll, in fact, is referred to as a 'portable temple'.[15] In its centre, there is an almost life size representation of Devnārāyaṇa, in front of which a makeshift altar is set up for the duration of the performance. Incense sticks are burnt here and offerings of grain and money are made by devotees throughout the performance. In addition to the performance of the epic during 'night-wakes'. Devnārāyaṇa, and his father, Savāī Bhoj are worshipped in a number of shrines and temples in eastern and southern Rajasthan.[16]

Whereas the *PM* essentially refers to a physical space (*kṣetra*) and the construction of order therein, the *BB* refers, in addition, to a temporal space, and

11. A translation and dicussion of this story is available in Malik, in press (b).
12. Gāyatrī's father makes Brahmā promise that henceforth no "horses, goats, sheep, and camel" will be sacrificed during the ritual, and that from them on ritual sacrifices (*bali*) will solely consist of offerings of clarified butter (*ghee*).
13. This feature may in past be attributed to the fact that the *PM* as a genre is designed to establish authority. Thus, the host of *Māhātmya*s and *Sthalapurāṇa*s whether they relate to sacred places, temples, or deities, all lay claim over the authentic origin and glory of the '*object*' of their narration.
14. On the diffusion and nature of pictorial narrative traditions, see Mair 1988. For the case of the Rajasthani hero Pābūjī, see 1991 : Ch.3.
15. See, also Smith 1991: 8 ff.
16. In contrast to the rich visual representations of the deity depicted on the *paṛ*, the temples contain aniconic representations in the form of rows of large, upright brick slabs (*ī̃ṭh*) that are either blank or pasted with red, blue, and yellow tinsel. In daily worship, these bricks are treated as Devanārāyaṇa, Savāī Bhoj, or sometimes Devanārāyaṇa and his four cousins. In the epic, however, the bricks are said to represent Devanārāyaṇa's wife, Rānī Pīpal De.

the 'management' of discontinuity through the mediality of 'time concepts'. This requires some explanation. To begin with the 'plot' of the *BB* is considerably more complex than that of the *PM* which, in a sense has a 'mono-plot'. The *BB* is extensively fabricated by 'substories' and 'subplots' so that it is difficult to identify a single, overarching plot. The narrative has, for example, two main parts whose overall thematic and ideological character differs distinctly from one another. In the first part, there are Śaivite themes of asceticism, self-sacrifice, violent offerings to the goddess, and, in the second part, Vaiṣṇavite themes of *bhakti*, incarnation, and divine healing. The first part deals with the heroic deeds of 24 Gūjar brothers who are born as the sons of the man-lion. *Bāgh Simh*. The 24 brothers die after a preordained period of 13 years in a battle against a Rājpūt chieftain. The second part is about Bhagavān's incarnation as Devnārāyaṇa, the miracles he performs and the revenge he and his cousins ultimately take on the Rājpūt chieftain. Whereas the first part is generally said to be marked by suffering (*duḥkha*), pain, and death, the second is marked by reunion, miracles and divine testimony (*parcyo*). The second part, thus, entails a reversal of the first part: death and defeat are followed by birth and creation, finally resulting in the establishment of Devnārāyaṇa's cult amongst his followers.

Given the complexity of the narrative as described above, it is perhaps more precise to talk here of recurring *themes* rather than a plot.[17] One such theme encountered in various episodes in the first part of the *BB* is the theme of death. The primary quality associated with death is sacrifice. Thus, the heroes' deaths can be appreciated in a framework of sacrifice which itself is an expression of devotion (*bhakti*).[18] Two examples of this can be found in the opening and closing episodes of the first part of the *BB* related below.[19] Both episodes deal with the same event which is the death of the epic's horoes. They die twice over in the two different ages (*yugas*). The first time is during the *satya-yuga* in the form of 24 sages who are disciples of Lord Śiva:

The first episode begins at a time when Brahmā is performing a *jug*[20]

17. The distinction between theme and plot is not a clear-cut one, since both refer to that aspect of a narrative which provides it with unity and meaning as a whole. I use the term 'theme' in order to underscore the fact that the *BB* is not ordered along the lines of an all-embracing plot or single idea, but has multiple themes.

18. See Malik, in press (a).

19. These and subsequent sections of the *BB* are taken from a longer translation previously submitted for publication in Malik, in press (a). I would like to thank the editors of that volume for letting me reproduce parts of the narrative here.

20. Brahmā's performance of a *yajña* — as we have seen above — is also the central theme of the *Puṣkara-Māhātmya*. As in the episode dealing with the skull-bearing ascetic previously related (*PM* ch. 6), here too Brahmā's *yajña* is disrupted by Śiva.

> in Pushkar — the famous pilgrim town in the district of Ajmer. Brahmā invites all the gods and Ṛṣis to his sacrifice. Among them is this group of 24 Ṛṣis living in a mountain chain running parallel to Pushkar. The Ṛṣis are disciples of Śaṅkar. Śaṅkar forbids them from attending the sacrifice, but they insist on going because they have received invitations from Brahmā. All of a sudden Śaṅkar grows ravenously hungry. The Ṛṣis suggest he eat the fruits growing in the forest in which they live. But Śaṅkar says this will not satisfy him. He wants more than plain fruit. But what else is available in the forest? There is no cereal or grain either. So what does Śaṅkar do? He turns to his disciples and begins consuming them one after another. After he has eaten them and satiated his hunger, he then visits Brahmā's sacrifice himself. The sacrifice comes to a halt because of Śaṅkar's misdeed.[21] He asks Brahmā how he should atone, whereupon Brahmā informs him that the only means would be to offer the Ṛṣis his own body in a future existence in which the Ṛṣis are to be born as the 24 sons of a single father.

The second time the heroes die is in their subsequent birth in the *kali-yuga* as the sons of the man-lion Bāgh Siṁh. Now they are collectively called the Bagaḍāvats. This time around the 24 brothers are devotees of Bhavānī, the goddess, who as a final token of devotion, demands a sacrifice of their lives on the battlefield in a battle against Rāṇā, the Rājput chieftain:

> In the battle some of the brothers continue fighting even after their heads have been severed by the Goddess' discus. But in the end all of them are slain and the Rāṇā is victorious. The Goddess assumes her awesome, terrifying form. Amidst the corpses of slain warriors, she squats on the battle ground, dripping with blood, stringing a necklace of the Bagaḍāvats' heads.

Besides the heroes, deaths, there are also other deaths in the narrative. The following lines relate two incidents, one concerned with the birth of the 24 heroes, the other with the 'sacrifice' of Śaṅkar's body. These points of cleavage, like the deaths of the heroes have one quality in common, namely that of regeneration and transformation:

> It is the reign of King Bisaldev of Ajmer. The populace is being terrorised by a lion that feeds on one individual every night. On one

21. Śiva's interference with Brahmā's sacrifice, parallels the myth of Śiva and Dakṣa's (a multiform of Brahmā) rivalry in the *Mahābhārata* and in Purāṇas. In these stories, Śiva, after being excluded from Dakṣa's sacrifice, destroys it and beheads Dakṣa.

particular night, a Rājpūt called Hari Rām[22] offers to take the place of a boy whose turn it is to be eaten by the lion. He sets up a trap for the lion and beheads the animal. Then in order to wash the blood off his sword and to cleanse himself of the sin of slaughter, he goes to the holy lake of Pushkar carying the lion's head on his shoulder. It is a full moon night (*pūrṇimā*). Exactly at the same time on the opposite bank a Brahmin girl who has taken a vow never to see the face of man is performing ablutions and bathing in the lake. While bathing, she sees the reflection of a man's body with the head of a lion of the surface of the lake, and conceives. She insists that Hari Rām marry her now, but he vacillates saying that such a marriage is not possible because she is a Brahmin and he a Kshatriya. Finally, however, King Bisaldev allows him to marry the Brahmin girl. After nine months their son is born. He has the head of a lion and the body of a man, and is named Bāgh Siṁh. Later because of his unusual and fearsome appearance, no one is willing to marry his daughter to him. He lives alone in a garden attended by a Brahmin cook. One day on the festical of swings (*ākhā tīj*), a number of young girls of various castes come to the garden attracted by Bāgh Siṁh's silken swing. The Brahmin allows them to use the swing on the condition that each of them circumambulate Bāgh Siṁh. While they are doing this, the Brahmin performs the necessary engagement rites. Unknowingly they are engaged to Bagh Siṁh. Later Bāgh Siṁh marries twelve of them. Each of his wives gives birth to two sons who are collectively called the Bagaḍāvats.

The Bagaḍāvats, whose mothers belong to different castes, are all married to Gūjar women. Of the 24 Bagaḍāvats, Savāī Bhoj is the most valorous. Each day Savāī Bhoj takes the Bagaḍāvats' cattle herds to graze on the slopes of *Nāg Pahāḍ*. One of the cows regularly leaves the herd and returns on its own in the evening. One day Savāī Bhoj follows the cow and discovers that it is being milked by the ascetic Rūpnāth. As compensation for milking their cow, Rūpnāth gives Savāī Bhoj a sack full of grain. But the brothers have no use for the small quantity of grain, so they feed it to birds. The next morning, however, they discover that the few grains left sticking to the scam of the sack have turned into gems.[23] They realise their folly and Savāī Bhoj returns

22. In one variant, Hari Rām is a Gūjar who later attains the title of *'Siṁh'* from King Bisaldev, as an acknowledgement of his heroic act of killing the man-eating lion. See Malik 1993b: 381ff.

23. This incident and following one in which Rūpnāth's body turns into gold, are typical of legends extrolling. Nāth Yogīs' miraculous powers. See Gold 1992.

to the ascetic to become his disciple. One day Rūpnāth has Savāī Bhoj heat a cauldron of oil and circle it, while he himself follows. While they are circling the cauldron, the ascetic tries pushing Savāī Bhoj into the boiling oil, but Savāī Bhoj leaps over with the help of his cowherd's staff. In the next round, Savāī Bhoj follows the ascetic and pushes him into the cauldron. Not so agile, the ascetic falls into the boiling oil. Instantly his body turns into solid gold. While Savāī Bhoj stands there repenting his crime, the ascetic reappears in the hermitage as though nothing had taken place. He explains that the golden image is a gift that will grant the Bagaḍāvats unending wealth for period of twelve years after which both wealth and life (*māyā-kāyā*) shall come to an end.

Creating time

The important point in the episodes concerning the birth of Bāgh Siṁh, Rūpnāth's offering of his body, and the deaths of the brothers is that they suggest a dual notion of time and personhood.[24] The notion of time and of personhood operating here is one which contains the possibility of repetition and transformation. And here lies a paradox: as such the narrative follows a sequence of events moving from a finite beginning to a finite end, creating, on one level, the linearity of time and enfolded within it the time limit of human life.[25] In the narrative and its tellings, there is a reference to what happend before, what is happening, and what will happen. Each of these temporal states, past, present and future are woven together by a causality of human action intertwined with fate. But the linearity of time that arises from the narrational structure of the *BB* is overlaid by a *concept* of time that offers the possibility of repetition and transformation. Again, like in the case of the *PM*, one could refer to this aspect of the narrative as the application of a 'cultural schema', namely that of the *yuga*. The usage of this 'cultural schema' concerning time, in turn, structures the response to discontinuity. It also defines the way in which human identity is perceived. Thus, the closure of linear time is juxtaposed with the open-endedness of cyclical time in which the temporality of human life receives an

---

24. The movement of 'individual' histories through a series of death(s), birth(s), rebirth(s), becomes possible only through a metaphysical notion of presonhood that is different to a 'Western' one. Whereas in the West persons are the product of time 'occupy' a physical body, and are born without any prior history, i.e., an individual begins with his *physical* birth, in India there are various notions of what constitutes a person. Creation may be connected to life-force or breath, or it may issue out of the Self (*Brahman*), which is 'present' in each person. Similarly aspects of a person's current personality exist well before (and after) his physical birth (and death).

25. See Ricoeur 1991 : 107ff.

extension: the heroes die in one epoch only to be reborn in another.[26] Furthermore, the fluidity of substance allows the slain lion's head to reappear on the body of Bāgh Siṁh, and Rūpnāth's mortal body to transmute into a solid golden one. While the narrative places events and characters in time past, time present, and time future, it also simultaneously extricates them from temporality. The past does not exist as memory alone, but also as substance in the physical presence of reborn heroes, a recreated Guru, and a refigured lion.

Constructing history

Similar to the case of the *PM*, in the case of the *BB* also, three levels of the construction of Order can be discerned. The first two levels, to repeat what has been said above, pertain to two distinct yet interwoven aspects of time. The first level refers to the linearity of time intrinsic to the sequential structure of the narrative, which like any other narrative, makes use of different tempi in situating events. The second levels refers to the instrumentation of a 'time concept' that reverses the inherent temporality of linear time. By framing the narrative in cyclical time, death and disjuncture are coupled with creation and coutinuity. While the first level pertains to the experiential structure of time resulting from a scccession of events, the second level relates to the application of a 'cultural schema' concerning time that challenges linearity. The third and last level to discussed here deals with the emergence of the narrative as a force in the domain of 'public discourse'. At this level we find the appearance of another crucially significant dimension of time, namely *history*. Thus, the narrative must be understood both as a statement of Gūjar history as well as a statement of the history of a particular region, namely Rajasthan. The application of a concept of time-cycles as 'cultural schema' or principle of order, therefore, provides temporal and moral depth to community identity. The order provided by the *BB* is, at this third level, the 'existential' order of history. Existential because it 'holds together' life events, such as birth, death, marriage, brotherhood, sacrifice, devotion, etc., in the context of social identity and historical continuity.

Concluding remarks

Earlier studies of religious narratives, perhaps because they were dealing with 'ancient' texts, tended to be content with a decontextualised and depoliticised examination of them —

> . . . conventions of scholarship had striven to keep the heat of politics

---

26. Whereas cyclical time and rebirth usually conjure up vision of determinism, *karma*, and fate (or even fatalism), here we find a striking reversal. Transformation and rebirth have a specific goal, namely to bring to an end unfinished business. Rather than serve a notion of mechanistic repetition, the narrative emphasises the *purposefulness* of being reborn.

> out of the cool world of Indic texts and the gentle warmth of folk expressions. (Appadurai, *et al.* 1991: 23)

However,

> this comforting compact between Indology, folklore, and anthropology has come unglued as fieldworkers begin to see . . . the links of text to social life, past to present, gender to genre. (*ibid.*).

Thus, the objective of narrative analysis can no longer be about the 'inside' of a text alone, but also about the text's capacity to engage in and create social and cultural configurations. Our understanding of narratives, to quote again a line from the same work, should revolve

> about narrative strategies, and about fictional realities and the realities engendered by fiction. (*ibid.*)

Following these remarks, the goal of this paper has been twofold: (1) to exanine the manner in which order (and by implication chaos) is constructed *in* and *through* two narratives taken from the contemporary religious culture of Rajasthan, and (2) to distinguish between the different kinds of order produced by these distinct narrative genres.

As a point of departure for examining the narratives, I began with the idea of the plot and later the theme as a primary orchestration of meaning. In the case of the *PM*, the plot is defined by the performance of Brahmā's *yajña* in Puṣkar. The kind of order produced by the *PM* is first and foremost *spatial*, since the aim of the text is to define what constitutes the *puṣkara-kṣetra.* The natural presence of the pilgrimage place — hills, lakes, rivers, land — are translated into the text as facets of the *kṣetra* that have the power to spiritually transform and physically heal pilgrims. This special capacity of the natural environment is further enhaced by the existence of temples, deities, and rituals. In the *PM* all these are intricately connected so that an order spanning the cultural, religious, social and physical fields is established.

In the case of the *BB*, one of the chief themes is sustained by a concept of *yuga*s. order here is essentially *temporal*, in the sense that continuity is sought over time. But time itself is indexed by the concreteness of critical life events, such as birth, death, rebirth, sacrifice, devotion and the experience of divinity. The inevitability of human life ingrained in the abstraction of linear time is, for once, reversed. Identity is then construed in the context of transformation, repetition, and regeneration. Finally, the order constructed here relates to the formation of the religious and historical self-representation of a community.[27]

---

27. In contrast to the *PM*, which emerges as a dominant, hierarchically placed 'public →

In both narratives it was suggested that their individual plots or themes refer to 'cultural schemas' that function as organisational slots. The *PM* and the *BB* make use of *yajña* and *yuga* respectively to rearrange disjuncture. Furthermore, the order contained within the texts extends beyond their narrative limits into the realm of 'public discourse'.[28] While the *PM* emerges as the authoritative *interpretation* of the physical, religious, and social environment of Puṣkar, the *BB* crystallises into a central statement about the history of the Gūjar community, and of Devnārāyaṇa, the deity they worship. In both instances, plot and theme respectively, through the application of key concepts, become *constitutive* of a 'redescription' of the world. The narratives cease to function as 'mere' stories — they begin to occupy the place of the thing we call '*reality*'.

References

Appaduri, Arjuna, Frank J. Korom, Margaret A. Mills (eds.) 1991, *Gender, genre, and power in South Asian expressive traditions,* Philadelphia: University of Pennyslvania Press.

Bailey, Greg, 1983, *The mythology of Brahmā,* New Delhi, Oxford University Press.

Gold, Ann Grodzins, 1992, *A carnival of parting. The tales of King Gopi Chand and King Bharthari as sung and told by Madhu Natisar Nath*, Berkeley: University of California Press,

Harlan, Lindsey, 1992, *Religion and Rajput women,* Berkeley: University of California Press.

Mair, Victor 1988, *Painting and perfomance,* Honolulu, University of Hawaii Press.

Malik, Aditya, 1993a, *Das Puṣkara-Māhātmya: Ein religionswissenschatlicher Beitrag zun Wallfahrtsbegriff in Indien,* Stuttgart, Fanz Steiner Verlag.

Malik, Aditya, 1993b, Avatāra, avenger, and king: Narrative themes in the Rājasthānī oral epic of Devnārāyaṇ. In *Flags of Fame. Studies in South Asian Folk Culture,* Heidrun Brückner, Lothar Lutze, Aditya Malik (eds.), Delhi, Manohar Publishers.

Malik, Aditya, in Press (a), Stringing a necklace of heads: Sacrifice and death in the cult of Devnārāyaṇa. In *The meaning of Death in South Asia,* Elisabeth Schoembucher, Claus Peter Zoller (eds.), Delhi, Manohar Publishers.

Malik, Aditya, in Press (b), Die Heirat Brahmās mit dem Hirtenmädehen Gāyatrī: Zwei Legenden von der Entstehung Puṣkaras. In *Festschrift für Hermann Berger*, Dieter B. Kapp (ed.), Wiesbaden: Otto Harrasowitz.

→ discourse' on Puṣkar, the *BB* needs to be seen as part of a 'decentralised', horizontally interactive nexus of contending historico-religious narratives in the region.

28. On the level of 'public discourse', both narratives need to be seen as part of a wider network of stories, commentaries, counter-narratives, etc. For example, in the case of the *PM*, its hegemonic representation of the 'origin myth' of Puṣkar is undermined by the Gūjar tale of Gāyatrī's marriage to Brahmā. Similarly, the *BB* engages in a 'counter-history' of pastoralists, farmers, potters, and leather workers that undermines the mainstream (Rājpūt) history of Rajasthan. Thus, for example, the *BB* provides an origin story of the Sisodiyā-Rājpūt clan that is radically different to the Sisodiyā's own claims. (See Harlan 1992 : 30, for a brief account of Sisodiyā origin stories.) In fact, given the social ranking of the narrative's main bearers one could even talk here of a 'subaltern' oral history that competes with the ruling class history of the region.

Melas, E. M., 1989, Etics, emics and empathy in archaeological theory. In *The Meanings of Things: Material Culture and Symbolic Expression.* Ian Hodder (ed.), London, Unwin Hyman.

Ortner, Sherry B., 1990, Patterns of history: Cultural schemas in the foundings of Sherpa religious institutions. In *Culture, Through Time.* E. Ohnuki-Tierney (ed.), Standford, Standford University Press.

Ricoeur, Paul, 1991, The human experience of time and narrative. In *A Ricoeur reader: Reflection and Imagination*, Mario J. Valder (ed.), Toronto: University of Toronto Press.

Sells, Michael A., 1994, *Mystical Languages of Unsaying,* Chicago: Chicago University Press.

Silburn, L., 1955, *Instant et Cause: Le Discontinu dans le Pensée Philosophique*, Paris.

Smith, John D., 1991, *The epic of Pābūjī,* Cambridge, University of Cambridge Press.

Valdés, Mario J., 1991, *A Ricoeur reader: Reflection and imagination,* Toronto, University of Toronto Press.

11

Dynamics of Cultural Communication
Ṛta and the Anthropology of Experience

S. C. Malik

Language, culture and communication

The modern era begins with the seventeenth century when more than ever before, the written word in an evolutionary sense, — language — with its other associations begins to dominate human behaviour. It reflects an over specialisation of a distinctive area of the brain; the role of the cerebrum which consists of two distinct halves — each functioning autonomously in sorting out information received, i.e., the left side is more logical, rational and involved with the use of language; the right being more intuitive and syncretic. But when this integral development of the nervous system breaks down and the two halves do not exchange information and get severed for one reason or the other, then a dualistic or split personality is formed. This oppositional duality reflects the psychological state of man today; the neurotic life dominated mostly by the linguistic context, distant from authentic first hand experience. All these developments suggest an over-specialisation of the left brain. One of the most conspicuous indication of this functional asymmetry, or lateralism, is the phenomenon of 'handedness' — right or left.

There are fairly obvious risks attached to a brain that operates on a double-plan system, the most outstanding being the danger that the two separate mental domains might vie with each other for control over the organism. Today, it is recognised that both hemispheres are involved in higher cognitive functioning, but that there is a division of labour and fundamental modal differences between the two sides. The two hemispheres process information differently, and are organised differently. It is not surprising, in view of the fact that they are separate entities, that they should have differing views of the world. In spite of their marked differences, there is a modal complimentarity in the functions of the separate hemispheres: one could generalise and say that the left tends to think in words, and the right intuitively, holistically in images. The combination of the two systems are far more effective than one on its own. Even if one may see with one eye our stereoscopic vision is essential, so also is stereocognition necessary to functionfully, in harmony and creativity. This is the only way one may respond to a universe and nature which is similarly organised but one which may never be revealed except in its own style of dynamic functioning — in all its various dimensions. (Fiumara: 1990)

Every individual brain is subtly organised in different ways, its psychic configurations creating unique patterns of ability and personality. Each individual psyche makes its own response to the inherent dualism of the mind/brain just as it responds to the cultural dualisms that are a feature of all social structures. In general, these perferences are made as unconsciously as those of the left/right dominance determining reflex itself: we are quite 'naturally' of an artistic or scientific cast of mind, or, for that matter, political orientation.

Thus, the divide between the East and West may also be seen, beginning with the seventeenth century, to be the dominance of the left brain activities as against the non-verbal, non-logical and 'fluid' methods of Eastern philosophies — the likes of which has disappeared in Western thought but is surprisingly perhaps making a return via the new vision of science itself. It is worth metioning that psychologists have noticed that the left brain has a distinct tendency to 'take over' and feel itself responsible for all the actions of an individual, even to the extent of rationalising those decisions made by its right partner that it has played little or no part in making. There is surely an analogy in the functioning of modern society, of rulers, political and other authority — the experts and their systems — who claim to know that they know what is best and have an overbearing attitude. One of the philosophical problems thrown up by the confirmation of the dual mechanism of the brain concerns the nature of consciousness. Modern science — relativity and quantum theory — has cast doubts on the nature of space, time, matter and evergy which are no longer tangible, solid 'things'.

This brief introductory background is necessary in the context of the dominance of the Western mode of communication widely prevalent all over the modern world. The stress in this paper, within the context of the theme of the seminar, is on an integral approach to the understanding of these two kinds of knowledge — the holistic functioning of cultures.

Contemporary man has not given due importance to the negative dimensions of expressive language, which is easily seen by the domination media — whether newspapers or audio-video means. All these developments have led to a social behaviour which reduces the unspeaking, non-expressive Other as a void, a negation. In many earlier non-industrial societies, the power of the unsaid was equally of crucial importance. We know that a large part of communication was carried out taking into account this 'unseen' aspect of the functioning of the brain which now has been lost in the use of mere expressive language — the constant chatter of the brain is the source of a great deal of anguish and sorrow for humankind.

The ground of modern man and his philosophies are grounded in only half a language, i.e., within any discourse the strength of listening is ignored. In fact, what one takes to be a form of genuine dialogue, is a mere speaking without listening. There is actually no authentic listening taking place. To illustrate, modern culture and society is working at hardware illustrated by the number of radios, TV sets and newspapers circulated. In terms of indicators of so-called development in the information-communication systems, it is totally ignoring a broad base of human communication networks that are deeply rooted in the cultural milieu characterised by oral traditions which represent a continuous creation in the now. (Finnegan 1992)

Hearing basically implies hearkening and heeding, and in this way listening is supposed to be a transportation of hearing proper into the realm of the spiritual. Obviously, in this sense it is not relished by a materialistic world. It is precisely this aspect of our culture that rationality has largely neglected. Today, social scientists, anthropologists and folklorists are doing a rethinking on what they are doing and looking at cultures from this alternate approach within the context of oral traditions. For example, to examine events and processes; to speak of shared experiences as an important aspect of anthropological knowledge; and, to see that integral listening means openness and a true dialogue.

However, modern culture's non-listening has given rise to two types of conceit, one of nations and the other of scholars who believe that what they know is as old as the world. The tacit, ubiquitous belief that recent Western logic represents the most reliable cognitive standpoint appears to characterise this worldwide modernism. Has not listening, as an ancient art, been gradually lost in the noisy inflation of discourse and by the infestation of pseudo-symbolic language? Or, conversely, could it be that the vital, ecological rationality has exhausted itself in its overwhelming production of talking and since it is more interested in hunting than in cultivation? Has this intellectual heritage not caused the conceptual connections of other traditions to disappear? Has it not given rise to an idea of truth which is befitting for the vacuum it has created?

In short, Western knowledge in this excessiveness of rationality and logocentricity, has left little room for listening. In fact, there is one voice only as the accredited source of knowledge, i.e., the celebrated science-power equation revealed in the coincidence of technological development and socio-political hegemony. This is why unless listening, a part of this holistic approach, comes to be seen as a radical and valid point of departure, the biosphere will turn out to be uninhabitable. This is why a 180-degree turnabout is essential, and a change of route is worth the attempt at the level of world-view and philosophic foundations.

The mythic domain

Myths arise out of a broad base of the collective unconscious. There are, however, many meaning given to myths and their nature; a debate has been going on for many millennia, say whether myths are distorted memories of historical events, are they moral or psychological insights, and many other beliefs and speculations about myths. It is not possible here to trace some of these ideas in their historical setting. What one can say is that with colonial, expansion, new information was received about different peoples all over the world. By the middle of the nineteenth century, ethnologists and anthropologists attempted to deal with this new data in terms of some all-embracing new schemes of organisation, viz., evolution of language, culture, and mythology. In this way, the early stages were represented by various indigenous cultures within some value-laden theoretical ladder wherein mythologies were seemingly irrational obsessions of these people and the ancients — a prelogical, as James Frazer said, mode of thought that did not allow them to distinguish between Man, Nature and Cosmos. Even later, Durkheim with his functionalist approach to myth and culture, explained it in terms of social function, customs and attitude rather than on looking into some deep philosophical meaings in myths. Of course, Freud viewed myths a primitive humanity's disguised expressions of unconscious sexual and aggressive compulsions. Both Durkheim and Freud who influenced most of the first half of the twentieth century, sought to identify religion with illusion and explain myth by reference to physical, social or psychological phenomena. Later, it was realised that something was missing in this collective dissection, analysis and classifications of myths.

Though not universally, but many psychologists, anthropologists and historians have abandoned this reductive approach. This radical new way sees myths as doors to a realm of experience that was, and is, both real and profoundly meaningful. Mythologies simply are not a study of economic, social and cultural meanings. In them lies the primacy of the sacred that is present in all traditions; and this is not present in any evolutionary order. These reveal and clarify their common motifs, a universal pattern is revealed, e.g., rock, trees, rivers, and clouds are parts of a whole in which the Cosmos is alive and conscious; it partakes of the same intelligent force by which humankind itself is animated and acts as a link between the inner dimension of spirit and the outer world of form. In this domain, every individual knows that his/her life is the embodiment of a larger principle — norm, *ṛta* — so that even the most mundane activity has an overarching significance because every act is not performed as a personal, private act but as part of a Cosmic drama. In short, the respect for the sacred is derived from an awareness of the creative process of Nature, and it implies a hesitancy to arbitrarily intrude on those processes in which time and space are themselves sacred.

Almost all non-industrial human cultures in the past and even today have traditions belonging to this simple yet magical, harmonious atunement with Nature and the Cosmos. There is a mythic unity in the spiritual and religious realms, for, repeatedly in America, Africa, Greece, India, Australia and so on, in different ways, cultures have pursued this Cosmic unity in varied ways both metaphorically and literally. It is a sacred world-view which lacks any sense of sectarianism or dogmatism because there seems to be an understanding of the universal order and meaning of existence that guides one in relationship to social order, Nature and Cosmos. Indigenous people have never assumed that Nature exists for the benefit of Man; rather humankind owes a responsibility to mother Earth and all its creatures — plants, and animals. They, in fact, are apologetic for exploiting the earth for their food, and clearly see the Universe as aware and benevolent. In this sense, there has been a decline of humanity, for religions of today appear as remnants of a formerly universal spiritual traditions which had the original sense of a sacred purpose.

Modern Science — Physics — unlike Classical Physics is recapitulating in many ways the ancient spiritual world-view of integral living. But in these new formulations, is it possible to discern any sense of the sacred? And, whatever the name given to this ultimate source — this universal ground of Being — is no modern invention. Indigenous peoples all over the world were masters of holism before this term was coined!

Convergence of modern science and ancient insights

Humankind today faces a crisis at many levels, despite (or because) the magnitude of resources available as a consequence of tremendous technological and scientific growth. The idea of 'progress and development' begins with the positivistic-reductionistic, empiristic and anthropocentric enterprise in Europe in the senveteenth century. Underlying contemporary challenges are certain unquestioned assumptions (e.g., rationality, linear time, subjectivity *vs* objectivity, nature *vs* man). Although outdated by Modern Science, these paradigms dominate decision-makers who continue to ignore many of the alternate world-views of indigenous-non-Western cultures which are very relevant today. This is the perspective of interconnectedness, simultaneity and multilayerdness of reality; of a seamless whole, a continuum in which we — earth with its creatures and the universe — are all enmeshed within a Unified Force-Field, Energy or Consciousness. This overarching energy-field is expressed in various cultures through the mythic domain within which experiencing takes place, allowing for the psychic maintenance of socio-cultural variations. This domain is crucial in understanding indigenous cultures; it is the source wherein lies our collective memory. Modern man has ignored this dimension at its own peril, although it is trying to create a new world order with the myth of history, the myth of materialism and the myth of science; believing as if together these will provide anwers to all our prayers, to all our questions about existence. This seeking for answers — one's identity — in externalities alone has increased desperation and alienation; it has encouraged revivalism and fundamentalism. Clearly, this myopic unidimensional viewpoint has brought upon us many diabolical scenarios for the planet and its creatures. Has not imagination and intuitive knwledge as experience, which is the essence of living cultures, taken a backseat?

The viewpoint suggested above may be disturbing since it challenges earlier frameworks and the unexamined certainties. The study of this area by many disciplines is inhibited by the essentially linear or non-contextual historical tradition that provides the presuppositions of scientific enquiry in the West. But these instruments of Western rationality are not applicable to other cultures, wherein rational principles are discoverable through their own world-view, i.e., a text within its own context which is peculiarly non-linear or contextual. This is to be understood in the way complementary frameworks in Quantum Mechanics are created by different contexts of measurement — frameworks that are mutually exclusive (and, therefore, non-linear) but ordered to one another in a lattice structure (and, therefore, complementary). Complementary frameworks involve changes in the embodied subjectivity of the knower. Knowing about cultures, therefore, cannot be done with the head, on the conceptual soil of Europe, nor new models formulated about culture and development without sounding the deathknell of this culture and civilization which is still a living body. Lived experience of such cultures seldom arises by describing the surface of their world; this knowledge must act, reflect, and communicate experiencing since it is this Consciousness of man on which man counts and man get hold of it in him/herself.

The reference here is more to Western thought which has become a cultural determination for all men. The first determination, for instance, in the problem of the One and the Many, was the identification of the One with Thought; and the second that this Thought was Being. This notion has become common to the individual both in the East and the West; that is, Be-ing identified with the word which proclaims in this fashion as able to control universal human behaviour, to this logic. But this will not allow us to reach the shores of other cultures which do not take Thought and Be-ing to be identical. It is possible to understand these cultures through the action and meaning given in their cultural 'texts', implicitly and explicitly; abandoning one's own theoretical knowledge, i.e., the starting point will be that Thought is a subset of Be-ing. The latter, for instance, is not an element in the conceptual system — it creates a reference to a domain of things, processes and events and it exists independent of any human involvement. Be-ing is primal and as mentioned in Buddhist tradition "What is evident (*pratyakṣa*) to men is concealed (*parokṣa*) to the gods and what is concealed to men is event to the gods."

These ways of looking at the world may further be illustrated by the responses from philosophers of the West and the East, to the question 'What am I?'. Socrates, as quoted by Plato attempts to bring together the what and I of the question by trying to figure out the x-what and thereby have the answer to the dictum: 'know thyself'. There would be a long list of each of the identifications given to the 'what' of man in the History of Western Philosophy — this figuring out the whatness of man or what it meant except were it not for existentialism or phenomenology. But in every answer provided, the phenomenon itself was forgotten as meaningless. In this way, the what became a strictly linguistic question, or some sort of an empirical problem which could be answered by adding up sets of empirically discovered characteristics or as a substance, etc. In contrast, in other cultures, it is not the what nor the subsequent possible identifications with the 'I' which would give an answer to the problem, but rather the AM-BEING of the question. What is being looked at it is neither the 'whatness' nor even the 'I' as the source of enquiry but to go to the core of both the 'what' and the 'I', i.e., existence itself, the AM-BEING which every question-asking-subject is before he even bothers to figure out essences, or substances, whatever else becomes fashionable within a community to ask. In the modern world, this dictum has become a question of achievement, of seeking self-identity, personality through several frantic steps of one order or the other. (de Nicolas: 1976)

The main point of this comparison is not to prove anyone nearer the truth than another, or to arbitrarily establish contact points between East and West. It is clear that man must realise "himself as 'this', 'that', 'here', 'there'; since, originally and finally man-was-able-to-become one or another or several in an infinite repetition of this first affirmation of existence-as-capacity. It functions as the original space" out of which all forms and names derive; as such, i.e., as original space, it is the container of all human possibilities.

Thus, one can say that there are the two sources of knowledge — the indirect (called understanding, imagination, etc.) and the direct (called sensibility, perception, etc.); the two sources of knowledge are termed 'non-sensuous' and 'senuous' sources — neither better nor worse except in the manner of how we deal with the world. Instead of negating each other, these might be seen as complementary. In short, there are many ways of viewing the world and describing it without any one way being pre-eminent over the other. If this is not the case in the modern world, it is because of certain preconceptual visions which are exclusivists and not inclusivists, and are adhered to dogmatically. The need is to transcend one's own framework. These two distinctive ways are available to man to view the world; the dominant 'common sense-Classical-Physics viewing' and the 'Modern-Physics-Eastern viewing' of the world. Man's condition is such today that he is bound to use both viewpoints, if he is to slove the problem of 'what-is-really-the-nature-of-things'.

Modern Physics, and the Eastern world-view assumes that whenever we are in search of anything, we are primarily in contact with a totality, the most 'real' aspect of any entity being the total pattern. Our perception of 'it' defies any atomicity or real identification. It is only secondarily that classification of individual entities is made possible, and for this we revert to ordinary symbolic manipulation. For example, one no longer says, 'Here is an electron' but says 'Here is an area where the field is strong'. In this view, 'what is' appears as a quantum, a whole, a totality; the identifiable parts of this totality are artificially created for purposes of linguistic communication and conceptualisation: they are artificial subpatterns. The separation is totally false in relation to 'what is'.

The impact of this idea is to note that we are living in a continuum, in the present, where the distinction between the living and dead, between moving bodies and bodies at rest, etc., no longer holds good. Man is now in nature, not seeing something distinct from himself. In this way, we shall have to describe things in new and better way; sometimes creating and selecting or abstracting. The human condition is such that both ways are essential, if man is to feel at home, and this is what Complimentarity means,

> It is not that there are songs to be discovered but that the symphony was already there — sometimes in one note or in one song because both are necessary in knowledge.

This freedom is necessary if one wants to stop reinforcing what one already knows. The historical accident of the discoveries of quantum mechanics and their relation to linguistic communication, complimentarity, indeterminacy, and vision, makes our project of understanding cultures easier.

Anthropology of experiencing the other

Perhaps the greatest shortcoming in cultural studies is the hidden presupposition that our linguistic criteria are the only ones by which all men and cultures should be measured or reduced — the positivistic view of language where the logic is universal irrespective of how the people use it. It is essential, therefore, that we do not presuppose what Culture is before we discover it. Culture is always incomplete, always on the move; this making gives it a certain indirection as an open phrase hanging in mid-air.

The knowledge we formulate about the 'other' is filtered or refracted through the knowledge we have built for ourselves, i.e., we are interpreters of cultures and can observe 'others' only through our own cultural and experiential biases. But this is not all so subjective, for at any given time there are accepted norms of what knowledge is conceived to mean, i.e., the knowledge of the 'self' and of the 'other' comes together in terms of some subjective and creative understanding; say, about new sights, sounds, rhythms, silences, feelings and tastes amidst many other cultural paraphernalia (Hastrup *et al.*, 1994). This does not mean that language is not important in that culture and that they are not linguistically sophisticated. It is just that in the natural flow of interaction, especially in music and dance and so on, there is something behind the words — a hum of another kind — which takes into account a large sensory inventory which cannot be frozen into the written word that becomes the so-called ethnographic record. The human approach to a cultural model must encompass all 'experience' even if in terms of categories — taste, smell, sound, shape, colour and so on. Moreover, while linguistic categories may be gradually learnt, cultural learning may just have to be picked through sheer participation — doing the right thing at the right time, by feeling something beyond language that give some meaningfulness and vibrance before these are classified and explained away. One can of course only attempt to approximate to the verbal and non-verbal experiences in terms of the shared experience, and as far as possible it is to share emotions — if at all in any case. May be there can be a lived understanding of the situation, event and process.

We need to consider our model along these lines; the multiplicity of perspectives. Modernism has imposed a single perspective in dealing with human language and human culture. Cultures have to be seen as a whole, linguistic or otherwise. It is to see the presuppositions and criteria on which life is ground, to discover a different way of viewing and listening. This perspectival vision thus does not rupture the continuum between thought and action, viewing and action. To reduce and measure man by the image of his thought carries inevitable consequences: For one thing, what is not an image, a thought, is outside of man, a mystical power, a god or a devil; while whatever is human must of necessity be only that which appears or is an image. For another, the only possible role for man to play in a world grounded on thought is to systematically reduce and control all his possibilities to the reality offered by the image; it is to condemn man to a programme of desensitisation. The integrating way to see this in many cultures is to put an axe to this tendency, so that all perspectives are kept alive simultaneously.

It has been overlooked that most social experience about cultures lies beyond language, both 'theirs' and 'ours'. Cultures are not things, objects, theoretical frameworks. The error lies in the production of anthropological-ethnographic-knowledge which has ignored experience, personal and social. Language categories fragment the experience of both the 'self' and the 'other', i.e., there is an inherent unidimensionality and linearity involved in this domain of objective rationality which blocks out experience (subjectivity and intuition). The contention here is that this need not be so in any exclusivistic terms as both domains are crucial for understanding cultures in general and specifically in India.

Clearly, the spoken or written word-prose involves one of the senses, and not the other senses (say, smell, touch, feelings, sight, rhythm and so on) which express vividly what cultures are all about, especially Indian civilisation. It is dominated by oral means of transmission of heritage where songs, music, dance, poetry — the Arts in a broad manner are important. The first step is to rethink earlier axioms and assumptions of the research involved. An awareness of the issues and seeing that such fusion is possible between the two poles, is itself an important step in contributing to methodological frameworks. The verbal and the non-verbal encounters merge into a continuum since often minimum words are needed in this form of communication. The emphasis is on the fact that the total representations of the senses in understanding other cultures or representing them is crucial. We may call this as knowing the taste or essence of the culture and a removal from that spatial ambience does not replicate the same essence of this aspect of culture — it is out of context.

In short, over and above the intellect, linguistic utterances, the full range of bodily senses — experience — is an important means for approaching others' experience — beyond the linear, preordained format. In no way does it imply that the linguistic means, are therefore, redundant or subordinate to this form of knowing. One may call this grounded knowledge, a most appropriate medium available which has been disembodied in the name of objectivity.

Understanding other cultures is only possible when they are experienced comprehensively; the internalisation of the holistic social and cultural experience is crucial since it allows one to move beyond conceptual worlds of people, to a totality that comprises thoughts, feelings and emotions. In fact, this is the only way which allows for a fuller understanding of both cognitive and embodied knowledge. Understanding cultures is not about information categories, it is a learning process that can only come via experiencing. This is especially true for India.

The context of ṛta in Ṛgveda

There are many ways of viewing the world and describing it without any one way being preeminent over the other. The need is to transcend one's own framwork, this creation of pseudo-problems through an idea of 'either/or' framework, taking the atomisation of language and its separateness of the things of the world as real: subjects and objects, man and the world, agent and re-agent, observer and the observed, life and physiology, mind and bodies, I and other.

Ṛgvedic man (other such cultures) refused to create new problems by separating the inseparable, and searched instead for that other way of viewing the world which happens as a result of transcending common sense language and its viewpoint. The point is of not having a philosophy but doing philosophy, beyond a single set of possibilities, and liberate man from these various controls, inner and outer.

This is not only a way of viewing the world but one of interacting with it; making freedom possible by falsifying all controls through the knowledge of the controls themselves. The positivistic view of language along with its own ground of meaning has to be dropped, and the researcher has to be free from this belief. This freedom is necessary if one wants to stop reinforcing what one already knows, e.g., the achievements of a method that allowed fixed notions about nature, society and the individual. But there is the absolute falsification of this method, since we find ourselves trapped in a continuous crisis of nature, society and the individual. However, while the crisis of nature does not bother us too much, the crisis of society and the individual hit us closer to home, where it hurts. This is where man's fourth dimension comes in, where critical philosophy and meditation coincide.

Cultures thus have to be seen as a whole, on two points at least: (1) the conscious ordering of the structures of experience, and (2) the dynamic activity produced through the conscious ordering of these structures. It is to see the presuppositions and criteria on which life is ground, how through structures and the activity based on metaphysics, ontology, logic and epistemology, etc., are combined in order to discover a different way of viewing and listening. This perspectival vision thus does not rupture the continuum between thought and action, viewing and action. In short, the basic structure of this situation is then a human consciousness, consisting of both a subject and a field of objects, toward which the consciousness is turned intentionally.

From this perspective, every movement is the whole, the whole is in every movement. This is the fully realised presence of a total system of possibilities embodied in every movement. In presupposing a field opened by sight, for modern man, vision came to be based on a linear kind of movement, which disclosed a perspectival, three-dimensional space and linear time. In contrast, in the *ṚV*, the audial space-time structure opened by sound was articulated not only by rhythmic and cyclically recurring movements, but movement itself became the base of all contexts (structure) and the source of meaning within each and every field of experience. (de Nicolas, 1976)

Thus, the integrating way is to see that all perspectives are kept alive simultaneously. The implied philosophical activity, say in the *Ṛgveda*, holds that the internal language of images is essential to both human experience and human progress in such a way that both become dependent for their functional efficacy on a clear understanding of the language of the images themselves. The *ṛṣis* of the *ṚV* resolve the philosophical activity of integrating different images by means of the language of the sacrifice, a sacrifice of complementary integration which leads to new creation through sharing in an effective way of viewing human action (*dhiḥ*) according to the effective body of common law or norm (*ṛta*).

The *ṚV* mind was certainly not after abstract definitions of essences. It was worried about what existence really meant, the concrete act of existing; and the observation of this act was their whole concern from the *asat* to vision. It is the 'sheer-being-able-to' that takes the name and form of the existing actuality.

The main point of this comparison is not to prove anyone nearer the truth than another, or to arbitrarily establish contact points between East and West. It is clear that man must realise himself as 'this', 'that', 'there'; since, originally and finally man-was-able-to-become one or another or several in an infinite repetition of this first affirmation of existence-as-capacity, which is the *asat* of *ṚV*. It functions as the original 'space' out of which all form and name drive; as such, i.e., as original space, it is the container of all human possibilities.

For Western readers, this again might be understood, this space, as some 'visual' model leading to a visual synthesis of their human experience as is common when speaking about 'vision', including senses of ears, mind, eyes, etc., that one reads into the language. But are we dealing with a 'visual' model or of an 'audio-aurol' model? The vision spoken here has nothing to do with looking, but the model is grounded on 'sound', not 'sight'. (de Nicolas, *ibid.*) Western Philosophy from Aristotle onwards, has equated vision or contemplation with gazing at human life from the heights of theory; the soil of vision and contemplation has remained theoretical. The only form of transcendence possible within such determined confines is either, the decapitation of theories by other theories, or a system of dialectics by which the process of executing theories is accelerated, leaving in its wake a world empty of human creation but uniformly nominalistic.

On the other hand, in the *ṚV*, *asat* is a tonal context ruled by the criteria of music, the ground of transcendence, the origin of all organised perception, the original ground any and all sounds count on in order to sound. It is simply silence that embraces a whole spectrum of sound, from its absence to its plenary confusion. The flesh wants to be music; for this was the beginning. Sound emerges as all of organised sensation and of all communication; sheer vibration, energy, possibility — the sounding silence from which the worlds, gods, and man emerge, is the space of discourse. But modern man has deprived himself of the possibility of returning to his origins and that of others. This is the only sin path of *ṛta* could not tolerate, for it deprived man from the eternal return to his origin, and tried to reduce the multiplicity of embodied-songs to one theoretical voice. Contemporary man and contemporary science, especially psychology, needs to dwell on this sin; for unless memory and imagination are freed from the theoretical constraints limiting their movement, man and woman cannot recover their body completely. Not allowed to reach the beginnings of the human body we all carry with us, the present crisis of contemporary man and woman. The *ṚV* insight needs not only verification but to recover our own act of creation and the power to revive it. "We have forgotten the Dragon, the Snake, the Silence, and the Flesh that wants to be music." (de Nicolas, *ibid.*)

If one does not agree with this view then one is agreeing to the method of the natural sciences, as the only method whereby man and his 'body' may be understood, explained, predicted and controlled. A necessary condition of the method is that in experimental observation one variable must be constant; the 'body' as an organism must be conceived as historically resting, while the mind may be conceived as historically moving. Even if the approach to the study of body has changed with improved istruments, it still implies that we have better explanations of the body than before, while it stays unchanged. The idea of predictability and control is facilitated by this notion, which is repeatable. Hence, the idea of behavioural control or generic manipulation is the result of this journey. The historical man is thus denied human freedom of creation, of freedom which present-day education inhibits completely. The memories of body buried, imaginings and rhythms are unable to be released.

The Western and Eastern scholars, have tried to attribute a visual model to the *ṚV ṛṣis*, or presupposed such a visual model as the synthesis of their sensorium. It is common place that man's sensory perceptions are abundant and overwhelming; but it should be eqully evident that it is impossible for man to attend to all of his sensory perceptions at once. Every man is part of a civilisation which is committed to an organisation of the sensoriun stressing certain types of perceptions and neglecting others. This may be a telling clue about specific cultures — historically speaking — that any given culture is committed to one prominent way of sensory perception, and that their way is not necessarily ours, is at the root of many of our misunderstandings and misinterpretations of other cultures. This Western 'visual' culture is at the worst odds to understand and interpret a culture like the *ṚV*, where the stress is not so much on the visual, but rather on the oral-aural. There is in this field of exploration a sensorium synthesis in the *ṚV*; it is at once varied, vast and intricate.

It is obvious, when talking about the whole-human-sensorium, that this refers to the world of sight, sound, taste, smell, touch; the relations of touch to sight and to sound, the relations of those sense perceptions to our expressions in the vocabulary of our vernacular, the relations of those sense perceptions to our self-identification and to the perceptions of others, i.e., interiority and exteriority. What might not be so obvious is that a synthesis based on sound as a primary model of organising sensation contains a multiplicity of preceptions that will certainly have a different character that, say, a synthesis based on primarily sight-perceptions alone.

A society bent on sight-perceptions and on the fixedness which such a priority in perception carries with it, is mostly concerned with surfaces, with objectifying, with fixed spaces and with objects in such space; a society so perceptually inclined cannot stand the light, but only its reflection!

In the *ṚV*, then there is sound, which is the greatest key to interiority among all of our senses, even though interiors of a certain kind are also felt through touch and kinaesthesia. But it is only through sound that interiors as interiors are manifested. Sound is the greatest clue we have to interiority, our own and that of others. It is only sound which makes true interiority communicative.

Sound discovers interiors by invading them physically; the hearer vibrates not merely emphatically but in physical bondage (resonance) with the sounding body. Sound is absolute presence; it is an activity rooted in the present. Sight may provide a lot to think about, but it is only in sound that all the thinking is done. No wonder that sound, the word, has been attributed with power, even magical power. In this way, *ṚV* culture which stresses sound as the primary organiser of sensation, both sensation and thinking will have a different structure than the same process in culture which stresses the visual. No thought or object is sensed or thought in isolation, but within 'sets', 'groups', 'horizons', or simply contextual structures. The root of contemporary man's crisis is that while his culture tries to reduce his body to simply the names of an organism, contemporary man's body still remembers its origins in sound and refuses the nominalistic amputation. (de Nicolas, *ibid.*)

By focusing on the criteria of sound, the measures of the structures of the language of Existence (*sat*) are discovered in the *ṚV*. It would appear that the *ṛṣi*s did not have the atomisation of names and forms in mind; but rather, the establishment of an effective activity centered at the heart itself of that powerful *māyā* (force), originator of any and every activity; and which moved according to the norm (*ṛta*) through song (*vāc*). Therefore, in the *ṚV*, and by the silent criteria it presupposes, the act of creation is not a single, definitive act; but rather, an act which is repeated at every sound point.

There is also the world of touch, sight, taste, smell, etc. These are the multiple perceptions of structuring of the world in terms of the human body. Today psychiatry sees the appearance of multiple personalities as a threat to reason and is, therefore, labelled it as sickness; monotheistic personality has always been the prototype of modern culture and a fortiori of psychitary — schizophrenia — at a time when whole cultures are being fragmented into multiple personalities, in painting, music, literature, and even the natural sciences. The fragmenting personality becomes fragmeted into numerous centres of spontaneity, relativity, discontinuity, and disorganisation. We were not trained to survive without the monotheism of personality, and are unable to cope with psychological polytheism, except as an excuse for punishment and control.

In the *Ṛ V* context, the existence of fragmentary, autonomous systems is not only acknowledged, but no social life is possible without them. However, a polytheisic personality allows for the condition of survival when one of our psychic centres cannot hold and things fall apart. Polytheism in the human body is a psychological response to the challenge of breakdown and disintegration; it is a model for integrating disintegration. But this psychological aside cannot be easily understood in a culture ruled by the criteria of sight. *Ṛ V* methodology draws its main clue to interiorising all perception, the whole sensorium from sound, which found the model of complete, absolute instantaneity and communication in sound. In one way, it was the instant way to become the total presence and power of absolute and efficient communion. While the other sensory media provided discontinuity, sound gave the eternal presence. The total presence of speech and the discontinuity of sight are both reconciled in the common origin of sound, through *vāc*. This process presupposes an internal activity that is much in opposition to the Western activity that is suggested by the Western model of sight. Realising the intimate unity of all existence, *Ṛ V* methodology tries to recapture it in an auspicious moment of inspired vision. (de Nicolas, *ibid.*)

On the model of sound, and by its criteria, the *Ṛ V* offers us a completely different picture. The space is the musical scale, and it is neither here nor there prior to song; space and song are simultaneous. Time, again, is not prior to the singer, and the singer is no other than the song; the singer's body shares its dimensions with the structure of the song. The human body is polytheistic, multiple personalities as the body becomes the multiple perspectives it sings. Since the body remembers all its previous incarnations, and since the human body was born in sound and ruled by its criteria, its therapy does not lie in submitting it into psychological monotheism, but rather in releasing its lost memories, its silent music: The human body has the right to innovation and continuity.

In the *Ṛ V*, the individual, the society, the cosmos at large, are not three different entities, even though related, but rather society, cosmos and individual are all one body; this embodiment may be changed, modified, enlarged, make smaller, but in no way can it be radically gotten rid of. The effort of those same 'seers' was directed towards building such a common body as would make human existence most communicative, pleasurable and likable.

The *Ṛ V* philosopher-poets were very much aware of this 'tacit' dimension, i.e., that the structure of subjectivity is the sturcture of the embodied knower, the subject.

Different kinds of sense perceptions were understood simultaneously and as such influencing each other's growth. The distinction between both ends, subjective and objective, was understood by the *ṛṣis* as an apparent discontinuity — time, brought about by the sensorium itself and its discontinuous perceptions. These ends could be regathered in a continuous efficacious instant-moment, a space, by falling back on the infinity of an organising force, underlying — and found inside of *nitya* — all discountinuity.

In summary, there are three main clues that guide one in the *ṚV*:

1. A unitary and indivisible originating power — *māyā* — moves in accordance with the movement of the Norm — *ṛta* — and appears wherever the chant sound — *vāc*.
2. This coincidence of power, norm and chant occurs at any sound-point, any pitch being possible tonal centre for any kind of tonal structure.
3. God, heroes, Dragons, etc., are only the prototype — *pratirūpa* — and the embodiment of multiplicity of perceptives — *pararūpa* — generated from a common origin — *sayoniḥ* — the musical octave, conceived as a field admitting many alternative structures (i.e., 'tuning systems').

Thus, the movment of the *ṚV*, the trajectory of its path, is pointing straight at the heart of the stillness; for the path of the *ṚV* is none other than the power to still what moves and set in movement what is still. All this only may be known through meditation so that the human body is transformed. It is time to still the mind, historically moving for so long; time to set the body in motion, which has been historically resting for so long; let it become music again.

References

Finnegan, Ruth, *Oral Traditions and the Verbal Arts*, 1992, London.

Fiumara, Gemma Corradi, *The Other Side of Language — A Philosophy of Listening*, 1990, Routledge, London.

Hastrup, Kirsten and Hervik, Peter, *Social Experience and Anthoroplogical Knowledge*, 1994, Routledge, London and New York.

Malik, S.C., *Modern Civilization — A Crisis of Civilization*, 1989, New Delhi, Abhinav.

———, *Matter is Consciousness*, in *Prakriti*, 1995a, IGNCA, New Delhi.

———, *Holistic Science and Consciousness*, in *Prakriti*, 1995b, IGNCA, New Delhi.

———, *Re-conceptualising the Sciences and the Humanities — An Integral Approach*, 1995c, Manohar, and Nehru Memorial Museum and Library, New Delhi.

———, *Interface of Science, Consciousness and Indentity*, Forthcoming, 1996, IGNCA, New Delhi.

———, de Nicolas, Antonio, T., *Meditations Through the Ṛgveda — Four Dimensional Man*, 1976, Nicolas Hays, New York.

12

Order : The Old and the New

Baidyanath Saraswati

I AM moved and enlightened to hear from the learned participants of this seminar how sciences and scriptures view cosmic order and Chaos. I admit that there is the difference. There is also the convergence. But science cannot turn into scripture and scripture cannot turn into science. What can one do, within the limits of human knowledge, is to accept that there are many ways of capturing the elements of reality — each valid in its own right.

What I propose to present this afternoon is a construction of the tribal vision of order. My task is difficult. For, tribal culture does not have a conceptual scheme of its own. Nevertheless, the exploration of the tribal vision of the cosmic order is exciting and challenging in so far as it is founded entirely on the remembrance of the origin of life. Their memory is presented in the myths, ceremonies, symbols and patterns of living that have been scrupulously maintained through oral transmission for the millennia.

Ours is a culture with self-explanation. Tribal culture is without self-explanation. I have tried to understand their sensitivity to the memory and potency of cultural tradition through continued involvement with them as also within the framework of my own tradition. In the midst of such limitation, I admit, I cannot travel deep into tribal thought. My intention is to provide a glimpse of the world-view they foster.

The fivefold order

Tribal cosmogony refers to a fivefold order that sets forth the timeless sequence of creation, preservation and dissolution.

The First Order is set in 'nothingness': In the beginning, there was nothing; nothing at all but water or clouds and mist or two eggs, that shone like gold. In that state of nothingness, life was there above the primeval water, hidden deep in the clouds and mist, or in the two whirling eggs. With such vibration of life, the beginning was not an absolute vacuity.

The Second Order causes primary creation of elements from the element of the First Order. The First creation was asexual: The golden eggs broke open. From the one came the earth, from the other the sky. When the sky made love to earth, every kind of tree, grass and all living creatures came into being. The early phases of creation were marked by total integration of all that exists. Every element has its own life and all elements are interrelated.

The Third Order causes natural identity and differentiation in terms of colour, direction and form. Smell is another element of the Third Order. It makes communication between the form and the formless possible.

The Fourth Order causes the return to primordial state. Water is the self-existing element from which all other elements originate and to which they all return. Dissolution is a process of regeneration or recreation of order.

The Fifth Order is the order of all orders. It repeats the scenario of the world in which everything has its proper place, and everything grows and allows others to grow. It is inviolable.

In tribal perception, our world is continuous with the other world or worlds. There are also transition zones filled by primordial waters. Life in this world is repeated in the other world in a similar order. Worlds are communicable. Tribal eschatology reveals that the ontological experience of life and death is the same. Death brings to man only yet another existence. The errant soul moves on in the cosmos from one abode to another.

The fivefold process

What gives the tribal picture of the cosmos credence is the theory of elements, widely known to ancient peoples. Its basic assumption is that like the rest of the material world man is made up of elements such as water, earth, fire, air and sky, which at death disintegrate and dissolve into nature. The elements are subject to a fivefold process. Briefly:

ORIGINATION

As stated before, all forms of life originated from the state of nothingness. There are different stories of creation. Metaphorically speaking, every kind of life originated from Love (when the Sky made love to Earth), or from Compassion of the Cosmic Mother, or even from Strife (when two original beings living in the waters quarrelled and in the fight that followed they killed each other and from their flesh the world was formed).

BUILDING

Elements of nature have a binding ability. Each element has a form, a location, and a dependent relation with another element.

INTERLOCKING

Form and life are cross-linked. By entering into a form, the formless life acquires qualitative distinctions. It gives different expressions to different forms or species. Accordingly, it is called by different names.

OVERLAPPING

Elements have both personal (material) and universal (spiritual) attributes. Water and egg, which appeared in the beginning, embody have a fundamental feature of sacredness. The other primal elements, such as earth, air, fire and sky (with the sun, moon and stars) have also a similar indwelling sacred attributes. However, not all elements are spiritually vibrant all the time and at all places; but they can be made so in a ritual way.

TRANSCENDING

Cosmogonic myths describe how the limits of the natural state are transcended. The state of primordial solidarity was transcended, as the eggs broke open and the physical world revealed itself. The natural order of self-origination was transcended by the origin of the male-female principle. The order of self-organisation of each element was transcended by the interlocking of various elements. The order of the pluriverse was transcended by the overlapping of spheres in dream and trance. Life transcends the limits of the form. Death transcends all attributes of elements, including the limits of time (with a small 't'). There is no intrinsic disorder in nature. Dissolution is an integral aspect of the transcendent order of nature. Transcendence is the order of all orders. It is inviolable.

The old and the new

Taking the fivefold order and the fivefold process together we can make a few general statements on the 'Old Order' of culture.

Tribal myths deny the uniqueness of man in so far as his origin in concerned. Man is not unique even in the possession of knowledge. Primordial knowledge came to him from birds and animals. The priests of all creatures were born ahead of human beings. Man is not the creator of knowledge. Cosmic intelligence is the self-existent source of all knowledge.

Tribal culture is ordered as the honeycomb cells in a beehive. In other words, all things in tribal culture are interdependent like honey and bees.

Nature is repetitive. Hence the natural order of culture is also repetitive.; Tribal culture remains true to the old order, that is, the primal order. Many examples can be cited. Ritual order prevails over the human order. Ritual is repetitive. As stated before, the priests of all creatures were born ahead of human beings. The priest is the controller of the social order. The office of the priest is hereditary. In some cases, political organisation is separated from ritual organisation. The office of the chief is hereditary. Thus, the control system in both the cases is repetitive — confined to a particular family or clan (that is, kingship order). Tribal culture is a republic of the old in which the degree of freedom necessarily depends on such factors as age (that is biological order), signs of nature as revealed in dream and trance (that is, transcendental order), age-old customs and traditions (that is, social order). For the tribal people, myth is a body of revelatory knowledge of the unseen reality. Hence myth has a critical value in their way of life. It is believed that the primal form of culture is itself an imprint of the nature that brought about its material manifestation at the beginning of creation. In the tribal world-view, nature and culture are held in symbiotic relation. It would be a mistake to think that tribal culture is static. Following the fivefold natural order it undergoes through a fivefold process of origination, building, interlocking, overlapping, and transcending. Seen in this way, one can say that the 'Old Order' or the primal form of culture moves and it moves not. In using this Upaniṣadic metaphor, what I wish to say is that the tribal culture has historically moved in time and yet its critical intuition of understanding the Ultimate remains unmoved.

When extended into the domain of human affairs, the 'New Order' is totally opposed to the 'Old Order'. The forces of the 'New Order' throughout the modern world are geared up to the overthrowing of the old world-view. The new system of knowledge prides itself in being autotelic, that is, human thought is and ought to be pursued for its own sake. This claim is consistent with the general theory of human evolution that makes man the *telos* of his own thoughts and deeds. Hence, the New world-view, which is emerging as a result, has demoted the old world-view from its central place to be replaced by such concepts as organisation, complexity, information, modernisation, newness. It signals the demise of the 'Old Order' of culture. It reduces human beings to consumers and conquerors of nature and leaves no room for experiencing the wealth and the wisdom of nature. The 'New Social Order' places its emphasis not on the image of human development, but on the image of technological development. The 'New Order' is thus neither cosmocentric nor anthropocentric: it is essentially technocentric. It has produced technological communities totally bereft of humanistic perspective.

What happened when the 'Old Order' meets the 'New Order?' To answer this, let me briefly state the tribal situation in north-east India: efforts are being made to textualise the tribal oral tradition. As things stand, the enterprise of script and language movement is faced with such problem as hybridisation and loss of tribal dialects. The quest for tribal jurisprudence is threatening the age-old matrilineal system. In writing tribal theology deep problems have arisen. The elements chosen for the construction of Khasi theology, for instance, are such that cannot be reconciled with the indigenous belief system. In making visual text of tribal artistic manifestations, the Old context is lost and the New context is totally devoid of religious value. There is, inevitably, a snag. The New Order causes internal crisis, destroys the very texture of the tribal oral traditions and takes away all its vigour and vision. Anthropologists are content to ignore the situation — the infinite destruction and disorder — on the basis that however large and deep the loss may be, there is still a formidable process of retribalisation and retraditionalisation. This is where the New modernity seems to force itself on us. However, taking the tribal situation to its logical conclusion we are led to believe that the 'Old Order' of the 'nature-integrated' culture and the 'New Order' of technocratic modernity cannot coexist, or absorb into a unity through the transformation of each. What emerges as a result, is not a 'New Order' but chaos and Disorder.

13

Gandhi's Vision of Ṛta

Ramjee Singh

The unfolding cycle of the holy sprit

The basic and fundamental problem of the philosophy of history is social causation. Historicity does not work in vacuum. It works in relationship in time, both of the present to the past and the present to the future. However, we should not forget that human history is linked up with cosmic history. Individual is a part of the cosmos. Hence, they brought 'the mediation of imponderable spiritual forces' in the explanation of 'social and political phenomena'.[1] History at this point ceases to be science of the individual and becomes a science of the collective.[2] It also concerns not only the tangible and the visible but goes beyond the world spirit (Hegel), ordered cosmos (Greek), the play of the Law (*ṛta*).

Gandhi's philosophy of history is rooted in spirituality. According to him,

> Human society is a ceaseless growth, an unfolding in terms of spirituality.[3]

Spirituality is affirmation of eternal moral order or *ṛta*. Gandhi perceived that

> whilst everything around me is everchanging, everdying, there is underlying all that change a living power, i.e., changeless that holds all together, that creates, dissolves and recreates.

And he replies:

> I see it as purely benevolent, for I can see that in the midst of death

---

1. V.P. Varma, Philosophy of History in the Bhagavad Gita, *The Philosophical Quarterly*, Amalner, Vol. XXX, No.2, July 1957, p. 94.
2. Jean-Francois Bergier, New Tendencies in Economic History, *Diogenes,* No. 58, Summer, 1957, p. 107.
3. *Young India*, 16.9.1926.

> life persists, in the midst of untruth truth persists, in the midst of darkness light persists.[4]

This is the law of nature or *ṛta*.

There is repulsion enough in Nature but there is greater attraction. There are quarrels but there is more of love — which is an expression of soul-force. Being natural it is not noted in history.[5] Hence, Gandhi was convinced that,

> the sum total of the energy of mankind is not to bring us down but to lift us up, and that is the result of the definite, if unconscious, working of the law of love.[6]

He found that

> life persists in the midst of destruction and, therefore, there must be a higher law than that of destruction. Only under that law would a well-ordered society be intelligible and life worth living.[7]

Ṛta as truth

Amarakośa, a popular lexicon of Sanskrit language, gives the synonym of *satya* (Truth) as fact or reality (*ṛta*). Nothing is or exists in reality except Truth. For Gandhi, truth is the sovereign principle, which includes numerous other principles.

> This truth is not only truthfulness in word, but truthfulness is thought also, and not only the relative truth of our conception but the Absolute Truth, the eternal principle, that is God.[8]

Nothing is or exists in reality except Truth. That is why Truth is perhaps the most important name of God. To Gandhi, therefore, God and Truth seem to be synonymous.[9] There are innumerable definitions of God because his manifestations are innumerable. But Gandhi says, "I worship God as Truth only."[10] Truth is not only an epistemological and ontological concept, it is also axiological. Hence, truth to be truth must also be good and beautiful. However, naturalistic ethics holds the contrary view that whatever is true is true, it cannot be good. But we should remember that truth itself is a value concept as truth is a value attached to reality.

---

4. *Young India*, 11.10.1928.
5. M.K. Gandhi, *Hind Swaraj*, Ahmedabad, Navjeewan Publishing House, 1944, p. 45.
6. *Young India*, 12.11.1931.
7. *Ibid*., 1.10.1931.
8. M.K. Gandhi, *An Autobiography*, Ahmedabad, Navjeewan Publishing House, Introduction, p. xv.
9. K.G. Mashruwala, *Gandhi Vichar Dohan*, New Delhi, Sasta Sahitya Mandal, 1968, p. 1.
10. M.K. Gandhi, *An Autobiography*, Introduction, p. xv.

To Gandhi, Truth is not only the nature of reality, it is also its ultimate ideal. Thus, like *ṛta*, Truth is not only the law of our social being but also the basis of our morality. This is in consonance with the spirit of Indian philosophy where there is almost an identity between the Ultimate Reality and Ultimate Value of life. Apart from the existential and in axiological meaning of Truth, in the epistmological meaning, truth is an attribute of knowledge. Gandhi tries to equate knowledge with truth. He says,

> Where there is Truth, there is also knowledge which is true. Where there is no Truth, there can be no true knowldege. This is why the word *cit* or knowledge is associated with the name of God.[11]

Commonly speaking, there is a difference between ontological truth and epistemological truth. But this epistemolgical dualism between the object of knowledge and knowledge evaporates on a higher plain of consciousness, as we find in the religious and mystic experience of the Upaniṣadic thinkers, the Sufis and the neo-Platonic mystics. The *Bible* also says, "I am the way, and the truth and the life."[12]

What is of 'that world' (*āmusmika*) prossesses *sat* and *ṛta* in their fullness. What is of 'this world' only partially possesses *sat* and *ṛta* in their incomplete manifestaion. The function and being of *this* world requires the support of the being and function of *that* world which is a higher reality. According to the *Ṛgveda*, X.190, *ṛta* and *sat* were born of *tapas* (austerities or sacrificial heat). In the transcendental world, *ṛta* (order) and Being (*sat*) have been eternally there. At the empirical level, in the making of the world, the first process of order and law is the outcome of the rituals performed by the *devas* (Gods). Here we can note that *hiraṇyagarbha* or *puruṣa* are not the creators of the world. Ṛgvedic Gods have functions analogous to those of Plato's demiurge (demiourgos).

Ṛta as vrata

Ṛta after from being the cosmic order is also the moral order. *Ṛta* originally meant 'the established route of the world but gradually it also became the path of morality or the law of righteousness'. Thus, *ṛta* is the right path. He keeps count of good and evil deeds of mortals and is responsible for meeting out rewards and punishment to them. In this way, the *Law of Karma* is a detailed version of the Vedic concept of *ṛta* in its application to the moral life of conscious human creatures. The religio-philosophical world-view of the Vedas envisaged an ultimate reality which is both transcendent to and immanent in the visible world. The visible world depends on a

---

11. M.K. Gandhi, *In the Search of the Supreme*, Ahmedabad, Navjeewan Publishing House, Vol. II, p. 10.
12. New Testament, St. John, 146.

transcendent order which is the abode of a moral or spiritual law. This reminds us of Wordsworth's invocation to Duty:

> Thou dost preserve the stars from wrong;
> And the most ancient heavens, through thee,
> are fresh and strong.

What *law* is in the physical world, that virtue is in the moral world. Varuṇa, who was first the keeper of the physical and cosmic order becomes the custodian of the moral order (*ṛtasya gopa*). In the *Ṛgveda*, there is prayer to the Gods: "O Indra lead us on the path of *ṛta*, on the right path over all evils."[13] We feel that there is a law of rightousness in the moral world, conforming to the order of nature. Where law is, disorder and injustice are only provisional and partial. *Ṛta* is the truth of things, disorder (*anṛta*) is falsehood, the opposite of truth.[14] The good are those who follow the path of *ṛta*, the true and the ordered. Ordered conduct is called a true *vrata*. *Vrata*s are the ways of life of central feature of a good life. Varuṇa, the perfect example of the follower of *ṛta* is of unalterbale ways (*dhṛtavrata*). When ritual grew in importance, *ṛta* became synonym for sacrificial ceremony (*yajña*). There are duties both to Gods and duties to man.[15] Kindness, hospitality, charity and help to poor are reckoned as virtues[16] and sorcery, witchcraft, seduction and adultery, etc., are vicious.[17]

To Gandhi, for truth realisation, the eleven rules of conduct (*ekādaśa vrata*) came as the unfailing weapon of which Truth is the means and God is the end or we can also say that God is the means and Truth is the end. As a matter of fact, in our sincere quest of truth, it is hard to differentiate between ends and means, as they are convertible terms in Gandhi's philosophy of life. Gandhi's emphasis upon rules of conduct and virtues are necessary not only for a spiritual life but also for the maintenance of the social order. This is also the Gandhian way of emphasising the importance of *dharma* or righteousness and duty in the scheme of four-fold aims of life (*catuḥ-puruṣārtha*). From *dharma* alone proceed prosperity and happiness. Even the doctrine of *karma* lends additional emphasis to the importance of righteous conduct. There is no escape from the consequences of good and evil actions done by a person. This means that man is not free but he is born with numerous obligations. Even Lord Rāma, Kṛṣṇa and the mighty Viṣṇu could be made to suffer on account of a wrong done by him. This is the law of *karma* which affirms the prevalence of a

13. *Ṛgveda*, X.133.6.
14. *Ibid.*, VII..56.12, IX.115.4; II.6.10; IV.5.5, VII.47.3; VIII.6.2.
15. *Ibid.*, X.117.
16. *Ibid.*, VI.5.I.2.6.
17. *Ibid.*, VI.104.8; IV.5.5.

moral order in the universe alongside the natural order. Hence, Gandhi was perfectly justified in extolling the values of righteousness or in this words the idea of 'Ethical Religion', which is in consonance with the spirit of *Rāmāyaṇa* and the *Mahābhārata* where they are very much preoccupied with *dharma* and much less to the religious ideal of *mokṣa*. The last verse of the *Gītā* with the wish and prophecy that victory would go to the party which honours eternal moral law is significant. Hence, Gandhi laid emphasis upon accepting the eleven vows to embark on the experiment of self-realisation. Just as for conducting scientific experiments there is an indispensable scientific course of instruction, in the same way strict preliminary discipline is necessary to qualify a person to make experiments in the spiritual realm.[18] Gandhi did not regard God as a person. Truth for him is God and God's Law and God are not different things or facts in the sense that an earthly king and his law are different. Because God is Idea, Law Himself, therefore, it is impossible to conceive God as breaking the Law.[19] *Ṛta* stands for law in general and immanence of justice. It corresponds to the Universals of Plato or Chinese notion of Tao or Hegelian categories of universals of logic as 'God before the creation of world of any planet'.

Conclusion

Gandhi was a scientist as well as an intuitive seer. It was a common supposition in India, and more so in Europe and America that he was an opponent and a foe of science. Nothing can be farther from truth than a charge of this character. But in his humble opinion there were limitations even to scientific search. However, he distinguished between science of matter and science of spirit and advocated a synthesis of science and spirituality. There is difference between 'anti-science' and 'beyond science'. Gandhi was never anti-science which is equal to anti-reason which is worse than superstition. The concept of *ṛta* is neither anti-reason though it is also 'beyond reason'. *Ṛta* is law of moral causation hence we cannot call it as anti-reason. But so far *ṛta* is considered as immanence of spiritual power through the pursuit of moral causation, it is an intuitive perception. In fact, there is no conflict between scientific and intuitive approaches to the concept of *ṛta*. Even the pursuit of science itself is a moral commitment and an ethical truth. We cannot derive from science why some people love science, or why there should be science at all? Science rests on the law of physical causation but we cannot say that why science is the search for truth — a selfless unfailing devotion to truth? Truth is all that earnest scientists seek. But what is truth? There is no objective criterion of truth. Are there no truths except mathematical, and positively scientific? What about ethical and metaphysical truths? *Ṛta* is such an ethico-metaphysical truth which can be conceived or perceived only intuitively. This is 'beyond reason', but we should remember that

18. *Young India*, 31.12.1939.
19. *Harijan*, 23.3.1940.

the path 'beyond reason' is through reason, and never through anti-reason or bypassing reason. Intuition is inclusive of knowledge and reason (*jñāna vijñānam sahitam*). As human history cannot be properly understood without social and moral causation. Life is a unity. It cannot be divided into watertight compartments. Similarly, universe is not a chaos, it is a cosmos. That is the Law, prevailing all over. This moral nature of universe is unfolding cycle of the ultimate reality or spirit. Hence, it is also Truth (*satya*). Hence, Gandhi's vision of means-end-symmetry and synthesis is also born out of this inexorable universal law of moral causation. Even the Creator God cannot but obey this inflexible law which is firmly fixed in the universal order.

14

Social and Political Order in Chinese Tradition and Future Development

Tan Chung

China has the size of a whole continent and a mini-world of people (not less than 1/5 of humanity in history)[1] all under a single political umbrella. This geo-politico-human phenomenon gives rise to two kinds of problems. First, there is human density and closeness with every Chinese having little share of environmental and social space. Privacy and individual freedom as enjoyed by the modern people of Western cultural milieu was and still is alien to the Chinese lifestyle. In Chinese social reality, every individual is born not to live as an individual, but to become one among many. Except the happenings of the last fifty years, virtually no Chinese had ever has a separate bed to sleep after birth, and the majority of Chinese in the last three thousand years has never slept in bed alone between birth and burial. When we discuss Order in China, we have to keep this human closeness in mind.

I

From the infancy of Chinese civilisation, Chinese eyes, born in their thousands of pairs, saw order in Nature. They noticed the order of the four seasons, one following the other. They saw daily the sunrise and sunset with such dead punctuality. They wondered why the moon could not remain constantly round and bright, but noticed the thirty-day gap between every two full moons without variation, hence using it for the measurement of time. Spring came to them as the season of thaw, but autumn meant fall, with leaves and petals littering the ground. Summer brought heat to them while winter was severely cold — also the order of the Nature. They sighted that the most brilliant sky before sunset was the prelude to darkness and the dead

1. Having studied the Chinese historical vicissitudes for forty years, I feel emboldened to say that in the last three thousand years when China could be conceived as one political entity, it was populated by no less than one-fifth of humanity at any given point of time. During the nineteenth century, when China had four hundred million people the whole world did not have two billion.

of night. They compared the not-too-infrequent reunion and separation of the near and dear to the wax and wane of the moon. They were impressed by the two constantly moving phenomena, i.e., *xingyun liushui* 'the sailing clouds and flowing water'. They noticed that fish lined up when they swam: *yu guan er xing* 'Fish form a string when they move'. Water and human dynamism move towards the opposite directions as the Chinese say:

> *Ren wang gaochu zou, shui wang dichu liu.*
> Water flows downwards while humans climb upwards.

The moon, they noticed, chased the sun in the sky but never tried to overtake — what the subordinate should do to the master. One of the earliest songs said to have been composed more than four thousand years ago goes thus:

> *Ri chu er zuo, ri ru er xi, zao jing er yin, geng tian er shi,*
> *dili yu wo he you zai?*

> I start to work at sunrise
> I return to sleep at sunset,
> I dig my well for water to drink,
> I till my land for food to eat.
> How can God mean anything to me?[2]

Here, we see the Chinese people trying to fashion their living, according to the rhythm of Nature, but not to depend on Nature or any external assistance. For the last four thousand years, the Chinese farmers had tried to live in this 'natural economy' until its rhythm was broken by the latest wind of commercialisation in the last one and half decades.

Only the leisured and privileged in China could have the time and mood to appreciate the orderly Nature. The majority of Chinese society burrowed their heads inside the labyrinth of human chaos. From day one, the Chinese civilization overconsumed its energy in order to establish the human order. It was their endeavour to come out of the human chaos that they fixed their eyes on the orderly manner in which Nature conducted itself.

One important realisation of ancient Chinese sages was the absolute necessity to lead the humans to progressively move away from the beasts — not just physically, but also mentally. The early man-apes (I use here a modern terminology) lived among the beasts and behaved like beasts. Then, they went through a process of *de-brutalisation*. Mencius, (372?-289 BC), who was the Vivekānanda to Confucius (551-479 BC, China's Ramakrishna in a way), often asked: 'How much are humans different

2. Tan Chung, Classical chinese Poetry, in *Classics of the East* series, Calcutta: The MP Birla Foundation, 1991, p. 3.

from beasts?' Even though the difference (between humans and brutes) was slim most of the humans had shed it, and only the 'noble persons' (*junzi*) could maintain it.[3]

We can fully imagine why Mencius made such a stern remark. In the infancy of Chinese civilization, the elders who shouldered the responsibility of establishing social order were often not respected — even not distinguishable from the rest. Manners, or the want of them, contributed to such a chaos. There was no criterion to differentiate the right behaviour from the wrong — nor were there the right examples, right directions. Humans had just graduated from chaotic sex relations and established the family system. But, in a Chinese joint family, men and women lived too close under the same roof to facilitate the maintenance of social decorum. It was out of all such circumstances that emerged the Chinese concept of *xu*, *bie*, and *li*. These three Chinese concepts can be understood as we proceed to examine them.

Li is an overall concept which embraces both *xu* and *bie*. The word *li* literally denotes 'ceremony', but is, in fact, the Chinese symbol for order and the reinforcement of order. The Chinese political culture can be summarised in one sentence: '*Yi Li zhiguo*' (To make the country in order by means of *li*). Among the nine basic Confucian classics, there is *Liji* which is known to non-Chinese scholars as the *Book of Rites*. This book compiled more than two thousand years ago was meant to be the moral guide of the Chinese society — with forty-nine chapters and hundreds of taboos all about social order. I wonder whether any other civilization has thrown up such a comprehensive codification about human order.

Let me take out a few comments from *Liji*. First, there is the general observation that 'Humans are safe when they observe *li*, they are in danger when it is wanting.'[4] This proposition strengthens what Confucius has highlighted about he principal approach of governance: '*daozhi yi de, qizhi yi li*' (To lead the people with virtue and discipline them by *li*).[5] The importance of *li* in concrete terms, as *Liji* says:

> Without *li* we cannot decide and stabilise the relationship between ruler and subject, senior and junior, father and son, elder brother and younger brother.[6]

It further says:

> A parrot can speak language yet remains a flying bird. A chimpanzee

3. *Mengzi* (Mencius) *juan* 8, 'Lilu' B.
4. *Liji* (Book of Rites), chapter 1, "Quli" A.
5. *Lunyu* (Analects), chapter 2.
6. *Liji*, chapter 1.

> can speak a language yet remains a brute. Presently humans don't observe *li*, though they speak a language, they have the hearts of the brutes. Without *li* these humans are like brutes — father brutes living with son brutes.[7]

Xu literally means the sequential order *Liji*'s reiteration to it amounts to impose a queue on the activities of the hierarchical strata of Chinese society. The Book quotes Confucius to say that it is important to 'understand clearly the propriety between father and son, and the *Xu* between a senior and a junior'.[8] The Book also dwells on ceremonial details in observing *Xu*. For instance, it prescribes that being a son one should not live (sleep) in the south-western corner of the room (because that position was regarded as a position of honour), should not sit on the middle mat, should not walk in the middle of the road (when walking with family members), and should not stand in the middle of the gate (when the seniors were around). The son should not share the mat with his father. The Book also prescribes that at the call of the father the son should stand up immediately without uttering any sound. So should the younger brother do when the elder brother calls.[9]

Liji also prescribes that while sitting in public, men should not mix with women (like the Indians do even today). Men and women should not hang their clothes together. They should not share the bath towels. Passing anything over to the opposite sex by hand is also taboo. Brother should not converse with sister-in-law, says the Book.[10] Mencius was asked an embarrassing question about this when he was lecturing on *li*. Asked whether he thought it was conforming to the spirit of *li* that a brother could not touch his sister-in-law. "Should he stretch his hand to save the sister-in-law when she is about to be drowned?" came the next question. Mencius, who was particularly sensitive to humanism, shot forth his reply: 'If he does not extend a hand to the drowning sister-in-law, he is a wolf.' The next moment he realised that there was a dichotomy, so he added; 'Men and women not touching each other is *li*, but extending a hand to the growing sister-in-law is expendiency.'[11] Here, there is the principle of *bie* which literally means 'distinction'. That ancient Chinese culture reiterated the distinction between the two sexes was chiefly to restrict the incidences of permissiveness than the obsession of male chauvinism which, of course, can't be ruled out.

Bie (distinction) should help Chinese social order to maintain the distinction between the ruler and the subject, the senior and the junior, father and son, elder

7. *Liji*, chapter 1.
8. *Ibid*., chapter 8, *Wenwang Shizi*.
9. *Ibid*., chapter 1.
10. *Ibid*.
11. *Mengzi*, *juan* 7, *Lilou* A.

brother and younger brother, husband and wife, when asked by the king of Qi state what should be the ideal government, Confucius replied:

> *Jun jun, cheng cheng, fu fu, zi zi . . .*

This quotation betrays the peculiar syntax of Chinese language. It mentions four persons: *jun* (ruler), *cheng* (subject), *fu* (father), *zi* (son), and repeats them. The sentence rendered into English would read: 'Ruler be as ruler; subject be as subject; father be as father, son be as son.'[12] How stupid a saying it appears! But, there is profound meaning in these pithy formations. The repetitions tantamount to drawing an inviolable boundary between ruler and subject, father and son, which should be extended to all other hierarchical Chinese social relationships. In other words, if the ruler deviates from the established norms for the institution of a ruler, say, not showing exemplary behaviour, there will be chaos in the country. If the subject does the same, say, trying to become a ruler (by armed revolution or usurpation), there will be chaos. So are other social distinctions inviolable.

An important Chinese moral value closely connected with order is *Zheng*. The paleographic form of its writing or is the drawing of a footprint under a horizontal line, suggesting standing in an erect position. Confucius was very particular about this *Zheng* (proper mannerism) order. If the meat pieces were not cut properly (in proper sizes, etc.) and served to him he would refuse to eat them.[13] He further instructed that his disciples should stand erect when they rode the art (bullock-cart in those days) with hands holding the rein.[14] It is from this posture-consciousness that the Chinese tradition has developed the concept of correctness. *Zheng* becomes not just a one-time action, but a way of life. Confucianism persuades all Chinese to adhere to this way of life so that the society become orderly.

Mencius, while expounding the Confucian teaching about the importance of the moral example of the ruler, made the following remark:

> *Jun zheng mo buzheng. Yi zheng jun er guo ding yi*
>
> When the ruler is correct, all his subjects will not deviate from correctness. Just by making the ruler correct the country will be in proper order.[15]

II

Confucius and other sensitive thinkers who lived in the fifth century BC had already realised the problems arising from human closeness of China. Confucius propounded

12. *Lunyu*, chapter 12, *Yan Yuan*.
13. *Ibid.*, chapter 10, *Xiangdang*.
14. *Ibid.*,
15. *Mengzi*, *juan* 7 , *Lilu A*.

the concept of *ren* which is self-explanatory from its written symbol:

> The left side is a modern written form of the ancient
> which is the sketch of a person's profile.
> The right side = is the sign for 'two'.
> This ideogram = or = thus unfolds a human situation of how to deal with the other person in one's immediate concern.

Confucius conceived with deep social insight that at a specific juncture the society in its capsuled form consists of only two persons: self and the other.

Starting from this basic human reality, Confucius made *ren* the highest value in humanity. In other words, *ren* is Confucius' prescription to the social problems created by China's human closeness. To translate the word of *ren* into English is an impossible task as such a concept is totally alien to the English and other Western cultures. But, the nearest equivalent so far attempted is 'co-humanism'. We may even cal it 'self-versus-the-rest ethics'.

What Confucius has underlined is not China's uniqueness. Such a self-and-other relationship exists in all other societies as well. But it is interesting that while the Western culture generates only the concept of Individualism, not *ren*, the Chinese culture generates only the concept of *ren*, not Individualism. The difference between the two lies in:

> Individualism = self
> *Ren* = self and its relations with the rest

A primary Confucian principle is: Don't just develop and enrich yourself, you have the bounden duty to develop and enrich the rest just as you do to yourself.

> *Ji yu li er li ren, ji yu da er da ren.*
>
> If you want to establish yourself, establish others; if you want to make yourself prosper, you make others prosper.[16]

If China had not developed Confucianism, it might have acquired the concept of Individualism. But, as Confucianism had an early development in China, the concept of Individualism was deprived of its market. I should hasten to add that there is a wide gap between the ideal society of Confucius and the real society which has existed in China from the time of Confucius till today. We have always had a Confucian Social Order and a Minus-Confucian Social Order where Individualism might reign supreme. However, due to the Chinese human closeness, Individualism could never have flourished without bringing chaos to China's social order. So, it is the Chinese

16. Quotation from *Lunyu*, chapter 6.

human ecology which has predestined the dominance of the Confucian Social Order over Individualism, leaving the Minus-Confucian Social Order very little room to manoeuvre. In this way, the Confucian Social Order is the antibody of Chinese society against the growth of Individualism.

It is wrong to conceive Confucianism as the antithesis of individual development. The above quotation shows that Confucius also favoured individual efforts to better one's fortune and career. He only wanted you to take others along in the development, instead of trampling on the shoulders and heads of others to reach the top. Here lies the superiority of Confucian *ren* over Individualism.

The *ren*-oriented human relations of China shows both strength and weakness. The crux of the problem is how to make such a society both orderly and robust. Society is like the human body and the individuals are its cells. When the cells as not healthy and vigorous, the body can't be strong and robust. One of the reasons why China, in the course of the last two thousand years, had often been conquered and defeated by less numerical human collectives was due to the indoctrination of Confucianism. For, in the Confucian scheme the society is conceived like a pyramid of the following description:

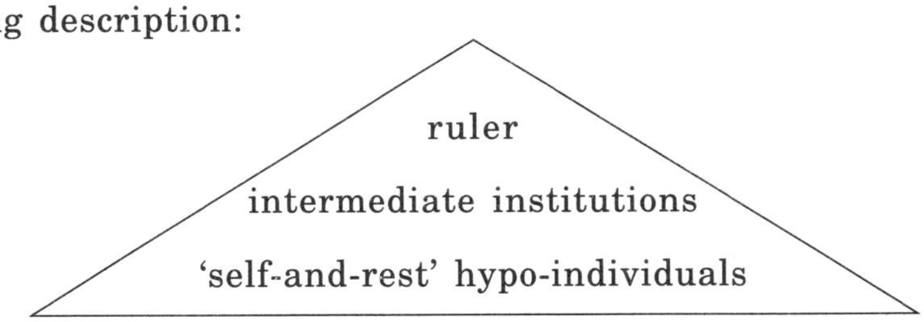

In comparison to the individuals of other societies (like those of the Mongol and Manchu who had conquered China), the Chinese individuals were like hypo-individuals, neither having a full opportunity of development, nor willing to assert their own individuality and develop their innate talent to the full. In other words, the Confucian social order had reduced the Chinese people to lesser-individuals — less selfish, less ambitious, less assertive, and less dynamic. The culture of Confucianism has killed the social ability of throwing up great thinkers, great scientists, great social reformers, and great revolutionaries. Only in times of Chaos when the Confucian social order was eclipsed could there emerge daring individuals who rose in arms to challenge the political regimes. Most of such individuals were put to the sword before they could put their names on the rosters of Chinese heroes. A few of them succeeded and established their own ruling dynasties as the patriarch of generations of the 'Son of Heaven', i.e., emperors. Strangely, it was these heroes who, having enjoyed the holiday of Confucian moral bondage and immediately after fulfilling their individual ambitions, invited Confucianism back to checkmate other individuals who might emulate their now heroic feats. So, even Individualism in

China had found Confucianism the best protector of the booty stolen from China in the absence of guardian Confucianism.

In spite of all this, we have to understand Confucianism to gain an insight into China's cultural dynamics. The Confucian world-view can be summarised by his main theme as enshrined in *Daxue*, or *Great Learning*. He says:

> Since the ancient times till today, those who want to introduce enlightenment to the universe should first put their own state in order. Those who want to put their own state in order should first put their own family in order. Those who want to put their own family in order should first perfect their own personality. Those who want to perfect their own personality should first put their own heart [mind] in the right place. Those who want to put their own heart in the right place should first make their own attempts serious. Those who want to make their own attempts serious must first obtain the wisdom. Obtaining wisdom depends upon finding the order and rhythm of things.[17]

Confucius has, in this immortal observation, provided the guidelines of an orderly society — in fact, an orderly world. He has united individual ambition with the societal aspiration. In this progression of the development of individuality (not individualism), Confucius has prescribed a 'self-and-the-rest' programme all along the course. Of course, this ideal individual is not any one who lives among the hypo-individual multitude, but the exceptional one who is destined to be the ruler, in fact, the sage-ruler. Thus, in the Confucian scheme, not all individuals in the society are hypo-individuals, super-individuals, too, can come out of the colossal human multitude. In this way, Confucianism has downgraded individualism on the one hand and upgraded individuality to the highest dimension on the other. The Confucian prescription for the creation of an ideal social order lies in the synthesis of individual aspiration and the orderly function of the entire human race. Confucianism is an attempt to combine individualism and collectivism and make them harmonious in coexistence, if not in symbiosis.

The Confucian Social Order, as the above quotation has elaborated, makes it mandatory that the real social leader has the other person in mind at every stage of his development, and sinks the self-and-the-other orientation into the core of his world-view. A good leader and ruler of a country is necessarily a good father, good husband, and a good human being — and, of course, a good researcher and good academic (as the last part of the quotation shows). That is what the Confucian 'Great Learning' is all about.

---

17. Quotation from *Daxue* (The Great Learning), chapter 1.

III

Order is the result of networking which assumes a colossal dimension in Chinese civilisation. The nucleus of Chinese networking is the family. The Chinese term for country is *guojia*, with the first syllable denoting the state, and the second denoting family. This close association of family with state traces the genesis of state in China. We know that China as a state was created by a great number of tribes merging themselves into one political entity. The close kinship ties of the tribal element has never been lost in the historical vicissitudes of this multi-tribal creation that is China. The concept of *Jia* (family) symbolised this tribal kinship even when the concept of *Guo* (state) started gaining supremacy over *Jia*. Three thousand years ago *Guo* was the symbol of the king while *Jia* was that of the aristocrats. For a long period (may be more than a thousand years) certain government appointments, such as the official historian called 'Shi', were hereditary — demonstrating the importance of family institution in China. Uptil the sixth century there were certain families among the subjects (other than the royal family) who used to monopolise key government posts. When the Tang Dynasty introduced the Imperial Examination System and introduced meritocracy into the state governance during the seventh century, it created a social revolution of *hansu* (poor commoners) usurping the domination of the distinguished families in the government.

Once the emperor of Wei, Cao Pi (reigning from 220 to 226), asked his subordinate guests in a banquet:

> If your ruler and your father are seriously ill at the same time, and you have only one life-saving pill, to whom will you give, the ruler or the father?

This sharp question aroused murmurs among the guests. Finally, one of them daringly spoke out what was the consensus: 'Father'[18] This story is cited by Prof. Yu Ying-shih of Yale University to prove that while family is natural relationship, that of the state (between the ruler and subject) is unnatural. Political loyalty is out of compulsion, which was the remark of the famous Neo-Confucian scholar, Zhu Xi (1130-1200).[19]

When Dong Zhongshu (179-104 BC), the famous Han courtier-scholar codified Confucianism as the state idealogy, he formulated a social order which corresponded

---

18. *Sanguo zhi* (Annals of the Three Kingdoms): *Weishu* (the Wei state), *juan 11,* Biography of Bing Yuan.
19. Yu Ying-shih, "Cong jiazhi xitong kan Zhongguo wenhuade xiandai yiyi" (The modern significance of Chinese culture reviewed in terms of its system of values), in *Wenhua: Zhongguo yu shijie* (*Culture: China and World*), volume I, Beijing: Sanlian Bookshop, 1987, p. 67.

to the celestial order. As the moon follows the movement of the sun, the same should the subject do to their ruler, the son to his father, and the wife to her husband.[20] Here, Dong Zhongshu tries to establish a symbiosis between the ruler and the subject, father and son, husband and wife, in the same pattern as *Yang* and *Yin* (the former first and the latter follows). There is a hierarchical order in these four symbioses: *Yang* dominating *Yin*, ruler dominating subject, father dominating son, and husband dominating wife.[21] I should imagine that both the modernists and femininists would hate these hierarchical orders and think them harmful to social progress, but we cannot deny that these orders had contributed to the stability of China in the past.

The mutual complementality between the state order and family order is not only a great asset of Chinese culture, but has also benefited the development of other East Asian countries. The modern phenomenon of the East Asian countries — Japan, South Korea, Taiwan, Hong Kong (though not a full-fledged independent State), China, Vietnam and Singapore — fast catching up with the Western countries in industrial development is often attributed to the working of the Confucian social order in which family order plays a vital part. Conversely, USA and other Western countries are increasingly realising the social weakness due to the want of a well knit family system. The increasing incidences of juvenile delinquency in USA is closely connected with the loss of family affection and care, guidance and education among the young.

In the Confucian social order there are five basic equations: (1) ruler and subject, (2) father and son, (3) elder brother and younger brother, (4) husband and wife, and (5) between friends. The first four are hierarchical but also reciprocal, only the fifth equation is based on equality. Dong Zhongshu and other Han scholars have tried to link these five equations to the five elements in Chinese cultural tradition: metal giving birth to ruler-subject relationship, wood to father-son, fire to brothers elder and younger, water to husband-wife, and earth to friends.[22] There is no scientific base for such human-nature linkages, but the very idea outlines the Chinese consciousness in building their socio-political superstructure closer to their natural environment.

Liji quotes Confucius for saying that: "Sages treat the universe as one family, China as one person."[23] This will not only gladden the exponents for 'Global Village' today, but might place Confucianism to the service of future Globalisation. Yu Dunkang, a modern Chinese scholar, makes a reference to this and further points to the Chinese tradition of *jiuzu* (nine generations: four in the past and four in the

20. Dong Zhonshu, *Chunqiu fanlu jiyi* (Basic discourse on the jewels of Spring and Autumn).

21. See Ren Jiyu, *op cit.*, p. 334.

22. See Ren Jiyu, *op cit.*, p. 500.

23. *Liji*, chapter 9, *liyun*.

future, in addition to that of the present) and *wufu* (five kinds of dresses for funeral). The connection between the two is to observe mourning (including expressing sympathy and empathy) to anyone who is related to oneself in nine generations.[24] Here is the Chinese networking by enlarging the family ties to a large number of people as a solid prop of the political unity of China. It is well known that all the governments prior to the founding of the People's Republic of China had, for two thousand years, reached their long arms only up to the level of the county (equivalent to the Indian district). Below that level, the clan (the enlarged family networking) took over the maintenance of socio-political order. The erstwhile imperial government of China had the law to kill all the relatives in nine generations of a rebel leader called *zhu jiuzu*. In China's governance, we see the devolution of power at the grassroot to the family networking which, in turn, shouldered a collective responsibility. This collective punishment has been stopped only in China's republican era.

At another level, Chinese culture transplants family symbols to social intercourses. For instance, both in the past and even today, the elder-younger brotherhood has been widely extended to the society. If two Chinese becomes friends, they treat the self as *di* (younger brother) and the other as *xiong* (elder brother). In modern times after women entered social life, they have been sharing this equation too. The famous Chinese writer, Lu Xun (1881-1936), used to address his girl friend and future wife, Xu Guangping, as 'elder brother'. There is a new vogue among academics in modern times of using four categories: *xuexiong* (academic elder brother), *xuedi* (academic younger brother), *xuejie* or *xuezi* (academic elder sister) and *xuemei* (academic younger sister). The second and fourth are generally used for one's own student, or someone who is much younger in age. Otherwise, to attribute the other as 'elder' brother or sister) is just a courtesy not in strict observance of age seniority. Elders addressing youngers as 'elder' is good Confucian ethic, if not logic. The Confucian family was and is truly the most expansive and dynamic element in Chinese culture pertaining to social bonds.

What will be the social bonds after another decade or so if China's one-child family norms are strictly implemented all over China — by then the social relationship of brothers and sisters would virtually disappear? Family planning will eventually abort one of the five Confucian relationships (that of the brothers), but the family bonds of Chinese society may not necessarily be weakened. Even the 'academic' brothers and sisters will survive, if not multiply, for the symbolism of 'brother' and 'sister' is immune to the abortion in real life.

The discussion of 'academic' brotherhood brings us to another social bond, i.e.,

---

24. Yu Dunkang, "Rujia lunli sixiang yu Zhongguo chuantong wenhua" (Confucian ethics and traditional Chinese culture), in *Wenhua: Zhongguo yu shijie, volume* 3, p. 308.

teacher-taught relationship. In popular Chinese religion there are five deities: *Tian* (Heaven), *Di* (Earth), *Jun* (ruler), *Qin* (ancestor), *Shi* (the institution of teacher personified by Confucius). Confucius was one of the earliest teachers of great fame in China, but he was never esteemed as a deity before the advent of Buddhism in the country. Buddhism gained its popularity in China by eclipsing the authority of Confucian teaching on the one hand, while elevating Confucius to the status of *gurudeva* on the other. Without the influence of Buddhism, Confucius and even Mencius whose advice was keenly sought by the kings never obtained the honour of *guoshi* (imperial teacher), but three Indians, Buddhacinga Kumārajīva, and Amoghavajra, enjoyed such as honour on Chinese soil. It was in 739 that the Tang Emperor Xuanzong offered a posthumous title of *Wenxuan Wang* (King of the popularisation of culture) to Confucius. In 1012, the Song emperor Zhenzong added the wording of *Zhisheng* (most venerable) to Confucius' honorific title. In 1530, the Ming emperor Shizong honoured Confucius as *Zhisheng Xianshi* (most venerable teacher-god).[25] The Gurudeva finally arrived via the Indian influence. In the last ten years, the Buddhist terms, *Shifu* (teacher-father), *Shixiong* (academic elder brother) and *Shidi* (academic younger brother) have been in vogue not only among scholars, but also in the communities of crafts and trades. The teacher who imparts a skill to a pupil is regarded by the latter as father, while the fellow-students under the same teacher are *Shixiong* and *Shidi* which become the Chinese versions of the Indian term *gurubhai*. From such examples we see Indian input to the networking of Chinese family bonds beyond the family bondage.

Another foreign concept entering the Chinese social order is the Western word 'comrade', which got widespread in China immediately after the founding of the communist regime. During the Mao Zedong era, the Chinese word *tongzhi* (comrade) became the most correct and fashionable social calling disregarding whether the person so address was a communist or not. At one time, the word *nu tongzhi* (female comrade) almost totally replaced that of *nuren* (woman) which always smacked the vestige of male Chauvinism. In the post-Mao period, the universality of 'comrade' in Chinese society is down, but not out. The writ still runs within the Communist Party that once a 'comrade' always a *tongzhi* — be it father or mother, or son or daughter, or brother or sister. In some sense, this new trend constitutes a de-familisation of Chinese social relationships. However, this Chinese translation of 'comrade', i.e., *tongzhi*, was a very ancient concept denoting bosom friendship. The popularity of this term in present-day life combines both a Western influence and a revival of China's traditional values.

IV

How to create order in a human collective of the dimension of 1/5 of humanity that

25. *Ciyuan*, encyclopaedia, Beijing: Commercial Press, 1984, vol. 3, p. 2588. *Zhisheng Xianshi.*

is China? Confucianism which is a voluntary persuasion cannot provide all the necessary guarantees by acting alone. Politics in China has not just been order-sensitive, but also diligent in order safeguarding. Creating the necessary safeguards is always the endeavour of Chinese politics.

Sima Qian, born in 145 or 135 BC China's Herodotus, commented in his 'Introduction' to *Shiji* (Records of a historian), the first of a series of Dynastic Annals of China, that all the discourses of ancient Chinese philosophical schools revolved around the topic of *zhi* — the Chinese word for 'order'. This Chinese *zhi* is simply a brutal coersion — a human imposed socio-political order. The etymology of *zhi* (with waterwritten on the left part) is connected with the harnessing of river floods. The legendary Great Yu (who may be comparable to the Indian culture hero, Rama) set an example by digging channels to let floods flow out of human residence areas. So, in this word *zhi*, there is the lesson that one must abide by the natural order in order to maintain human order.

Here, I must introduce the thinking of Laozi which has a bearing on our study of 'order' in Chinese tradition. Laozi (also spelled as Lao Tse) was contemporary of Confucius and an equally great thinker. Laozi's basic teachings are predicated in the ancient philosophical concept of everything as a unity of two opposite elements — *Yin* and *Yang*. In Chinese parlance this is described as *Yin Yang Xiaozhang* (*Yin* and *Yang* grows at each other's expense). If *Yang* represents order, success, triumph, *Yin* represents disorder, failure and defeat. When order expands, disorder contracts; when success prevails failure recedes; when triumph reigns defeat is dormant. Also true is the vice versa. Then, Laozi's Law of Reality rings: *Fanzhe Dao zhi dong* (The movement of Tao tends to go towards the opposite). When order reaches its optimum disorder will follow; when one is at the top of success one will have failure in store; when triumph is being celebrated it augurs for the coming defeat.[26] The spirit of *wuwei* propounded by Laozi and expounded by Lu Jia is to realise this alternation between *Yin* and *Yang* and try to moderate one's course by avoiding going towards the extremes. *Wuwei* does not mean to sit idle to do nothing and achieve nothing. It only advocates a middle course between commission and omission. As the experience of the Qin Dynasty shows that too much administration, institution, and law proved to be counter-productive, the momentum of *Wuwei* tries to find an outlet to the human dilemma of order and Chaos. When one drives unwittingly towards the opposite direction of one's own destination, the more one drives, the father one becomes separated from the goal of one's drive. In Laozi's thinking the best way to

26. *Laozi* is a small text left behind which is also called *Daode jing* (Canon of Tao). There are stray references to a contemporary of Confucius,called *Lao Dan,* who might be the author of this text. The text reveals a very profound ancient Chinese thinker, but unfortunately the bulk of his teachings and writings is lost.

establish order is to do nothing to establish it. Order will emerge without human effort. As we say in modern times that the best driver of a car is not to drive it, but to allow the car to drive itself. Laozi's famous saying of *Wuwei er zhi* (literally "Order is achieved by having no achievement"), tries to warn humans that they should do well to let the natural order reveal its true self, and avoid creating an artificial order contrary to the natural order. In this sense, Laozi was a great environmentalist. In not listening to his teachings, humans are suffering the consequences of over-imposition of the human order on the natural order.

V

That the Chinese culture shows an obsession for *zhi* also speaks of the tremendous difficulty in ruling the mini-universe of people as well as managing a colossal governing edifice. Chinese are said to be the ancestors of bureaucratism. Bureaucracy was absolutely unavoidable to keep one-fifth of humanity under one political roof. However, from historical experience, the downfall of a ruling dynasty was often caused by the corruption of the reigning edifice to begin with. Only when the ruling machine was rotten to the core that the Chinese people rose in arms to overthrow it. Much thought and effort in the history of Chinese political development had gone into the art and networking of governance.

First, there should be the correct orientation about the governance. There was a historical debate between *renzhi* and *fazhi*. The two prefixes to *zhi* (order) here stand for human (*ren*) in the former, and 'law' (*fa*) in the latter. According to the first school which gravitated towards Confucianism, it was the quality of the humans in the ruling machine that clinched the issue of Order. No matter how perfect was the paraphernalia of governance, in the hands of bad rulers and administrators it would be totally in vain. The other school, usually described as the Legalists (*fajia*), did not directly contest this Confucian proposition, but raised the slogan of *Yi fa zhiguo* (to bring order to the country by means of law). Deep beneath this debate was the contention whether human nature was good or evil. Mencius reieterated the innate good nature of humans, while his contemporary, Xunzi (313? - 238 BC) argued to its contrary. Xunzi came much closer to the Christian concept of humans born in sin, but did not reflect the mainstream of Chinese ethos.

It is important, I think, for humans to have faith in their own good nature. Mencius observed that: 'Everything is inbuilt within the self.' (*Wanwu jie bei yu wo*).[27] It is this immense trust in the good nature of self and fellow humans that human engineering has meaning. The feasibility of establishing and maintaining order in society lies in human trust. First, there should be education to remove ignorance and misguided notions from the masses. Second, the ruler and ruling elite should

27. *Mengzi*, chapter 13.

set good examples for others to emulate. Confucius explained to his disciple who asked about the meaning of goverment, and said: 'Government means correctness. When the command is correct who dares to be incorrect'.[28] In saying this, Confucius actually placed the pun in Chinese language.

The Chinese script for the word 'government', i.e., *zheng* contains two parts. The left side denotes 'correctness', while the other side (archaic form) suggests 'hand action'. I have no idea who invented this word, but the creation is perfectly in tune with the Confucius thinking. The ideogram presents a scenario of the governement being an institution to generate, create, establish, maintain, and safeguard 'correctness' — moral correctness, i.e., virtue. Therefore, the Confucian orientation of 'human governance' is to establish an infrastructure wedded to virtue and moral correctness. Such an infrastructure can only be made of human personalities, not any system, institution, or regulation.

However, experience has taught the Chinese politicians and governors that without systems and regulations a virtuous government can hardly be created, and can never be maintained even after its creation. Chinese culture has adopted a double stand in respect of the debate I alluded to earlier, viz., let Confucianism look after human consciousness and let Legalism run its writ. Such a two-pronged approach was established through accumulated experience. This can be illustrated.

By the end of the third century BC a group of lumpen proletarian led a peasant revolution and became the founders of the Han Dynasty. They were comrades in arms with bonds fastened by vows as sworn brothers. When they sat with the new emperor, Liu Bang (their ring leader who became the Han Emperor Gaozu and reigned between 206 and 195 BC), to discuss State matters, they invariably turned the imperial Court into a fish market, fighting duels not only verbally, but often times with swords. As the supreme ruler of a great empire, Liu Bang had to evolve an elaborate order for the Court sessions. Earlier, the creator of imperial system of China, Emperor Shihuangdi of Qin (who reigned between 221 and 210 BC) did not evolve an elaborate Court ritual with the result that an assasin went up to the dais which was exclusively for the emperor to attempt assassination. The emperor panicked and ran around a pillar while his guards watched helplessly because it was His Majesty's explicit order that no one except the royal master was allowed to ascend the dais. Only when the courtiers shouted to remind the emperor that he had a sword on his back that saved the situation.

These episodes in Chinese history resulted in the most elaborate measures being created to protect the Chinese emperor and the dignity of the imperial proceedings. There is the unusual Chinese phenomenon of the imperial palace being called the 'Forbidden City'. The Chinese wording is *jincheng* with the first syallbe *jin* denoting

28. *Lunyu*, chapter 12.

'to forbid'. This gave rise to a bad English translation of 'Forbidden City', and a even worse misinterpretation that the Chinese palace forbade the entry of commoners.[29] In fact, the inmates of the Chinese imperial palace numbered no less than several thousands. The emperors of the Tang Dynasty (618-907) had the reputation of keeping three thousand beauties as imperial consorts. Each of these imperial ladies had at least half a dozen service people who were all commoners. There was no palace elsewhere in the world where so many commoners flocked and flowed in and out everyday. The English writer (whosoever he might be) who first coined the word 'Forbidden City' to translate *jincheng* was probably unaware of the connotation of *jin* for imperial guards. The true meaning of the Chinese word *jincheng* is that is a well guarded fortress, and tresspassing is absolutely *forbidden* (hence the word *jin*). But, there was the most elaborate paraphernalia of reception and protocol to regulate the entry of royal aristocrats as well as commoners in and out of the palace.

Jia Yi (200-168 BC), who played an important role in establishing the Han imperial order, likened the status of the emperor *vis-a-vis* his subordinates to the sun's positioning among the stars. He observed that

> the subordinates should not take liberty with the master while the humble should not impinge upon the distinguished. When the hierarchy is not violated, the top position becomes respectable; and when the subordinates do not cross the limits, the master's position becomes secure.[30]

He went a step further to say that 'rank, power, dress, order (instruction)' were instrumental in distinguishing the high from the low. These external signs, he reiterated, were particularly important for people to recognise a person's social position from a distance.[31]

Jia Yi's observations helps us to gain an insight into the Chinese concept of Order. Order in the Chinese context of a multitudinous human collective under a singular political governance is predicated on not only hierarchy, differentiation, and ranking, but also on the distinguishable external signs to legitimise these. Thus, when a person is born in China, he/she has to get not only a slot in the social hierarchy, but also a set of paraphernalia that goes with the specific slot. I would think that such an imposition on a human being is universal, while the form and degree may vary from one country to another. Just as a person loses one's freedom to exhibit

29. I have come across such an interpretation when I was assisting Dr. Madhu Khanna in preparing the exhibition materials about the Chinese city Beijing, hence I feel the necessity to include this paragraph.
30. Ren Jiyu, *Zhongguo zhexue fazhan shi: Qin Han*, (History of development of Chinese philosophy: Qin and Han dynasties), p. 141, quoting Jia Yi's *Fu yi* (Discourse on dress).
31. *Ibid.*, quoting Jia Yi's *Deng qi* (on ranks).

one's naked body in public immediately after birth, one must exist in an orderly society being dressed and oriented in a particular manner to which one has no choice. Order and personal liberty are fundamentally incompatible values.

However, when the Han courtier-scholars examined the causes of the downfall of the previous Qin Dynasty which had a pitiable short life of 15 years only between 221 to 206 BC. One of the scholars, Lu Jia (who died in the beginning of the second century BC) attributed it to the excessive measures for maintaining order by the erstwhile regime.

> The more there were government activities, the more chaotic the country became; the more laws multiplied, the more furious was its observance in the breach; the more soldiers were deployed, the greater number of enemies it created.[32]

It was based on the Qin failure of over-administration and excessive application of law that the Han government began to advocate Confucianism and replaced Legalism by it as the ruling ideology. The fundamental difference between Confucianism and Legalism lies in the latter's total reliance on the rule of law, while the former wanting the Law to have a human face — dispensing with punishment as far as possible by way of education and persuasion. Incidentally, Lu Jia was also the famous courtier who convinced the first Han emperor (who had little cultural refinement) that though power could be seized by sitting on the horseback, it could not be administered from that position — meaning that brutal physical force can't accomplish an orderly rule.

We see from above examples the dichotomous situation of political order in China. On the one hand, since there is such a colossal human collective generating all kinds of disruptive forces, there is the need of a powerful governing machine. On the other hand, the governing machine cannot deliver the goods without a human face, hence the importance of abiding by the Confucian principles which is described as the Chinese or Confucian humanism.

VI

I often liken the Chinese socio-political system to the solar system in which we exist. The source of energy and dynamism of the solar system is a powerful and brilliant centre, while that of the Chinese system lies in the central authorities. When the Chinese system functions orderly and smoothly, it is because the central authorities are sagacious, thoughtful and considerate of popular welfare. In the

32. Ren Jiyu, *Zhongguo zhexue fazhan shi: Qin Han*, p. 138, quoting Lu Jia's book *Xinyu* (New words), chapter on *Wuwei* (No commission).

normal situation in China, both in the past and in the present, political initiatives are always taken from the top. The wisdom of Chinese culture gravitates towards the ruling elite. But, when the top leadership falls in dotage, it no longer accommodates and reflects this wisdom, and fails to maintain its brilliance and power. Then the cultural wisdom dissipates from the central authority. At such a juncture, heroes emerge from the masses to become the rallying points of wisdom and power. This is tantamount to political initiatives taken from below. We have here the alternate movements of political initiatives: initiatives from above when there is order, initiatives from below when there is disorder.

During the Tang Dynasty, emperors initiated debates about the merits of unitary system as compared to the alternative federal government. Liu Zongyuan (773-819), a famous courtier-scholar, was for the former. His argument was that provinces never rebelled against the central authorities, while feudal States did — always. Ouyang Xiu (1007-1072), another famous courtier-scholar of later times who was also the chronicler of the Tang history, commented on this subject by saying that: with the federal-feudal lords, there would not be any avalanche, while with the unitary system, the tail would not be too big for the head to bother.[33]

Unitary from of government had won the day. China has been famous for her tradition of 'great unified oneness' (*da yitong*). I think this is not a random choice, but dictated by the very nature of China's geo-socio-human context. Here, I want to add the ecological dimension also. The Chinese civilization took shape around, 4,000 years ago, which was the period of the legendary, Yu, harnessing the river floods. From that day on, China grew into a larger and larger entity with the participation of various races through voluntary union or conquest. Within this Chinese civilization, the dominant economic pursuit was the water-and-earth culture, i.e., agriculture. When we look at the political map today, we see China in the enviable position of having two of the earth's ten greatest rivers. *Yangtze* and *Huanghe,* running within her international boundary — a facility which no other country enjoys. This ecological advantage of China is partly God-sent, and partly the realisation of a process of China-building jointly pursued by the Han, Mongol, Manchu, and other races. One cannot envisage that neither the entire nation would allow, nor it would be wise for any part of this country to destroy this advantage in future.

As an individual living inside this colossal entity, there is both pleasure and excitement on the one hand, and inconvenience and sacrifice on the other. It is interesting to notice the coagulative force that such a politico-cultural colossus holds on both its inmates and its diaspora. It is based on the willingness of Chinese individuals to suffer the weight of the administrative machine that contributes to

33. Ouyang Xiu (comp.), *Xin Tangshu* (New Annals of Tang Dynasty), *juan*78, end comments on *zongshi* (personalities of the royal family).

the soundness of order in Chinese politics.

The two thousand-year-story of how order worked in China, is a mixed bag of achievement and failure. About half of the two thousand-years Chinese lived in war and social turmoil. Only from 1949 onwards till today has China enjoyed an unprecedented long holiday from civil war, yet there were several major man-made disturbances during which people suffered a great deal. Before this period, there was the spell of "a small disturbance every year, and a big scale disorder every ten years". Half of the total historical of imperial China, the reign authorities were of foreign origin, settling there after conquest. The scale and frequency of changing fortunes, fleeing homes, separation of near and dear, disease, death, famine, etc., could not be compared by the history of any other nation.

During the time of disorder in China, the following signals were sounded which I will present in Chinese historical parlance:

1. *Zhu hun yushang, ren yuan yuxia.* (The Master/ruler above is a dotard, while the masses are complaining.)
2. *Nei luan wai huan* (Internal chaos coupled with external threat.)
3. *Qun hao jing xing* (Heroes/rebels vie with each other in gaining ascendancy.)

The third signal is the silver lining in the above picture. With the emerging new heroes among the masses, the Chinese socio-political system regains its vitality to end a hopeless situation. The scenario here is that the vitality of Chinese system is passing down from the top to the bottom.

To go back to *Yin* and *Yang*, we should conceptualise a constant entity in which two volatile factors interact with each other. When *Yang* is strong *Yin* falls weak, and vice versa. Order and disorder fall into such a scenario. Thus, *Tianxia yi zhi yi luan* (the world alternates between Order and Disorder), was the rhythm of political development as conceived by traditional Chinese thinkers.

In all periods of Chinese history except one, Chinese rulers made it their primary endeavour to create and safeguard Order and prevent and suppress Disorder. This was because their own ruling position was built on the socio-political order of China. The exception came during recent past when Chairman Mao Zedong, as the supreme leader of China, launched the Great Cultural Revolution to throw away the leash and create a countrywide chaos. He did this on purpose to inject new dynamism and vitality into the Chinese socio-political body. He was also confident that great disorder created by the Cultural Revolution would usher in a new era of Great Order. For one thing, this was a movement that had made a Humpty Dumpty out of the Confucian social order, but not necessarily succeeded in promoting Individualism. For another, even Mao himself realised without admission that destroying the paraphernalia of political order in China was too dangerous a game to be repeated.

Understanding the Chinese scenario of order from an Indian viewpoint, we must travel to another peak from the commanding height of the Indian background. Prof. Tu Weiming of Harvard University who delivered a series of lectures in Delhi and other Indian cities and institutions described the East Asian governance under the Confucian influence as 'maximum government' in the sphere of education and introduction. My feeling is that such a governance is often detrimental to the full development of individual creativity and talent. The Indian tradition is quite the opposite. Ancient Indian teachers favoured the creation of both physical and spiritual space for the taught. The early Upaniṣads speaks of all human beings arising out of *ākāśa* and returning into *ākāśa* which is the sky, the Heaven, the matrix of dimension.

So, we have two different cultural traditions of India and China. In the Chinese tradition, there is the attempt of caging the human minds, while in the Indian tradition, the human mind is set free and the sky is the limit. In the Chinese tradition, there is the attempt of brain-washing the masses, while in the Indian tradition there is absolute freedom of thought. In the Chinese tradition, there is self-restrain in criticising the government, while in the Indian tradition criticising the establishment becomes a routine amusement. In the Chinese tradition, writers exercise self-censorship and see that no negative observations against anyone going into black and white, while in the Indian tradition the pen is often viciously offensive, and at times inking accusations without verification of facts, running the risk of being chastened in legislative and judiciary houses.

The usual distinction of the two countries brought out by modern commentators is the Chinese dictatorship *vis-a-vis* the Indian democracy. This distinction is rather superficial. The Indian dynamics lie in its diversity and centrifugalisation. China is just the opposite, orienting towards uniformity and centripetal tendencies. The rebellions in India, both past and present, have been more localised than of all-India dimension (exceptions, of course, were also there). In Chinese history, most of the armed rebellions moved their forces towards the imperial capital with the aim of capturing it and, thus, controlling the entire country. The difference here does not mean that Chinese rebels were more ambitious than their Indian counterparts. But, they knew from past experience that unless they controlled the entire country, their rebellion could not endure — sooner or later, it would be crushed by other forces that would have an all-China appeal. The dynamism of power struggle in China had this holistic character in which the capital city invariably became the target of all civil wars in China. Historians and archaeologists in China have established the typical Chinese phenomenon of both greatest building activities and greatest destructions taking place in the Chinese imperial capitals which has no parallel in other countries.

Confucius made an interesting observation that: "Poverty is not my worry, restlessness is."[34] Despite this remark, he also understood that poverty and restlessness were symbiotic in China. Conversely, order and prosperity are also symbiotic. The Chinese aspiration of *Taiping* is an interesting concept which is a different dream to different people. To the rulers of China, it was generally associated with *wushi* (no trouble). Literally, the term *Taiping* can connote both 'grand peace' and 'grand equality'. The Taiping Movement which erupted in the middle of the nineteenth century was the greatest destabilising movement in the entire Manchu period. Those rebels who rose in arms to fight the Manchu tyranny could not have used the symbol of *Taiping* for 'grand peace'. They must have conceived an utopia in which the Chinese peasants could enjoy prosperity and orderly life after removing the tyranny. I often thought that the concept of *Taiping* in the minds of the *Taiping* soldiers must have had an element of grand equality. As the concept of equality was an Indian gift to China, and the Chinese word *pingdeng* was a translation of the Sanskrit term *samatā* (Buddha was known in China as *Pingdengwang*, i.e., *samatārājā*), it may not be out of order to conceive, *Taping as mahāsamatā*. Thus, order to the Chinese masses is one thing, and to the Chinese rulers another.

What is the present aspiration for order on the part of the Chinese people? I think is consists of four major yearnings at the present juncture. First, they wish China to be rich and strong. When they see China going that direction, they can tolerate the mistakes and failings of the government in other aspects to a great extent. Second, they want peace and order. They shudder at the memories of war, of fleeing their settled homes, of the Cultural Revolution. They don't want the Tian'anmen types of movement to recur. Third, they want to have a better and better material life, and most of them prefer to enjoy it in their home place. The present Chinese government policy of mobilising the initiatives of all local government at all levels, to develop their native places with central and neighbouring assistance, is welcome to the majority of Chinese people. Many of the adventurers who went away from their home places in search of fortune have sent their remittance back regularly, some have even returned to start new enterprises like those which they are familiar in other lands. Traditionally, Chinese were soil-bound. Although about 7 per cent of China's population today are knocking the doors of the big cities and affluent areas along the coast, the majority of Chinese population still stay put at their home-places or neaby areas. Fourth, Chinese people want to share the economic development of the country which they have directly and indirectly contributed. They resent that preferential policies are granted to selected parts, not to the entire country. Presently, the majority of Chinese live better than the past, and the country

34. *Lunyu*, chapter 16.

bumpkins have chances to travel by cars, trains, and some even by aeroplanes. They are happy to receive the modern style of life in the thousand year rural setting along with the comforts brought by the new lifestyle. But, they would not wish this upward trend to discontinue, and they are joining China's national endeavour in achieving affluence and prosperity. Fifth, they resent the powerbrokers and corrupt officials, particularly those in their localities, for the eating away of the national fruits of economic resources. They intially fear the officials which is a fear that has been passed down by their ancestors for millennia. But, with increasing education, information, and wisdom, they become less fearful, and are voicing increasing protests against corruption and harassment of government functionaries. Right now, the Chinese government is fighting corruption at selected places, and is trying to replace bad grassroot officials whenever evidence is collected. This gives hope to the people that the present regime as a whole can still be trusted. With such an overall situation the Chinese government is not bothered by the international condemnation of China's human rights failure. But, it is paying serious attention to the regions where people show signs of rebellion, and trying to remove the popular grievances. The government of China has two trump cards in its hand: stability and development. When these two cards don't slip from its grip, it can ensure order in the country. Besides, these four yearnings there may be other demands, but direct election and multiparty system rank quite low in their priority at the present moment. Whether these demands will rise higher and be loudly voiced in future one cannot say for certain.

Order is not a subject which can be discussed without taking the socio-economic life of a country under consideration. What I have discussed in this paper are some aspects concerning a large agricultural country which China had been until a few years ago. Today, China is experiencing a rapid process of industrialisation which has partially or totally destroyed some of the fabrics of the agrarian order of China. As Confucianism was built on this agrarian order, and the Communist movement has already made Confucianism a Humpty Dumpty, what will be the emerging new socio-political order in China is very difficult to predict.

One major question being asked is whether China would remain an entity of the 'great unified oneness', or disintegrate and become several independent states. One of the reasons for those to anticipate China's disintegration is China's rapid transformation into a market economy which resulted in greater and greater regional disparity. However, marketisation, in one way, is also a unifying force, which leads to, as many say, to globalisastion. Another strong element working for globalisation is the communication revolution — in another 20 years' time the electronic mail may become as popular as paper mail. In such a new global trend of globalisation China's order of unified oneness may be strengthened instead of being weakened.

PART III

ṚTA: MANIFESTATIONS IN THE ARTS

15

The Geometries of Self-organising Systems
From Chaos to Pilgrimage

John McKim Malville

Introduction

ALTHOUGH our universe has been expanding for the last 10-15 billion years, the meaning and beauty of the cosmos appear to be contained in systems of ever diminishing size. The cumulative effect of gravity over the past 15 billion years has been the aggregation of matter and energy into smaller and ever more complex systems.

Besides gravity, there are many other processes that have led to the production of complex biological and socio-cultural systems on the planet Earth. Most of those systems may be described as dissipative self-organisers. The seminal work that led to an understanding of these systems is due to Illya Prigogine and his colleagues at Brussels, who showed that stable states of great complexity can exist outside of thermodynamic equilibrium. Prigogine characterised these as dissipative structures, as they require a constant flux of matter and energy. Within the past decade discussions of self-organising systems have been broadened to include complexity, non-linear dynamics, and chaos theory.

An important feature of these systems is that their novel geometries emerge from within themselves and are not imposed from the outside. This paper sketches the development of such emergent geometries from the primordial Big Bang to the human landscape of cities and pilgrimage. At the first instant of our cosmos, when the universe emerged from the state of Primordial Chaos, there was no geometry by which matter was ordered. The first geometry that appeared involved very large-scale aggregations of matter, comparable in size to that of clusters of galaxies which today span hundreds of millions of light years. With time, the geometrical arrangement of matter trickled downward, and order emerged in smaller and smaller objects such as galaxies, stars, and planets. Not until small, cool planets made their appearance in the universe could the microcosm begin its co-evolution upward, as electrical forces glued atoms together to form molecules and molecules together to form living systems.

Near the intersection of the co-evolving macrocosm and microcosm lie the cosmic city and the pilgrimage centre. In our comparison of these two social-cultural systems, we conclude that the cosmic city with nearly perfect alignment to the cardinal directions, enclosing walls, and elegant symmetries is in reality a closed system which has lost much of its evolutionary vitality. By contrast, the pilgrimage centre remains open to a vigorous circulation of people and ideas and remains at the edge of creative chaos. As opposed to the design of the cosmic city, the geometric structure of the pilgrimage landscape is not preordained by emerges spontaneously from inside. Pilgrimage centres, such as Varanasi, Chitrakut, Mecca, and Jerusalem are more robust, felxible, and long-lived than imperially mandated cosmic cities.

Dispersion and convergence

To the eyes of the astronomer, the geometrical order of the large-scale universe is due to the control of matter by gravity. The dominating cycles of our lives arise from a precise order imposed upon the natural world by gravity: the sun rises every 24 hours, awaking the earth's billions; the moon is reborn every 29.53 days, establishing the rhythm of the calendar; the land is swept by seasons every 365.24 days; Jupiter returns to Aquarius every 11.9 years, energising millions to move across the face of India toward Prayag for the *Kumbha Melā*; the earth has orbited the sun for 4.5 billion years.

Originally identified by Isasc Newton as a universal force of attraction between masses, gravity is now understood to be not a force at all but the consequence of curved space-time. Free particles move along pathways known as geodesics which converge upon each other in the positively curved space-time that is our home. Without the influence of gravity the natural tendency of both matter and energy would be to disperse into ever more widely scattered states.

Such dispersion is evident in those processes that are only minimally influenced by gravity such as photons of light. The energy that emerges from our sun flows past the earth into the depths of space, never to return until a time far into the future when all of space and time may collapse in upon itself. In the case of these dispersing and thinning solar photons, entropy steadily increases in obvious accordance with the Second Law of Thermodynamics. In a like manner, the photons from the primordial fireball, which was last present in our universe some 15 billion years ago, have dispersed, thinned, and cooled. In their quantity, these cool photons dominate the universe. For every particle of normal matter, such as protons, neutrons, and electrons, there are approximately one-billion more photons. Ours is a universe primarily of light; diminishing, fading, thinning light which is becoming randomised and cooled.

Rare in this sea of light are particles of matter which have come together through the convergent influences of gravity. Matter has progressed through a series of self-organising systems, from clusters of galaxies, galaxies, stars, solar systems, to planets. Each smaller state is characterised by a new ordering principle, greater complexity, and enhanced departures from thermodynamic equilibrium. These clusters of matter are dissipative systems, through which energy passes, and are complex and orderly because they 'export' disorder and entropy to the surrounding universe. Only if there is a huge reservoir of space outside of them that can absorb their outflowing energy, can these ordered self-organising systems continue to exist. Both components of the universe are needed; order and disorder, cosmos and chaos. Disorder can exist entirely by itself, but order cannot survive without disorder.

Order, chaos and complexity

The *Oxford Dictionary* defines Order as sequence and succession as in alphabetical or chronological order or as a regular array in which every part is in its right place. Chaos is the opposite of order: formless, random, and primordial. Chaos is utterly without order or arrangement.

Complexity is a more elusive concept, but basically it involves multiple interacting parts, different types of order, and a combination of order and disorder. While lacking in complexity and information content, chaos is ripe with promise and can lead to complexity. Innovation emerges from chaos while excessive order suppresses novelty. Complexity and information are greatest somewhere between perfect order and total randomness (Pagels 1988).

We receive information from the world as a time sequence of items acquired through our senses. The message makes sense when it contains a certain amount of order, although too much order can bore us. A simple form of such a date string is a series of binary digits, 0 or 1 which may signify either yes or no. An ordered string of binary digits could contain a clear-cut pattern of 0 and 1 such as 111111111, 0000000000, or 101010101. A completely chaotic and disorderly sequence might look like 10110001010100.

Those one-dimensional date strings which are at opposite extremes, either highly ordered or totally random, contain little or no information (*fig.* 15.1). By contrast, the complex binary string, lying between confirmation and novelty, can contain immense amounts of encoded information, such as a radio transmission from the Viking spacecraft on Mars or a sequence of amino acids of the DNA molecule.

Fig. 15.2 demonstrates a two-dimensional progression from Disorder to Order as dots are connected by lines. When no lines have been drawn there is total

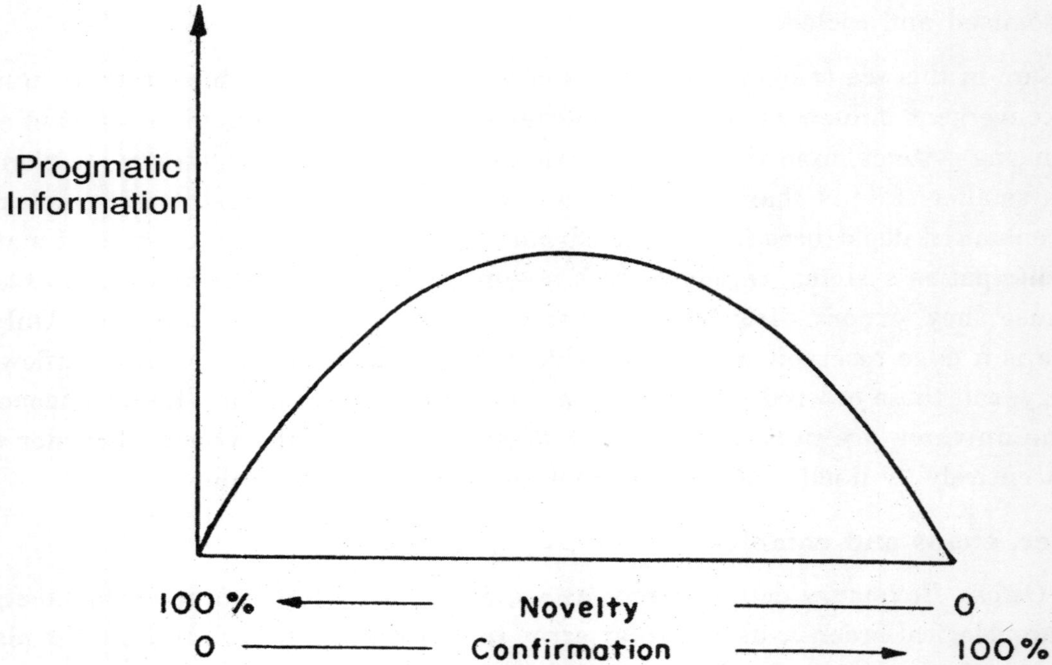

Fig. 15.1. Information content of systems lying between order (confirmation) and disorder-chaos (novelty).

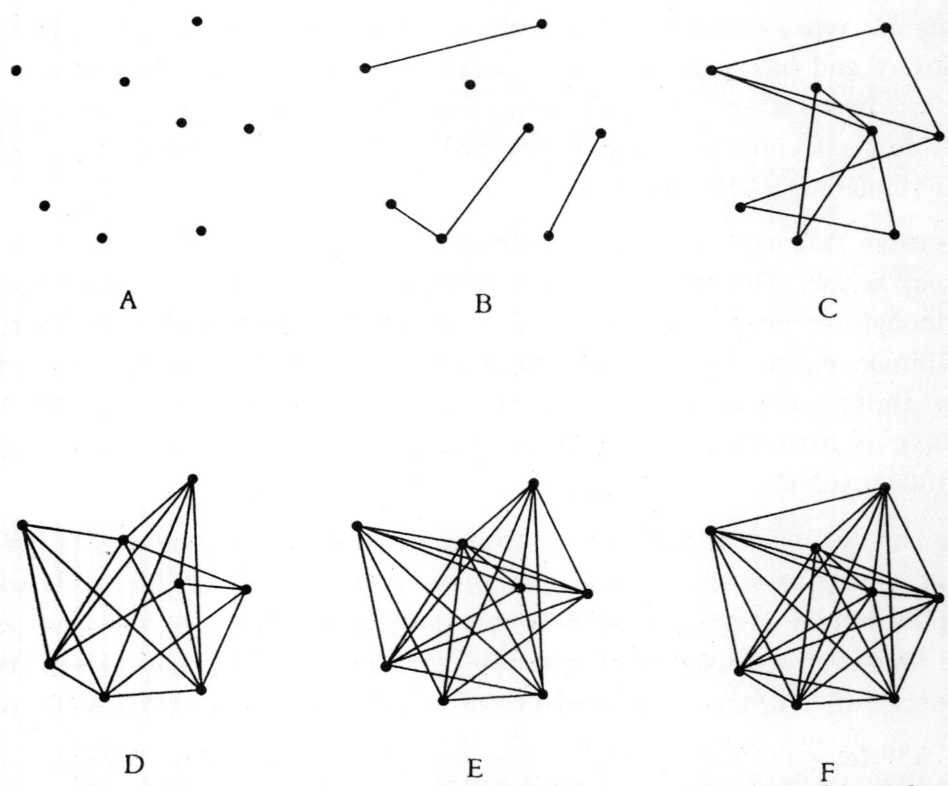

Fig. 15.2. Patterns connecting eight points; from disorder to complete order (after Gell-Mann 1994).

Disorder: no connections have been made; no pattern has been started. The information content of the collection increases as choices are made and some dots are connected while others are left alone. Finally, in the extreme case where all possible connections have been established, all potential order has been realised, and the information content has again fallen to zero. There is nothing unique about the completed pattern, and no message is conveyed by such complete order.

PRIMORDIAL CHAOS

> The universe may have started in chaos, which is often represented in cosmogonic myths by the symbolism of darkness, water, and the unknown. — Long 1963

> Darkness there was at first darkness hidden;
> Without distinctive marks, this all was water.
> — *Ṛgveda*, X.129

> There was nothing standing; only the calm water, the placid sea, alone and tranquil. Nothing existed. There was only immobility and silence in the darkness, in the night. — Popol Vuh

> To dwelt within breathing-space of immensity.
> The Universe was in darkness, with water everywhere.
> — Maori

> In the beginning God created the heavens and the earth. The earth was without form and void, and darkness was upon the face of the deep; and the Spirit of God was moving over the fact of the waters.
> — Genesis

> In the beginning there was Chaos. Out of it came pure light and built the sky. — China

> He says there was a time in which all was darkness and water, wherein strange and peculiarly shaped creatures came into being.
> — Babylon

> In the beginning there was Chaos, nothing but void, formless matter, infinite space. — Hesoid, *Theogony*

Today's astrophysical cosmogonies also include chaos. One current model for the earliest moments of the universe starts with an impenetrable state known as Primordial Chaos which ended 10-43 seconds after the onset of expansion. During that strange period energy, space, and time were overpowered by uncertainty and indeterminacy. There was no orderly sequence of time or space. Each packet of energy and mass has uncertainties than itself. There was no platform of space-time upon which events could play. Causality did exist. Since physics is dependent upon causality, Primordial Chaos cannot be probed by the questioning fingers of physics. Only when Primordial Chaos ended did our measurable and ordered universe appear.

NON-LINEAR CHAOS

Another precise definition of Chaos has developed during the last two decades that refers to non-linear processes which amplify small initial fluctuations to unpredictable outcomes. The term first appeared in scientific literature in 1975 (Li and York 1975) and was more broadly developed by the mathematical biologist, Robert May (1976), in a paper entitle "Simple Mathematical Models with Very Complicated Dynamics".

A dramatic example of the non-linear amplification of initial conditions has been provided by Stephen Hawking (1991), who points out that if the density of the universe one second after the onset of expansion had been only one part in a trillion (a thousand billion) greater, the universe would have collapsed due to the mutual gravitation of matter after 10 years. Had the universe been one part in a trillion smaller, expansion would have been so rapid that it would have been essentially empty after ten years.

Weather prediction is a familiar example of the process of chaos. Sight uncertainties of wind, temperature, or pressure can result in major uncertainties in weather patterns and, as a consequence, long-term predictions are not possible (Lorenz 1963). Since nothing in the natural world can be measured with absolutely perfect precision, the amplification of miniscule uncertainties by non-linear processes can lead to huge uncertainties in outcome.

The process of choas injects novelty, freshness, and surprise into a system and is essential for the evolution of life. Kaufmann (1995) describes complex biological systems as existing at the 'edge of choas' where they have the greatest creative impulses, greatest flexibility in responding to environmental threats, and evolve most rapidly. As a system is forced further and further from equilibrium, it becomes increasingly subject to transformations at bifurcation points, when the tiniest effect will push it into one mode or another (*fig.* 15.3).

EQUILIBRIUM AND FIXED POINT ATTRACTORS

Two types of stable systems exist in our universe. The most stable configuration is that of thermodynamic equilibrium, which is characterised by a detailed balancing of all internal processes. Every emission of a photon of light is balanced by an absorption of exactly the same kind of photon. Every process leading to the concentration of matter is balanced by an equal and opposite rarefaction of matter.

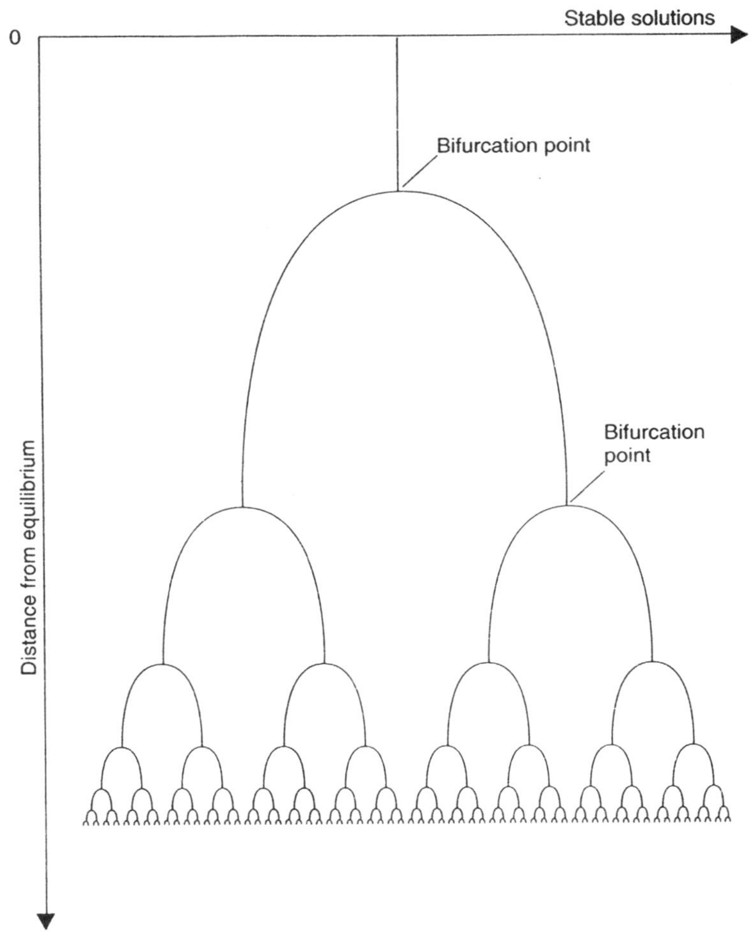

Fig. 15.3. The development of bifurcation points as the system is driven further from equilibrium. At each bifurcation point the future is undecided (after Convery and Highfield 1995).

Because all processes are so precisely balanced, complexity has no chance to grow as every process which might enhance complexity is balanced by an equal and opposite process. No information can be accumulated in an equilibrium system.

If left alone, an inhomogeneous gas with regions of differing density and composition will spontaneously move toward equilibrium and uniformity. Every drop of ink placed in a glass of water will evolve toward the equilibrium state in which the ink molecules are uniformly distributed throughtout the water. A pocket of hot gas surrounded by cooler material will evolve toward a uniform temperature.

The movement and evolution of these systems toward the stable equilibrium state can be described mathematically in terms of an 'attractor' that pulls the non-equilibrium system, like moths are drawn to a light. In the case of equilibrium, the attractor is known as a fixed-point attractor as all systems move inward towards the unmoving centre of attraction. Water poured into a funnel moves as if it were attracted toward a fixed-point attractor. Swinging pendulums gradually slow their motion and come to rest as if they were attracted to the motionless state (*fig.* 15.4).

SELF-ORGANISING SYSTEMS AND STRANGE ATTRACTORS

The second type of stability is found in self-organising systems. Although such systems may depart significantly from equilibrium. Prigogine and his colleagues were the first to demonstrate that there are configuration that are stabilised by internal cycles of matter and energy (Prigogine 1980, 1981; Jantsch 1980, 1981; Nicolis and Prigogine 1989). Prigogine identified these stable states as dissipative systems because they need to export low grade erergy to the environment. The heat proudced by a fertilised chicken egg is an example of energy dissipation resulting from self-organisation.

As a system moves further and further from equilibrium and the symmetries of opposing processes are increasingly broken, the system may become more complex and fragile. The human brain, utterly dependent upon the flow of blood and oxgyen, is an example of a very complex, self-organised system that is far removed from equilibrium. When a complex system becomes disconnected from its environment, it will sink into equilibrium.

The dynamics of these non-equilibrium stable systems may be described in terms of a 'strange attractor' which induces unpredictable behaviour and sudden transformation. Instead of pursuing the goal of a fixed-point attractor, self-organising systems strive to reach an ever-changing, ever-unpredictable goal, which is essentially unachievable. Without actually using the term, Prigogine and his colleagues (Prigogine *et al.* 1972) described the evolution of life in terms of a strange attractor which constantly thrusts biological systems out of equilibrium. Thus, in

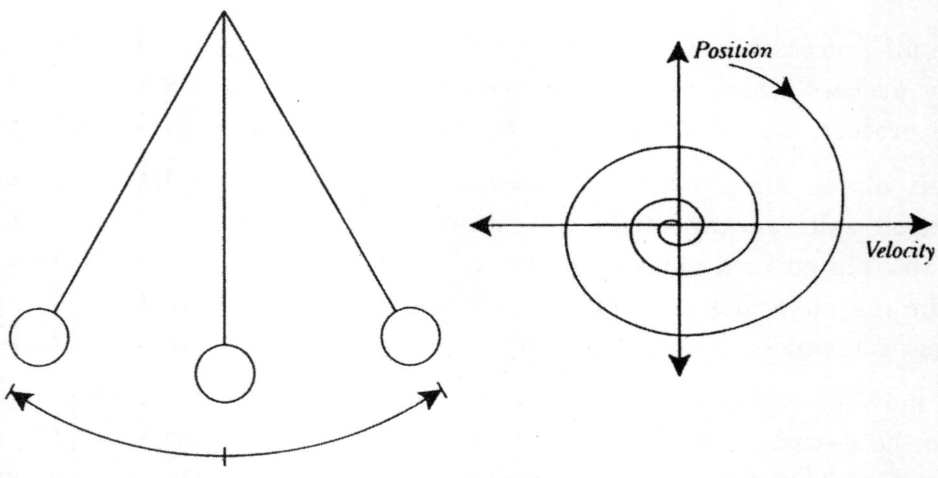

Fig. 15.4. Free swinging pendulum moving toward its fixed point attractor as its motion is dissipated through friction. Regardless of initial conditions, the pendulum always moves to the same fixed centre (after Cambel 1993).

order for evolution to continue each successive system must be driven a little further from equilibrium and, as a result, the complexity of successive systems can increase. Those mutations that inadvertently move a biological system backward toward equilibrium may die out because they may be less competitive.

The biosphere of the earth is an excellent example of a self-organising system that is stable, dissipative, far from equilibrium and under the control of a strange attractor. We can judge a system's departure from equilibrium by its internal temperature differences, i.e., a system is in equilibrium when every part has the same temperature. Our system includes the hot sun and cool intersteller space. The earth is bathed in radiation from the sun produced at a temperature of 5800K; the biosphere itself has a temperature close to 300K; and we radiate energy into surrounding space which has a temperature of 3K. Like an internal combustion engine, the biosphere needs a cool resevoir in which to dump its thermodynamic debris. If the attractor that provides the dynamics of the biosphere were to lose its strangeness, the biosphere would move toward the death of thermodynamic equilibrium. Such a transformation will occur some five billion years in the future when the sun ceases to shine and the earth cools to equilibrium with surroundings space.

Table 15.1 contains a summary of characteristics of self-organising systems.

Large-scale systems

In its beginning, the universe passed through successive stages of primitive order. First there were clumps of matter; then great patterns developed as walls and holes in the distribution of galaxies appeared. The first self-organising systems may have been huge clusters of galaxies covering hundreds of millions of light years and containing thousands of galaxies. They achieved stability, although space was expanding about them, because of a balance between divergent motion and the convergent effects of gravity. Galaxies are held together by a similar balance, but that balance has created a new order and a new geometry that has the form of rotating disks of stars. These vast rotating disks containing the matter of hundreds of billions of stars, acquired new geometries in the form of spiral arms (*fig.* 15.5). The emergent complexity of the galaxy includes outward moving density waves which form the spiral arms, hot and cool stars, dense nuclei containing black holes, and extensive halos of stars.

As they formed within galaxies, stars acquired new geometric structures, new evolutionary behaviour, new forms of magnetic fields, and novel chemical composition. New Principles of order appeared when the first stars appeared. Entirely unprecedented elements were created in their interiors and new 'laws' of physics were engaged which connected the interior space of the atomic nucleus to

Table 15.1
Characteristics of Self-organising Systems

1	2	3	4	5	6
Openness	***Non-equilibrium***	***Symmetry breaking***	***Self-reference***	***Metastability and super-criticality***	***Indeterminacy***
Openness to the environment is an absolutely necessary condition for self-organisation and complexity. Circulation of matter and energy through the system are required for its survival. If obstructions or enclosing walls are created and the system becomes isolated form its environment, it will move toward the death of equilibrium. Openness implies symbiosis with the environment. The self-organising system and its environment are dynamically coupled and mutually interdependent.	Departure from equilibrium is a second necessary condition for complexity and self-organisation. When a system is too close to equilibrium, the balance of opposing processess precludes the growth of complexity or the storage of information. At equilibrium, the system achieves uniformity, stasis, and death.	A geometrical pattern with exact symmetry has no uniqueness and no information contents. Broken symmetries are necessary for variety, surprise, and complexity.	Self-organisation develops without dependence upon external authority. The emergent geometry of the self-organising system is not a copy of the macrocosm. Through a series of internal loops involving the movement of people, energy, and information, the self-organising system develops an autonomy of its own.	The closed, equilibrium system maintains stability by suppressing fluctuations. As the self-organising system departs further from equilibrium and becomes increasingly complex as small fluctuations are amplified. The metastability of the system means that small fluctuations that reach a certain threshold may rapidly transform the system.	Because of the amplification of small random fluctuations, outcomes of change are unprdictable. The self-organising system is open to the future, does not have a goal or telos, and does not follow a perordained pattern or teleology.

Fig. 15.5. Spiral galaxy in Andromeda. (photo by Palomar Observatory, California Institute of Technology)

the macrocosm. The geometry of a star is more complex than that of the cloud of gas from which it was born. Large stars develop an internal complexity that is too great to sustain, and they self-destruct into supernovae, scattering their interiors into surrounding space (Malville 1995).

Solar systems utilised those scattered remains to build planetary systems with a consequent immense increase of complexity. The rings of Saturn provide a dramatic example of the emergent geometry of a self-organising system (*fig.* 15.6). The geometry was truly new. Within the rings orbital resonances, gravitational tides, 'shepherd' satellites, and electrostatic forces combine to create a beautiful and intricate system.

Biological systems

Aroung 3.6 billion years ago life appeared in the warm, nutrient-rich oceans of the planet Earth, perhaps only 200 million years after its oceans of magma had cooled. For the first billion years of its existence, the earth had been bombarded by rock and ice debris, causing temperatures in its outer layers that were too great to allow the formation of life. But once the appropriate conditions were reached, life appeared

Fig. 15.6. Rings of Saturn. There are thousands of rings surrounding the planet. The smallest rings in the photograph are 10 kw. across. The colour diffrences reveal particles of different sizes and chemical conposition. (photo by NASA)

rapidly. However, for the next three billion years, life changed very little and consisted only simple bacteria, algae, and plankton. At a remarkable time, 543 million years ago, the Cambrian explosion occurred, and like dropping a salt crystal into a supersaturated salt solution, life swarmed and exploded in number and variety. Virtually the entire animal kingdom appeared within a period of 10 million years. The sudden burst of complexity and variety has been proposed by Kaufmann (1995), as an example of the fecundity of chaos. Described in other terms, the biosphere was pushed so far out of equilibrium that it reached the state of super-criticality and non-linearity such that very minute fluctuations had major consequences. This surge of life in the Cambrian explosion produced new order, new purpose, and new meaning for the earth's creatures. It was the result of both stochastic (random) processes and deterministic laws of chemistry and physics.

The microscopic fluctuations that drove the Cambrian system across an instability threshold into new structures had been present before the explosion. Microscopic fluctuations constantly test the stability of a system. Within a stable structure, negative feedback processes dampen these fluctuations, and as long as the fluctuations remain below a critical threshold the system remains stable. The greater the system is pushed out of equilibrium, the greater is its metastability. The early earth was far from equilibrium: warm oceans surrounded by cold space, heated by a nearby star, filled with complex molecules, rocked by volcanic explosions, and lightning discharges. The earth was teetering at the edge of chaos and was pushed over by the smallest of a template-bearing molecule of life. Stabilising negative feedback processes were then replaced by exponentially-growing positive feedback, and new forms of order swept through the system.

Socio-cultural systems

The first cities, which appeared during the thrid millennium BC, were also stable, self-organising stages in the evolution of the microcosm. Like a galaxy, star, or fertilised egg, the city is a dissipative non-equilibrium system, with its own particular geometry, purpose, and ordering principles. The first major examples of urban order and 'cosmic' geometry appeared suddenly in the Indus Valley between 2600 and 2550 BC, giving the appearance of rapid self-organisation ('a paroxysm of change', Possehl 1990), similar to that of the Cambrian explosion (Jansen 1991; Parpola 1994). A variety of stimuli may have initiated the vast modifications of socio-cultural behaviour that led to the Mature Harappen culture: the onset of maritime trade, a new ideology, and a powerful new writing system. Towns with monumental architecture appeared along rivers, dimensions of bricks became standardised, a system of weights and measures appeared, sophisticated sanitation, drainage, and water supply systems were incorporated into the cities. The geometry of the macrocosm was imposed upon the Harappan city through cardinal orientations and an orthogonal gridwork of streets and structures (*fig.* 15.7). The technique for establishing true north that employs the gnomon may have been invented by the Harappans.

Parpola (1994) suggests that the burst of creativity was paralleled by the development of a complex astronomy, which had been building momentum for perhaps 500 years, from the time of the heliacal rising of Aldebaran on the vernal equinox near 3000 BC. In Parpola's reading of the Indus script, a sophisticated astronomy is suggested by possible references to stars, asterisms such as the Pleiades, and the planets (*navagraha*s, such as Mercury, Venus and Saturn). The 28 stations of the moon (*nakṣartra*s) may have been first recognised at that time by the Harappans.

Order and the cosmic city

Ironically, the seeds of the eventual decline of the Indus valley civilization may have been present in the great achievements of the mature Harappan culture that were expressed in its uniformity and order. Major technical innvoations in

Fig. 15.7 Mohenjo-Daro. The axes of the city are approximately cardinal with the exception of sections that are rotated clockwise up to 10 degrees.

observational astronomy and city planning are demonstrated by the geometrical order of the Harappan cities. While these innovations are fascinating examples of ancient science, they reveal the imposition of an external non-human geometry upon the inhabitants of the Harappan cities. The human microcosm was forced to fit into the imagined cardinal geometry and orthogonality of the macrocosm. The society which had experienced such an astonishing burst of innovation may have been imprisoned by its rigid symmetries and orthogonal geometries. Real and symbolic walls may have been erected between an inside 'sacred order' and an outside 'profane disorder', and these barriers may have limited the circulation of new people and new ideas into the city.

Nearly 1,000 Harappan cities were built throughout an area of 1.25 million squere km. While there is reason to believe in system-wide administrative control, there is no evidence of royal or priestly authority or even of strong military power. Walls surrounding the city appear to have defined social classes and differentiated inner and outer space rather than provide protection from enemies. Starting with the Shang dynasty (1700-1100 BC), there was a similar tradition in China of establishing capitals that aspired to be copies of cosmic geometry, i.e., cardinally aligned with north-south axiality, and a concentricity with the palace in the centre (*fig.*15.10) (Meyer 1991). Every capital was meant to be identical, and it mattered little exactly where on the landscape of China it was built.

The Chinese capital has been often used as the paradigm of the universal cosmic city that articulated a parallelism between heaven and earth (Carrasco 1987; Wheatley 1971; Meyer 1991). Rome, Tenochtitlan, Teotihuacan, Babylon, and Anuarādhapura have been identified as similar 'cosmocised sacred cities' (Meyer 1991). Other examples in India are Śiśupālgarh (*fig.* 15.8) and Wārangal (*fig.* 15.9). Since the Chinese capital is an uniquely Chinese example of geometric symmetries and Confucian ideals, (*fig.* 15.10) it is conceivable that few other cities outside of China achieved comparable degrees of social order and sclerosis.

While these cosmic cities are often praised as masterpieces of city planning, they are also examples of closed systems. During their early phases many undoubtedly functioned as self-organising systems and nurtured a host of creative impulses. However, in some of the cities a self-aggrandising agenda by the rulers may have dominated city planning, causing the city to be designed as a miniature copy of the macrocosm. Kingship and the power of sacerdotal elites were legitimised by geometric connections to the larger cosmos. As the cosmic city matured and began to value order over innovation, centralised authority over individualism, and stratified society over social mobility, many of thse cities closed in upon themselves resulting in diminished innovation and novelty.

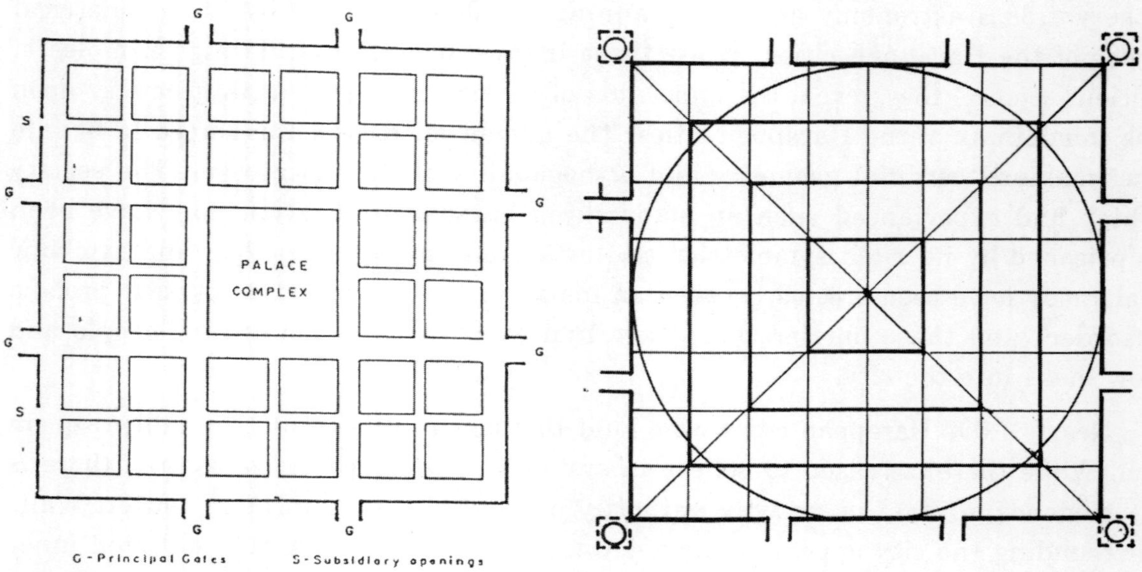

Fig. 15.8. Śiśupālgarh and its possible geometrical design (Joshi 1996).

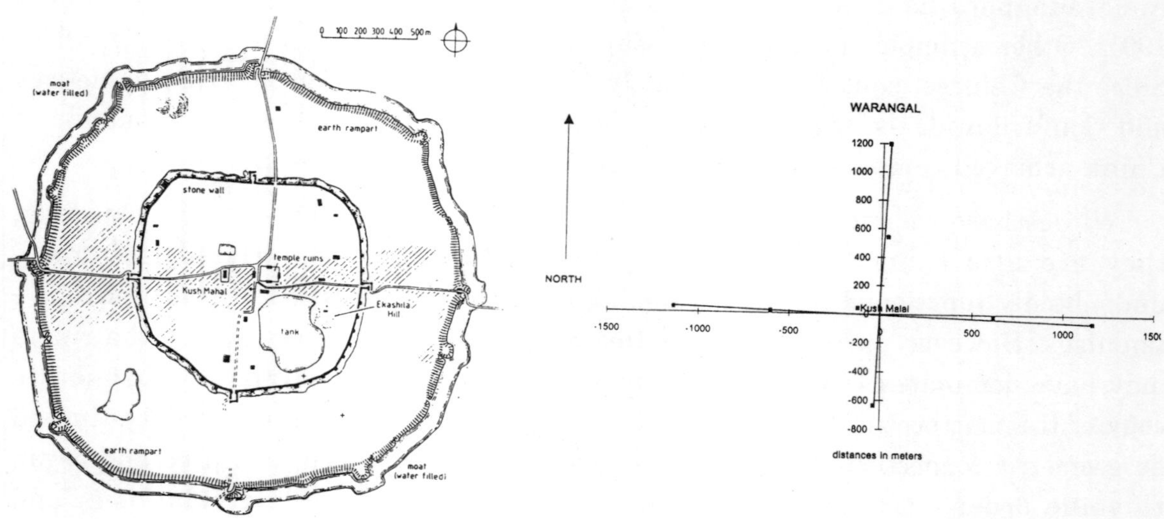

Fig. 15.9. Warangal (Michell 1992) and recent GPS determinations of the centre-points of the gates using differential measurements. The axes of Warangal are rotated by 2.4 degrees clockwise from true cardinality.

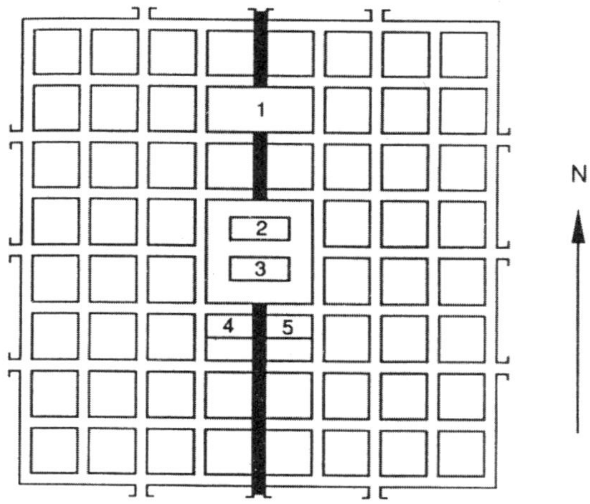

Fig. 15.10. The ideal Chinese captial based on the Zhouli.
The ruler's palace lies in the centre (Meyer 1991).

Within Beijing, the public was excluded from the emperor's rituals; the elegant geometric patterns and symmetries of the Forbidden City were not for public consumption (*fig.* 15.11). It was at threat of death for citizen even to view the emperor's procession through the streets from the Forbidden City to the Altar of Heaven at winter solstic (Meyer 1991). In chinese society, individuality was minimal as, in accordance with Confucion ethics, the emperor suppressed all kinds of disorderly and chaotic behaviour (Tan Chung 1996). Confucianism effectively precluded individualsim and 'killed the social ability of throwing up great thinkers'. Periods of social choas were necessary for the emergence of individuals.

> Most of these individuals were put to the sword before they could put their names on the roster of chinese heroes. A few of them succeeded and established their own ruling dynasties
>
> — Tan Chung 1996

These successful few would, in turn, invite

> . . .Confucianism back to checkmate other individuals who might emulate their own heroic feats.

Pilgrimage, with its robust individualism, unpredictable outcomes, and potential for evoking innovations from below, had no role in Beijing. The city was never the site of a country-wide pilgrimage movement. Instead of pilgrims coming with new ideas and brief dreams of egalitariansim, visitors to the city came primarily bearing tribute to domonstrate submission to the emperor (Meyer 1991).

Emergent geometries of pilgrimage

Pilgrimage provides an entirely different method for organising human space at

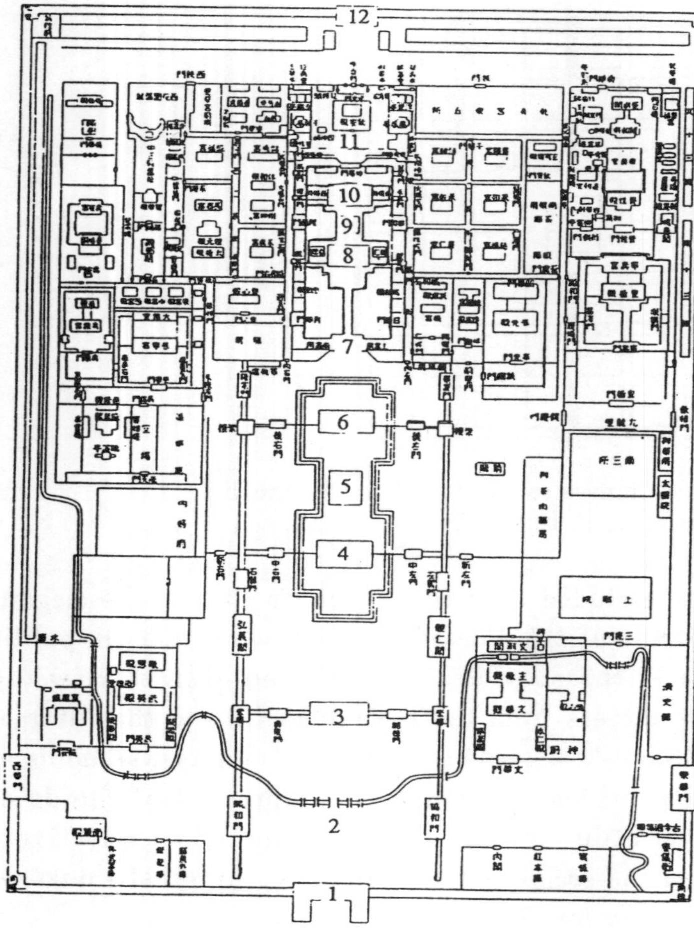

1. Meridian Gate (*Wumen)*
2. Golden River
3. Gate of Supreme Harmony (*Taibemen*)
4. Hall of Supreme Harmony (*Taibedian*)
5. Hall of Middle Harmony (*Zbongbedian*)
6. Hall of Protecting Harmony (*Baobedian*)
7. Heavenly Brightness Gate (*Qianqingmen*)
8. Palace of Heavenly Brightness (*Qianqingqong*)
9. Hall of Peaceful Unity (*Jiaotaidian*)
10. Palace of Earthly Tranquility (*Kunninggong*)
11. Imperial Garden
12. Martial Spirit Gate (*Sbenwumen*)

Fig. 15.11. The Forbidden City (Meyer 1991).

both global and local scales of size. Ideology, not cocercive power, energises these self-organising systems and establishes their emergent geometries. Pilgrims mark out large-scale patterns in the landscape in their travelling to a pilgrimage centre; by their feet they appropriate the land into the realm of human experience (Tilley 1994); once they have reached the pilgrimage centre, they walk through complex geometries of encirclement. Some pilgrimage centres are organic cities, which grew entirely by themselves, without imperial mandate or formal planning. Contrary to Meyer's (1991: 157) assertion that "there is no recognisable geometry of form, no evidence of overall planning . . . no orientation or axial way" in the organic city, many pilgrimage centres have highly complex geometries.

Movement is the essence of pilgrimage. It is the single most significant condition for a ritual to be identified as pilgrimage. Movement separates pilgrims from home; carries them through unfamiliar and often difficult landscape, across physical and metaphysical thresholds into liminal space; and returns them to the ordinary world often as changed individuals. An example of an emergent pilgrimage geometry is found in the great Maharashtrian pilgrimage to Paṇḍharpur and is shown in *fig.* 15.12.

Openness is a fundamental feature of pilgrimage. Through the act of separation from the familiar world, the pilgrim becomes open to new perspectives. Equally as important, the pilgrimage centre is open to individuals from a variety of different places and backgrounds. The circulation of pilgrims from village to pilgrimage centre creates a religious space that transcends regional diversity and social stratification and opens up possible pathways for individual social mobility (Bhardwaj 1973; Preston 1985). Like the stirring of the cosmic ocean to create *amṛta*, the institution of pilgrimage stirs the cultural landscape, produces new life-giving options and prevents the stagnation of equilibrium.

These self-organising pilgrimage systems are not the 'complex adapative systems' (CAS) that have been the focus of considerable attention by archaeologists at the Santa Fe Institue (Gell-Mann 1994; Gumerman and Gell-Mann 1994; Tainter and Tainter 1996). The initiation of pilgrimage and the growth of complexity in the pilgrimage landscape are primarily adaptive repsonses to the challenges of a changing environment. The old system, prior to the onset of pilgrimage, was not necessarily

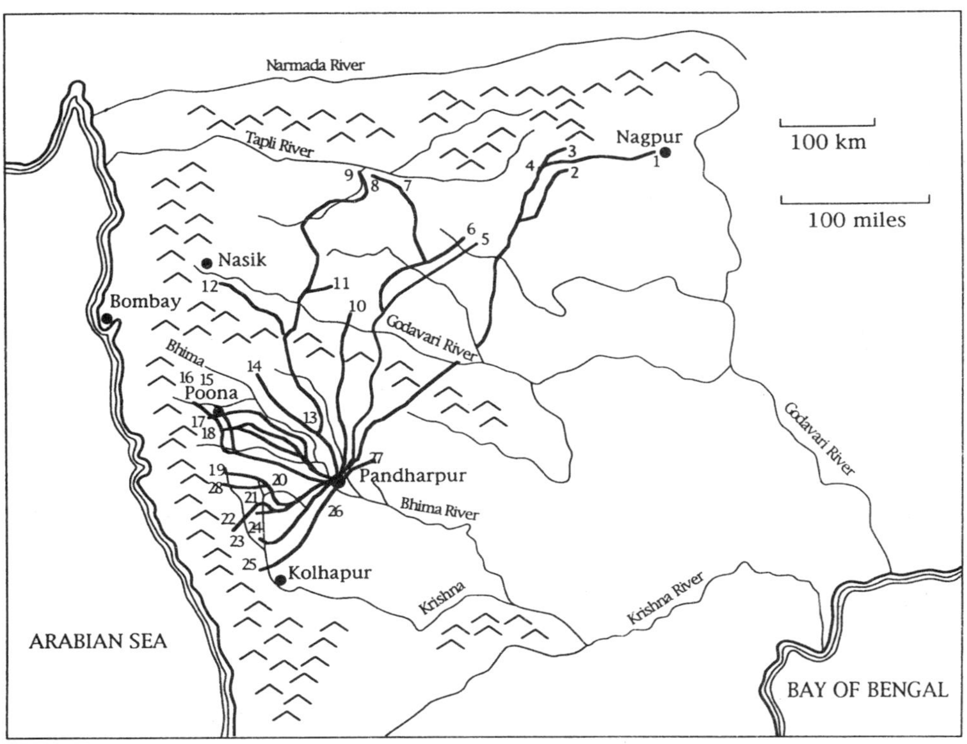

Fig. 15.12. Paṇḍharpur with 28 pilgrimages routes (*pālkhīs*) (after Stanley 1992).

unsatisfactory of dysfunctional. Innovations of pilgrimage are not tested by the environment. Some of the choices made by pilgrims are, in fact, decidedly non-adaptive as judged by standard economic criteria, such as those of the Wakaris of Maharashtra who spend their entire lives on pilgrimage walking back and forth between Paṇḍharpur and Alaṇḍi (Mokashi 1987). In its extreme expression, the complex adaptive system may undo itself by seeking equilibrium, order, and static security (Jantsch 1980).

The critical event leading to the onset of pilgrimage may be relatively miniscule but is greatly amplified by non-linear societal processes. A pilgrimage tradition may start with a charismatic leader, a strange vision, a miraculous cure, or simply a novel idea. In the case of the Paṇḍharpur pilgrimage, the initial event was modest but clear in its egalitarian and filial messages. While Puṇḍalīk, the devoted son, is massaging his father's feet, he is visited by Lord Kṛṣṇa. Not willing to stop helping his father, he tosses a brick to the god, on which to stand above the wet ground. Kṛṣṇa, in the form of Viṭobā, becomes so impressed by the demonstration of filial devotion by Puṇḍalik that he decides to remain standing in that place forever (Mokashi 1987).

In Table 15.2 cosmic cities and pilgrimage centres are compared. The cosmic city, in its mature phase of rigidity and closure, fails to meet most of the criteria of self-organisation. Pilgrimage contres, on the other hand, persist as self-organising systems because of their openness and flexibility. The religious symbols they embrace are agents of change, serving as dynamic mechanisms for integrating people of difference backgrounds (Preston 1980). In their multiplicity of meaning and stimulation of renewal and transformation, these religious symbols serve as 'strange attractors' to the pilgrim and play a major role in the self-organisation of the pilgrimage centre. Like the biosphere which contains it, the pilgrimage centre is always in a state of flux.

SIZE AND STABILITY OF THE PILGRIMAGE LANDSCAPE

"The more important a scared centre, paradoxically, the more flexible and numerous are likely to be the meaning it encompasses" (Coleman and Elsner 1995: 208). The self-organising pilgrimage institution may be very large and remarably stable. More than 100 pilgrimage sites or *tīrtha*s stretch from Himālayas to the tip of the Indian sub-continent and from the Bay of Bengal to the Arabian Sea (Bhardwaj 1973). The north-south line between the pilgrimage sites of Badrīnāth in the north of that of Rāmeśvaram in the south is 23,000 km in length and departs from true north-south by less than 20 km. Symbolically, the north-south line connects the regions of birth and death. The east-west line between Purī and Dvārakā spans 1,700 km.

As an institution, Hindu pilgrimage has been in place since the composition of

Table 15.2

Order and Complexity in Self-organizing systems

Properties of Self-Organizing Systems	Cosmic Cities	Pilgrimage Centres
1. Openness and Symblosis	NO Closed systems Boundaries at city walls Inside/outside distinction	YES New ideas, new visions, new people Little control over exchange with outside No boundaries Dynamically coupled with environment
2. Non-equlibrium	NO Attempt to achieve political and economic balance	YES No balance Little social stratification Flux of people and ideas
3. Symmetry breaking: new geometries	NO Highly symmetrical geometries All cosmic cities are similar Strong centrality: throne or temple	YES Geometrical symmetries not important Unique Circumambulation
4. Self-reference: no external authority	NO Exact copy of macrocosm Sympathetic magic between macrocosm and microcosm Legitimizes authority	YES Individualistic behaviour Innovative and creative Local traditions and mythologies Antistructure
5. Metastability and Super-critically	YES Initial rapid growth Negative feedback at maturity Stablility, order, and lawfullness Supression of innovation Little fundamental change	YES Initial rapid growth Remains at the edge of chaos Super-criticality may result in transformation to greater complexity or self-destruction
6. Indeterminacy	NO Intent is to remain forever Teleological Established future	YES Individualistic & idiosyncratic Teleonomic (emergence of purpose) Uncertain future

the *Mahābhārata* as early as 300 BC (Bhardwaj 1973). The pilgrimage centre of Vārāṇasī is one of the oldest consitnuously occupied cities of the world, extending from at least 700 BC to the present (Eidt 1977). In addition to Vārāṇasī (Kāśī), other long-lived major pilgrimage centres of north India mentioned in the *Mahābhārata* include Citrakūṭa, Prayāg (Saṅgama), Gayā, and the sources of the Gaṅgā and Yamunā rivers.

The pilgrimage geometry of Islam with Mecca at its centre contains a vast pattern of alignments which are symmetrical about that centre. Its large-scale geometry is established by the *qiblā* or the local direction of Mecca. The *qiblā* establishes the direction one should face for reading the *Korān*, the call to prayer, ritual slaughter of animals, and burial of the dead, as well as the alignment of mosques. At first the *qiblā* was simply the direction the pilgrim would start walking toward Mecca. The need to establish the *qiblā* with precision stimulated the growth of Arabic astronomy, and the ninth-century methods were available for determining the *qiblā* at any location on the earth. The resulting geometry of moving people, rituals and aligned structures centered on Mecca stretches across more than one-quarter of the circumference of the planet, along the 8,000 km between Andalusia and Samarkand (King 1982, 1993). Mecca was first visited by pilgrims in AD 629-30.

In the American Southwest, Chaco Canyon may have been centre of a regional system covering as much as 200,000 km and containing over 130 communities, which were tied together by a geometric network of roads (*fig.* 15.13). The precise nature of the Chaco regional system has not been established, but pilgrimage is one possible mechanism for its self-integration (Malville and Malville 1995). The roads converging on the Canyon may have been the routes of pilgrimage, its great houses may have been pilgrim hostels, and its trash mounds may contain the remains of pilgrimage festivals.The greatest burst of building activity in Chaco Canyon occurred in a five-year period AD 1050-55 when the construction labour jumped by more than 600 per cent compared to the previous 25 years (Lekson 1984). These rapid changes have the characteristics, of the self-transformation of a metastable system. The resources deficiency, marginal levels of subsistence, and climatic fluctuations of the Chaco basin could have prevented the system from achieving equilibrium and thrust it into super-criticality.

THE CHAOS OF PILGRIMAGE

There clearly must be a powerful 'attractor' to cause the pilgrim to journey far and undergo sometimes extreme physical hardships and personal sacrifice. In its dynamics, changing nature, and multivalency, the attractor of pilgrimage shares features with the strange attractor of chaos theory. In his description of complex systems, Cambel (1993: 4) could well be describing pilgrimage:

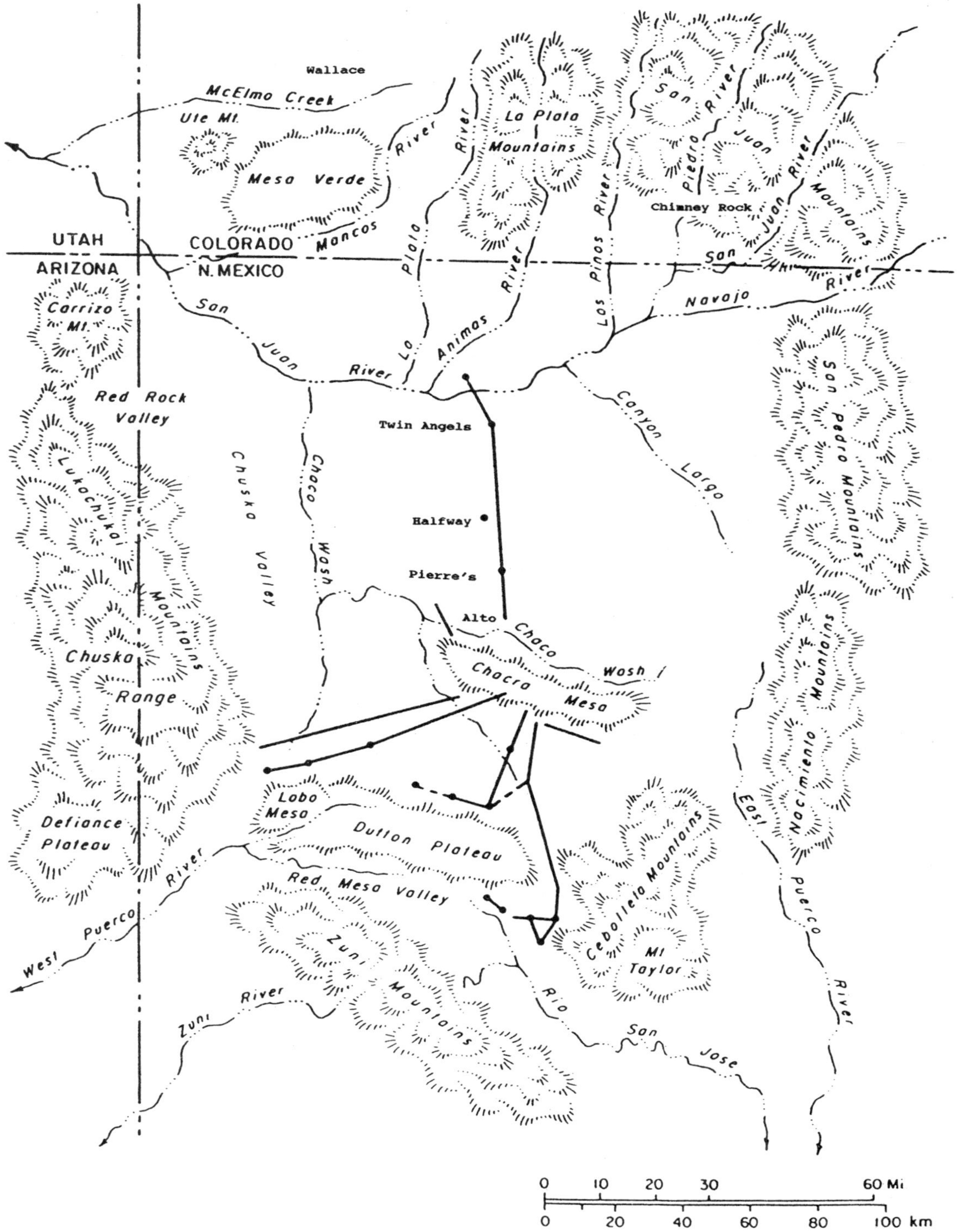

Fig. 15.13. Roads of Chaco.

> Complex systems are dynamic and not in equilibrium; they are like a journey, not a destination, and they may pursue a moving target.

The journey of the pilgrim as described by the Turners (1978), involves liminality which they liken

> to death, to being in the womb, to invisibility, to darkness, to bisexuality, to the wilderness, and to an eclipse of the sun or moon.

The Turners have been criticised for overly idealising the communitas of pilgrimage in which they assert that norms of social status and social interactions are temporarily abandoned and replaced by 'antistructure', spontaneous association, and 'social death' (Morinis 1992). The social chaos of communitas is an ideal which is clearly approached by certain individuals in certain settings, such as the Maharashtrian pilgrimages to view Viṭhobā at Paṇḍharpur (Mokashi 1987) and Khāṇḍobā at Jejuri. Turner has noted that pilgrimage is energised during periods of social chaos and rapid social change.

INTERNAL GEOMETRIES OF PILGRIMAGE CENTRES

A common feature of many pilgrimage traditions is that once the pilgrimage centre has been reached, pilgrims engage in circumambulation of important shrines, special objects, and/or hallowed space. By encircling the centre, pilgrims may perceive and comprehend the cosmic totality of which they are a part, reenact its cosmogony and its rhythm, and be merged with it (Saraswati 1985). It is the geometric complexity of these pilgrimage *maṇḍala*s that interests us most in the present context.

The Muslim Hajj includes both the often very difficult journey to Mecca and a seven-fold circumambulation of the *Ka'bā*. After cirlcing the *Ka'bā*, pilgrims visit the Mountain of Mercy at Arafat some 20 km to the east and then the three stoning pillars at Mina.

After engaging in an arduous trek, pilgrims to Mt Kailās circle the mountain along the 33 km *kora*, which involves crossing the Dolma Lal at 5490 m. After 13 circumambulations of the outer *kora*, pilgrims may follow the inner *kora* or *nangkor* which circles the smaller peak south of Kailās, which Hindus call Nandī. Pilgrims may also follow a longer circuit around Lake Mānasarovar visiting its seven *gompā*s.

After reaching Pueblo Alto, the terminus of the North Road, Pilgrims to Chaco Canyon may have followed a circular route that took them to the great houses of Chetro Ketl, Tsin Kletzin, and Pueblo Bonito and the great *kiva* of Casa Rinconada (*fig.* 15.14). No road apparently enters Tsin Kletzin from the south. The only roads and stairs which reach Tsin Kletzin come in from the north and may pair with the double set of roads and stairs which proceed southward from Pueblo Alto (*fig.* 15.14). As viewed from Tsin Kletzin, the original centre of Pueblo Alto is within 7-8 minutes

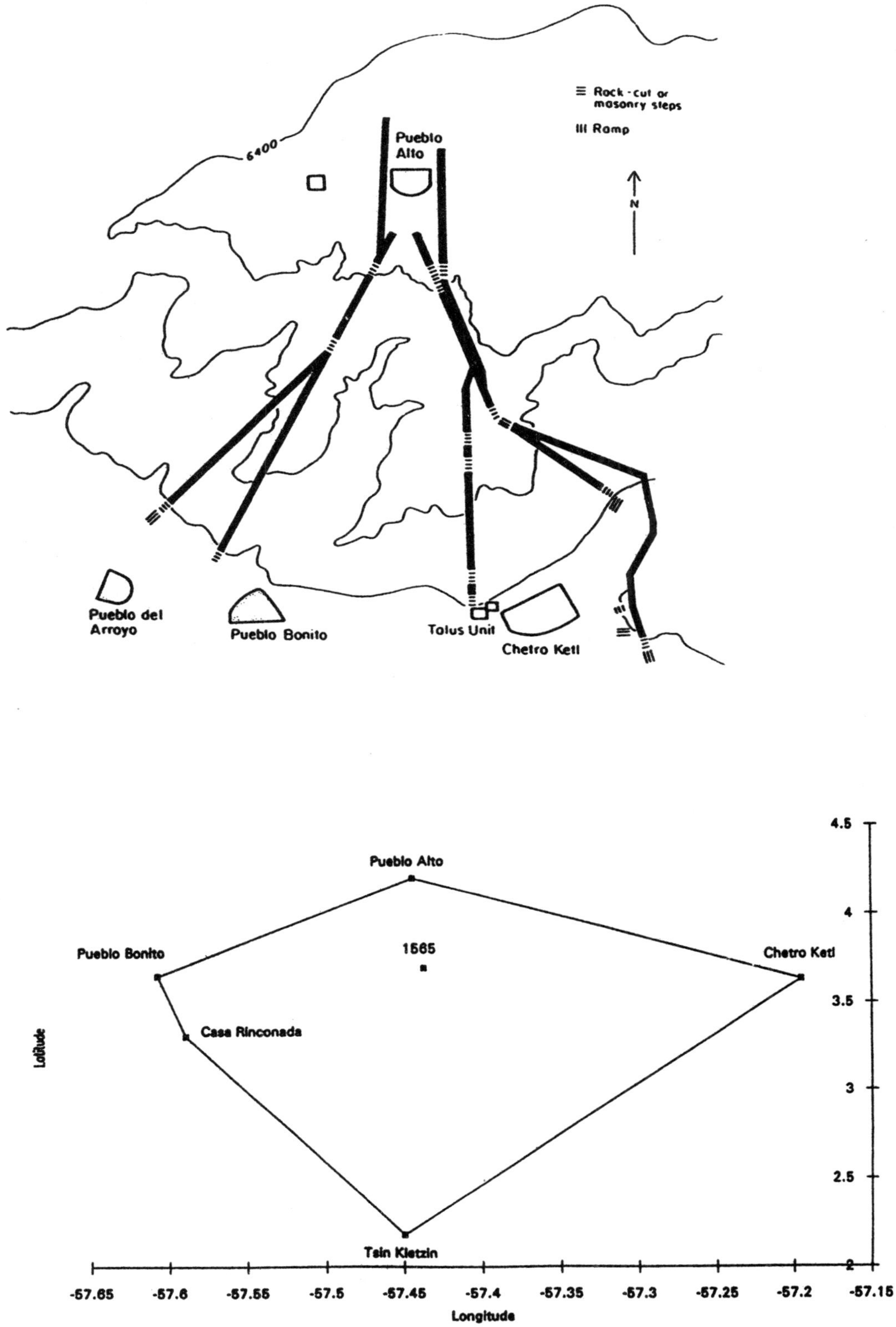

Fig. 15.14. Possible pilgrimage circumambulation route in Chaco Canyon.

of arc of true north, and at night pilgrims could have watched the heavens wheel over the centre of Pueblo Alto.

The pilgrimage landscape of Kāśī (Vārāṇasī) contains an almost bewildering collection of intertwined pilgrimage circuit's of extraordinary complexity and variety, the most prominent of which have been described and analysed by Singh in a number of important papers (1987, 1991, 1993, 1994a, 1994b). Who created this complex geometry of movement we shall never know for certain, but it was not the result of an imperial agenda or formed city planning.

Singh (1994) provides numerous examples of the geometries of these circuits, which include the most popular Pañcakrośī circuit, the spiralling routes of the Avimukta, Antargṛha and the 56 shrines of Vināyakas. The complex geometry of the later involves the eight cardinal and intercardinal directions and the seven realms of the heavens. Both Vināyaka (*fig.* 15.15) and Antargṛha circuits spiral seven times into the centre (*fig.* 15.16).

Another geometrical pattern in Vārāṇasī created by the 14 sun temples, many of which are contained in a regular triangle centered on the ancient centre of Kāśī, now the shrine of Madhyameśvara. The shrine lies close to the perpendicular bisector of the longest (north-south) side of the triangle, only 45 m from the midpoint of its 2.5 km length (Malville and Singh 1995; and Malville 1995) (*fig.* 15.17).

Citrakūṭa provides further examples of highly ordered geometric patterns in pilgrimage landscape, which include the *pradakṣiṇā* route encircling Kamadagiri hill, icons of Rāma and Lakṣmaṇa, and alignments to the solstice sun (Dubey, Malville, and Singh 1996) (*fig.* 15.18). The natural landscape contains three series of sub-*tīrtha*s, each of which establishes an isosceles triangle. Because of the special relationship between Rāma and the region of Citrakūṭa, these triangles appear to represent the arrow and bow that are the identifying of Rāma and Lakṣmaṇa.

The symbolic arrow from Hanumāndhārā to Vālmīki Āśrama bisects the largest triangle into angles of 13.9 and 14.4. That arrow aligns with sunrise on summer solstice. The two long sides of the triangle, Vālmīki Āśrama to Atri Āśrama and Bharatakūpa, are 29.4 km and 32.15 km, respectively.

The second line of sub-*tīrtha*s extends from Bharatkūpa to Hanumāndhārā and aligns with the sun when it sets at summer solstice. These two solstic lines intersect close to Hanumāndhārā such that an observer standing above it would see the sun at summer solstice rise in the vicinity of Vālmīki Āśrama and set above Kamadagiri hill. The second isosceles triangle is also remarkable in its symmetries. Two sides have lengths of 9.3 km and 9.6 km. The line from Bharatkūpa to Hanumāndhārā bisects the central angle with a precision better than 1 per cent with angles of 11.66 and 11.45 degrees.

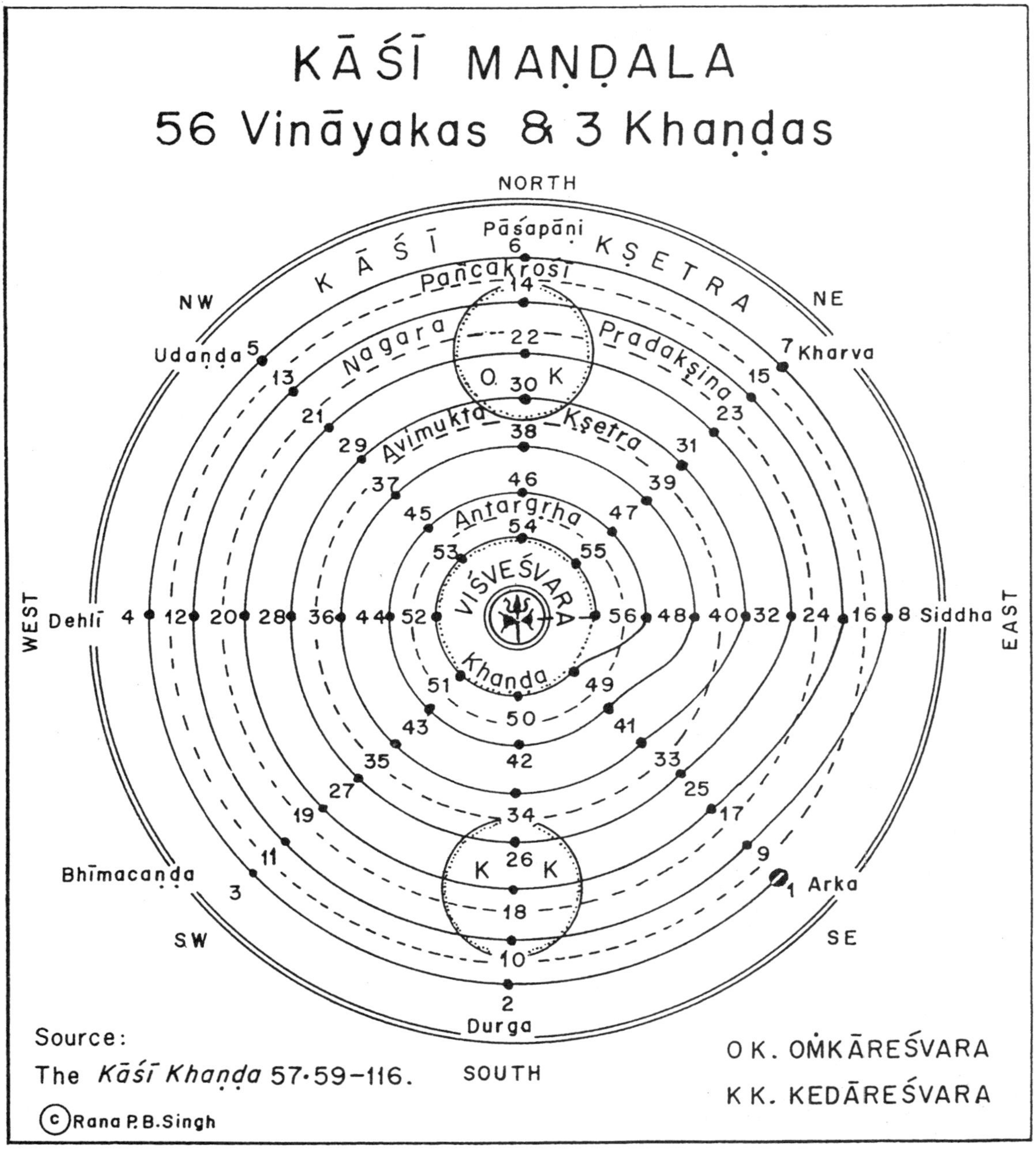

Fig. 15.15. Vināyaka pilgrimage *maṇḍala*, Kāśī.

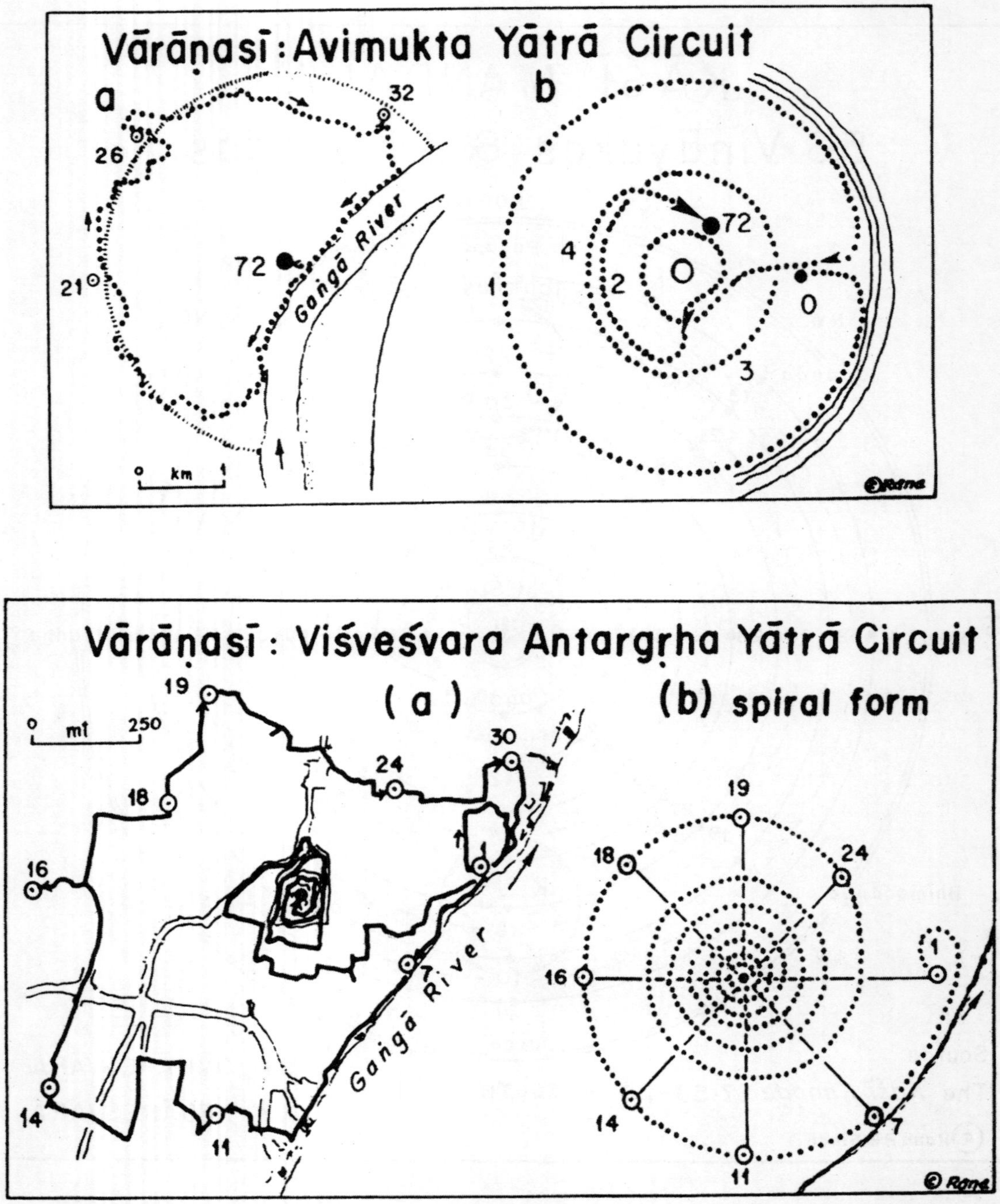

Fig. 15.16. Pilgrimage routes of Kāśī: Avimukta and Antargṛha circuits (Singh 1993b).

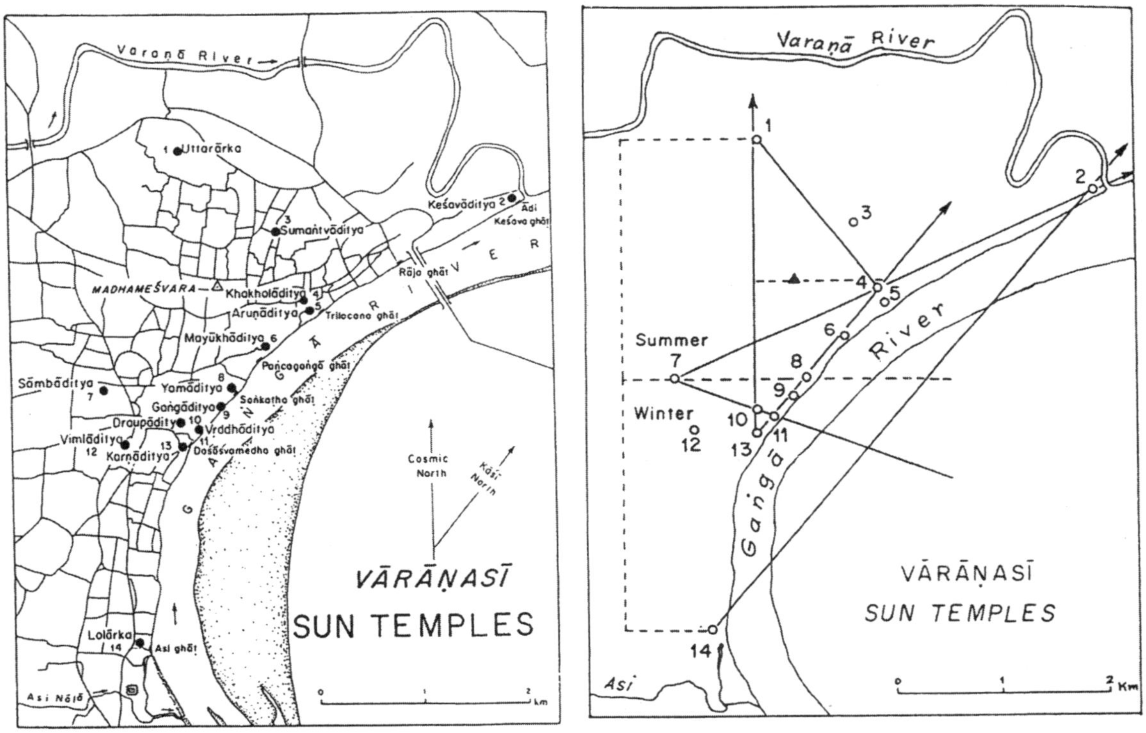

Fig. 15.17. Ādityas of Kāśī.

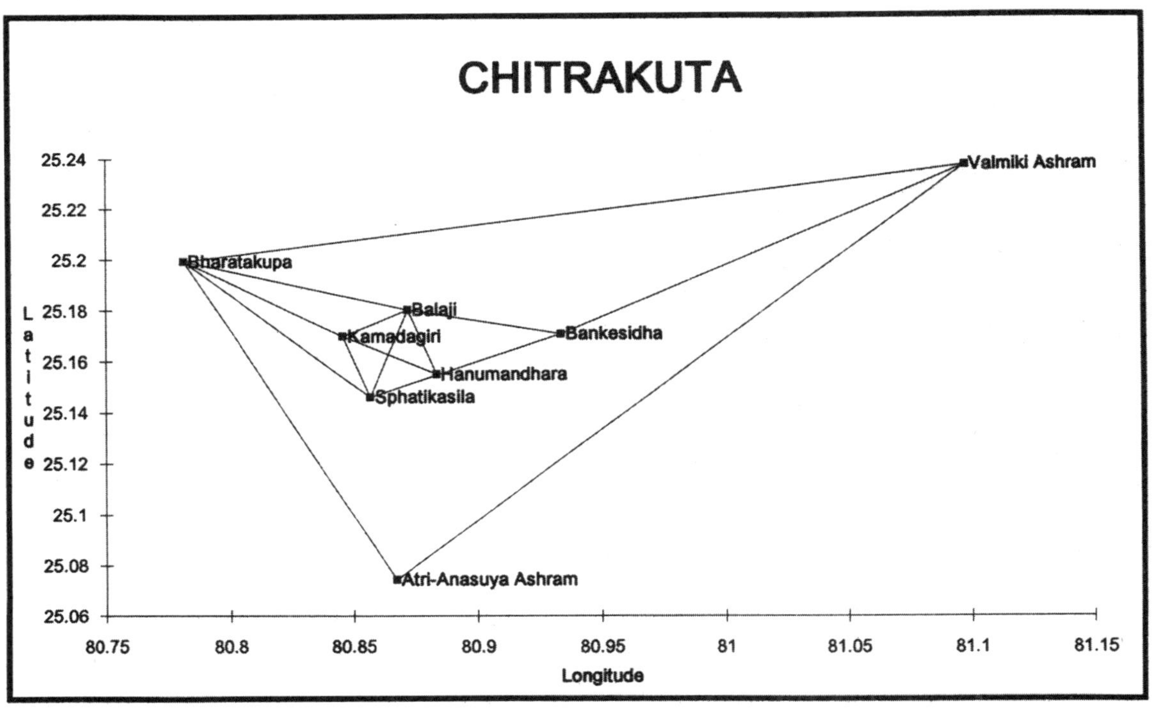

Fig. 15.18. Geometry of Citrakūṭa.

At the smallest level, the third isosceles triangle is formed by Kamadagiri, Bālājī and Sphaṭikaśilā; the longest sides have lengths of 2.4 km and 2.7 km, respectively. An individual on the summit of Kamadagiri would see the summer solstice sun rise near Bālājī and the winter solstice sun rise near Hanumāndhārā.

Concluding remarks

Whether it be the spiral galaxy, star, ring around Saturn, or pilgrimage, new geometries with each transformation of self-organising systems. Chance and necessity combine to generate unprecedented and unpredicatble systems, the birth of which brings new meaning and purpose into the world (Mondod 1971).

After an initial burst of creativity and self-organisation, the cosmic city may settle into a state of equilibrium and stagnation brought on by its externally imposed rigid geometry, social stratification, and enclosing walls. By contrast, the open pilgrimage system may remain robust and in the state of super-criticality for a considerable time.

Comparison of the two types of geometries displayed, repectively, in *figs.* 15.11 and 15.12, summarises remarkably well the differences between cosmic city and pilgrimage. The geometry of the cosmic city is linear, Cartesian and exclusive while that of the pilgrimage centre is circular, convergent, and inclusive. The cosmic city seeks legitimisation by copying the periphery; pilgrimage seeks union with the centre. Centripetal/centrifugal, inner/outer, sacred/profane, order/chaos are distinctions that are articulated in the geometry of the cosmic city but are dissolved in the geometry of pilgrimage.

Pilgrimage can be remarkably resilient and resistant to changing political forces. During the Muslim invasions of India, temples and shrines were destroyed, but the sites remained in people's memories and continued to be visited. The great city of Vijayanagara was built at the pilgrimage site of Pampā-tīrtha, which had been in existence at least since AD 689. While the city was destroyed some 250 years after its founding, the vitality of pilgriamge centre of Hampī continues to this day. Great cities rise and fall, but pilgrimage remains. The longevity of pilgrimage centres, such as Jerusalem, Mecca, Vārāṇasī, and Citrakūṭa demonstrate the remarkable resilience of these self-organising systems, which are delicately balanced between order and chaos.

References

Bak, Per, and Kan Chen, 1991, Self-organised Criticality, *Scientific American*, 46-54.

Bhardwaj, Surinder Mohan, 1973, *Hindu Places of Pilgrimage in India: A Study in Cultural Geography,*Berkeley, University of California Press.

Cambel, A.B., 1993, *Applied Chaos Theory: A Paradigm for Complexity*, Academic Press, Boston.

Carrasco, David, 1987, 'Myth, Cosmic Terror, and the Temple Mayor', in *The Great Temple of Tenochtitlan. Center and Periphery in the Aztec World,* pp. 124-62, Berkeley, University of California Press.

Coleman, Simon and John Elsner, 1995, *Pilgrimage: Past and Present in the World Relgions,* Cambridge, Harvard University Press.

Convey, Peter, and Roger Highfield, 1995, *The Frontiers of Complexity: The Search for Order in a Chaotic World,* New York, Faweett Columbine.

Dubey, D.P., J.M.Malville, and Rana P.B. Singh, 1996, Chitrakut: A Hindu Tirtha and its Cosmic Geometry, in *Ancient Cities and Ancient Skies: Cosmic Geometries and City Planning in India*, ed. by J.M. Malvile and L. Gujural, New Delhi, Indira Gandhi National Centre for the Arts, In Press.

Edit, R.S., 1977, Detection and Examination of Anthroposols by Phosphate Analysis, *Science* 197,1327-33.

Gell-Mann, Murray, 1994, *The Quark and the Jaguar: Adventures in the Simple and the Complex*, New York, W.H. Freeman and Co.

Gummerman, George J. and Murray Gell-Mann, 1994, *Understanding Complexity in the Prechistoric Southwest*, Reading: Addison-Wesley.

Hawking, Stephen, The Future of the Universe, *Engineering and Science* LV (1) 13-21.

Jansen M., 1991, The Concept of Space in Harappen City Planning — Mohenjo Daro, in *Concepts of Space: Ancient and Modern*, ed. by Kapila Vatsyayan, pp. 75-82, New Delhi, Indira Gandhi National Centre for the Arts.

Joshi, M.C.,1996, Application of Geometry in the Planning of an Ancient Settlement: Sisupalgarh, A Case study, in *Ancient Cities and Ancient Skies: Cosmic Geometries and City Planning in India,* ed. by J. M. Malville and L. Gujural, New Delhi, Indira Gandhi National Centre for the Arts. In Press.

Kaufmann, Stuart, 1993, *The Origins of Order: Self-organisation and Selection in Evolution*, New York, Oxford University Press.

———, 1995, *At Home in the Universe*, New York, Oxford University Press.

King, David A., 1982, Astronomical Alignments in Medieval Islamic Religious Architecture, in *Ethnoastronomy and Archaeoastronomy in the American Tropics*, ed. by A. F. Aveni and G. Urton, pp. 303-12, New York, New York Academy of Sciences.

———, 1993, Folk Astronomy in the Service of Religion: The Case for Islam, in *Astronomies and Cultures*, ed. by C. L. N. Ruggles and N. J. Saunders, pp. 124-38, Niwet, University Press of Colorado.

Lekson, Stephen, H., 1984, *Great Pueblo Architecture of Chaco Canyon*, New Mexico. Albuquerque, University of New Mexico Press.

Long, Charles H., 1963, *Alpha. The Myths of Creation,* Chico, Scholars Press.

Lorenz, E. N., 1963, Deterministic Nonperiodic Flow, *Journal of Atmospheric Sciences*, 357, 130-41.

Malville, John McKim, 1995, Cosmogony and the Elements: The Intuition of Cosmos in Science and Myth, in *Prakṛti: The Integral Vision*, Vol. 5, *Man in Nature*, ed. by Baidyanath Saraswati, pp. 17-36, New Delhi, Indira Gandhi National Centre for the Arts.

Malville, John McKim and Nancy J. Malville, 1995, *Pilgrimage and Astronomy at Chaco Canyon*, New Mexico. Paper Presented at the National Seminar on Pilgrimage, International Society for the Study of Pilgrimage, Allahabad, January 1995.

Malville, John McKim and Rana P. B. Singh, 1995, Visual Astronomy in the Mythology and Ritual of India: The Sun Temples of Varanasi, *Vistas in Astronomy*, 39,431-49.

May, R. M., 1976, Simple Mathematical Models with Very Complicated Dynamics, *Nature*, 261, 459-67.

Meyer, Jeffrey F.,1991, *The Dragons of Tiananmen: Beijing as a Sacred City*, Columbia, University of South Carolina Press.

Michell, George, 1992, City as Cosmogram: The Circular Plan of Warangal, *South Asian Studies*, 8,1-18.

Mokashi, D. B., 1987, *Palkhi, An Indian Pilgrimage*, Albany, State University of New York.

Morinis, Alan, 1992, Introduction: the Territory of the Anthropology of Pilgrimage, in *Sacred Journeys, The Anthropology of Pilgrimage*, ed. by A Morinis, pp. 1-28. Westport, Connecticut, Greenwood Press.

Nicolis, Gregoire, and Illya Prigogine, 1989, *Exploring Complexity*, New York, Freeman.

Pagels, Heinz, 1988, *The Dreams of Reason*, New York, Simon and Schuster.

Parpola, Asko, 1994, *Deciphering the Indus Script*, Cambridge, Cambridge University Press.

Possehl, Gregory L., 1990, Revolution in the Urban Revolution: the Emergence of Indus Urbanisation. *Annual Reviews of Anthropology*, 19: 261-82, Palo Alto: Annual Reviews.

Preston, James J., 1980, *Cult of the Goddess, Social and Religious Change in a Hindu Temple*, Prospect Heights, Wavelened Press.

Progogine, Illya, Gregoire Nicolis, and Agnes Babloyantz, 1972, Thermodynamics of Evolution, *Physics Today*, November, pp. 38-44.

Prigogine, Illya, 1980, *From Being to Becoming. Time and Complexity in the Physical Sciences*, New York, W.H. Freeman and Co.

Prigogine, Ilya and Isabelle Stengers, 1984, *Order Out of Chaos: Man's New Dialogue with Nature.* New York, Bantam Books.

Saraswati, B. N., 1985, Kashi Pilgrimage: the End of an Endless Journey, in *Dimensions of Pilgrimage*, ed. by M. Jha, pp. 91-104, New Delhi, Inter-India Publications.

Singh, Rana P. B., 1987, The Pilgrimage Mandala of Varanasi (Kashi), *National Geographical Journal of India*, 33:493-524.

———, 1991, Pancakroshi Yatra, Varanasi: Sacred Journey, *Ecology of Place and Faithscape*, Varanasi, Tara Book Agency.

———, 1993a, Varanasi: the Pilgrimage Mandala, Geomantic Map, and Cosmic Numbers, in *Banaras (Varanasi): Cosmic Order, Sacred City, Hindu Traditions*, ed. by Rana P. B. Singh, pp. 37-64, Varanasi, Tara Book Agency.

———, 1993b, The Sacred Geometry of India's Holy City, Varanasi. Kashi as Cosmogram, in *The Spirit and Power of Place*, ed. by Rana P. B. Singh, pp. 189-216, Varanasi, National Geographical Society of India.

———, 1994a, Time and Hindu Rituals in Varanasi: A Study of Sacrality and Cycles, in *Pilgrimage Studies: Text and Context*, ed. by L. Gopal and D.P. Dubey, pp. 67-72, Allahabad, The Society of Pilgrimage Studies.

———, 1994b, Sacred Geometry of India's Holy City, Varanasi: Kashi as Cosmogram, *National Geographical Journal of India*, 40:189-216.

———, 1995, Varanasi: Ganesh Images and Shrines in the Cityscape, in *Pilgrimage Studies*; *Sacred Places, Sacred Traditions*, ed. by D. P. Dubey, pp. 209-20, Allahabad: The Society of Pilgriamge Studies.

Singh, Rana P. B., and John McKim Malville, 1995, Cosmic Order and Cityscape of Varansi (Kashi): Sun Images and Cultural Astronomy, *National Geographical Journal of India*, 41: 69-88.

Stanley John M., 1992, The Great Maharashtrian Pilgrimage; Pandharpur and Alandi in *Sacred Journeys. The Anthropology of Pilgrimage*, ed. by A. Morinis, pp. 65-86. Westport, Connecticut, Greenwood Press.

Tainter, Joseph A. and Bonnie Bagley Tainter, 1996, *Evolving Complexity and Environmental Risk in the Prehistoric Southwest*, Reading: Addison-Wesley.

Tan Chung, 1996, Social and Political Order in Chinese Tradition and Future Development, in *Cosmic Order and Chaos*, ed. by M. Khanna, New Delhi, Indira Gandhi National Centre for the Arts. In this volume.

Tilley, Christopher, 1994, *A Phenomenology of Landscape*: *Places, Paths, and Monuments*, Oxford Berg Publishers.

Turner, V. 1969, *The Ritual Process: Structure and Anti-Structure*, Chicago, Aldine Publishing Company.

Turner, V. and E. Turner, 1978, *Image and Pilgrimage in Christian Culture Anthropological Perspectives*, New York, Columbia University Press.

Wheatly, Paul, 1971, *The Pivot of the Four Quarters*: *A Chinese City*, Chicago, Aldine Publishing

16

Order and Plenitude

Creativity and Aesthetic Experience

Kamlesh Dutta Tripathi

BHARATA equates *nāṭya* with *yajña*. Dramatic presentation is a sacrifice in the sense that it is a *kriyā* or creative activity and thus, it may be explained satisfactorily in terms of primal creative act. The performer is initiated into the role of First Creator and the act performed by him is rooted into the 'fullness', i.e., *rasa*-experience of the poet-playwright. The aesthetic meaning or the poetic meaning (*kāvyārtha*) enshrined in the dramatic text is germinally present in the heart of the poet-dramatist, which finds its manifestation in the dramatic text and the same is communicated to the spectator through performance and performer. This creative activity may be visualised as the act of first creation. The primordial act of creation has been viewed as a divine sacrifice in the Vedas.[1]

Thus, cosmic creation is a unity of the divine act and sacrifice performed at the human plane is the re-enactment of the same in order to sublimate the fragmented action of the limited self in this world of dichotomy and pluralism.

The unity of macrocosm and microcosm is a principle shared by Vedic as well as Āgamic traditions. Hence, aesthetic creativity at the microcosmic level is essentially similar with the macrocosmic creative act. It is, therefore, not surprising that theatre which has been identified with *yajña*, is a means of rediscovering and realising the sublimation of the action at aesthetic level and, therefore, it may be viewed in terms of wholeness of the cosmic sacrificial act.

The dramatic text is the very basis of theatrical performance and it has been explained in terms of a series as well as unity of action which ultimately transcends the sequentiality. Therefore, the inner structure of the dramatic text has been viewed as the stages of action (*kāryāvasthā*) on one hand and the *artha-prakṛti* (means of

---

1. *Vedic Experience*, Raimondo Panikar, pp. 348-9, Motilal Banarsidass, Delhi, 1977.

realising the goal) on the other, which demonstrates ultimate unity of action even at the level of ordinary life and its portrayal in theatre.[2]

The ordered manifestation of the 'full' as multiplicity leads ultimately towards the same unity and 'plenitude'. Upaniṣads declare:

> In the beginning it was 'fullness', and from this 'fullness' everything came, that is, became, and to it everything will return.[3]

The *pūrṇatā* or 'plenitude' and *ṛta* or cosmic, sacrificial and moral order — the twin Vedic concepts form the ideational foundation of the entire Indian Aesthetics.

Āgmas/Tantras share and develop this notion of *kriyā*, as transcending the triad of the will, knowledge and action ascending to the complete harmony of 'Śiva' and

---

2. The very structure of the plot (*itivṛtta*) in Sanskrit Drama has been visualised in terms of an act, i.e., that of the hero and its fruition. It has five stages — *prārambha* (beginning), *yatna* (the strivings), *prāptāśā* (the hope of attaining the result), *niyatāpti* (certainty of achieving the result), and finally *phalaprāpti* (the attainment of the result). The fourth stage has been alternatively explained as some hindrance or restrain in attaining the goal and then ultimately attaining it. The concept of *arthaparkṛti* (lit. the nature of the means of attaining the desired result) viewed in terms of the means of realising the goal and *anusandhāna* or 'reflection' over course of action is also quite in consonance with the concept of *nāṭya* as an act.

   Abhinavabhāratī explains: *arthaprakṛti* entitled *bindu*, in terms of reflection over continuing course of action, which is presented in drama and which leads to the fruition (*Abhinavabhāratī*, N.S., IXX, 23, Baroda, edn.).

   Thus, *nāṭya* as a poetic/dramatic text as well as a perfoprmance has been viewed in terms of *kriyā*, i.e., creative activity. In fact, *nāṭya* is a symbol for all creative activity in the realm of arts. All actions portrayed in the plot, the body of the play, are germinally and creatively present in the heart of the poet/playwright and blossom into the dramatic action and *bhāva* and *rasa* evoked through them.

   Just as a tree grows from a seed and from the tree comes flowers, and from flowers fruit, so also *rasa*s are root, and from them are all *bhāva*s derived.
   — *Nāṭya-śāstra*, VI.3,8, Pune, 1989

   This is further emphasised by Bhaṭṭanāyaka in his *Hṛdayadarpaṇa*.
   The poet does not regurgitate *rasa* until he is completely filled with it.
   — *Locana*, *Dhvanyāloka*, I.5

   And this is the reason why Bhaṭṭa Tauta, the celebrated teacher of Abhinavaguptapādācārya, quite in tune with Bharata, identifies *nāṭya* with *rasa* on one hand and Veda on the other:

   Rasa consists of aesthetic pleasure, and *rasa* alone is drama, and drama alone is the Veda. — *Locana*, *Dhvanyāloka*, p. 336, Benaras, 1940

3. पूर्णमिदं पूर्णमदः पूर्णात पूर्णमुदच्यते।
   पूर्णस्य पूर्णमादाय पूर्णमेवावशिष्यते।।
   — *बृहदारण्यकोपनिषत्*, 5.1.1

   — Tr. *Vedic Experience*, pp. 347-8

'Śakti' or the 'supreme consciousness' and His first 'Vibration' as 'self-consciousness' and 'freedom'. They declare, there is no consciousness without 'self-consciousness' or the 'awareness of the 'self'. Kṣemarāja, the great disciple of celebrated Abhinavaguptapādācārya, declares in his *Spandasaṁdoha*:

> The Supreme Lord is both — the pure (*vimala*) great light (*mahāprakāśa*) (of the Universal Consciousness) and perfect power of self-awareness (*parāmarśa-śakti*). His power of self-awareness is one (although it appears as *unmeṣa* as well as *nimeṣa*). Proclaimed in Āgamic scriptures by means of countless names, it is vibration (*spanda*) as the subtle motion (*kiñcit-calattā-rūpa*); Radiance (*sphurattā*); wave (*ūrmi*); strength (*bala*); spontaneous emergence (of the Supreme 'I'-consciousness) (*udyoga*); the heart (*hṛdaya*); the essence (*sāra*); the power of letters (alphabet which holds within itself, entire universe and in which letters are arranged in a different order, i.e., from *na* to *pha*) (*mālinī*) and the Supreme Power (*parā*).[4]

Thus, Vedas speak in terms of sacrifice explaining it through the principle of cosmic order and dynamism and Āgmas speak in terms of universal and supreme 'I'-ness or *parāhantā*. The cosmic energy has been viewed as *ṛta* in the Veda and the potentiality (*śakti*) of the 'self' has been seen as *vimarśa* or the 'self-awareness' in the Āgamas. *Ṛta* is the 'cosmic order' as well as the 'sacrificial order'. Its correspondence with the Āgamic concept of *śakti* reveals the truth that *ṛta* is the dynamic cosmic power.

> It is the primordial dynamism, that is inherent in everything and also possesses its own inherent essence, a unifying force that could be said to be very soul of sacrifice.[5]

This explains why *ṛta* in the Vedas appears as superior to and independent of the gods, yet at the same time they preserve and protect it. Gods protect *ṛta* as well as they abide by it.

Ṛta and *satya* are born of the *tapas* of the Supreme and they are identical, mutually dependent and complementary to each other, so much so that one cannot operate without the other. *Śatapatha* (6.4, 4.10) and *Taittirīya Brāhmaṇas* (6.7.7.4) emphasise the complete identity of both:

---

4. इह परमेश्वरस्य महाप्रकाशात्मतो विमलस्यापि एकैव परामर्शशक्तिः किञ्चित्त्चलत्ता भासरूपतया स्पन्दः इति, स्फुरत्ता इति, ऊर्मिः इति, बलम् इति, उद्योगः इति, हृदयम् इति, सारम् इति, मालिनी इति परा इत्याद्यनन्तसञ्ज्ञाभिः आगमेषु उदद्योष्यते।
— *स्पन्दसन्दोहः* p. 5, K.S.T.S, Bombay, 1917

5. *Vedic Experience*, pp. 349-50.

ṛtam satyam, satyam ṛtam
and
ṛtam satye dhāyi । *satyam ṛtam ṛte dhāyi* ॥

Ṛta (righteousness) and *vrata* (law) are also practically synonymous terms. Ādityas in general and Varuṇa and Mitra, who belong to the class of Ādityas — in particular, are connected with *ṛta*. Agni, Soma and Dyāvā-Pṛthivī are also the protectors of *ṛta*.[6]

It may be pointed out that the concept of *ṛta* includes the principle of harmony. Complimentarity presupposes harmony. Hence, at social level, *ṛta* gives rise to the notion of ultimately harmonious a society, its hierarchical nature is just a secondary aspect.

In the realm of arts, this concept results into the principle of 'movements' and 'rest' and ultimate harmony of the two. The concepts of *ṛta* and *satya* blossom into a seemingly paradoxical position. The two opposite notions of 'motion' and 'stillness' are simultaneously present in the concept of *ṛta*. Notion of motion is reflected in the process of creation and emergence of finite time as *saṁvatsara*, *ṛtu*, *māsa* and *ahorātra*, etc. The concepts of *rātri* (night), *samudra-āraṇya* of the cosmic waters reflect the underlying stillness and unity.

All differentiation takes place in time and space. Time is the first manifestation of the power of differentiation or diversity. The sun and moon not only manifest the time, they also reflect the state of plurality.

Ṛtu (season), variously viewed as 3, 4, 6, and 7 in number, as the division of *saṁvatsara*, is a fixed time for the respective sacrificial acts and again it is the notion reflected in the succession of seasons. This motion aspect has been beautifully rendered in the metaphor of *saṁvatsara* as a bird:

tasya saṁvatsaram mukham, grīṣmaśca varṣā ca pakṣau hemantaśca puccham । — *Tāṇḍya Brāhmaṇa*, 2.25.2[7]

The notion of 'order', 'motion', and 'stillness' inherent in the concept of *ṛta* are the foundation of Indian moral-ethical and aesthetical thought.

Transgression of *ṛta* is a sin, for it amounts to turning one's back to the plenitude (*pūrṇatā*). To be intent towards the plenitude is the righteousness. It generates

6. *Vedic Experience*, Prof. K. Chattopadhyaya, pp. 49-50. Centre of Advanced Studies of Philosophy, Benaras Hindu University.

7. Comp.

वसन्तःशिरो ग्रीष्मो दक्षिणपक्षः वर्षा पुच्छं
शरदुत्तरपक्षः हेमन्तो मध्यम्
— *तैत्तिरीयब्राह्मणम्* — 30.10.41

merit which enables one to realise the plenitude, the *amarattva* or immortality and *jyoti* or light, whereas turning one's back to *virāṭ* or the macrocosm and *pūrṇa* or the 'full' is a sin. The more one is inclined towards the narrow goals of the pluralistic world and is forgetful of *samaṣṭi* (totality, collectivity), the more sinful he is. This forgetfulness towards *samaṣṭi* and being engrossed with the narrow individualism, causes 'attachment' (*rāga*) and hatred (*dveṣa*), the root of all sinfulness. Therefore, the realisation of the 'fullness' is the highest spiritual goal. The invocation of 'Varuṇa' is a testimony to this awareness of totality, infinity and plenitude.

> The beautiful name of what God, among the immortals, shall I praise.
> Who will again hand me over to Aditi (literally — boundlessness), so that I may see my Father and Mother.[8]

The child of 'boundlessness' invokes Varuṇa for realising the same 'boundlessness'.

The fetters are many: the highest, the middle and the lowest and the condition for realising the 'boundlessness' consists in following the 'law':

> O Varuṇa. loosen from us the highest, the middle and the lowest fetters.
> O Āditya, we shall then, following thy law, become sinless before Aditi.[9]

---

8. कस्य॑ नू॒नं क॑त॒मस्या॒मृता॑नां॒ मता॑महे॒ चारु॑ दे॒वस्य॒ नाम॑।
को नो॑ म॒ह्या अदि॑तये॒ पुन॑र्दात् पि॒तरं॑ च दृ॒शेयं॑ मा॒तरं॑ च।।
— *ऋग्वेदसंहिता*, 1.2.4.1

Translation, Prof. K. Chattopadhyaya, *ibid.*, 5.52.

9. उदु॑त्त॒मं व॑रुण॒ पाश॑म॒स्मद् अवा॑ध॒मं वि म॑ध्य॒मश्रे॑याथ।
अथा॑ व॒यमा॑दित्य व्र॒ते तद् अ नागसो॒ अदि॑तये स्याम।।"
— *ऋग्वेदसंहिता*, 1.24.15; Tr. *ibid.*, p. 53.

Varuṇa can punish the wrong-doers and can pardon those who are penitent or confess their guilt. Varuṇa and Mitra or Varuṇa pardons the trangression in the rituals. For *prāyaścitta* or 'expiation of faults', the expiatory ceremonies are performed. *Tāṇḍya* and *Taittirīya Brāhmaṇas* describe these ceremonies meant for the expiation of such transgressions taking place in *daśarātra* and *agnihotra* ceremonies respectively. In the *avabhṛta* ceremony of the *agniṣṭoma* also such 'expiatory acts' are prescribed. Varuṇa is the deity mentioned there. It may be emphasised here that *prāyaścitta* is required here for the fact that lapses and transgression is act, cause lack of 'fullness'.

The emphasis over the Order and the prescribed way in a sacrificial performance has been interpreted by Martin Haug in terms of a mechanical act. Sacrifice has been conceived by him "to be a kind of machinery in which every piece must tally with the other". The point raised by Haug may be elaborated a little. Slightest discrepancy in the performance of even a minute ritualistic details may spoil the whole sacrifice. But if the sacrifice is duly performed down to the minutest detail, there was no power which could arrest or delay the fruition. It is true that there is an emphasis over the strict observance of the injunctions, but it may be viewed otherwise. Sacrifice is the 'fullness' of the action. It is

→

Thus, the Vedic notion of morality is deeply rooted in one's awareness of plenitude, integral reality and order. Dr. Radhakrishnan has rightly observed that if ethical thought is profound, it will give a cosmic motive to morality.[10]

The earnest desire of being 'one' and 'full' cosmically, reflected in Vedic path of *karman*, assumes another dimension in the Upaniṣadic path of *jñāna* and Āgamic path of 'submersion' and 'resting' in the 'self'. Although the dualistic and even the materialistic schools of Indian philosophy have their own aesthetic theories, which is evident in some of the interpretations of *rasasūtra* and in the aesthetic theories of *rīti* and *alaṁkāra*, yet the *dhvanivādin*s from Ānandavardhana to Mammaṭa through Abhinavaguptapādācārya on one hand and Rūpagosvāmin/Jīvagosvāmin, Madhusūdana Sarasvatī and Paṇḍitarāja Jagannātha on the other, develop the aesthetic theories on the sound foundation of the Āgamas and Vedānta. The *rīti* school expounded by Udbhaṭa and others has been equated with the materialism or *jaḍavāda* of Cārvākas by Ānandavardhana and Vidyānātha,[11] for, it fails to see the soul of poetry and confines to the body of the poetry only. An old commentary of Cakradhara on *Nyāyamañjarī* identifies fragments referred anonymously in the text as quoted from certain Udbhaṭa's commentary on the aphorism of Bṛhaspati, the exponent of materialist school of philosophy.[12] This Udbhaṭa may be identical with the Udbhaṭa, the exponent of *rīti*.

The *alaṁkāra* and *vakrokti* schools, although viewed as confining to the dualism of the embellishment and that which is embellished, yet may be seen in a wider

---

→ precisely the purification of our fragmentary ordinary action and the sublimation of our action has been taught for the realisation of the 'plenitude' through the path of *karman*. Thus, the bedrock of the entire Vedic moral and ethical thought consists in being aware of the cosmic unity and 'plenitude' and forgetting 'plenitude' is the source of sin.

The entire question if 'sin' and *hīna karman* (deficient act) or *karmalopa* (loss of some prescribed part of the ritual) may be viewed as an obstruction in realising the wholeness of the act. The 'sin' may be an impediment created wilfully, whereas *karmalopa* or *hīna karman* is generally committed unintentionally. Therefore, *prāyaścitta*s have been prescribed for the lapses.

In the realm of arts and aesthetics, the obstruction comes from the side of our total involvement in differentiation, pluralistic approach, and, therefore, total forgetfulness towards our own unfragmented Self. This is the prime source of obstacle in the relishing of *rasa*. The power of art may be seen in its capability of removal of these obstacles.

In the creative process, deficiency of creative act lies in the occurrence of blemishes of *doṣa*. Hence, there is the emphasis over removal of *doṣa*s, they are seen as the obstacles in attaining the perfection.

10. *Eastern Religion and Western Throught*, p. 82.

11. *Dhvanyāloka-Locana*, p. 44, Varanasi, 1965, Ekāvali, Vidyānātha, 1/3 and Taralā, p. 21, Hyderabad, 1981.

12. *Nyāyamañjarī*, p. 100, ed. Gaurīnātha Śāstri and Cakradhara thereon, Varanasi, 1982.

perspective from the angle of creative process. The act of embellishing may be viewed as a process offering the perfection and the fullness to that which is being embellished, the term, *alam* in the sense of *paryāpti* or 'sufficiency' indicates the same direction. One of the meaning of the term *ṛta* in the expression of *ṛtapeśas* or 'having a perfect shape' (*Ṛgveda Saṁhitā* I.66.1) is 'perfection'. This notion of *ṛta* might have been viewed as instrumental to the concepts of *alaṁkāra* and *vakratā*.[13]

But, the philosophy of Śaivite Advaita, which flourished in Kashmir, explains the riddle of the world satisfactorily and offers a pervasive theory of aesthetics based on the notions of cosmic unity of *ṛta* and the realisation of the 'plenitude' enunciated in the Upaniṣads and the Āgamas. The *Svāntantryavāda* of Kashmir Śaivas successfully unfolds the principles germinally present in the *Nāṭya-śāstra* of Bharata.

The notion of *vāk* or speech as 'consciousness' found in the Vedas and the philosophy of the speech developed by the grammarians, blossoms into the aesthetic theory of *dhvani*. Resonance, the attribute of sound, when extended from sound to the area of semantics, offers an enchanting theory of aesthetics.[14] The causal-theory

---

13. Prof. Reva Prasad Dwivedi has developed this notion of *alaṁkāra* in his work entitled — *Alaṁkārakārikā*, pp. 52-80, Chaukhamba Surbhārati Studies-1, Varanasi, 1977.

14. The aesthetic theory of *vyañjanā* is based on the assumption that a single sentence, or a single word or even a part of a word may evoke or reveal an entire universe of meaning which is different from the denotational and connotational (related to denotational) meaning. The process of revelation of the meaning suggested by the denotational and connotational word and meaning is much, like the illumination of an object by the lamp. It is the manifestation of an already existing but unmanifest object. Thus, it is a process of evoking the unmanifest implicit level of meanings and thereby, ultimately revealing the supreme meaning, i.e., the plenitude of the Self.

    There is a unity of experience from poet/artist to aesthete through the poetic text/piece of art. This is the reason why *dhvanivādins* emphasis the autonomy of the poet/artist and the piece of art.

    The freedom of poet enables him to create the laws for his own creation.

    The comparison and contrast of the poet with the creator shows the Vedic background of this notion of poet as the Creator.

    Delineation of the *vibhāva*, *anubhāva*, etc., (*vibhāvādi-pratipādana*) is the distinctive feature of Sanskrit theatre tradition. The principle is applicable to the all forms of *kāvya* and, to certain extent, all the other art-forms. Principle of delineation has given rise to theory of 'glorious retelling' of the *bhāva*, instead of 'reproduction' of things or events.

    The *rañjana* or the power of instant pleasant appeal present in theatre, poetry and in all the forms of art, brings about the removal of the obstacles created by subjectivity and multiplicity and prepares the aesthete for *rasa*-experience.

    The purification and transformation of the objects of life when the same are presented in art, as well as the purification of sense-organs, as well as that of internal faculty →

of *satkāryavāda* and its corollary, the process of manifestation or the *abhivyañjana* or *prakāśana*, gives rise to the theory of *dhvani* or *vyañjanā* and the concept of *rasa* as the state of 'submersion' or 'absorption' into the 'plenitude' and the manifestation of the true nature of the 'self', Śiva as pure unity and the *sāmrasya* of *prakāśa* and *vimarśa*, the freedom of Śiva, the immanence as well transcendence of Śiva and the world as His play, lay the foundation of the philosophy of aesthetics enunciated by the exponents of *dhvanivādin*s in general and Abhinavagupta in particular.

The notion of aesthetic experience transcending the temporal and relational reality is very much present in the *Nāṭya-śāstra* itself. Prof. Vidya Nivasa Mishra beautifully elaborates this point:

> Bharata in his *Nāṭya-śāstra* propounded the theory of *rasa* under a compulsion or imitation of life as perceived in a definite time and space. For him, the suchness of life was to be conceived first, then the enactment had to follow suit. . . . Both the actor and the spectator are to prepare themselves for a new experience, experience of suchness of life. *Rasa* or this experience is not a 'thing in itself', formed prior to the act of consciousness by which it is perceived, but it is the consciousness itself (therefore, the perception) which freed from all practical desires, becomes *rasa* or an aesthetic expression.[15]

Thus, transcending the temporal and spatial existence and realising the unsegmented and 'fuller being' is the nature of aesthetic experience. The universe of art and the inner aesthetic experience cannot be defined in terms of mundane reality. Only in this sense art-creation and the aesthetic-experience is something like uncommon

→ which grasps them, the process of the depersonalisation and universalisation in order to fill the emptiness occurring in our life with the object of arts which are relatively free from such deficiencies as *arjana* (acquiring), *rakṣaṇa* (preserving, protecting), and *kṣaya* (perishability), etc., form the cardinal principles of Indian aesthetics. The process of purifying the sense-organs and the inner faculties in order to meditate and realise the *samādhi* in Yoga may be compared with the aesthetic process. Universalisation enables one to transcend the relational reality of time and space. Finally, the rise of *sattva* culminates into the 'submersion' and 'rest' into the consciousness, i.e., *prakāśānandamaya-nira-saṁvid-viśrānti*. This view of the art-creativity and the aesthetic experience as emerging from the dynamic 'plenitude' of the poet and the artist and leading the aesthete back to that fullness is the crown-jewel of the Indian Aesthetics.

15. The Aesthetic experience of *bhakti-rasa* — An Article in *Follow the Notes of Flute*, p. 35, Sahitya Akademi, New Delhi, 1987.

and supersensuous.[16] Otherwise, it is as close to us as other experiences of life. In fact, art-experience is an intermediary experience between worldly and spiritual ones and shows the possibility of realising the transcendental spiritual experience.

The emphasis on ecstasy in Indian thought does not tend to world and life negation as argued by some scholars, on the contrary, it offers an opportunity of better and fuller experience of the world and life.

Such a theory of creativity and aesthetic experience was made possible by the emergence of notions of *ṛta* and *pūrṇa* in the Vedas and the notion of *Śiva-śakti-sāmarasya* or the harmony of *Śiva* (consciousness) and *Śakti* (his potentiality as self-consciousness) in Śaivite Āgamas. In fact, *sāmarasya* is another term expressing the same notion of the dynamic 'plenitude'. All creativity as an activity is the free manifestation of the 'plenitude' and this activity is an ordered one. 'Chaos' arises from losing sight of that 'plenitude' and 'order'. Manifestation of multiplicity with the awareness of 'plenitude' and 'order' is the *krīḍā* or *līlā* (play) enunciated in Āgamas and Purāṇas, whereas forgetting the 'plenitude' and the 'order' is an impurity and sin, hence the fetters. This may be emphasised here that the adherence to and awareness of 'order' does not mean accepting the *status quo* 'and rejecting the idea of change and novelty. In fact, this awareness of plenitude renders all changes as new and beautiful.

In fact, awareness of and adherence to the 'cosmic order' (*ṛta*) is staying in *dharma* and forgetting it results remaining in *adharma*. Dissolution (*saṁhāra*) is going back to same unity, if it is realised through the conscious process. It is a spiritual (yogic) process leading to the realisation of the tranquillity of 'plenitude'. But for them, who are foregetful of their essential nature of 'plenitude' and 'freedom', this 'dissolution' happens as the inevitable process of nature and, therefore, they remain fettered.

In the realm of art also, aesthetic experience is the realisation of the same 'plenitude' as *rasa*. Although the process of *rasa* realisation is different from that of *yoga* or *upāsanā* (worship, religious meditation), yet the similarity between the spiritual and aesthetic ways of realisation of the state of 'plenitude' cannot be overlooked.

Thus, the concept of *ṛta* and *pūrṇatā* are not confined to Indian metaphysics, spirituality and moral law, but they equally permeate the traditional Indian aesthetics. We need not deny this fact in quest of assigning full autonomy to Indian Aesthetics and trying to free it from Indian metaphysics and epistemology.

16. *From Sensuous to Supersensuous* — K.D. Tripathi, *Prakṛti*, Vol. 3, Indira Gandhi National Centre for the Arts, New Delhi, 1995. Also see *Indian Arts: Background and Principles* — Dr. Kapila Vatsyayana, in *Rūpa Pratirūpa*, ed. Dr. Bettina Baumer, Biblia Impex Pvt. Ltd., New Delhi, 1982.

17

Reflection of Cosmic Order in Buddhist Stūpa

M.C. Joshi

OF pre-Buddhist origin, a *stūpa* as a structure was highly venerated and worshipped by the Buddhists in India especially during early phases of the history of Buddhism. According to ancient tradition, its other synonyms are *caitya* and *dhātugarbha* in Sanskrit or *dagobā* in Sinhalese which is pronounced as *pagoḍā* in Burmese. In literal terms, a *stūpa* denotes a made-up heap of earth or of any other material to serve a specific purpose. In the *Ṛgveda*, a collection of flames of fire has been styled as *stūpa* (VII.2.11).[1]

It seems that the *stūpa* originated in the form of a platform or alter (*citi*) or a tumulus piled at site of a funeral pyre (*citā*) as some kind of burial or memorial generally with a tree or a wooden post planted in its centre, and on this account it was also called a *caitya*, the tree on it as *caitya-vṛkṣa* and the post as *caitya-yūpa*. The *Śatapatha Brāhmaṇa* preserves a reference to circular (*pari-maṇḍala*) and quadrangular (*catussrakti*) *caityas*[2] which were perhaps being raised traditionally as the memorials for departed personages of significant status. The same text also mentions that the circular variety of the *caityas* was popular with the easterners (*prācyas*) or the people of eastern India. Regarding the tradition of non-Buddisht *stūpa*, an interesting evidence could be seen in a Sāñcī relief depicting *jaṭila* ascetics engaged in fire-sacrifices with *stūpas* (without any crowning member) in the background suggesting their connexion with Jaṭila cult of Brāhmaṇical origin.[3]

The term *dhātugarbha* refers to a construction serving as a respository of *dhātus śarīra*, i.e., corporeal relics of a person. The ancient practice of erecting the *caityas* for the dead is also confirmed by a statement attributed to Buddha following an enquiry by Ānanda, his favourite disciple, in connexion with the disposal of his own

---

1. Vasudevasharan Agrawala, *Bhārtiyakalā* (in Hindi), Prithvi Prakashan, Varanasi 1966, p. 132.
2. Vasudevasharan Agrawala, *ibid.*, p. 136.
3. Debala Mitra, *Sanchi,* Seventh Edition, New Delhi, Archaeological Survey of India, 2001, fig. 2, East-gate, rear face, north side of southern pillar, p. 22.

body after his passing away as indicated in *Mahāparinibbāna sutta*.[4] According to this reference, Buddha told Ānanda that following the cremation of his body a *stūpa* should be constructed on his mortal remains at the meeting points of four roads (*catuṣpatha*) in the same manner in which the *cakravartin*s or the great rulers of yore had been honoured by raising memorial *stūpa*s (*catummahāpathe rāño cakkavattissa thupaṁ karonti*). After his *parinirvāṇa* (decease), Buddha's bodily relics were divided amongst eight claimants, all of whom are stated to have erected *stūpa*s over their share of relics in their respective localities, according to Pāli texts, in the honour of Buddha. The available archaeological evidence suggests that the archaic Buddhist *stūpa*s, which were made of solidified earth, had a circular plan, possibly with a peaked or hemispherical elevation but other details about them have not been clearly ascertained.

Keeping in view the antiquity of Buddhist *stūpa* we may like to refer to one of the epigraphs of emperor Aśoka which mentions that during his fourteenth regional year he doubled (enlarged) the *stūpa* of Kanakamuni, the fifth human (*mānuṣī*) Buddha[5] before Śākyamuni, the seventh one in the line. According to northern Buddhist tradition, Aśoka is said to have constructed 84,000 *stūpa*s over the fragments of the *dhātu*s of Buddha after recovering a portion thereof from the earlier *stūpa*s, redistributing and re-enshrining them in newly built *stūpa*s, at various important sites within his kingdom. The tradition seems to be somewhat hyperbolic in contents but not totally devoid of truth. There is archaeological evidence to show that the *stūpa*s built by Aśoka on Buddha's relics were styled as Dharmarājika *stūpa*s because they contained within them the mortal remains of Dharmarāja (Buddha). Such *dhātu*s were perhaps considered to be ever alive as indicated in an inscribed record on a relic casket from Shinkot (Pakistan)[6] reading in the context of despositing Buddha's remains (in a *stūpa*) as *pratithavita pranansamedam śarīra bhagavata sakamunisa* (*partisthapitam praname-tam śarīram bhagavataḥ śākyamuneḥ...*), i.e., installed (in the *stūpa*) living corporeal remains of Buddha Śākyamuni.

The idea to preserve the mortal remains of a person fully or partially in a structural memorial was, most likely, based on the age-old concept of sympathetic magic conditioned by the belief of inseparability of connections between an organism and its constituents[7], even after the former had become lifeless or detached from its

4. Rahul Sankrityayana, *Buddhacaryā*, Benaras (Varanasi), Mahabodhi Society 1952 p. 502.
5. Dines Chandra Sircar, *Select Inscriptions*, second edition, Calcutta, University of Calcutta 1965, pp. 102-06.
6. *Ibid.*, pp. 103-05.
7. M.C. Joshi, 'From Symbolic Pillar to Preaching Buddha' in *Roop-Lekha*, LXIV-LXVI, March 1997, New Delhi, p. 67.

original position. The bodily relics of Buddha and his living personality thus had an inseparable relation with each other, suggesting that every bit of his bone represented the Buddha through the *stupa* raised on his remains. Aśoka's attempts to establish more *stūpa*s with fragments of Buddha's original *dhātu*s seem to have been solely guided by the belief that every Buddhist intending to worship the *stūpa* in his locality must feel the living presence of the Master therein.

On the basis of the available archaeological evidence, what appears to be probable that Aśoka or his contemporaries gave a formalised shape to the archaic and traditional form of the Buddhist *stūpa* by providing it a circular stone or brick-lined base (with solid superstructure), sourrounded by a railed circumambulatory at the ground level and *hārmikā* and *yaṣṭi* (central pole) with one *chatra* or more *chatra*s, at the top. In the post-Mauryan period and later, the *stūpa* architecture underwent further development with some of the conspicuous elements in the form of four gates, double balustrades, flights of steps, etc. In *stūpa*s of Andhra, a charming feature of the structure was groups of *āyaka* pillars facing the cardinal points. The important *stūpa*s, particularly the *mahā-stūpa* or *mahā-caitya*s, were enriched with varied kind of sculpted decoration on railings, gates and elsewhere. What is to be noted in regard to the elevation of the *stūpa*s is that their solid structure from first century BC, onwards with *medhi* (basal terrace) was built on in many cases on a wheel-shaped plan. From around sixth century AD onwards, remains of quadrangular multi-terraced *stūpa*s are also available and subsequently this form travelled to Nepal and Southeast Asia also with several elevational modifications, their basic source being Indianized ziggurat called *Jerūka* or *eḍūka*, often equated in Indian tradition with Sumeru.[8]

As we have already indicated, the *stūpa* was basically devised as a circle which was turned in some cases into a *svastika*, as examplified by *mahā-caitya*s of Bhārhūt and Sāñcī, with the addition of four gates (*toraṇa*s) each attached to a railed passage leading to ciruclar processional path.

Associating the term with Vedic traditions, Agrawala calls it *dik-svastika*[9] and suggests its symbolic relationship with the element of the creation of the universe. It also symbolises the *prāṇa-śakti* or solar energy and motion in an established order. The idea is also supported by circular simple brick-lined ring and wheel-shaped plan of the *stūpa* which also had conceptual links with Vedic tradition in the opinion of Kapila Vatsyayan. In fact, both types of plans bear a similarity with

8. Paul Mus, *Barobudur* (English translation), 'Foreword' by M.C. Joshi, IGNCA, New Delhi, 1999, pp. ii-v.

9. Agrawala, *op. cit.*, pp. 133, 150, 158-59.

Vedic *ratha-cakra*[10] *citi* used in *kāmeṣṭi* sacrifices. According to *Sāṅkhyāyana Brāhmaṇa*, the Calendar year is visualised as a divine-wheel (*devacakra*) and identified with immortality. Another notable feature, the *yaṣṭi* in centre of *stūpa* also shows close links with Vedic concept of *skambha* and *yūpa* with *catrāvalī* representing the Supreme Being the upholder of the order reminding us of the Buddha, the sustainer of the *dharma*, his capacity as the mover of the dormant Wheel of Law.

We may recall that in the *Atharvaveda*, *skambha* is regarded as suppoprt of all existence as a cosmic post (X.7.44 and X.1.93) and *Bṛhadāraṇyaka Upaniṣad* equates life principle with it.

The ideal of *skambha*, which is referred to as *agikhanda*, i.e., *agni-skambha*, i.e., a column of light[11] as a cosmic representation of Buddha was also utilised by Aśoka in the dramatic performances organised by him to propagate *dharma* as mentioned in his major Rock Edict IV. The actual inscribed lines read:

> '. . . *aja devānaṁpiyasa piyadasino rāño dhamācaraṇena bherighoso aho dhamaghoso' vimāna dasana ca hasti-dasaṇā ca agi-khaṁdāni ca añani divyāni ca rupāni dasayiptā* . . .'
>
> 'On account of the presentation of visuals illustrating dramatically celestial mansion/car, divine elephant, and flaming-column and other celestial forms, the sound of the announcer's drum (indicating the holding of the performances), turned into the sound of *dharma* due to the righteousness practised by Priyadarśin, the Beloved of the gods (Aśoka).'

Perhaps all the three dramatic visuals represented the life of the Master, viz., *vimāna-darśana*, illustrating his presence in the heaven before his birth, *hasti-darśana*, expressing his concept, and *agni-skambha*, manifesting his enlightened body. Thus, the column of light or fire in these shows organised by Aśoka represented him within the established norms of Theravāda Buddhism, symbolically. This inference is well-supported by the flaming pillar motif used in the Amarāvatī reliefs. The highly polished Aśokan pillar at Sārnāth originally with a crowning *cakra*, most probably was installed at the site of the First Sermon (*fig*.17.1), as a symbolic representation of Buddha, utilising the traditional concept of *skambha*, preaching the law.

---

10. Remains of a few *ratha-cakra cities* have been exposed by DR. R.S. Bisht of the Archaeological Survey of India at Dholavira (Gujarat), the famous Harrappan settlement outside the habitation in probably funerary context.
11. M.C. Joshi, *op. cit.,* pp. 65-66.

Fig. 17.1: Sarnath, Lion-Captal of Asoka in original form — symbolic representation of Buddha

The use of term, *yaṣṭi*, in context of *stūpa* as the evidence of Buddha's symbolic representation can be inferred from an early inscritpion on one of the rails of Sāñcī (*stūpa* 1) recording *bhagavato pamana-lathi* perhaps is intended to indicate the rod or the post as the representation of the Lord (Buddha). The *yaṣṭi*, thus, in the *stūpa* represented the Supreme-Enlightned Being under his name Lokanātha or Lokajit who presided over the *loka*s of the *deva*s, *manuṣya*s and *pitṛn*s. The association of *stūpa*s with *pitṛn*s is also suggested by the Shinkot Casket epigraphs which make a statement that no periodical offering of *śrāddha*, water and *piṇḍa* to ancestors could be made to the *stūpa* containing the relics when it was in a state of neglect.

The variety of reliefs on the important *stūpa*s (*mahā-caitya*s) at Bhārhūt, Sāñcī, Amarāvatī, Mathurā, etc., particularly on the rails, *toraṇa*s, and other structural members also confirms the conceptual presentation of different *lokadhātu*s and associated elements. It is on this account that the sculptural depictions cover the life of Buddha, his previous births, i.e., *Jātaka* tales, representations of earlier human Buddhas and in some cases also the future Buddha (Maitreya), scores of divinities including Lakṣmī, the Mahārājika Lokapālas, Celestial Beings, *kumbhanāda*s, *yakṣa*s, *yakṣī*s, etc., besides sight of heavens, illustrations of *kalpalatā* and other sacred motifs, symbols, etc., executed on the *mahāstūpa*s can be treated a kind of archaic Buddhist cosmography. Our speculation is further supported by Svastika-shaped circular plans as *mahāstūpa*s at Bharhut and Sāñcī suggesting solar symbolism of the structures. The great *stūpa* at Amarāvatī (*mahācaitya*) with four gates each facing a cardinal direction also indicates the same idea i.e., the cosmic form of Buddha represented by concept of time in the terms of present, past and future. Similarly according to Agrawala, *stupa*s like that of Sāñcī also embodied in it the idea of three worlds as a part of the Dharmakāya of Buddha (*figs.* 17.2 & 17.3).

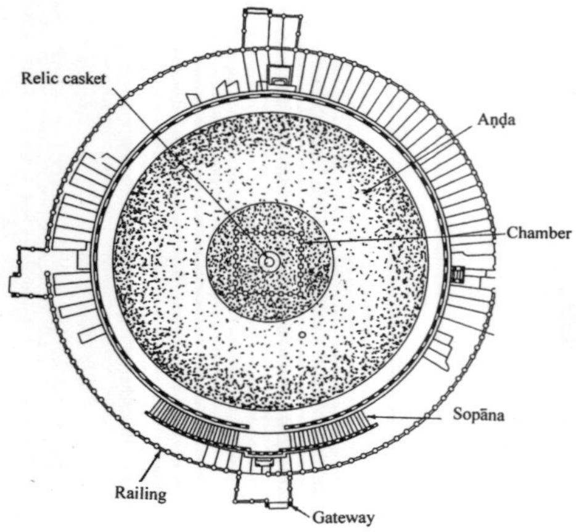

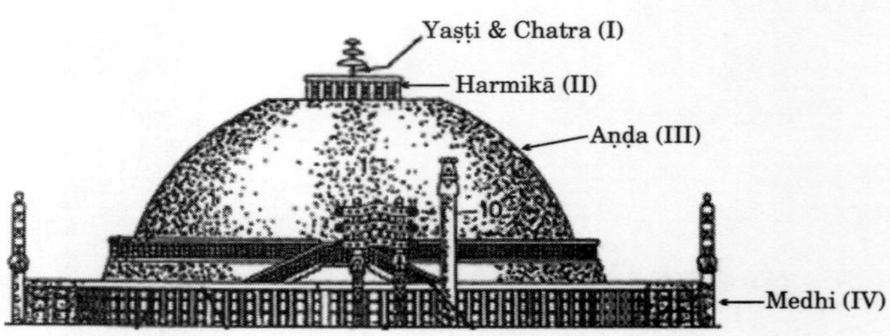

* [I] = Enlightement [II] World of gods
[III] Space or *Antarikṣa* [IV] World of mortal and below World of Pitṛins and Nāgas
[* As defined by V.S. Agrawala, *op.cit.* p. 35]

Fig. 17.2 : Plan-Great *Stūpa* at Sāñcī and its elevation

Fig. 17.3: Drum-Slab from Amaravati *Stūpa* in the British Museum
(After Robert Knox, *Amaravati,* (London 1992) No. 72)
A: Future assuring enlightenment; B: Past; and C: Present

Architecturally, the arrangement of diverse constituents in a *stūpa* was not only harmonious but aesthetically rythmic, as the part of an order which has been compared in Buddhist texts with the Cosmic Body or *dharmakāya* of Tathāgata. The Tibetan Buddhist traditions associated with the raising of a *stūpa*, which are in fact based on the lost Sanskrit work *Caityavibhaṅga* and *Vinayoddhṛta-Sūtra*, mention it as symbolic of Tathāgata's Dharmakāya or Cosmic body. The essence of Buddha's *dharmakāya*, according to these traditions, is supposed to consist of his intellectual attainments including elements of consciousness, mystical powers, factors for enlightenment, tenets of eightfold path, five faculties, various qualities like *karuṇā*, etc., which are to be represented in some form in the *stūpa* structure to suggest the reflection of Buddha's *dharmakāya*. Another notable point in Tibetan tradition pertains to writing of *mantra*s invoking *Sarva-Tathāgata*s (multiple Buddhas) on a scroll to be placed at the base and sides of *yaṣṭi* of the *stūpa* when it is installed. The opening words of one of the *mantra*s calling the *yaṣṭi* as *sarva tathāgata vipulayaṣṭi* are not without some religious significance. Another Mahāyānic text, *Amitāyur-Dhyāna Sūtra* supporting the idea under discussion states that a *Tathāgata* is one whose (spiritual or Cosmic) body is the principle of nature (*dharmadhātu-kāya*).

A reference in the *Aśokavadāna*, a text of about the first century AD or so, connected with story of Upagupta, a great *Sarvāstivādin* monk of Mathurā also deserves to be mentioned in the present context. It relates to the subjugation of Māra, the god of desire, by Upagupta by putting the former in hard fetters of bones. When Māra prayed for his release, Upagupta told him that he is prepared to do so provided the god of desire (*māra*) appears like an actor before the monk in the physical form of Buddha, the Lord of three worlds; because he has seen so far only the cosmic form (*dharmakāya*) of Buddha[12] and not his actual body in human form (*rūpakāya*) similar to a golden mountain.

The verse under reference reads:

धर्मकायो मया तस्य दृष्टस्त्रैलोक्यनाथस्य।
काञ्चनाद्रिनिभस्तस्य न दृष्टो रूपकायो मे।।

The text was composed at a time during the proto-Mahāyānic phase of Buddhism when a large section of the Buddhists strongly felt the urge to worship Buddha's image in human form and wanted to have justification for it. The present story, however, gives us a clue about *dharmakāya* concept of Buddha represented probably through the *caitya*s and *stūpa*s as already discussed above. The term Trailokyanātha, used for Buddha in the above cited verse may not be without a purpose, because the structure of a Buddhist *stūpa* represented the three worlds.

12. M.C. Joshi, *ibid*., p. 75.

In the present sequence may also like to refer to the *Saddharma-puṇḍarīka-Sūtra*, an early Mahāyānic text, recording the mysterious appearance of a bejewelled *stūpa* in front of Buddha Śākyamuni. Bodhisattva Mahāpratibhāvana, who also witnesses this phenomenon, enquired about the nature of this *stūpa* from Śākyamuni. The latter then clarified to the Bodhisattva that this *stūpa* contains within it, the essence of (an earlier) Tathāgata's own body. Subsequently, he opened this *stūpa* in the centre and showed inside it seated *Samyak-Sambuddha Prabhūta-ratna*, alive in a state of *samādhi*.

This story reminds of multiple *stūpa* structures around the main edifice (*caitya*) at Borobudur with seated Buddha sculpted in round inside of them indicating that this kind of artistic treatment might have been indirectly inspired by a similar concept.

A significant role was played in the development of the architecture of the Buddhist *stūpa* by the Vedic concepts of *hiraṇyagarbha* (present in *aṇḍa*) and *skambha* (visible in *yaṣṭi*) Buddhist cosmos in a *stūpa* with a wheel-base symbolising movement within a system. The whole fabric of the edifice was dominated by *yaṣṭi* under crowning *chatra*s, symbolic of the Supreme Enlightened Being, as the Master of the Order embodying the *lokadhātu*s and looking in all the directions with compassion, to guide everyone to the eternal bliss of *nirvāṇa*. This is well indicated by the pair of painted eyes, on each side of the *stūpa* towers of Nepal. (*fig.* 17.4)

Fig. 17.4: Kathmandu (Nepal), *Stūpa* of Svayaṁbhūnātha
(After Percy Brown, *Indian Architecture, Buddhist & Hindu*)

The terraced-*stūpa*s, whereof the remains date in India from about the Gupta period onwards are equally interesting. Extant at Sārnāth, Nālandā, Pahārpur, Leh, etc., these terraced *stūpa*s consist of three, five or seven square terraces, successively receding in size in an upward direction and ultimately turning the whole edifice into a stepped pyramid with a shirne or *stūpa* at the top. Such a structure looks somewhat similar to an ancient Ziggurat in shape and the architectural type has been mentioned in Indian tradition as *eduka* or *jeruka* showing their links with the term Ziggurat. They appear to be a representation of some mountain,[13] like the Ziggurat itself. In the light of Henri Frankfort's statement, the form and concept of West-Asian Ziggurat could be better understood:

> The temple tower or the Ziggurat was sacred structure. The names of some of them, known in later times, indicate that they were intended, not merely to resemble, but to be mountains. The Ziggurat of the storm god Enlil was called, "House of the Mountain, Mountain of the Storm, Bond between Earth and Heaven". In Mesopotamia, "mountain was a religious concept of many-sided significance. It stood for the whole earth, and within it, therefore were concentrated the mysterious powers of life which bring forth vegetation in spring and autumn, and carry water to dry river beds. . . . The mountain, then, was the habitual setting in which the superhuman became manifest, the Sumerian, in erecting their Ziggurats with immense common effort, created conditions under which communication with the divine became possible.

We feel that *stūpa* in the form of a stepped pyramid, like Ziggurat were intended probably to represent the sacred moutain Sameru. In the Buddhistic context of Sukhāvatī, the abode of bliss, we told that the Tathāgata's holy and fully enlightened body there looked like Sumeru, the mythical mountain, elevated above all the regions surpassing all the quarters shining, glittering and blazing. It is, thus, another form of cosmic representation of Buddha.

The idea is well reflected in one of the verses of the lyrical poem *Buddha-Bhakti Śataka* by Ramacandra Bharati, a Bengali poet[14] of the twelfth century AD who used to live in Sri-Lanka. The verse reads as under:

> नागालयोपरिधरालयचक्रवालं
> मूर्ध्नित्रिकूटगतकाञ्चनशैलश्रृंगे ।
> बोधिद्रुमूलनिहिताक्षयधातुबिम्बं
> बिभ्रन्नमामि शिरसाजिनचैत्यमग्रम् ।।२०।।

---

13. Banister Fletcher, *A History of Architecture,* London, B.T. Batsford Ltd., 1959, p. 58.
14. *Buddhabhakti Sataka* by Ramacandra Kavi Bharati, with Newari translation by Sthavira Aniruddha, Kantipur (Kathmandu), Newari Samvat 1-78 (AD 1959) śloka 20.

> I offer my homage to the prime Jina *caitya* (*stūpa* containing Buddha *dhātus*) under the Bodhi tree, rising on the earth from the nether world (world of Nāgas) in a circular form with (its lofty) top simulating the Trikūṭa peak of the Golden Mountain (Meru) and containing (within) eternally alive mortal relics (*dhātus*) bearing the reflection (of Buddha).

It is significant to note that Kharostī inscription of the Kuṣāṇa period, originally, perhaps from Swat area of Pakistan referes Buddha's relics as eternal[15] in the same way in which Shinkot inscription (Sircar, *op. cit,* p. 104) uses the expression '*prāṇa samedaṁ śarīra*' in the contexts of Buddha mortal relics as 'infused with life'.

It may also be relevant to invite the attention of scholars to a wall painting probably from Balawaste originally in Central-Asia and now in the National Museum of India. It depicts Buddha's cosmic form with several motifs and symbols within his iconic human form. P. Banerji rightly identifies it as a representation Vairocana Buddha.[16]

The notable symbols and motifs on the body of Vairocana are sun and moon, flaming pillars, marks of *vajra*, sacred gems, *śrīvatsa* symbol on the chest, a sacred jar, a running horse, snake and auspicious motif like triangles and circles. It is an elaboration of the cosmic form incorporating several elements from different traditions within the framework of evolved Mahāyānism.[17] Basically, it reflects the same concept which is available in the early *mahāstūpas* with their sculpted limbs.

---

15. H.W. Bailey, 'A Kharostī Inscription of Seṇavarma, King of Odi' in *Journal of the Royal Asiatic Society,*No. I, 1980. pp. 21 ff.
16. P. Banerjee, *New Light on Central Asian Art and Iconography,* New Delhi, Abha Prakashan, 1992, p. 48, fig. 16.
17. Also see; Lama Anagarika Govinda, *Psycho-Cosmic Symbolism* of *Stupa,* Dharma Publications, California, 1990.

18

Meditative Architectonics and Borobudur

Lokesh Chandra

MEDITATION, visualisation, cultivation or contemplation is beyond matter and beyond mind in the incandescence of being, the *agnim īḍe purohitaṁ* of the *Ṛgveda*. It is the diaphany of the divine in human consciousness radiating from the depths of a glowing universe. It is to find the bonds of being from non-being: *sato bandhum asati niravindan* in the words of *Ṛgveda*. While the root *paś* means 'to see, behold, look at' as a biological act and gives the word *paśu* 'animal', the root *dṛś* refers to *darśana*, seeing with the spiritual eye, insight, visualising by divine intuition to manifest the unseen. In the ancient Indo-European world, realisation was central to human transcension, as distinct from revelation in the Judeocentric traditions. Revelation is the body of truth which is made known by prophetic traditions. The truth is bestowed on man, and it is not verifiable. It is a communication to a lower mind and demands accommodation. Realisation, on the other hand, is seeking by humans, beyond historical rigidity, a transfiguration of the individual into the majesty of the Divine. The Persian word *dīn* 'religion' is from ancient Avesta *daena* which is a common word in the *gāthās* of Zarathustra, meaning 'inner self of man, faith'. It is the Ṛgvedic word *dhenā* in the sense of 'speech reflecting the inner thoughts of man'. Ascent to the divine was a human effort and not a divine condescension. Epic moments of man 's life are fragments of divine splendour, or as the *Bhagavad Gītā*, 10.41 says:

> *yad-yad vibhūtimat sattvaṁ, śrīmad ūrjitam eva vā* ।
> *tad-tad evāvagaccha tvaṁ, mama tejo' ṁśa-sambhavam* ॥

Contemplation needs a visual symbol. In the words of Lessing (1942:101),

> The paitings serve as a support (*ālambana*), a starting point in the meditation, as a means of mental self-identification with the deity in the process of *sādhanā* 'realisation'.

Besides paintings, the sacred edifices themselves are symbols and catalysts for contemplation. The world 'contemplate' itself is derived from *con* 'with, together' +

templum 'sanctuary, temple' + the verbal suffix, *-ate*. The Chinese Buddhist master Shandao (AD 613-82) pointed out that paintings and architectural structures enhance meditation. There are two methods of cultivation: (i) recitation (*nianfo*) and (ii) visualisation (*guan*). As a master of the Pureland School, he promoted the use of Pureland illustrations of the *Amitāyur-dhyāna-sūtra*, as meditating agents. The role of architectural elements is one of mediation between the heavenly and earthly experience. There are sixteen visualisations in Shandao's system. If one meditates on the Jewelled Ground (third *guan*) he is acquitted of sins of life of eighty billion *kalpas*. If one meditates on the Jewelled Trees, Jewelled Pool, and Jewelled Pavilion (4,5,6 *guan*), one is acquitted of sins of countless billions of *kalpas*. In the cave complex of Tun-huang, visualisation is practised through meditating upon the large Buddhas, as well as on the grandiose architectural layout. *Prāṇo vai virāṭ:* immense is the Divine.

Characteristics of structures for meditation

They are (i) eleborate and vast complexes, as well as (ii) multi-storeyed as indicative of the several planes of spiritual ascension or *dhyāna-bhūmis*. (iii) They illustrate a number of texts in ascending order of evolution. They co-ordinate multiple-level teachings. They are based on the principle of *p'an-chiao* 'classification of doctrines', that one particular scripture contains the highest truth and other scriptures belong to a sequence of evolving stages of *dharma*. These complexes (iv) encode the cosmology and theophany of several doctrines leading to the summum of meditation. (v) As such they illustrate several paradises, with illustrations of thousands of deities, and are significantly termed *sku.ḥbum* 'myriads of deities' in Tibetan and *ming-oi* in Turkish with the same meaning. They are known as *ch'ien fo t'ung* 'caves with thousands of Buddhist images' or *wang fo t'ung* 'caves (*t'ung*) with myriads (*wang*) of Buddhist images (*fo*)'.

Three kinds of structures

(i) *guhā* (ii) *śatadvāra*, and (iii) *Sumeru.* The cave complexes (*guhā)* are grottos excavated in mountains. Some of their examples are *Bamiyan, Ming-oi* at Kizil, Tun-huang and Yun-kan. The cave has been a syllogism of the soul in India from ancient times: *guhā nidhī nihitau brāhmaṇasya* (*Atharvaveda*, 11.5.10) means that the treasures of the sacred lore of a brāhmaṇa are hidden in a cave. *Śatapatha Brāhmaṇa* 11.2.6.5 equates the *guhā* with the heart (*tasmād idaṁ guheva hṛdayam).* Jean Laroche echoes the same sentiments in his *Memories d'été:*

Une maison dressé au coeur
Ma cathédrale de silence.

A house that stands in my heart
My cathedral of silence.

Brahmā resides in the *guhā*, the supreme space (*brahma yo veda nihitaṁ guhāyāṁ parame vyoman* — Indische Stüdien 2.217.

The second type of edifices were *śatadvāra* with 'hundreds of doors', called *sgo.maṅ* (literally 'many-doored') in Tibetan. They were tapering pyramidal structures with several chapels. The chapels had hundreds of icons and their walls were covered with murals all over. The walls outside were bare and simply plastered. The term *śatadvāra* occurs in Pāṇini 4.1.123. The *Gyantse Kumbum* is an outstanding example of this type of meditational architecture. It can be studied in the detailed descriptions by Franco Ricca and Erberto Lo Bue, *The Great Stupa of Gyantse* (London) where they have indicated the scriptures followed in each chapel. Such *kumbums* were spread over Tibet, and a number of them have survived the political holocaust. The *kumbums* generally culminate in the erototropic Inner Tantras of Vajrayāna.

The third type of edifices are the stepped pyramidal mountain structures known as Sumeru. They are solid inside and the icons and bas-reliefs are sculpted on the visible exterior walls. The sanctification of the outer walls and balustrades exposed to the fury of elements is the symbolisation of open space as Brahmā. In the *Chāndogya Upaniṣad* (7.12.2) the open firmament is worshipped as Brahmā (*sa yaḥ ākāśaṁ brahmeti upāste,* CHI.4.386). The sky provides a comparison with the highest state in the Bodhicaryāvatāra 1.19 (*avicchinnāḥ puṇyadhārāḥ pravartante nabhaḥsamāḥ*). They represent the phototrophic Outer Tantras of Mantrayāna.

Planes of meditation

Buddhist scriputeres have various gradations of meditation:

(i) The *Amitāyur-dhyāna-sūtra* has 16 meditations (*guan).*

(ii) The *Daśabhūmika-sūtra* has 10 levels of meditation.

(iii) The *Abhidharmakośa* has 3 realms (*tridhātu*) with 32 states and 8 *dhyāna-bhūmis*.

(iv) The *Gaṇḍavyūha* has 54 stages.

The cosmology of meditation at the Borobudur

The Borobudur immortalises the meditations of its architect Guṇadharma, who retired in Mount Menoreh to contemplate. According to tradition, he is integrated into this mountain range where the silhouette of his chin, mouth and nose can be seen. It is a Sumeru or *adhara* for the pavilion of the deities of the *maṇḍala*. I have detailed its Sumeru or architecture in CHI.4.56f. A miniature Sumeru (Jap. *Sumi*) is placed on the altar under the *maṇḍala* to this day in Japan to integrate the cosmos and the *maṇḍala*. The Borobudur is a complex *temenos* which synthesises three meditaitonal systems: (i) three realms (*tridhātu*) of the *Abhidharmakośa* (ii) the 54 stages of the *Gaṇḍavyūha* of the *Avataṁsaka*, and (iii) *Vajradhātu-maṇḍala* of the *Caryā-Tantras*.

Symbolism of the Barobudur has to be perceived on three planes: (i) symbolism of the architecture of Sumeru, (ii) meaning of the bas-reliefs on the walls and balustrades, and (iii) their correlation with *Abhidharma*.

(i) Buddhaguhya's commentary on the *Sarva-durgati-pariśodhana* (as cited by Wayman 1973:92f) gives the symbolism of four-sided Sumeru and the *maṇḍala* as follows:

four corners	four knowledges
four gates	four kinds of marvellous action (*Khedubje* 232)
four arches	four boundless states
four staircases	four means of conversion
arches adordned with	
garland	infinite compassion
eight posts	eight liberations
lions	one with great compassion of means is not frightened of *saṁsāra*
bulls	infinite marks of right powers
gates adorned with	
silk, five-coloured (*pañcarāga*)	five kinds of knowledge
tassels, three-coloured (*trirāga*)	pure nature of body, speech and mind
pendant necklace of pearls	Bodhisattva's joy
garland of pearls	set of requirements for *samādhi*
bells, combined with necklaces	purity of speech, to teach *dharma* to living beings
yak tails	no shifting of the mind of enlightenment
adorned with mudrās of	
diamonds, round fence of	wisdom-knowledge (*vidyā-jñāna*)
jewels, garland of	all sorts of merits
lotus	great compassion of skill in the means while being unattached

svastika	union of means (*upāya*) and insight (*prajñā*)
lines, i.e., threads	contemplation of the mind of enlightenment
eight lines	four-directional threads and four inner threads
eight kinds	eight auspicious symbols on the body
outer gate projections	means of entering by *samādhi* comprehension.

The commentary of *Buddhaguhya* explicitly states that adornment is to clarify the apperception of inner symbols.

(ii) The bas-reliefs of the Borobudur are intended as supports for the meditative system of the *Abhidharma-kośa* and *Lokaprajñapti* of the *Abhidharma*. *Abhidharma* is supplemented by the *Pāramitā-yāna*, *Avataṁsaka* and *Mantrayāna*.The four systems are represented as follows:

	Genre	*reliefs*	*text*	*walls*
1.	Abhidharma	160	*Lokaprajñapti*	hidden base
2.	Pāramitāyāna	120	*Lalitavistara*	Ia
	Pāramitāyāna	120	*Jātakamālā*	Ib
	Pāramitāyāna	600	*Avadānas*	IBa-b, IIB
3.	Avataṁsaka	388	*Gaṇḍavyūha*	II, III, IIIB, IVB
	Avataṁsaka	72	*Bhadracarī*	IV
4.	Mantrayāna	504 Buddhas	*STTS*	all round

The *Lokaprajñapti* is extant in a few Sanskrit fragments from Gilgit, Turfan and Japan. The complete text is available in Tibetan and Chinese translations. The Chinese translation (K 967) was done by Paramārtha of Ujjayinī in AD 558. Prof Ryusho Hikata has identified the panels of Lokaprajñapti (CHI.4.75-76) as the realms of *kāmadhātu*. The *Jātakamālā* and *Lalitavistara* reliefs on the inner wall of the first gallery are the practice of *pāramitās*. The *Avataṁsaka* is the *Gaṇḍavyūha* represented on 110 panels. The number 110 has been studied by Fa-tsang who lived from 643 to 712. They are the 54 sections of the *Gaṇḍavyūha* (*Gv.*) as follows:

(i)	The ten degree of faith/*śraddhā*	*Gv.*1
(ii)	The ten abodes/*vihāra*	*Gv.*2-11

(iii) The ten degrees of action/*caryā* *Gv.*12-21

(iv) The ten degrees of diversion/*pariṇāmana* *Gv.*22-31

(v) The ten stages/*bhūmi* *Gv.*32-41

(vi) The ten *vimokṣa* *Gv.*42-52

(vii) Mañjuśrī, *Sāmantabhadra* *Gv.*53,54

The Chinese Buddhist master Chih-i (538-97) worked out an elaborate course of contemplation designed to lead the Buddhist practitioner to the goal. He integrated the doctrines of a number of *sūtra*s. To him, intellection and contemplation was always indispensable to the other. He has presented an enlightening exposition of the above seven stages (i-vii) of the *Avataṁsaka* (Hurvitz 1962:363-7). Hurvitz has detailed the life and thought of the Chinese master in 372 pages.

The large images of 504 Buddhas in various *mudrā*s represent the Vajradhātu system of Mantrayāna (as explained by the author in CHI.4.81f).

(iii) *The psycho-cosmic system* of meditation is given at length, in the second, third, fifth, sixth and eighth chapters of the *Abhidharmakośa.*The diverse topics of the mind are produced in the three realms (*dhātu*): *kāmadhātu*, *rūpadhātu* and *ārūpyadhātu*. They are the realms of deisre, of subtle form and non-form. These three realms consist of 32 states. The second chapter establishes a classification of the mental states in the three *dhātu*s: four kinds of minds (*citta*) belong to the *Kāmadhātu* (Pr.1.310), six types of minds in the sphere of *rūpadhātu* (Pr. 1. 317), and four kinds of *ārūpyadhātu* (Pr.1.318). There are seven abodes of consciousnesses (*vijñāna-sthiti*'s) in the three *dhātu*s (Pr .2. 374) which are infinite like space (2.370). To raise oneself above one's natural state (*prakṛti-avasthā*) in order to become disgusted with the *kāmadhātu*, one has to enter a state of absorption (*anāgamya-phalaṁ sarva-dhyānānāṁ*) which is the threshold, the frontier (*sāmantaka*) of the First *dhyāna* (Pr.3.xix) of the *rūpadhātu*. The *rūpadhātu* or universe of subtle form is inhabited by *rūpāvacara deva*s. The lower senses of touch, taste and smell are eliminated, while the mental, visual and olfactory faculties remain. It represents four stages in the advancement of meditation. It comprises from the first to the fourth *dhyāna-bhūmi*. Whoever produces the higher knowledge of *abhijñā* in the First *dhyāna*, creates a being that can only be the *brahmaloka* of the universe. The eighth chapter of the *Abhidharma-kośa* is concerned with the nature of *dhyāna* as states of absorption and as states of existence in the universe of *rūpadhātu* and *ārūpyadhātu*. It discusses the components of each *dhyāna* (Pr. 4. 1215).

The three realms (*tridhātu*) with their thirty-two states are as follows:

KĀMADHĀTU/Realm of Kāma

(1-4) The four unhappy states (*durgati*)

1. *Naraka*/hells
2. *Tiryag-yoni*/animals
3. *Preta*/suffering ghosts
4. *Asura*/demons (those who love aggression)

(5-11) The seven happy states (*sugati*)

5. *Manuṣya-loka*/humans

(6-11) *Deva-loka*/six heavens of *kāmāvacara devas*

6. *Caturmahārājika*/Four Guardian Kings
7. *Trāyanstiṁśa*/Indira's heaven
8. *Yāma*
9. *Tuṣita*/Full of Joy
10. *Nirmāṇarati* / Delight in Own Creations
11. *Paranirmita-vaśavartin*/Delight in Other's Creations

RŪPADHĀTU/Realm of Subtle Form

(12-14) First *Dhyāna*

12. *Brahma-pāriṣadya*
13. *Brahma-purohita*
14. *Mahābrahmā*

(15-17) Second *Dhyāna*

15. *Parīttābha*/Limited Lustre
16. *Apramāṇābha*/Infinite Lustre
17. *Abhāsvara*/Radiance

(18-20) Third *Dhyāna*

18. *Parītta-śubha* / Limited Aura
19. *Apramāṇa-śubha* / Infinite Aura
20. *Śubha-kṛtsna*/Steady Aura

(21-28) Fourth *Dhyāna*

21. *Anabhraka*
22. *Puṇyaprasava*
23. *Bṛhatphala*

24. *Abṛha*

25. *Atapa*

26. *Sudṛśa*

27. *Sudarśana*

28. *Akaniṣṭha*

ĀRŪPYADHĀTU/Realm of non-form, inhabited by *arūpāvacara* gods

29. Fifth *Dhyāna*: *Ākāśa-ānanty-āyatana*/plane of Infinity of space

30. Sixth *Dhyāna*: *Vijñān-ānanty-āyatana*/plane of Infinity of consciousness

31. Seventh *Dhyāna*: *Akiñcany-āyatana*/plane of Nothingness

32. Eighth *Dhyāna* : *Naiva-saṁjñā-nasaṁjñ-āyatana* / plane of Absolute Nothingness

The *kāmadhatu* comprises four happpy states (*durgati*) and seven happy states (*sugati*). The first four are represented on the hidden base of the Borobudur:

	reliefs
1. hells	86-92
2. animals (*triyag-yoni*)	93-94
3. *preta-loka*	95
4. *asuras*	96

The seven happy states (*sugati*) pertains to human existence and the six *kāmāvacara devas*. The human world is shown on reliefs of the hidden base from relief 97 to 160. The six heavens of the *kāmāvacara devas* are sunstituted by the life of Lord Buddha and various *avadānas*.

The four *dhyānas* of the *rūpadhātu* are planes of meditation and hence formless. The seventeen states (12-28) of these *dhyānas* represent meditative planes of impersonal immensity (*brahman*), radiance (*ābhā*), aura (*śubha*), and beyond them all to the most subtle. They are immaculate (*an-abhraka*), outdo immensity (*a-bṛha*), excel austerities (*a-tapa*), and go beyond (a) the subtlest (*kaniṣṭha*). They are betokened by depictions of the *Gaṇḍavyūha* on the second and the third walls as well as on the third and fourth balustrades of the Borobudur. The last state of *akaniṣṭha*, the twenty-eighth, is the culmination of the *rūpadhātu*, the realm of subtle form. *A-kaniṣṭha* means the most subtle (*kaniṣṭha*) state, ultimate subtlety that cannot (a) be surpassed. Vairocana dwells in the *akaniṣṭha* heaven. He is the culmination of the *Yoga-Tantras*.

The Realm of non-form, the *ārūpyadhātu*, being beyond form, cannot and is not configured. Thus, it culminates on the summit of existence (Pr.1.83) as the open space (*ākāśa*) on top of Borobudur : unconditioned, formless.

The correlation of the realms of *dhyāna* to the Borobudur can be tabulated as follow:

Kāmadhātu		*Borobudur*
1-4	four unhappy states (*durgati*)	hidden base
5	world of humans	hidden base
6-11	six *deva-loka*s	Ia (life of Lord Buddha)
	six *deva-loka*s	Ib, IBab, IIb (*avadāna*s)
Rūpadhātu		
12-27	four *dhyāna*s	II, III, IIIB, IVB, (*gaṇḍavyūha*)
28	culmination : *akaniṣṭha*	Variocana
Ārūpyadhātu		
29-32	beyond depiction	open sky

The Borobudur is the visual symbol for *dhyāna* or meditation. Its bas-reliefs are the physical seeing and the *dhyāna* accompanying them is spiritual visualisation. The biological phenomenon of the root *paś* 'to see' and the divinity of *drś* 'to envision' are complementary to meditational ascent. Living images for meaningful meditation. The three realms of *kāmadhātu, rūpadhātu* and *ārūpyadhātu* are not horizontal existences, but psychological states. As the *yogacārins* say: "The threefold world is only mind" (Pr.1.41). Residing in one realm, the consciousness has potentialities to move forward or backward to other realms. Freed from all materiality, the ascensional being attains the supreme. *Dhyāna* is a process of transumuting the lower states of consciousness into the higher states, from the worlds of sense-desires to the realms of finer forms and finally to the realms of the formless, to the Absolute Sublime.

References

Lokesh Chandra, *Cultural Horizons of India*, vol. 4, New Delhi: Aditya Prakashan,1995.

Ryusho Hikata, 1980, *The wall reliefs of the hidden base- 160 panels, International Symposium on Chandi Borobudur*, Kyoto (25-27 September 1980),97-100.

Leon Hurvitz,1962, Chih-i, *Mélanges Chinois et Bouddhiques*, vol.12 Bruxelles.

Ferdinand D. Lessing and Alex Wayman, *Mkhas grub rje's Fundamentals of the Buddhist Tantras*, The Hague, Mouton,1968.

Ferdinand D. Lessing, 1942, *Yung-ho-kund*, Stockholm.

Leo M. Pruden's English translation of Louis de la Vallee Poussin, *Abhidharma-kośa-bhāṣyam*, vols. 1-4, Berkeley, California, Asian Humanities Press, 1988-1990.

Alex Wayman, 1973, *The Buddhist Tantras*, New York, Samuel Weister, 1973.

19

Manifestation of Order in Art

The Iconic Scheme at Khajurāho

Devangana Desai

SUPPORTED on the back of the Vāstupuruṣa, originally the disorderly demon of the Site who is stabilised by the divinities settled upon him, the temple is "a renewed conquest of disinitegration".[1] The grid of the *Vāstupuruṣa-maṇḍala*, with its 64 or 81 squares, underlies the plan of the temple, and the configuration of its divinities (*pada-devatās*) is ritually present, though not seen in the temple's iconography.

What is seen in the iconic scheme of the temple, particularly from the eighth century AD onwards, is an alternate cosmic order[2] represented by the eight guardians of space called *dikpālas*, the eight atmospheric divinities called Vasus, the nine planets, and so on. In the *Vāstuśāstra* texts that deal with the building of the temple, the entire cosmos is invoked to come down and pervade the physical body of the temple, from its finial to the base. The temple itself is conceived of as a model of the cosmos, and also as *puruṣa*, the humanised Supreme Being.[3]

In the tenth-eleventh century, Khajurāho in central India represents the Indian temple in its highly evolved stage. The architectural expansion and the sculptural profusion of the temple that we see here was accompanied by conceptual developments in Tāntric-Purāṇic religious systems regarding the idea of the Supreme Being and its manifestations, the One and its many forms. A concept of far-reaching importance in the monotheistic religious systems of Khajurāho's Viṣṇu and Śiva temples was that of the emanation of cosmic elements (*tattvas*) from the Supreme Being in the process of creation of the universe, and their reabsorption back to the

---

1. Stella, Karmarisch, *The Hindu Temple*, 1946, Motilal Banarsidass, Reprint, 1976, pp. 96-7.
2. Michael, Meister, "Muṇḍeśvarī : Ambiguity and Certainty in the Analysis of a Temple Plan, *Kalādarśana*, ed. Joanna G. Williams, American Institute of Indian Studies, New Delhi, 1981,pp. 86-7.
3. M.A. Dhaky, Prāsāda as Cosmos, *The Adyar Library Bulletin*, Vol. XXXV, 3-4,1971.

primordial centre in the process of dissolution.[4]

There are hundreds of images on the exteriors and interiors of the Khajurāho temples. Are they randomly put on the walls? What is the order of their arrangement? We shall explore the manifestation of order in the mature temples of Khajurāho. The Khajurāho architect or *sūtradhāra* was described in the inscription as *dharmādhāra*, who has his base in *dharma* or rule of conduct. Also he was knowledgeable in the *Viśvakarmā-śāstra*, architectural lore in the tradition of Viśvakarmā. (*Epigraphia Indica*, Vol. I, p. 146, verse 60). He has a well-planned scheme for the temple.

We notice at least four varied expressions of order in the iconic scheme of Khajurāho temples.

I

Firstly, there is a hierarchical order of cardinal and peripheral images in relation to the centre, which can best be illustrated in the grand Kandarīyā Mahādeva temple. The centre of the temple is a luminous source which radiates its power in cardinal directions through the graded images of its manifestations. Through the medieval language of hierarchy and prescribed modes of thinking the architect of the temple is conveying the truths of cosmological insight which today also strike a note, and which modern physics would explain in terms of the Big Bang, Expansion and Collapse of the Universe.

The *Śiva-liṅga*, the principal object of worship, is installed exactly in the centre of the dark, cave-like *garbhagṛha* (sanctum). This is symbolically the womb-house of creation and reabsorption. The pinnacle of the *śikhara* lies exactly above the *liṅga*. It is the cosmic axis uniting heaven and earth. It is specifically described as *jagataḥ mūlastambha*, the primordial pillar of the universe, in a Candella inscription (*Epigraphia Indica*, XXXI, pp. 163 ff). It is with the *liṅga* as the centre that a centrifugal movement radiates in the four cardinal directions of the temple.

A unique icon of Sadāśiva, placed in the hall of the temple, shown as four-footed, *catuṣpāda*, metaphorically suggests the four *pāda*s or parts of the Śaiva system. Conceived as *sakala-niṣkala* (differentiated and undifferentiated), or *vyakta-avyakta* (manifest-unmanifest), Sadāśiva is the intermediary and a link between form and formlessness.[5] Sadāśiva is the key figure who helps us to unfold thisŚiva temple's methphysical order as well its iconic scheme.

---

4. Devangana Desai, Man and the Temple—Architectural and Sculptural Imagery of the Kandarīyā Mahādeva Temple of Khajurāho, in *Eastern Approaches*, ed. T. S. Maxwell, Oxford University Press, 1992, 141-54.

5. T.A. Gopinatha Rao, *Elements of Hindu Iconography*, Vol II, ii, pp. 361-96.

From Sadāśiva emanates Maheśa, the third main *tattva*, who is conceived of as manifest (*vyakta*) aspect of Śiva. He is the *sakala* or differentiated aspect of Śiva who manifests through 25 *līlā-mūrti*s, such as dancer, bridgegroom, slayer of demons, and so on.

Stella Karmrisch, in her exposition of the sculptural scheme of the Elephaṇṭā Caves near Bombay, has observed these triple levels of meaning of Śiva, viz. (1) *Śiva-liṅga* as sign of unmanifest, (2) Sadāśiva as manifest-unmanifest, and (3) Maheśa as manifest.[6] Recently, Doris Srinivasan has also noticed these three levels of Śiva's presence in the sculptural imagery of the Śiva temples of many regions of India from the sixth century AD onwards.[7]

At Khajurāho, in addition to the triple levels of manifestation, we see also Rudra, Viṣṇu and Brahmā included in the scheme.[8] In the Śaiva system,[9] Rudra emanates from Maheśa, Viṣṇu from a crore part of Rudra, and Brahmā similarly from Viṣṇu. The Śaiva hierarchical scheme is to a large extent reflected in the sculptural scheme of the Kandarīyā Mahādeva temple.

In the main cardinal niches of the Kandarīyā Mahādeva we see Maheśa *līlā-mūrti*s as Andhakāntaka, Naṭeśa and Tripurāntaka. Viṣṇu is hierarchically shown smaller in size than Maheśa, and Brahmā, still smaller is represented at the plinth level. (*fig.* 19.1)

There are hundreds of images of Śiva on the exterior wall. They do not have the majesty of the great god but seem to represent the lesser aspects of Śiva such as Vidyeśvaras and Mantreśvaras, described in Śaiva texts.[10]

Thus, various images of this well-organised temple can be seen as evolutes, hierarchically positioned in relation to the central principle.[11] The devotee in his circumambulation of the temple proceeds through various aspects of Śiva, the graded manifestations, until he reaches the *antarāla* (vestibule) to have *darśana* of the emblem of the Supreme Śiva.

6. Stella Kramrisch, The Great Cava Temple of Śiva in Elephanta : Levels of Meaning and Their Form, in *Discourses on Śiva*, ed. Michael W. Meister, Philadelphia and Bombay 1984.
7. Doris Srinivasan, From Transcendency to Materiality: Para-Śiva, Sadāśiva and Maheśa in Indian Art, *Artibus Asiae*, Vol L. 1/2,1990.
8. Davangana Desai, The Strucutre of Time in the Kandariya Mahadeva Temple of Khajuraho, in *Concepts of Time, Ancient and Modern*, ed. Kapila Vatsyayan, Indira Gandhi National Centre for the Arts, New Delhi, 1996, p. 344, Plate 5.
9. Devangana Desai, *The Religious Imgery of Khajurāho*, Franco-Indian Research, Bombay, 1996, pp. 151-2.
10. T.A. Gopinath Rao, *Elements of Hindu Iconography*, II, ii, pp. 392 ft.
11. Devangana Desai, Temple as an Ordered Whole — The Iconic Scheme at Khajuraho, *Journal of the Asiatic Society of Bombay*, Vol. 70, 1995, pp. 50, 52.

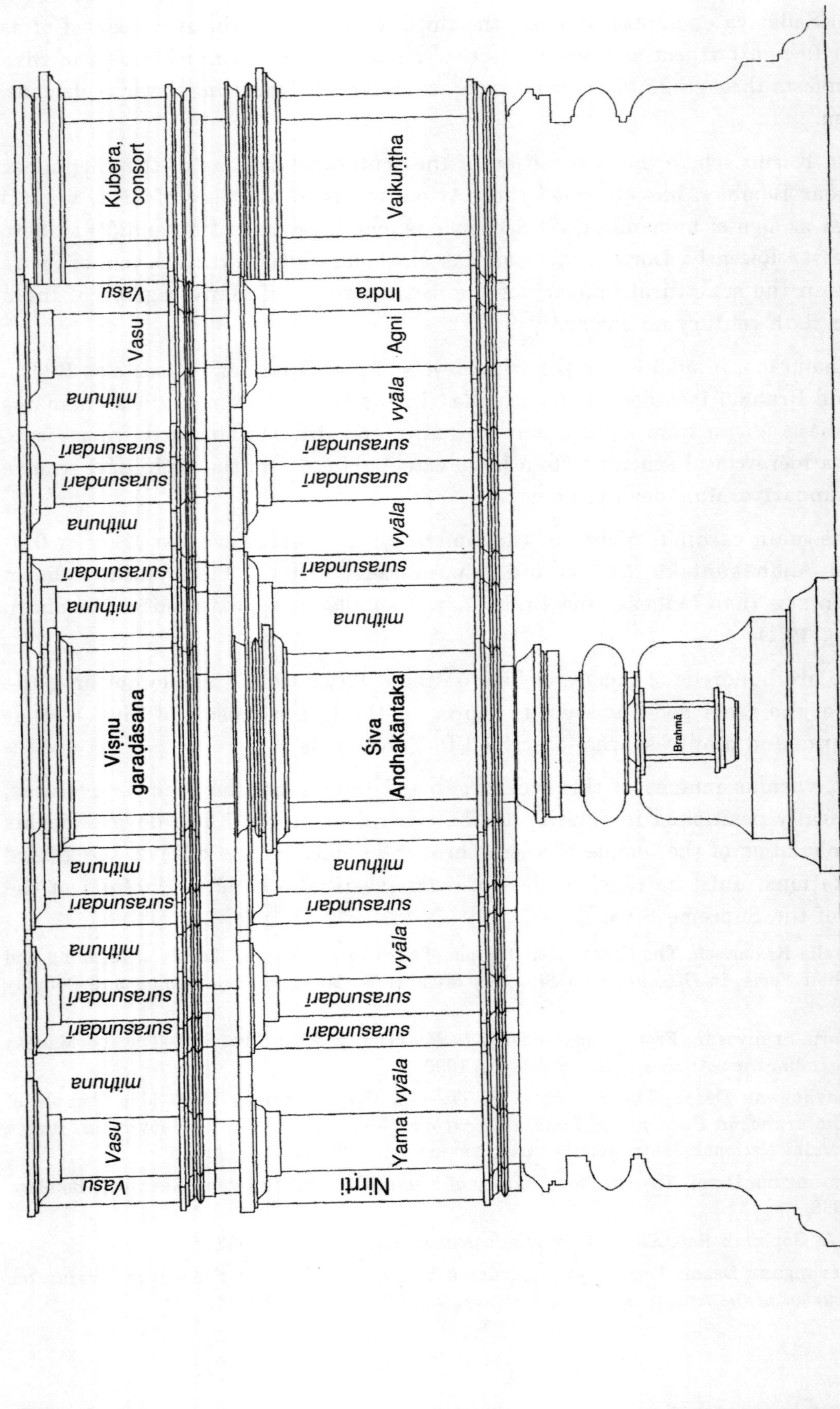

Fig. **19.1 Schematic diagram showing the arrangement of images, south elevation of the sanctum, Kandariyā Mahādeva temple, Khajuraho. (courtesy: Franco-Indian Research, Mumbai)**

Icons, which are but *nāma-rūpa*, name and form of the Formless, are not placed beyond the *śukanāsa*, the antechamber, which is the roof of the *antarāla*. Beyond this point what we see is the "ascent and descent and renewed ascent"[12] of the graded mini-spires, 84 in number,[13] leaning against the chest of the central *śikhara*. Here also, there is a hierarchical order in relation to the centre. There are series of graded mini-spires, each with its subsidiary spires, forming an integral unit themselves. Just as in a 'hologram', each fragment of the cosmos is a whole and complete in itself, and is like the large cosmos of which it is a part, the self-similar forms in different scales, as represented in the multitude of the peaks on the central *śikhara*, centering around its highest point, the finial, the cosmic axis, convey the perennial rhythm of creation, dissolution, and again creation.[14]

II

Another expression of order we see in the Khajurāho temples is in the pairing or balancing of polarities. The Lakṣmaṇa temple enshrines Vaikuṇṭha-Viṣṇu who is conceived of as *Daityārī* enemy of demons, in the inscription. Vaikuṇṭha has a composite form, of lion, boar and man.[15] According to the inscription of AD 954, placed in the porch of the Lakṣmaṇa temple, Vaikuṇṭha assumed this composite form in order to vanquish the three demons who were in a conjoint form. They had a boon of Brahmā that they could be slayed only by an identical form. (*Epigraphia Indica*, Vol. I, pp. 124, 130, verse 1). In the image of Vaikuṇṭha, the two side faces of lion and boar are balanced by the central *saumya* (placid) face of Viṣṇu. The spirit of fight against demonic forces of disorder is seen at the level of myth referred to in the inscription, and in the iconic imagery. Also the patron King Yaśovarman is called *Kuṇṭhitāri* (subduer of enemies) in the same inscription. The political and cosmic orders merge in the imgery of the Lakṣmaṇa temple.

The principal divinity Vaikuṇṭha is surrounded in the cardinal niches of the sanctum by the three incarnations of Viṣṇu: (1) Varāha, the Boar, who saves the Earth Goddess from the dark waters of the nether world, (2) Narasiṁha, the Man-Lion, who vanquishes Hiraṇyakaśipu, the demon of ignorance, as the *Viṣṇudharmottara Purāṇa* calls him, and (3), the horse-necked Hayagrīva, who restores the Vedas from a demon who had stolen them.[16]

12. Stella Kramrisch, *The Hindu Temple*, pp. 365-7, 371-2.
13. Krishna Deva, *Khajurāho*, 6th edn. ASI, New Delhi, 1980, p. 31.
14. Kirti Trivedi, Models of Cosmos, *Taj Magazine*, July, 1990; Adam Hardy, Architectural History and Ways of Seeing, in *Architecture Design*, July-August, 1993.
15. For a discussion on Khajurāho's Vaikuṇṭha images, see Devangana Desai, The *Religious Imagery of Khajurāho*, pp. 101-5, and Appendix B.
16. Devangana Desai, Hayagrīva at Khajurāho, in *Śilpasaṁvit* in Honour of Dr. U. P. Shah, ed. R. T. Vyas, Vadodara, 1996.

The demonic forces are dispelled and the other restored by Viṣṇu in his various incarnations sculpted on the sanctum wall. There are 12 *Kṛṣṇa-lilā* scenes[17] on the upper row of the sanctum wall, all, but one, of which represent the slaying or subduing of demons and dark forces. For instance, Kṛṣṇa subdues the snake Kāliya who had polluted the waters of the river Yamunā and created disorder in the land of Vraja.

Amazingly, the arrangement of the 12 *Kṛṣṇa-lilā* episodes on the wall of the sanctum is not in order or correct sequence (*fig.* 19.2), though the temple has a very well-planned sculptural scheme. The episodes do not follow the time sequence of the story of the *Bhāgavata Purāṇa* (section X) or other Purāṇas. For instance, *Pūtanā-vadha* is shown as the eleventh scene, and the second episode *śakaṭa-bhaṇga*, breaking of the cart, is shown as the eighth scene on the wall. Elsewhere, I have attempted to explain the apparent 'disorder' or seeming randomness of the *Kṛṣṇa-līlā* scenes of this temple.[18] Perhaps they have different purpose or logic other than that of linear time. *Kṛṣṇa-līlā* episodes in this temple, it seems, are not taken within *kārya-kāla*, the changing time of daily life, but *akhaṇḍa-kāla*, time without sections, of the Pāñcarātra theology. The Vaikuṇṭha temple, we must note, was associated with Pāñcarātra of the Kashmir school.[19]

The Kṛṣṇa scenes could also have a magic-protective function like the Kṛṣṇa-*mantra*s of the text *Kramadīpikā.* They could also have played a part in the *Ṛtucakra*, a diagram depiciting the presiding deities of the 12 months as described in the Pāñcarātra texts. The Pāñcarātrins worshipped 12 *vyūhantara* or emanatory forms of Viṣṇu, viz., Keśava, Mādhava, Dāmodara, etc., each in one month. Varāhamihira in his *Bṛhatsaṁhitā* shows his familiarity with the association of the 12 forms of Viṣṇu with the 12 months. In the Pāñcarātra texts these 12 emanatory forms of Viṣṇu are called 12 *mūrtipāla*s, gurdian deities, and connected with the *Ṛtucakra* diagram depicting the presiding deities of the 12 months.

Significantly, the artist the Lakṣmaṇa temple has placed the panels depicting demon-slaying near the panels representing Viṣṇu-Yogeśvara. Three unique Viṣṇu-Yogeśvara panels[20] are interspaced between the Kṛṣṇa subduing or slaying demons. By juxtaposing the Daityāri and Yogeśvara aspects of Viṣṇu, the artist balances the heroic and yogic aspects, or *pravṛtti* (activity) and *nivṛtti* (repose).

At more than one place in the Lakṣmaṇa temple, we see the pairing of Lakṣmī,

---

17. Krishana Deva, Kṛṣṇa-līla Scenes in the Lakṣmaṇa Temple, Khajurāho, *Lalit Kalā*, 7, 1960.
18. Devangana Desai, Kṛṣṇa-līlā in Temple Art of Khajurāho, in *Art, The Integral Vision*, A Volume of Essays in Felicitation of Kapila Vatsyayan, New Delhi, 1994.
19. V.S. Pathak, Vaikuṇṭha at Khajurāho and Kāśmirāgama School, *Journal of Madhya Pradesh Itihas Parishad,* No. 2, 1960.
20. *The Religious Imagery of Khajurāho*, photos 117-19.

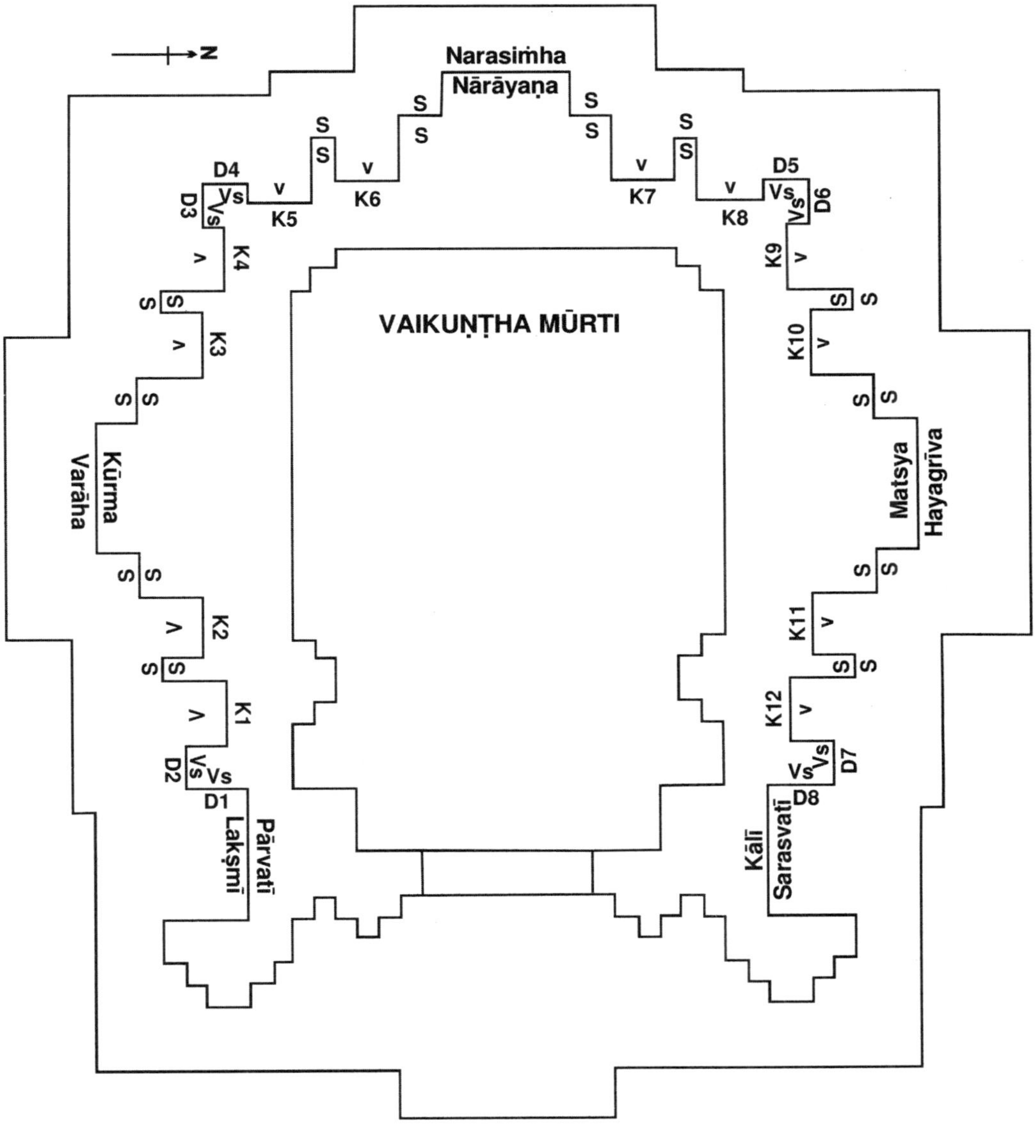

D= Dikpāla:
D1 *= Indra;* ***D2*** *= Agni;* ***D3*** *=Yama;* ***D4*** *= Nirṛti;*
D5 *= Varuṇa;* ***D6*** *= Vāyu;* ***D7*** *= Kubera;* ***D8*** *= Īśāna*
S *= Surasundarī.* ***V*** *= vyāla.* ***Vs*** *= Vasu*

K *= Kṛṣṇa-līlā;*
K1 *= Tṛṇāvarta-vadha;* ***K2*** *= Balarāma slays Sūta;*
K3 *= Chāṇūra-vadha;* ***K4*** *= Kṛṣṇa slays Kuvalayāpīḍa*
K5 *= Kāliyādamana;* ***K6*** *= Kṛṣṇa defeats Śala;*
K7 *= grace on Kubjā;* ***K8*** *= Śakaṭabhaṅga;*
K9 *= Ariṣṭāsura-vadha;* ***K10*** *= Yamalārjuna episode;*
K11 *= Pūtanā-vadha;* ***K12*** *= Vatsāsura-vadha*

It may be observed that there are 8 Vasus, 8 Dikpālas, 12 Kṛṣṇa-līlā scenes, 12 vyālas, 24 surasundarīs, along with Viṣṇu's incarnations on the three sides of the sanctum.

Fig. 19.2 Placement of images on the sanctum wall, Lakṣmaṇa temple, Khajuraho. (courtesy: Franco-Indian Research, Mumbai)

the goddess of wealth, and Sarasvatī, the goddess of learning, considered by the Sanskrit poets as of differing qualities. The architect places them in the south and north *kapilī* (juncture) niches of the sanction. He also places them on either side of the panel depicting Śiva-Pārvatī marriage, thus, suggesting their complementary role.

Very subtly and sweetly, the architect represents the two naturally incompatible animals, viz., lion and deer, sitting pacified on either side of Pārvatī in the penance grove. The atmosphere of the penance grove is so harmonious and peaceful that even the lion and deer sit on the left and right side of Pārvatī, who stands equiposided in *samabhaṅga*. And, further, the imagery is extended to the two goddesses flanking Pārvatī. The goddess Caṇḍikā on the left with fierce weapons and skull ornaments has a lion mount, whereas, on the right side, the goddess Tripurā sits meditating in *padmāsana*.

This imagery balancing the polar opposites is expressed on the *antarāla*, the passage joining the hall and the sanctum.

These two units, representing the temporal and celestial spheres, the world of men and the world of divinity, are joined in such a way in the *sāndhāra* temples (with inner ambulatory) that the juncture wall (*sandhi-kṣetra* or *kapilī*) is an overlapped portion, space common to both the hall and the sanctum (*fig.* 19.3). It can be taken from the side of the hall as well as from the side of the sanctum. It is the space 'which is here also and there also'. It is on this juncture that the Khajurāho architects found an appropriate space for employing puns and *dvisandhāna*, two-fold language.

That the architect of the Lakṣmaṇa temple was conscious of the *sandhi* of the two units is clearly illustrated by him by actually replicating in miniature form the joining of the two units, one with curvilinear *śikhara* representing the sanctum and the other with a pyramidal roof, standing for the hall.

It is on this juncture wall that he has employed the language of union and placed figures in conjunction. It also here that we see in the two contrasting sculptural figures a symbolic depiction of the two conflicting groups of discrimination (*viveka*) and delusion (*moha*), a significant theme in Indian religious literature, allegorised into characters of the Sanskrit drama, *Prabodhacandrodaya*, which was staged in the Candella Court. The disorder created by the forces of delusion is dispelled on the birth of *prabodha* (awakening).[21]

---

21. *The Religious Imagery of Khajurāho*, pp. 181-9, Appendix C;

    Also Sculptural Representation on the Lakshmana Temple of Khajurāho in the light of Prabodhachandrodya, *Journal of the National Centre for the Performing Arts*, Bombay, XI, 3-4, 1982.

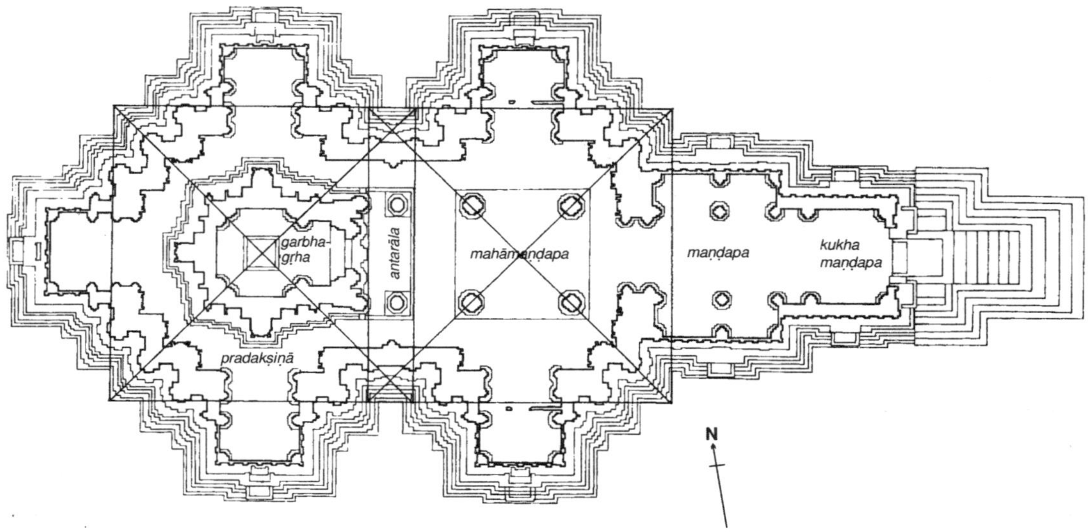

Fig. 19.3 Plan of the *sāndhāra* temple, Khajuraho (after Archaelogical Survey of India). (courtesy: Franco-Indian Research, Mumbai)

III

Sheer beauty of symmetry is felt in the arrangement of sculptural figures on the sanctum walls of the *sāndhāra* temples. There is a rhythmic pattern in the arrangement of *surasundarīs* (celestial females), *viyālas* (griffins), *mithunas* (couples) on either side of the cardinal niches, on the three sides of the sanctum (*figs.* 19.2 and 19.4). The Lakṣmaṇa temple, for the instance, has on each side of its sanctum wall, four *vyālas*, four *Kṛṣṇa-līla* scenes, and eight *surasundarīs*. The eight Vasus and the eight regents of space, the *dikpālas*, guard the sanctum against evil influences. The sanctum is conceived of as a *maṇḍala*.[22]

A symmetrical arrangement of motif is seen in door decoration of temples, with the *dvārapālas* (Gatekeepers), the river goddesses Gaṅgā and Yamunā on either side, and in the ornamentation of the *parikara* frames of the prinicpal images.

IV

Fourthly, there is a circumambulatory order of *pradakṣiṇā* in the placement of the Seven Mothers on the plinth of the two Śiva temples. Their placement on the temple is counter-clockwise (*prasavya*) as far as the devotee is concerned. The *mātṛkā* Brahmāṇī, who is first in the standard *krama* or order, is placed on the north, and is met with last when the devotee is completing his *pradakṣiṇā*, whereas the seventh *mātṛkā* Cāmuṇḍā, placed in the southern niche is met with first when the devotee circumambulates the temple. This apparent counter-cirumambulatory position

22. *The Religious Imagery of Khajurāho*, pp. 153, 156.

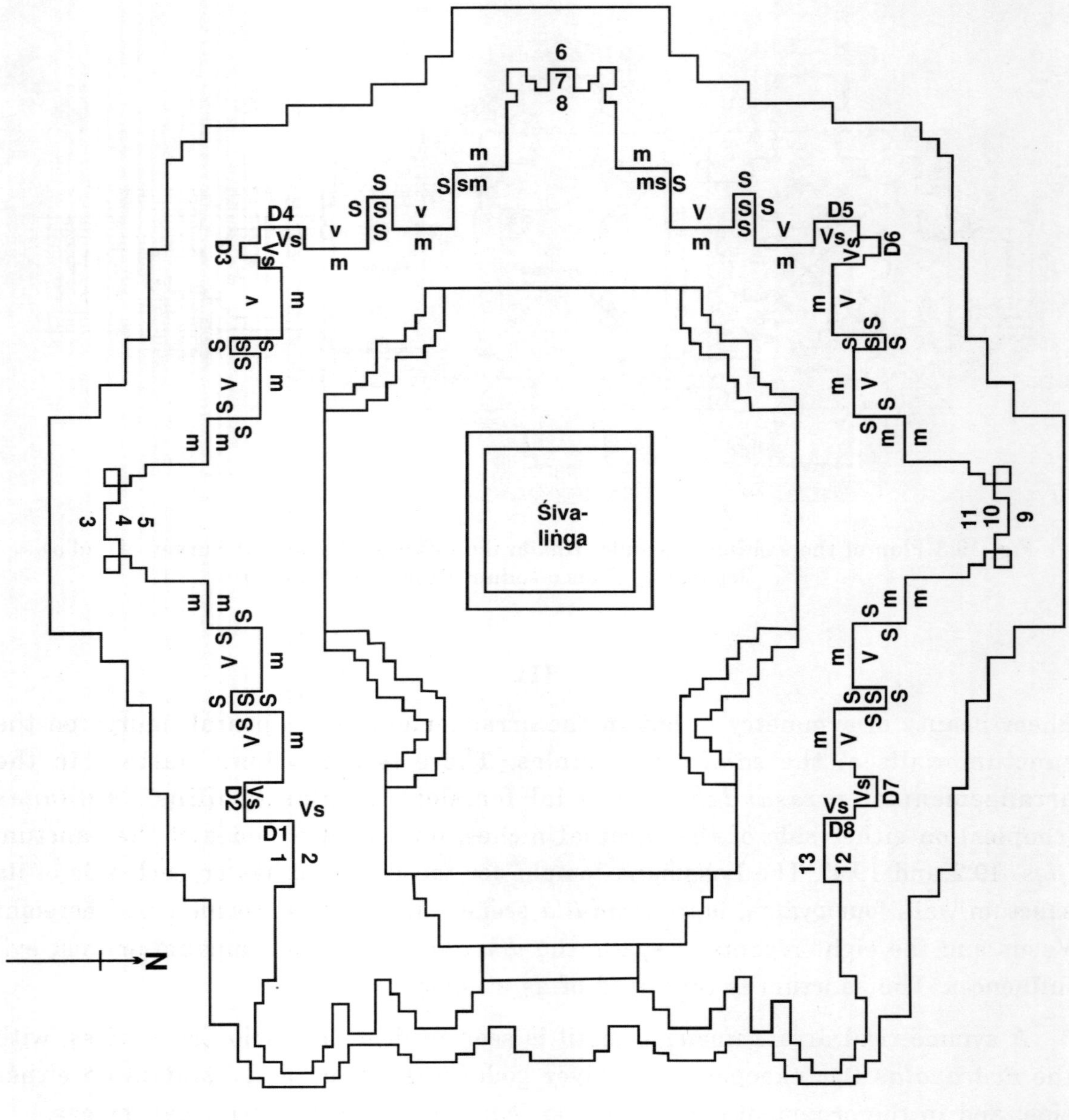

Key

D = Dikpāla

***D1** = Indra, **D2** = Agni, **D3** = Yama, **D4** = Nirṛti,*

***D5** = Varuṇa, **D6** = Vāyu, **D7** = Kubera, **D8** = Īśāna*

***M** = mithuna, **S** = surasundarī, **V** = vyāla*

***Vs** = Vasu*

***1**. Vaikuṇṭha, **2**. Kubera with consort,*

***3**. Brahmā, **4**. Śiva-Andhakāntaka, **5**. Viṣṇu on Garuḍa,*

***6**. Brahmā, **7**. Naṭeśa, **8**. Vīṇādhara Śiva,*

***9**. Missing, **10**. Śiva-Tripurāntaka, **11**. Viṣṇu-Lakṣmī,*

***12**. Lakṣmī, **13**. Śiva-Pārvatī*

Fig. 19.4 Placement of images on the sanctum wall, Kandariyā Mahādeva temple, Khajuraho. (courtesy: Franco-Indian Research, Mumbai)

results because the *mātṛkās* themselves are circumambulating the temple. The first *mātṛka* Brahmāṇī, led by the music-playing Vīrabhadra, has gone ahead in her movement in space, followed by the other six *mātṛkās* and Gaṇeśa (*fig*. 19.5).

The Mothers are performing an eternal circumambulation around the temple of *sthāṇu*, a point of stillness.

Similarly, the planetary deities, the *grahas* encirlces the Lakṣmaṇa or Vaikuṇṭha temple. There are nine niches on the socle starting with Gaṇeśa and ending with Durgā. Sūrya is stationed midway between the two, in the western niche. Up to now the other six handsome figures with *jaṭā* were not identified. But the frog mount of one of the figures helped me in identifying him as the planet Śukra (Venus),[23] and the identification of the rest followed (*fig*. 19.6). With excitment I could see the *grahas* encircling the Vaikuṇṭha temple. The planets are also associated with the five elements in Purāṇic tradition.[24] Maṅgala is associated with Fire, Budha with Earth, Bṛhaspati with sky, Śukra with Water, Śani with Air. In their placement in the Lakṣmaṇa temple we see the pairing of opposites. Thus, the Planets Śani and Śukra associated respectively with Air and Water are paired on opposite sides, as also Bṛhaspati (sky) and Budha (earth), Soma (moon) and Maṅgala (fire).

	5 Sūrya		
4	Soma (Moon)	Maṅgala (Fire)	6
3	Bṛhaspati (Sky)	Budha (Earth)	7
2	Śani (Air)	Śukra (Water)	8
1	Gaṇeśa	Durgā	9

Placement of *grahas* on the podium of the Lakṣmaṇa temple, Khajurāho.

The architect by placing the images of planteary divinities around the Vaikuṇṭha (Lakṣmaṇa) temple creates a cosmic imagery. The temple is likened to Mount Meru, the mythic world mountain in the centre of the Universe. The planets revolve around Mount Meru.

The devotee too follows the order of circumambulation around the temple, and gravitates towards the centre.

23. *The Religious Imagery of Khajurāho*, pp. 135-43, photos 142-8.

24. *Ibid*., p. 141, *MASI* No. 18, p.101, *Mastya Purāṇa*, Ch. 93.

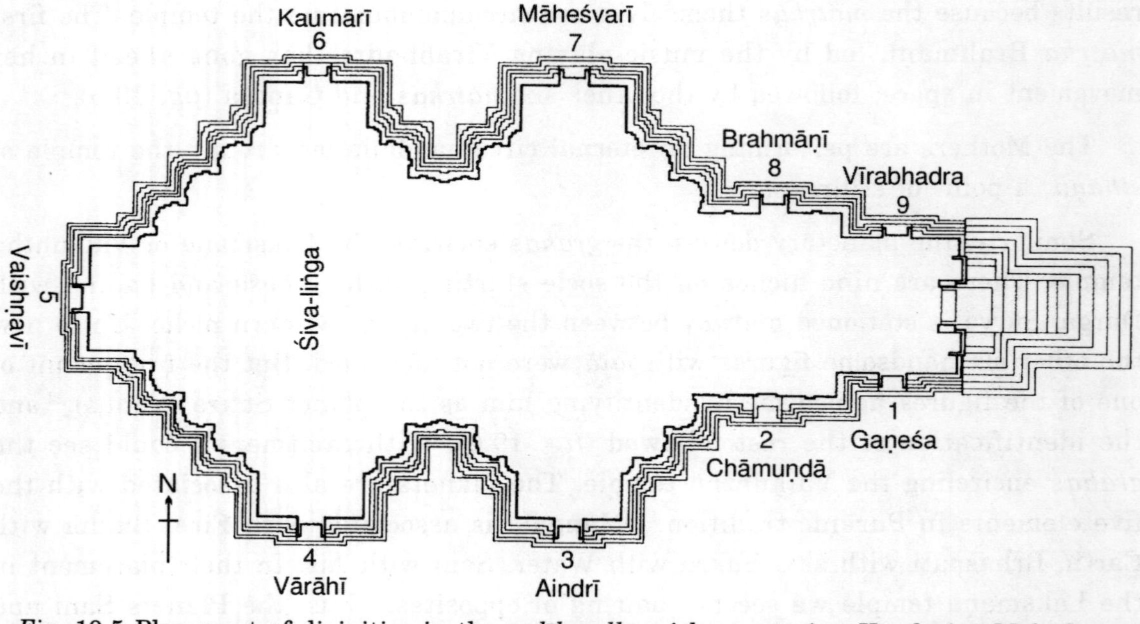

Fig. 19.5 Placement of divinities in the *vedībandha* niches, exterior, Kandariyā Mahādeva temple. (courtesy: Franco-Indian Research, Mumbai)

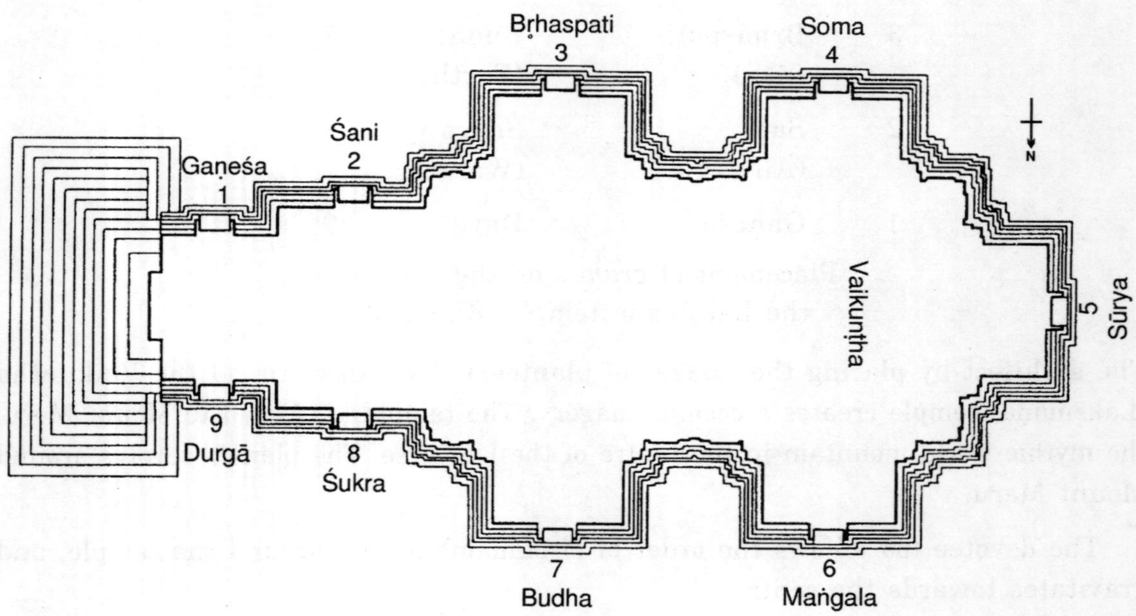

Fig. 19.6 Placement of divinities in the *vedībandha* niches, exterior, Lakṣmaṇa temple, Khajuraho. (courtesy: Franco-Indian Research, Mumbai)

In all the varied expressions of order that we see in the temple art of Khajurāho in medieval India, centrality is the overall order—seen in iconic manifestations in relation to the *Śiva-liṅga*, the gradation of mini-spires arrange rhythmically around the principal *śikhara*, the symmetry in the sculptural ornamentation on the walls and the door of the temple, and in the circumambulatory movement of the Seven Mothers, and the planetary divinities around the temple.

The architect has projected the temple as an integrated whole. The dynamics of the structure of the temple is like that of a vast banyan (*vaṭa*) tree with its interrelated order of the trunk, branches, twigs and leaves, all connected to a single whole. It is significant that the Supreme Being — *Śiva-liṅga* — is conceived in the Khajurāho inscription (*Epigraphia Indica*, I, p.140, verse 1) as unborn seed (*ajāyamāna bīja*) of a huge *vaṭa* tree. We can visualise the graded manifestations of Śiva as spread out in cardinal niches and peripheral walls of the temple. Though each individual image is complete in itself, often sheltered in a niché and attended by its own retinue of figures, conceptually it is not isolated but a part of the total system.

Finally, there is an amalgamation of the two orders—celestial and political — in the Khajurāho artist's portrayal of the mighty Boar, Yajña-Varāha, facing the Lakṣmaṇa temple in a specially built sanctuary. We see the Divine Boar who has just come out of the primeval waters after resuing the Earth Goddess from the nether region. It is a celebration of the victorious moment at the dawn of the present cycle of time. The vital Boar is covered with all the divinities of the Hindu Pantheon — 689 figures — in neatly arranged 12 rows of sculpture. Each divinity is in its place — the nine planets, the seven *mātṛkās*, the 12 Ādityas, the 11 Rudras, the river goddesses, the eight regents of space, and so on.[25] The order is restored.

Metaphorically, Varāha who rescues the Earth Goddess stands for the king who saves the earth. Such political-religious amalgamation of the myth of Varāha is known in central India from the fifth century onwards.[26] Here at Khajurāho we see the restoration of order at political and cosmic level. The powerful Varāha we installed possibly by the Candella King Yaśovarman, described as *Kuṇṭhitāri*, Subduer of Enemies, after he obtained the prestigious Vaikuṇṭha images from his *pratihāra* overlord. Both Vaikuṇṭha (Lakṣmaṇa) and Varāha temples are symbols of sovereign power. The political and cosmic orders merge in the representation of the mighty Varāha as well as Vaikuṇṭha-Daityāri.

Ṛta, Cosmic Order, is represented on a tenth-century circular stone slab, called

---

25. *The Religious Imagery of Khajurāho*, pp. 64-9, photos 64-8.

26. *Ibid.*, Also see Debala Mitra, Varāha Cave of Udayagiri — An Iconographic Study, *Journal of the Asiatic Society*, Calcutta, Vol,V. 1963.

antarikṣa-paṭṭa,[27] found from the Khajurāho region, and now preserved in the Dhubela Museum. The three footprints in the foreground of this circular slab symbolise the three strides of the solar Viṣṇu in the upper region, the earth, and the region below the earth. The unique slab illustrates the round orb of Sūrya, around which in the three rows are depicted the eight Vasus, the nine planets, the seven *ṛṣi*s, the twelve *rāśi*s (Zodiac), and so on.

While reading on the Vedic concept of *ṛta*, we note that *ṛta*, like the wheel, circumscribes the universe, regulates it and keeps it in place . . . and has for its physical basis the belt of the zodiac from which no luminary (*deva*) may deviate. . . . *Ṛta* is the path of the zodiac within which the apparent motions of *deva*s are confirmed and which is dotted by the *nakṣatra*s (constellations).[28] In the *antarikṣa-paṭṭa* of the Khajurāho region, carved 1,000 years back, we can see this expression of *ṛta* of the Vedic seers, which also anticipates the cosmic images observed by space scientists.

---

27. N.P. Joshi, Dhubela Saṅgrahālaya Kā Antarikṣa Paṭṭa, *Saṁskṛti Saṅdhāna*, (Hindi), IV, 1991.

28. V.M. Apte, in *The Vedic Age*, Bharatiya Vidya Bhavan, Bombay, fourth impression 1965, pp. 368-9.

20

Sṛṣṭi and Saṁhāra

The Dienergic Order in the Symbolism of the Śrī-Cakra

Madhu Khanna

GEOMETRICAL diagrams known as *yantra*, *cakra*, and *maṇḍala* form a very special class of religious symbols in Hinduism. Their forms and functions within the tradition vary according to their uses. The most important ones are those that serve as supports for daily ritual worship and as meditational aids to stimulate inner visualisations; others are employed in astrology and temple rites; some are meant for proficiency in occult arts, and many of these are used as talismans.

Meditational *yantra* or *cakra* are an indispensable constituent of Tāntric worship and are a substitute for the deity's iconographic image. Basically, a *yantra* used in this context is an abstract icon of some personification or aspect of the deity. Most Indian divinities have been assigned aniconic symbols in their specific *yantra*s. Whereas an anthropomorphic image is a static presentation, the *yantra* is a dynamic symbol of the totality of the cosmos. Hence, it is usually represented as an expanding form emanating from the central nucleus, a dimensionless point, the *bindu*. A linear configuration, the *yantra* usually has around its centre several concentric primal shapes, such as triangles, hexagons, circles, octagons, and rings of lotus petals. The figure's periphery is a square enclosure with four sacred doors opening toward the four cardinal directions. The seat of the principal deity is in the centre, while those of its emanations, or *parivāra devatā*s, are arranged concentrically in successive circuits known as *āvaraṇa*s ('veils').

This paper explores representation as a visual means to express the metadynamics of cosmic order as expounded in the theory of creation — as reflected in one of the most celebrated icons of Hindu Śākta Tantra, the *śrī-cakra* (also known as the *śrī-yantra*).

The *śrī-cakra* is conceived to be the aniconic symbol of goddess Tripurasundarī, who is known widely as Lalitā, Kāmeśvarī, Rājrājeśvarī, Tripurā, in her maiden aspect as Bālā Tripurasundarī or after her esoteric *mantra* as *śrīvidyā*. The cult of

Tripurasundarī is one of the most sophisticated and sublime streams of Hindu Śākta Tantra. The tradition came into prominence in the medieval period and has a very large corpus of literature in Sanskrit and vernacular languages in India. The *śrīvidyā* form of worship which exclusively centres around the worship of *śrī-cakra* was promoted fervently by Śaṅkrācārya through his four monastic seminaries. The *śrī-cakra* is an indispensable tool of *śrīvidyā* worship; and serves as a substitute for the goddesses inconographic image. Most Hindu divinities have been represented in their aniconic abstract symbol in their specific *yantra*s, or *maṇḍala*s in the Tantras. There is a very important distinction between a concrete, image of the deity (*mūrti*), anthropomorphic representation and a geometrical symbol of the *śrī-cakra* or a deity's *yantra*. Whereas in anthropomorphic image is a static presentation, the *śrī-cakra* is conceived as a dynamic symbol of the totality of the cosmos. Hence it is represented as an expanding from originating from the central nucleus, the *bindu*. Essentially a linear configuration, the *cakra* has around it self several concentric circuits composed of lotuses and triangles. The figure is bounded by a square enclosure with four sacred doors opening out to the cardinal directions. The *bindu* at the centre of the *śrī-cakra* is presided over by the goddess Tripurasundarī, while those of her emanations, or *parivāra-devatā*s are arranged concentrically in circuits. These are arranged in accordance with the hierarchical scheme of goddesses who preside over each part of the *cakra*. These goddesses are known as *āvaraṇa-devatā*s, so called because they conceal the luminous splendour of the deity in the centre. The most seminal, feature of the *śrī-cakra* symbolism is the manner in which it is to be understood by the devotee, as a fully manifested emblem of creation in the *sṛṣṭikrama,* in this mode the *cakra* is visualised *bindu* outwards as an expanding cosmos from the centre. *Śrīvidyā* masters have explained the evolutionary sequence of the theory of creation through the visual language of the *śrī-cakra* in the *sṛṣṭikrama*. However, when the *cakra* is understood in exoteric ritual worship and contemplative practice the figure is read in the opposite direction, square inwards, in orderly sequence which begins from the outermost periphery of the figure, the square moving inwards circuit after circuit, in nine stages. This is known as the *saṁhārakrama*, or the involution mode.

The term dienergic seems to be most appropriate to convey these two modes. It connotes, an orderly process involving the union of opposite principles, whose creative activity is expressed through the dynamic interplay of expansion and contraction, *sṛṣṭi*, and *saṁhāra*. The dienergic activity of the cosmos is a fundamental category of the theory of creation. By virtue of the fact that the *śrī-cakra* is a mirror of creation, the dienergic order of the twin cyclical movements: (*sṛṣṭī-saṁhāra*), emanation and involution, creation and dissolution (*prasara-viśrānti*), contraction and expansion (*saṅkoca-vikāsa*), thus forms the most fundamental articulation of the visual symbol.

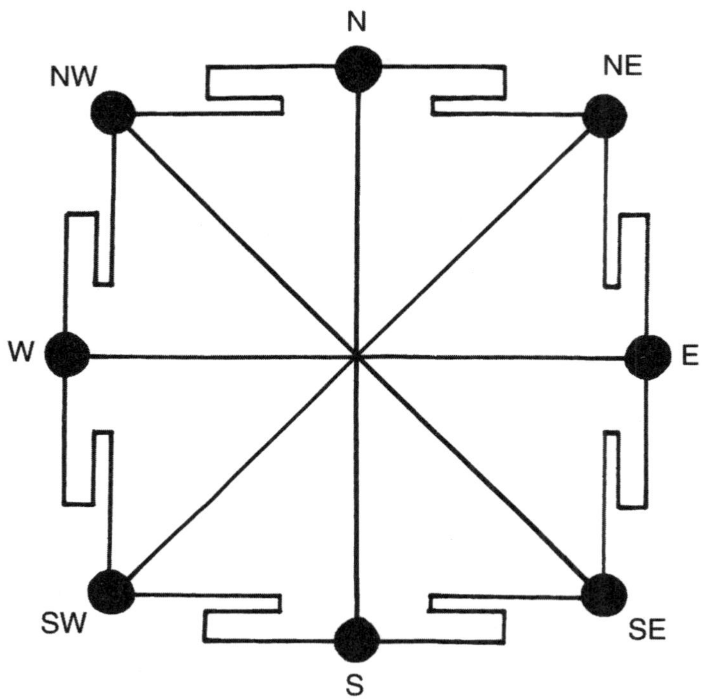

Fig. 20.1(a) *Sṛṣṭikrama,* the order of Evolution, movement from the *bindu* outwards.

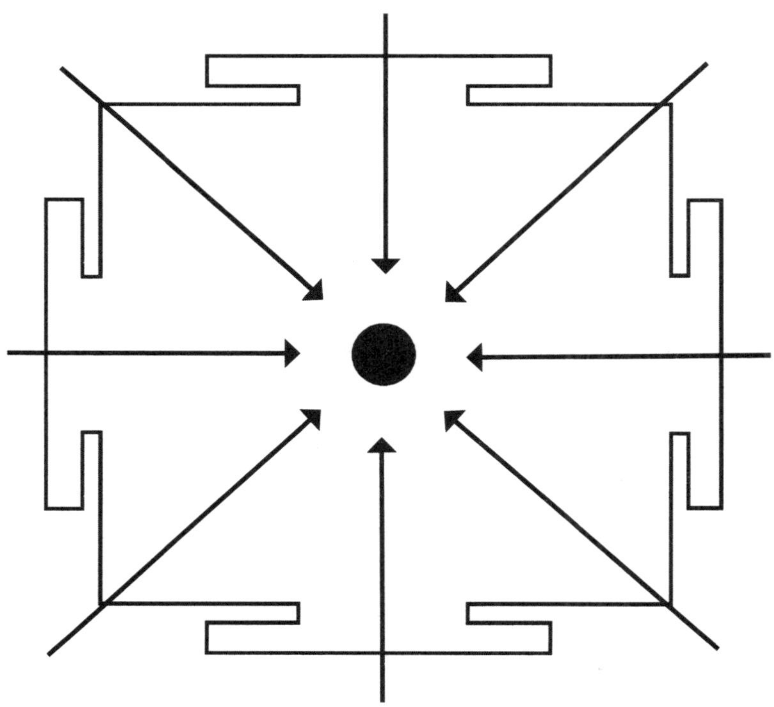

Fig. 20.1(b) *Saṁhārakrama,* the order of Involution, movement from the periphery to the centre.

The metareligions foundation of the cult of Tripurasundarī is firmly rooted in the *pratyabhijña*-based *trika* school of Kāśmīr Śaivism. The *śrī-cakra*, represents a graphic synthesis of the abstruse metaphysical theory of cosmogensis as expound by the *trika* school. According to *trika* school reality as an equilibrium of two contrary principles united in a harmonious relationship. The world emanates from a single all-inclusive transcendent essence called Parama Śiva, the silent seer of phenomena and the pulsing, mobile, energy, known as *vimarśa śakti* or cognitive energy. While Śiva, as the *prakāśa* is pure awareness *cit*, *saṁvid*, cognitive energy is his dynamic aspect. These two opposed yet complementary principles, are the ultimate cause of creation. *Vimarśa śakti* inheres in Śiva and they share equality throughout creation as one undivided whole. According to Śaiva philosophy evolution and involution of the cosmos is a ceaseless process. There is no such thing for Śaiva as absolute stasis or absolute dynamism. The point of stasis is inherent in the active emergent state of the divine. On the other hand, it is the innate nature of the active *śakti* to resolve into a state of rest (*viśrānti*). The Absolute reveals its divine splendour (*nijavibhava*) through these two modes of temporal succession. This vision of cyclic temporal order which is the very nature of the Absolute is the primary principle on which the cosmic dynamics of the *śrī-cakra* is based. Several Śaiva texts show how this creative act of cosmic descent and ascent is to be translated in the built-in dynamic of the *śrī-cakra:* which its means.

I shall first take up the stages of *sṛṣṭi-krama* as expounded in Śrīvidyā texts.

The sṛṣṭi-krama

The primal pre-creative stage of evolution is the state of total void, the purest principle of emanation, Parama Śiva. Śiva in his absolute state with his cognitive energy which is pure as a spotless mirror shine forth the luminous trans-phenomenal point:

> When the mass of sunrays of supreme Śiva is reflected back [on his body] from the spotless mirror of his cognitive energy, then the supreme point appears on the surface of consciousness lit by the reflected light.
>
> *paraśivaravikaranikare pratiphalati vimarśadarpaṇe viśāde pratirucirucire kuḍye cittamaye niviśate mahābinduḥ* ||[1]

1. *Kāmakalāvilāsa* by Puṇyānanda with comm. *Cidvallī* by Naṭnānandanātha, ed. and trans. by Arthur Avalon. Madras, Ganesh and Company, 1953, rpt., verse 4. (Alexis Sauderson's trans.) See: *Nityaṣoḍaśikārṇava* with comms. *Ṛjuvimarśinī* by Śivānanda and *Artharatnāvalī* by Vidyānanda, ed. by V.V. Dvivedi, Yoga Tantra Granthamala 1, Varanasi, Research Institute, Varaṇaseya Sanskrit Viśvavidyālaya 1968, Chap 1, 28-45. *Yoginīhṛdaya* with two Sansk. Comms. *Dipikā* by Amṛtānanda-nātha and *Setubandha* by Bhāskararāya, →

The first visual symbol to appear on the pure void of awareness is the *mahābindu,* the Supreme Point which rests in the centre of the *śrī-cakra*. This is also called *turīyabindu,* the Transcendental Point.[2] The transcendental state (*turīya*) is the universal awareness of 'I am all-inclusive' (*pūrṇo'ham*)[3] which spontaneously rises like a flash of light as modification of awareness shining in itself. This is the first moment of immanence when Supreme Śiva throbs spontaneously and observes himself. This is the stage at which the infinite powers of Śiva begin to be negated. Therefore, the limitless 'contracts', as it were, into a dimensionless point and has its first experience of cosmic location in the tractless void of consciousness which is the unchanging mirror of his essence. The Supreme transphenomenal point is Absolute as the supreme knower and is the body of Śiva and Śakti in union (*vedanārūpo bindu śivaśakti sāmarasyatanuḥ*).[4] Just as the scheme of the organism lies in its seed so the scheme of evolution lies in the form of potency in this seed of the whole world (*samastasṛṣṭibījam*). This point (*bindu*) then is the involuted state of creation when Śiva's power of awareness (*vimarśa śakti*) holds within her womb, the entire cosmos of 36 categories that will unfold as creation.

> Glory to the 'I' awareness which embodies consciousness whose form is the fusion of the fully manifested letters *a* and *ha*, the united body of Śiva and Śakti which has devoured all the spheres of the world within itself.
>
> *cittamayo'haṅkāraḥ suvyaktāhārṇa samarasākāraḥ śivaśakti-mithunapiṇḍaḥ kavalīkṛtabhuvanamaṇḍalo jayati* ।
>
> The two *bindu*s the white and the red hold the emission (of the categories) in a state of reabsorption when the Śiva and Śakti (which they embody) are separate. When they converge while preserving their individuality they cause the emission of the (universe as the) levels of the word and their object (i.e. 36 *tattva*s).
>
> *sitaśoṇabindu-yugalaṁ viviktaśivaśaktisaṁkucatprasaram vāgārtha-sṛṣṭihetuḥ parasparānupraviṣṭavispaṣṭam* ।।[5]

When Śiva and Śakti are concieved as an integral whole their symbol is the *bindu* of mixed colours (*miśrabindu*), white (*sita/śukra*) and red (*śoṇita/rakta*). The white

→ ed. Gopinatha Kaviraja. *Sanskrit Bhavana Granthamala*, 7, Varanasi, Research Institute, Sanskrit Viśvavidyālaya, 1963, Part 1, verses 2-15.

2. *Setubandha* by Bhāskararāya, Chaps. 1-8, 1963:2, p. 111.
3. *Cidvallī, op. cit.,* p. 16.
4. *Saubhāgyasudhodya* of Amṛtānanda-nātha, ed. V.V. Dvivedi in his edition on *Nityaṣoḍśīkārṇava, op. cit.,* pp. 306-21; 1, 24a.
5. *Kāmakalāvilāsa, op. cit.,* verses 5-6.

portion of the mixed point represents Śiva and the red, his power, Śakti. It is the holistic form (*samaṣṭirūpa*)[6] of the divine husband and wife (*divya-dampati*) in union.

The power and its possessor copenetrate in the intimacy of their union. They coalesce and part closing in 'like a bud' (*mukalībhavan*)[7] and expand outwards. These are the two phases of pulsation when the Absolute has a simultaneous awareness of the two moments of transcendence and phenomena in a single movement of awareness. First Śiva penetrates Śakti. This is the stage of extraversion of phenomena. Then Śakti is fused within Śiva; this amounts to the introversion of awareness. These two pulsations are the two phases of unfolding and enfolding that characterise the Absolute which is neither of these entirely but the unity of essence (*sāmarasya*) of both.

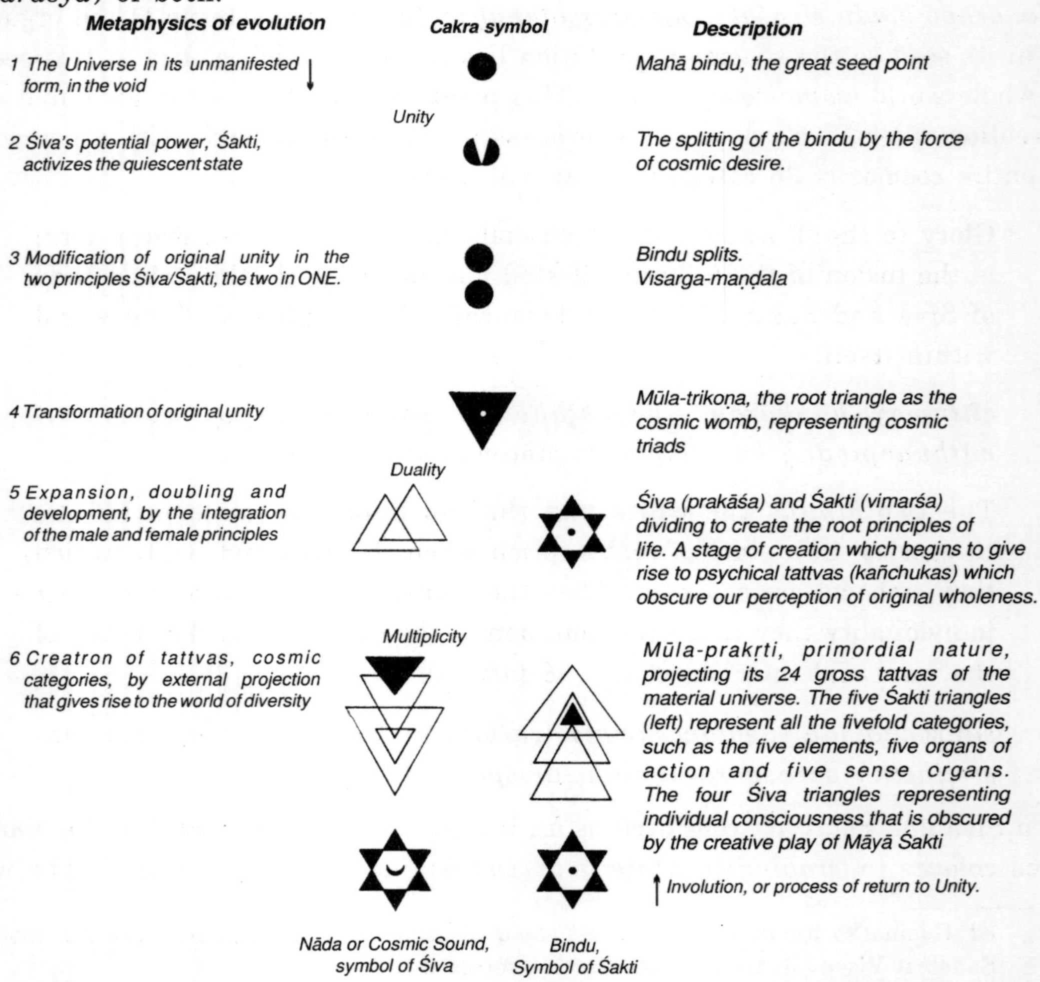

Fig. 20.2 Stages of the emanation of the *bindu* from a state of unity to multiplicity.

---

6. *Varivasyārahasaya* with comm. *Prakāśa* by Bhāskararāya, ed. with trans. Subrahmanya Sastri, Madras, 1976, p. 51.
7. *Cidvallī, op. cit.*, p. 18.

Due to the pervasion of cosmic passion arising through the mutual interaction of Śiva and Śakti, the transcendental point of mixed colour which is symbolised as the sun of awareness, becomes swollen, like a seed ready burst into life. At this stage cosmic evolution is triggered into action by the splitting up of original unity. There now appear two points, one white (*śuklabindu*) representing Śiva, and the other red (*rakatabindu*) representing his Śakti. These two points rest below the *bindu* of mixed colours. Though they appear as two, the pair is structurally indivisible even at this stage; they reflect the creative pulsations within the self-contained universal 'I'- consciousness. Together the three *bindus* are a condensed image of the universe glittering with the primal surges of contrary principles harnessed in supreme unity. The collective form of the two *bindus* is known as *kāmakalā-cakra:*

> The *bindu* (of mixed colours, white and red) which is I-consciousness and whose form is the fusion of this pair is the Sun. *Kāma* (so called) because it is desired and *kalā* are the two *bindus* embodying Fire and Moon.
>
> *bindur ahaṅkārātmā ravir etan mithunasamarasākāraḥ* ।
> *kāmaḥ kamanīyatayā kalā ca dahanenduvigrahau bindū* ॥[8]

The atomic *kāmakalā-cakra* encapsulates the very nature (*svarūpa*) of the Absolute-reality as dynamic equilibrium of the opposites. The *bindu* of mixed colour which is at the top is pure consciousness (*cit*) or Parama Śiva as the Sun. The two *bindus*, white and red, that lie below are the emission as *ānanda*, sublime bliss symbolising fire and moon. The playful dynamics of the two pulsations of the supreme point (*mahābindu*) and emission (*visarga* — two dots) in the transphenomenal moment of immanence is *kāmakalā*.

From the union of the white and red *bindus* characterising Śiva and Śakti flow the glittering waves of cosmic maifestation (*viśvalaharī*).[9]

In the next phase of its unfolding and evolution the supreme *bindu* transforms into the primal triangle (*mūlatrikoṇa*). The triangle is the second symbolic form of cosmic location to emerge from the blissful unity of Śiva-Śakti. It is known as the circuit of the womb of the supreme (*parayonimaṇḍala*).[10] The inverted triangle surrounds the infinitesimal nucleus, the *bindu* and rests in the centre of the *śrī-cakra*. In line with the theory of creation, the transformation of the *bindu* into a triangle is the contraction (*saṅkoca*) of Śiva into the cosmic triad of knowledge, knower and known. The emergence of the triangle marks the Śakti's awareness of her three cosmic energies: the Energy of Will, Cognition and Action that are related

8. *Kāmakalāvilāsa, op. cit.*, verse 7.
9. *Yoginīhṛdayadīpikā, op. cit.*, 1, p. 18.
10. *Artharatnāvalī, op. cit.*, 1, p. 18.

to the cosmic triads that make up the world. As a matter of fact all the attributes that characterise Tripurā's triadic nature are assimilable into the symbolism of the primal triangle. From the next stage on the expansion of the *śrī-cakra* takes place through luminous rays kindled by the flames of *prakāśa* and *vimarśa*. The combined light of their surging effulgence bursts forth from the luminous body of the triangle like pulsing vibrations (*spanda*) and transform into linear configurations of light.

After the initial crystallisation of primordial energy, the subtle principles of matter and spirit begin to make their appearance, and the whole process of creation alters course, as matter begins to dominate spirit. At this stage original unity splits into two streams, into subject and object in which all divisions and opposites appear. This phase of the *śrī-yantra* is indicated by the interaction of nine triangles.

Fig. 20.3 The traditional method of drawing the *srī-cakra* in the *ṣṛṣṭikrama,* the evolution mode, as outlined by the sage Lakṣmīdhara in his commentary to the *Saundarya-laharī*.

The triangles of the *śrī-cakra* are called nine cosmic wombs (*nava-yoni*) and parallel nine catergories of nature in the macrocosm. The triangles are in two sets: the four upward-pointing (known as *śrīkaṇṭhas*) emanate from the Śiva principle and denote the individual soul (*jīva*) and its vital energies; the five downward-pointing represent Śakti principles and from them emanate the material elements of the macrocosm — earth, water, fire, air, ether — their five corresponding subtle states (*tanmātras*) and all the human organs which react to the impressions of the senses. These are the organs which facilitate action (mouth, hands, feet, bowels genitals) and sense experiences (ears, skin, eyes, tongue, nose). The two sets of triangles are superimposed to show the imperishable unit of Śiva-Śakti. So united they form the creative cosmic field represented by forty-three smaller triangles, each presided over by a goddess, within the rings of lotus petals and the outer square fence. Metaphysically this stage constitutes the evolution of all the elements of nature: 'O Supreme One, the whole Cosmos is a *śrī-cakra* formed of the twenty-five *tattvas* — five elements plus five *tanmātras* plus ten *indriyas* mind plus *māyā*, *śuddha-vidyā*, Maheśa (Śiva), and Sadāśiva.[11]

Fig. 20.4 The fully created cosmos (*sṛṣṭi*) arising from the union of opposite principle in which the world of multiplicity, representing the 36 *tattvas* of creation is held together by the *bindu* in the centre, signifying cosmic bi-unity. The *cakra* is an expansion of the primal triangle. The dienergic order of the *cakra* is created by the primal triangle and the nine interperetrating triangles which result in the diagram of 43 trangles, each presided over by a deity.

11. *Bhairava-yamala* cited by Arthur Avalon in *The Serpent Power*, Madras, Ganesh and Company 1953, p. 145, for enumeration of 36 categories see: *Parāpraveśikā* of Kṣemarāja, ed. Mukunda Rama Shastri, Kashmir Sanskrit Texts Series No. 15, Srinagar, 1918, p. 7; *Pratyabhijñahṛdayam* by Kṣemarāja, Sansk. Text with trans. Jaideva Singh, Delhi, Motilal Banarsidass, 1980, *sūtra* 2 and 3 with note no. 17, pp. 122-24.

Saṁhāra-krama of the śrī-cakra

A devotee's spiritual journey from the stage of material existence to ultimate enlightenment is mapped on the greatest of *yantra*s, the *śrī-cakra*. The spiritual journey is taken in the *saṁhāra-krama* as a pilgrimage in which every step is an ascent from the world of multiplicity to the unity of the centre. Traditionally such a journey is mapped in nine stages, and each of these stages corresponds with one of the nine circuits of which the *cakra* is composed. Starting from the outer square and moving inwards, the nine circuits bear specific names, related to their characteristics; the first circuit (*trailokyamohana-cakra*) 'enchanter of the three worlds'; the second (*sarvāśāparipūraka-cakra*) 'fulfils all desires'; the third (*sarvasaṅkṣobhaṇa-cakra*) 'agitates all'; the fourth (*sarvasaubhāgyadāyaka-cakra*) 'grants excellence'; the fifth (*sarvārthsādhaka-cakra*) is the 'accomplisher of all'; the sixth (*sarvarakṣākara-cakra*) 'protects all'; the seventh (*sarvarogahara-cakra*) 'cures all ills'; the eighth (*sarvasiddhiprada-cakra*) 'grants all perfection'; and the highest (*sarvānandamaya-cakra*) is 'replete with bliss'.

As meditation nears the innermost triangle, a dramatic change takes place with the fading of the Śakti-clusters into the emptiness of the centre. The innumerable Śaktis of the earlier phases presiding over the circuits are reduced to three principles of existence, the Energy of Will (*icchāśakti*) the Energy of Knowledge (*jñānaśkati*) and the Energy of Action (*kriyāśakti*).

The ninth *cakra*, the *bindu*, is the symbol of final release. It is the summit of reality and represents the innermost centre of the consciousness, the abode of the supreme goddess Lalitā, whose mysterious presence is experienced in the depths of one's being. The *bindu* marks the end of the spiritual pilgrimage where outer life ends, the inner life begins; there is no shape, no form, all is immersed in the void.

The *śrī-cakra*'s nine *śakti*-clusters are thus nine levels separating the devotee from his primordial wholeness, or conversely, nine steps that can lead him through the principles or spiritual evolution. When the highest stage of exaltation is reached the *cakra* is internalised; it becomes a psychic complex. The truth of the cosmos, illuminated in the *cakra* is the *sādhaka* himself illumined, and his body itself becomes the *śri-cakra*.

In another type of meditation, the adept experiences both evolution and involution through the *śrī-cakra*. In deep concentration, the adept mentally constructs the entire image of the *śrī-cakra* from the centre, in the same fashion as the cosmos is held to unfurl itself in the process of evolution. After the whole image has been visualised, he begins his meditation from the outermost periphery of the figure. Moving inwards, enclosures after enclosure, he is symbolically involved in the 'dissolution' of all the cosmic principles projected by the nine Śiva-Śakti triangles.

In such meditation the adept lives through the whole drama of descent and ascent, as an act of purging his consciousness. He is summoned to and surrenders to initiatory death through which he is reborn. When he has attained the sought-after identity, the extended universe of the *cakra/yantra* symbolically collapses into the *bindu*, which itself vanishes into the supreme void.

Cosmic order

According to Śaiva evolutionary theory, the cosmos is to be viewed as a continuum. Whatever is born will develop, age, and dissolve again into the primordial reality that gave it birth. Like a circle, the cosmic order presents an interrupted continuity. hence, there never was a 'first', nor will there ever be a 'last' cosmos, not will there ever be a period at which the universe will have reached a static phase of total disintegration or total integration. There are three phases of the cosmic process: creation, preservation, and dissolution, a vision which Hindu iconography represents in the unified image of the Hindu trinity formed by the three major deities, Brahmā, the creator, Viṣṇu, the protector, and Śiva, the destroyer. The structural synthesis of the *śrī-cakra* illustrates the Indian view of cosmic time as a triad, with three phases of universal becoming. To match this, the gooddess Tripurā presiding over the *cakra* has three aspects: the young one (Tripurā-Bālā), the beautiful one (Tripurā-Sundarī, and the 'terrible' one (Tripurā-Bhairavī). Each of the three periods of cosmic time assimilates another triad, producing numerical association to the order of nine. Hence, the symbolism and basic structure of the *śrī-cakra* always revolve around a ninefold division which is basically an expansion of three. From its outermost periphery, the square, the *bindu*, the *śrī-cakra* has nine circuits, each with its own name and presiding *devatā* (*ante*). These nine circuits are divided into three groups of three circuits to denote the three phases of the cosmic cycle. These three major divisions which make up the nine circuits can be viewed philosophically as successive phases of creation, preservation, and dissolution. The following equation of ciruits of the *śrī-cakra* and cosmic phases is based on the *Tantrarāja Tantra* (Chap.V).[12]

First phase: CREATION

1.	The square	creation-creation	unity
2.	The circle of 16 lotus petals	creation-preservation	duality
3.	The circle of 8 lotus petals	creation-dissolution	duality

Second phase : PRESERVATION

4.	The 14-angled *cakra*	preservation-creation	duality
5.	The 10-angled *cakra*	preservation-preservation	unity

12. *Tantrarāja Tantra* with comm. *Manoramā* by Subgaganandanātha (Part 1, Chaps 1-18). Eds. Arthur Avalon and Mahamohapadhyaya Lakshman Shastri, Tantrik Texts, Vol. 8, London, Luzac and Company, 1919.

6.	The 10-angled *cakra*	preservation-dissolution	duality

Third phase : DISSOLUTION

7.	The 8-angled *cakra*	dissolution-creation	duality
8.	The primary triangle	dissolution-preservation	duality
9.	The *bindu*	dissolution-dissolution	unity

In the cosmic cycle no phase is absolute in itself but each is a synthesis of opposite principles, with the apparent disequilibrium neutralised by the principle of unity. In the first phase, for example, creation is seen as a vast cosmic activity in which certain froms of life are evolving, others are simultaneously vanishing, while some are static (preserved). In the second and third phases the same principle asserts itself, for while preservation or dissolution dominates, certain forms of life simultaneously evolve, are preserved and dissolve. Thus, each phase of the cosmic cycle is a dynamic whole, and while the Whole contains all the parts, all the parts assimilate the Whole. It is the dienergic order, that sustains the equilibrium of the *śrī-cakra*.

21

Ṛta : The Ordering Principle in the Cosmos and in Art

Chandra Rajan

THE Vedic *ṛta* is the eternal and immutable law, physical and moral that governs the entire universe and regulates every aspect of creation. The Vedic seers, the great *ṛṣis*, authors of the poems[1] of the *Ṛgveda Saṁhitā*, who are thinkers and philosophers, as well as poets, mystics and singers of sacred song, view *ṛta* as a power and principle as well as a divinity, exalting it to the higherst station in Vedic hierarchy, *parame vyoman*. The Vedas envisage three worlds rising above the earth (*bhūmi*). The third is *ṛta*'s seat in the empyrean. It is the world of eternal light and ineffable happiness that mortals yearn for; the paradise of mythology later named *svarga* (realm of light). The uppermost region in the universe is also referred to in the *Ṛgveda* as the World's Summit — *mūrdhan*. *Ṛta* has, however, a special place on earth as well — the sacrifical altar — *vedī*[2]. In fact, one of the two primary meanings of the term *ṛta-ṛtam* is the rite of sacrifice (*yajña*).

> इयं वेदिः परो अन्तः पृथिव्याः
> अयं यज्ञो भुवनस्य नाभि!
>
> *iyaṁ vediḥ paro antaḥ pṛthivyāḥ*
> *ayaṁ yajño bhuvanasya nābhiḥ!*
> — *ṚV*, 1.164.35
>
> This altar is the outermost bounds of the earth;
> This sacrifice is the navel of the universe.

Ṛta can, therefore, be perceived as holding a central place in Vedic metaphysics and a central position in the economy of the Vedic universe. Another perception of

1. A *sūkta* is literally what is well-articulated, well-wrought. It is better rendered by the term, poem, rather than hymn, which is commonly used in most translations.
2. *Yajña,* the rite by which things come into being; by which they are made; it is the re-enactment of the primal act of sacrifice that brought creation into existence. It has to be performed periodically to sustain creation.

the Vedic *ṛṣi*s adds to the profound significance of *ṛta* in the Vedic world. It is given pride of place as the primal manifestation, the first-born generated by incandescent heat (*abhīdhaḥ tapas*).[3] In the *Aghamarṣaṇa Sūkta* (*ṚV*, X.190) the seer (*kavi*), visions that moment at the Beginning before which nothing was. He witnesses the marvellous birth of *ṛtam*, twinned with *satyam;* the eternal law of the universe (or truth) and Being (or the Existent, the Reality) emerge together.

ऋतं च सत्यं चाभीद्धात्तपसोऽध्यजायत।
ततो रात्र्यजायत ततः समुद्रो अर्णवः।।

ṛtaṁ ca satyam ca abhīddhāt tapasaḥ adhyajāyata ।
tataḥ rātriḥ ajāyata tataḥ samudraḥ arṇavaḥ ।।

— *ṚV*, X.190.1

Eternal Law and Being were born
of blazing heat incandescent;
from that was born the Night;
from that the restless waters foaming.[4]

Satyam (*sat-yam*=is-ness) is what comes into being; it is the existent; Being. *Sat* derived from the root 'as' 'to be' signifies what *is*; what has come into existence; *A-sat* is its antonym signifying *what is not*; non-being, the non-existent. Because *ṛtam* and *satyam* emerge simultaneously and spring from the same matrix, they are coexistent and coessential. The twin birth of *ṛtam* and *satyam* says something else important. What *is, is ordered*. The *Ṛgveda* has another term for what *is*, but is un-ordered *tucchya*[5] undifferentiated mass of materiality; indiscriminate *chaos*, waiting to be ordered shaped into discrete forms of being. After these twins, everything

---

3. *Tapas* is also translated as fervour. Its primary meaning is heat.
4. Sri Aurobindo invariably translates *ṛta* as truth.

   This *ṛk* can also be translated somewhat differently because there are words in it that are bivalent:

   Truth and Reality were generated
   by blazing fervour;
   Then was the Night generated;
   after that the ocean with foam-waves.

   In later Sanskrit, *satyam* comes to stand for truth; what is, is real, what is real is true; there is a meshing of words and an interchangeability of meanings.
5. *tucchyena abhva-pihitam yad āsit*
   tapasas tat mahina ajāyata ekam.

   — *ṚV*, 129.3

   What lay hidden in chaos indiscriminate
   from heat, mightily emerged That One.

else comes in due order, because the ordering principle is already in place. Night followed by the Waters[6] and the Year, that is Time; after these come the twin celestial chronometers, the sun and the moon, followed by days and nights, the earth and the empyrean.

The Vedic seers vision *ṛta* as ranging over the vast spaces, moving straight to its farthest goal, laying out paths,[7] 'ordering' the manifest universe. At *ṛta's* command the waters flow; the dawns appear with unfailing regularity making the sky radiant, and the horses of the sun loosened to start their daily journey racing through space, and enlivening the world.[8] The word, *vāk* is the first-born[9] (*prathamajā*) of *ṛta*; and in some Ṛgvedic poems, the fiery, blazing creative force in the universe in its triple form, Agni itself, is glorified as 'born of *ṛta*'.[10] By the power of *ṛta*, the ancient sages, the Angirases cleft the cloud mountains to release the pent-up rain;[11] and *ṛta* rained plenitude on the earth. By its awesome power was the earth greened:[12]

> आविर्वै नाम देवतार्तेन परीवृता।
> तस्या रूपेणेमे वृक्षा हरिता हरितस्रजः।।
>
> *avir vai nāma devatā ṛtena parīvṛtā* ।
> *tasyā rūpeṇa ime vṛkṣā haritā haritasrajaḥ* ।।
>
> The divinity, Protector named, is mantled
> by the power of Divine Order;
> by her beauty are these trees green,
> hung with green garlands.

Ṛta is envisioned as a many-splendoured form in the Vedas:

> ऋतस्य दृढा धरुणानि सन्ति।
> पुरूणि चन्द्रा वपुंषे वपुंषि।।
>
> *ṛtasya dṛdhā dharuṇāni santi* ।
> *purūṇi candrā vapuṣe vapūṃṣi* ।।
>
> Firm-grounded are Eternal Law's foundations;
> manifold the splendours of its form.

---

6. The Waters of Creation, the space-ocean, that infinite and fathomless (*gambhiram*) reservoir of all the potentialities of being; the mass of materiality waiting to be shaped.
7. *ṚV*, 1.46.11.
8. *Op. cit.*, 1.164.37; 5.62.1.
9. *Op. cit.*, 1.164.37.
10. *Op. cit.*, 1.36.19; 6.13.3.
11. *Op. cit.*, 3.3.11.
12. *Op. cit.*, 3.56.13.

Looking around at the world in which they lived, the Vedic seers could not have failed to notice the unfailing regularity in the succession of events that flowed over the ever-changing face of the twin worlds — *rodasī* — heaven and earth and in their lives as well. It was an ordered universe — *ṛtāvari rodasī*. They intuited the presence of law that bound and held together the immumerable and disparate elements comprising the universe; weaving a pattern of the varied and variegated strands of being, of all forms of life, sentient and insentient; all existing and working in harmony within an intricate network of set and precise relationships. This law is envisages as integrating the several orders of being in the universe: cosmic, natural, human into a *whole*, a harmonious system. The intricate and interwoven network of relationships depending on place and function, rights and responsibilities maintains a delicate balance in the universe. Any infringement of this law upsets this balance and endangers Order. A similar view of this world as a vast and complex interrelated system is seen also articulated by the concept of the Great Chain of Being that was so powerful and dominant an idea in medieval European thought, so much so that the medieval Eurpoean mind was haunted by the desperate fear that a break in the chain, however slight, which might snap a link could inevitably result in the world lapsing back into chaos.

The law, *ṛta*, is inviolate; the divine order that it establishes on which depends order at all levels of the cosmos, is inviolable, never to be broken, never transgressed even by the great Vedic divinities, Varuṇa, Mitra, Agni, Indra, Sūrya, who are *ṛta* guardians — *ṛtasya gopāḥ*.The seers declare unequivocally that these powerful divinities, the Luminous Ones (*devas*) gain their might and majesty, their power and their very sovereignty over the universe through the inexorable power that is *ṛta;* by observing the ordinances of the Holy Law, following its dictate, its writ than runs right through the cosmos. These divinities, the Ādityas (born as Aditi, boundless space or Infinitude) are repeatedly celebrated in the poems of the *Ṛgveda* as 'ever true to the Eternal Law', 'knowing the Eternal Law', 'Strengthening the Holy Law'.

The Vedic seers are very precise in their use of words; they have a fine sense of nuances of meaning. In the *Ṛgveda*, *ṛta* is the eternal and inviolable law of the universe and it is the rite of sacrifice that is so central in Vedic faith and praxis; sometimes the word signifies water. We might assume that these are the primary meanings of twin terms *ṛta-ṛtam*. But, in course of time, the semantic area of the words becomes considerably expanded to include many other meanings. The dictionaries list a dozen or more meanings for *ṛta* and *ṛtam*: what is proper, right, fit, sincere, brave, etc., for the former; and custom, pious action, faith, wealth, carrying on one's livelihood, for the latter. No doubt language changes like all things that are living; words change their significations with changes in the world-view; they take on new meanings; or they drop out of use and are replaced. To what extent semantic stretching and loosening is desirable and meaningful is a moot point. *Ṛtam*, orderly flow, ever-moving, moving on, is wonderfully evocative of the manifold rhythms of the universe: from the majestic wheeling of celestial luminaries in space, the ebb and flow of tides, the endless procession of seasons and the regular movements of winds and clouds (as in the grand sweep of Megha in Kālidāsa's poem to which we shall come presently), to the beat of the human heart. But the word dropped out of use at some point; it is not met with in classical literature. And the all-important term, *ṛta*, itself appears to have been superseded or replaced at some point by another term, *dharma*.

The word *dharma* occurs rarely in the *Ṛgveda*; and when it does, it hardly comes mantled in the splendour and sacral aura that give the concept of *ṛta* form as a luminous entity (*deva*); and lends that form its beauty, its majesty and awesome power that the Vedic seers 'enrobe' it in, transforming what would otherwise have remained a mere abstraction, into what it is in their well-wrought poems (*sūkta*s) — the cosmic, creative force that supports the entire universe.

The new word, *dharma*, appropriated a wealth of meaning possessed by the word it superseded. But, its orientation shifted perceptibly as we meet it in later literature, moving from the mytho-cosmic linguistic economy of the Vedic world to a more mundane, if secular and social world of concerns and issues; the ethical dimension of the word and idea is foregrounded, valourised over the sacral. It is as *dharma* that the ancient and powerful of image, *ṛta* enters the world of art.

Vedic thought stands solidly, though not obtrusively behind the work of Kālidāsa to provide that work which emerges out of a philosophical context as all great works of art do, to provide it with depth and substenance; and returns us to it. *Ṛta*, reinscribed as *dharma*, provides that interconnectedness and interdependance of all forms of being in the cosmos, held together within a network of relationships based on hierarchy of place, power and responsibilities. *Dharma* is the guiding principle. By following *dharma*, life takes on meaning and gains fulfilment. Violating *dharma* brings suffering in its wake, entailing punishment and the need for expiation of the transgression. Wielding multiple meanings, such as, the law, duty, right action, virtue, moral and social order, the inherent quality in a person or thing (*sva-dharma*), *dharma* functions as a co-ordinating concept that brings the several meanings of the word together and integrates the religious, ethical, social and personal life of man in the same way that *ṛta* integrated all the multiple levels of being in the Vedic universe. As all forms of life sentient and insentient obeyed the command of *ṛta*, so also, non-human and insentient forms of being, such as the rain cloud, *megha*, follow their *dharma* in later thought and writing, as we shall see presently in our study of Kālidāsa's *Meghadūtam* (this is the work that I shall use to illustrate the role of *ṛta-dharma* as an ordering principle).

The terms *dharma* and its opposite, *adharma* are not named as such in *Meghadūtam*. No overt comments of approval or condemnation are found in the poem. Kālidāsa is a poet, not a preacher. Poetry works by indirection, by suggestion, employing the invaluable and subtle resources of the language, exploiting the potentialities of word and image that make a far more powerful impact on the responsive sensibility than a set of moral statements. Except for the odd observation now and then, Kālidāsa, like the Vedic seers before him, uses the strategies of language to make his point and articulate his vision of the existential condition; he employs images and allusions; the narrative structure with its symmetries, both contrasting and complementary; myth and legend; literary reminiscences; and the cadences of the verse, to rehearse the consequences of the violation of *dharma*, and also to set up *dhārmic* ideals. *Dharma* is not presented as an abstraction; its values and norms are integral to the structure. The *dhārmic* ideal is implicit in the vision that informs the poem shaping it from within.

An ordered world, a whole which is the world of the *yakṣa* and the beloved (*kāntā*), lies as a sub-text at the heart of the poem. It becomes fractured as a result of the violation of the law. Another world, the world of the law-abiding *megha*, the rain cloud, is created by the poem in contrast to act as a foil to it. But before laying out the manner in which the poem articulate its vision, a few introductory remarks about the poem itself are necessary.

Meghadūtam is a long lyrical monologue that employs a very effective blend of two distinctive modes of poetry, the elegiac and the celebratory modes that are interfused and not rigidly kept apart. The choice of *genre*, the lyrical monologue that marks a newmovement in classical poetry after the great period of the epics, is eminently suited to serve the twin purposes that the poem sets out to accomplish and accomplishes with extraordinary finesse and poetic tact. The two purposes might be characterised as the ethical-expiatory and the exploratory-celebratory. For the purposes of this essay, only the former aspect of the poem will be considered, though it is not easy to draw a hard and fast line of distinction between the two.

The poem has the barest possible outline of a story told in the first few stanzas. There are three characters: the speaker, a *yakṣa*, a celestial being exiled for dereliction of duty; the rain cloud, *megha*, whom he requests to carry a message of hope to his grieving wife in *Alakā;* the beloved herself (*kāntā*) who remains unseen. She is seen only through his eyes and heard through his voice, but her presence and her sorrow are pervasive in the poem. In fact, looked at from one point of view (and *Meghadūtam* is a multifaceted and many-splendoured work of the poetic imagination), she *is* the poem in the deepest sense.

The speaker of the poem, the exiled *yakṣa* and the beloved, the *yakṣī* are not named; and *megha*, the cloud is simply what the poem puts it forward as, a rain cloud, the first of the monsoon season. There is an element of depresonalisation at work here. The characters are stripped of particularity. 'A certain *yakṣa*' was found guilty of irresponsibility in carrying out the duties of his high office; this how the poem begins:

कश्चित्कान्ताविरहगुरुणा स्वाधिकारात्प्रमत्तः
शापेनास्तंगमितमहिमा वर्षभोग्येन भर्तुः।
यक्षश्चक्रे जनकतनयास्नानपुण्योदकेषु
स्निग्धच्छायातरुषु वसतिं रामगिर्याश्रमेषु।।१।।

kaścit kāntā-viraha-guruṇā svādhikārāt pramattaḥ
śāpena astam-gamita-mahimā varṣa-bhogyena bhartuḥ ।
yakṣaś cakre janaka-tanayā-snāna-puṇyodakeṣu
snighacchāyā-taruṣu vasatiṁ rāmagiri-āśrameṣu ।।

A certain *yakṣa* heedless of his appointed duties
and cursed by his lord to endure
a year's grievous separation from his beloved
dwelt exiled, his lustre dimmed, on Rāma's hill
in hermitage thick with shade-trees and waters
hallowed by the baths of Janaka's daughter
— *Megh*.1

Adhikāra signifies high office, a position of trust and authority in a political and/or administrative set-up or hierarchy, *pramattaḥ*, the adjective of *pramāda* 'meaning heedlessness, negligence, error, also carries a sense of intoxication and lasciviousness. The latter senses of the word are strengthened by the two terms used in the poem to characterise the erring *yakṣa*, namely, *kāmī* (passionate lover, passion-ridden), and *kāmārta* (sick with passion, tormented by obsessive passion).

The choice of the word, *pramattaḥ*, is highly significant. Heedlessness is the root cause of many of the human errors of ommision and commission. It is a symptom of the absence of inner discipline; a weakening of the moral fibre which results in a lack of keen awareness to discriminate right from wrong. This would result in a proneness to be indifferent, negligent, *heedless*. In religious thought, heedlessness is a serious shortcoming, a fault to watch out for (compare the parable of the seven wise virgins and the seven foolish ones in the Christian Bible). In iconography, in the great Cola bronzes of Śiva as Naṭarāja willing the world into existence through dance, the dancing deity stands on a deformed figure, stamping on it. This figure is called *mūḷayan* in Tamil, *heedlessness*.

By leaving the *yakṣa* without a specific name, the situation of a person guilty of transgression is generalised. He is *everyman*; any man who is neglectful and violates of specific orders by not carrying out duties entrusted to him. The *yakṣa* is no ordinary, petty official; he is a great lord in Alakā in whom his lord reposes trust; esteeming him worthy of placing in a high office involving special responsibilities. The violation is not particularised either. It is characterised by a single phrase: *svādhikārāt pramattaḥ*, swerving from the line of duty; the reason being to emphasise the inexorable fact, the truth even that the law, *ṛta*, *dharma*, is inviolable, no matter what. There can be no extenuating cirumstances. Therefore, the precise form that any kind of transgression takes is beside the point. The circumstances leading to and/or surrounding the dereliction of duty are not rehearsed because they are not relevant. *Dharma* has been flouted. The relationship between Kubera, Lord of the *yakṣa*s and his vassal, between master and subordinate, is broken. The delicate balance that maintains order in social structures and other structures as well, personal, political, administrative is upset. This could result in the unravelling of the whole interconnected network of relationships in the universe at any and/or all levels, as discussed earlier. Order, the very principle of *ṛta* (and *dharma*) is endangered. Punishment is immediate and swift. It has to be, to preserve order. Hierarachy is one of the forms of order. The violation of *dharma* brings suffering in its wake. Kubera's curse strips the *yakṣa* of his extraordinary powers, the *siddhi*s,[13] his glory (*mahimā*), his status; and he is banished from his home and his wife, from family and society. As a result, the world of the *yakṣa* and his beloved is fractured. They are both left rootless, alone, and unsupported. Further, alienation of many sorts comes into the lives of these two, to which we shall comes presently.

Though the names of the characters are not given and the precise nature of the *yakṣa*'s duties and the manner in which he failed are not described, the place and day of his wrongdoing is clearly stated; the precise relationship of Kubera and our *yakṣa* is also clearly defined.

Kubera is characterised as *bhartā*, the one who bears, supports, sustains and protects his world; the *yakṣa*-world in the Himālayas. He is the Lord of Riches, the riches of all earth, and what is more important, friend to the supreme, Śiva. In V.73 Śiva is referred to as *dhanapatisakhā* (friend of the Lord of Riches) and out of affection for His friend, Śiva has made Alakā situated on the ridge of Kailāsa and encircled by the holy Gaṅgā, His temporal abode, Śiva 'seated in her outer groves' illuminate Alakā perpetually by the moonlight streaming from his brow (8). The place of violation of *ṛta-dharma* is a specially holy place hallowed by the perpetual presence of Śiva, the Supreme. Alakā awash and radiantly luminous, is not illuminated by the ordinary light subject to change that we mortals live by.

Since Śiva is mentioned twice in the poem, where there is no narrative reason for doing so, it is reasonable to assume that there is a poetic reason for doing so.The

13. The eight suprahuman powers: to become minute or emormous, light or very heavy, to move freely, gain all desires, have lordship and possess total self-control.

yakṣa's wrongdoing seems to be somehow related to the Supreme and its terrestrial presence. At this point, the poem also introduces an interesting reference to another transgression, to another violation of *dharma*,[14] by another offender at another time, Kāma, who was burnt to ashes because he dared to violate the penance groves on Kailāsa where the Supreme *sat* in Yogic contemplation, lost to all thought of the world he had created. Kāma invaded this holy sanctuary, creating the untimely arrival of springtime in the cold season, setting all hearts on fire, filling all forms of being with desire, from the sages seated in meditation, to the cuckoo and the honeybee, though it was not their mating season. Dire punishment immediately followed, because Kāma had brought disorder into an ordered world, upsetting the balanced rhythms of life in nature and man. Similarly, the *yakṣa* by his wrongdoing had let disorder enter Alakā's ordered world.

मत्वा देवं धनपतिसखं यत्र साक्षाद्वसन्तं ।
प्रायश्चापं न वहति भयान्मन्मथः षट्पदज्यम् ।।

matvā devaṁ dhanapatisakhaṁ yatra sākṣāt vasantaṁ ।
prāyaś cāpaṁ na vahati bhayāt manamathaḥ satpadājyam ।।

Knowing well the Luminous Lord to dwell incarnate,
Friend to the Lord of Treasures, the god of love
Out of fear, refrains from drawing his bow
Strung with honeybees;

The day is also very sacred. It is the day of Viṣṇu's Awakening from his four month *yoga-nidrā* (110), known and celebrated as *Hari-Prabodhinī*. This only compounds the seriousness of the wrongdoing. The poem articulates the double violation of *dharma*, different in nature and relating to two distinct areas of the *yakṣa*'s or of any person's life. The *yakṣa*'s neglect of duties entrusted to him Kubera, his overlord and hierachical and social superior is socio-political, hierachic and administrative in nature. Kubera is ruler of a vast, opulent and powerful kingdom on whose prosperity some of the plenitude of the earth and the universe itself depends, for Kubera is the guardian of the nothern quarter of space; he is a *dikpāla*.[15] And to be entrusted with an important set of duties in this kingdom is a privilege bestowed on our *yakṣa*; an honour of which is not sufficiently appreciative. The *yakṣa* is a not a clerk pushing files in a corner in a government office handling trivialities, he is high official in the economy of the universe. Similarly, in the play, *Śākuntalam*, Śakuntalā obsessed by love for King Duṣyanta fails to honour a guest coming to her father Kaṇva's hermitage, despite the fact that her father had given her and not one

14. *KS*, canto 3: the episode referred to breifly here is described and narrated in great detail.

15. Literally: protector of the directions of space.

of his disciples the responsibility of offering hospitality to guests of the hermitage.[16] She was also punished for heedlessness, for neglect of specified duties. In the secular terms of our day and age, the *yakṣa* neglect of his responsibilities is disregard of the moral obligations of loyalty to the state and accountability that attaches to any high office. The other aspect of the violation of *dharma* is a religious one. It is disrespect to the supreme presence in Kubera's kingdom; to Śiva. Man owes a duty to the divine in his life. The disregard of the duty to the Lord of the Universe, who is above the *yakṣa*'s immediate superior, Kubera, is a prime instance of forgetfullness (heedlessness) of the need that is deeply grounded in human consciousness; the need to relate to the transcendent, through prayer, through ritual service and adoration, we do not know exactly what; we are not told in the poem. Leaving it unspecified is deliberate.

To all practical purposes the *yakṣa* and the beloved are mortals. They are humanised in the interests of reader-response. But it has to be stated that when celestial beings swerve from the path of duty (as they do in Purāṇic mythology) it only increases the enormity of the wrongdoing.

The *yakṣa* fantasises; holding his 'arms out to the empty air' to fold the beloved 'in a passionate embrace' (106) he realises how far away she is and fondly imagines that the Himālayan breezes blowing south touching his limbs have touched hers and hold her fragrance.

Moha (confusion) and *bhrama* (bewilderment) are signs of a disoriented state of mind. The poet seems to be interested in probing para-normal states of mind. Such states are always associated in Kālidāsa's works with wrongdong; violation of the law. In the play *Abhijñāna-Śākuntalam,* the king Duṣyanta is presented in a state of disorientation[17] as a coseaquence of his recognition that he has been guilty of serious wrongdoing in treating his wife, Śakuntalā, in a most callous and humiliating manner Dusyanta's violation of *dharma* (duty) has several aspects to it: rejection of a lawfully-wedded wife pregnant with his child, hurling insults at her in public, tainting her reputation, slandering her as a liar and whore; showing disrespect towards her father, sage Kaṇva. These violations of the flow from his initial transgression of foregetfulness (heedlessness) of duties and promises. As he himself describes it, he suffers from disorientation (*manasaḥ vikāraḥ*)[18], his mind veiled by the darkness of delusion (*moha-tamas*).

A careful reading of the poem (*Meghadūtam*) and the play (*Śakuntalā*) makes it clearly evident that Kālidāsa relates brooding depression, delusion and

---

16. *Abhijñānaśākuntalam*: 1.12.2; 4.1.

17. *Op. cit.*, 6.14. 26; 6.14-24.

18. *Op. cit.*, 7.31.

disorientation, with the sense of guilt that comes out of the knowledge of transgression; and he associates these abonormal states of mind with alienation of one sort or another: self-alienation or alienation from one's conscience, alienation from one's world, alienation from the divine.

In both the cases of King Duṣyanta in the play and the *yakṣa* in the poem, some sort of external force, a catalyst is required to rouse the guilt-ridden person; rouse him from the stupor and start the process of healing and restoration to normality. An act of almost fatal, physical violence inflicted on a very close and dearly-loved person, the *vidūṣaka,* rouses the king from the benumbing stupor that paralyses his will making him unable to act. The *yakṣa* cannot act; his will is paralysed, until the appearance of the rain cloud, *megha,* rouses him from his power-less-ness by reminding him of the sorrow of his dearly-beloved wife, grieving helpless. I use the word powerlessness advisedly, because the statement that the curse stripped the *yakṣa* of his 'powers' (*siddhis*) is only a figurative way of putting it. The curse articulates the mind-power, the power of thought of one individual Kubera in the poem, and the sage Durvāsā in the play, that impacts physically on another individual, the *yakṣa* and Duṣyanta. For a curse to take effect, the victim has firstly to have the basic ability to discriminate between right action and wrong and have a conscience; secondly, he has to believe in the efficacy of the curse, in mind-power as a controlling force; thirdly, he has to know and recognise his own transgression. The *yakṣa* explains to the cloud that he is asking it for its help, because he is 'banished from wife and kinsmen' by 'dinvine decree', *vidhivaśāt. Vidhi* can and does mean in the context both the divine decree of *ṛta,* the cosmic law (or *dharma*) as well as the law of the divine, of the Supreme, as carried out by its vice-regent, Kubera. Kubera incidentally is one of the four main regents governing the universe; the north, of which he is regent is special. It is the region of light and life and the presence of the Supreme on Kailāsa, seated in the outer groves of Alakā. The south, whose regent (*dikpāla*) is Yama, is the region of darkness and death.

Since the *yakṣa*'s will is paralysed by a sense of guilt and he cannot act, he is left with verbal action only; unpacking his heart and mind with words. The cloud has to act on his behalf.

The monologic form selected by the poet lends itselfr beautifully to the reverie that the Yakṣa has fallen into right after he is introduced, as one brooding, 'the golden armlet slipping down his wasted forearm'. (2) In his reverie, triggered by the sight of the rain cloud that brings joy to lovers-in-union, sorrow to lovers separated and restlessness to all, his thoughts and emotions are meshed with literary reminiscences, memories of love and experiences with his beloved as they flew though space over the vast stretch of land that now separates them, the vastness symbolising the enormous distance that keeps them apart as a result of the violation of *dharma* (duty). Again in his reverie, the *yakṣa* traces his route to Alakā from Rāmagiri in meticulous detail. As he travels back to home and wife by proxy, we the readers travel with him and the cloud with its entourage of wild geese, swans, egrets and other free and happy creatures, 'always heading north' towards Kailāśa.

There is method in the wildness, the disorientation of this forlorn lover, pining on a hilltop. The Orient, the East is the place of the rising Sun, the place of life and light. Dis-orientation is to be cut off from light; cut off from the springs of life. The West, the Occident is the place of the setting sun. The poem pointedly refers to the glory of the protagonist 'having set', *astam-gamita-mahimā.* (This comment relates to mythology, both Indian and Greek; it has nothing to do with twentieth century geo-politics.)

The *yakṣa*, disoriented, talks to the cloud, that is to himself, because the cloud that has to act for him, is his *alter ego,* his 'other self'. In the long message of the *yakṣa* to the beloved he instructs the cloud to say.

सोतिक्रान्तः श्रवणविषयं लोचनाभ्यामदृश्य–
स्त्वामुत्कंठाविरचितपदं मन्मुखेनेदमाह ।।१०२।।

sa atikrāntaḥ śravaṇa viṣayam locanābhyām ।
adṛśyas tvām at kaṇthā viracita padam man mukhena idam āha ।।102।।

he, gone beyond the range of hearing,
not seen by your eyes, speaks
through my mouth to you, these words . . .
framed by his intense yearning (102).

As the poem unrolls before our eyes, it presents a series of vividly drawn pictures of the landscape in exquisitely-crafted stanzas that glow like miniatures. It is a landscape that the exile knew so well from his pre-lapsarian days; and the poet as well, to whom this landscape lay on the palm of his hand, as it were, marked by opulent cities, hills and groves, fords and places of piligrimage, places made holy by hierophanies (Manākāla's shrine at Ujjain, Skanda's birthplace on a bank of reeds), and criss-crossed by great rivers and cascading streams.

The major portion of the poem (12-65) is taken up with the description of the route that the cloud has to traverse as it journeys north over the vast stretch of land between the Vindhyas where the sacred river Narmadā rises, to Alakā perched on the slopes of Kailāsa and encirceled by the holy Gaṅgā. Such is the power exerted by 'a willing suspension of disbelief' induced in a careful and responsive reader by great poetry, that we think, we imagine, as we read the exquisitely-crafted stanzas that the cloud is travelling the long road, taking us with it, and the message of hope and comfort and of 'happy days' to come to the beloved lonely and distraught in her mansion floodlit by the rays of moonlight streaming from Śiva's brow. But, we are brought to stark reality when we come to the end of the poem, and realise with amazement that we are still where we were at the opening of the poem, on the same hilltop. The cloud is still poised on the crest of the hill. The *yakṣa* has just come out of his reverie, at peace with himself and the world; tranquil enough to wish us his audience and the whole world well, as he speaks the *bharatavākya,* the stanza of benediction (the epilogue). Nothing has changed. Or has it? Yet, we have travelled long and gone great distances, and seen and heard much.

Why is the tormented guilt-ridden *yakṣa* at peace, finally? Is this the beginning of the end of the curse? Of the end of a period of transgression and disorder? Is *dharma* going to be restored to its inherent power and majesty in a world purified of self-willed wrongdoing?

In Kālidāsa's exquisitely ordered poetic universe, there are always wonderful surprises, waiting round the corner. The journy that the cloud undertakes on behalf of the *yakṣa* is no ordinary journey. It is a pilgrimage; a very special kind of pilgrimage too. The journey begins at Rāmagiri on the banks of an affluent of the holy river Narmadā which has its source at Amarakaṇṭaka,[19] a place of pilgrimage celebrated to this day, as specially holy by millions of Indians. But the pilgrimage proper starts at Mahākāla, one of the holiest shrines and places of pilgrimage in the country because it is a place of hierophany where the Supreme descended into time-and-place to reveal itself in the form of time for the benefit of the godly. The cloud arrives at the holy shrine, a cosmic centre because it is a place of hierophany, at the hour of twilight, having already made itself ritually pure by dipping in the holy waters of the Narmadā, sipped, its waters and bowed in adoration to the river, to participate in 'the evening rituals offered to the spear-armed Lord' officiating as the temple-drum; thundering out its devotion (*bhakti)* for the divine.

Two important facts have to be kept in mind in *reading* the poem in relation to the role of *ṛta-dharma* in it. The initial violation of *ṛta* resulting from the heedlessness of the *yakṣa* though it is presented as an act of disobedience to his lord, Kubera, is also related in some unspecified manner to the temporal presence of the Supreme Lord, friend to Kubera (*dhanapatisakhā*) dwelling in person *sākṣāt vasantam* on Kailāśa (73), 'seated in the outer groves' of Alakā (7), shedding eternal radiace on this favoured and blessed world, the *yakṣa*-world. The term *bhartā* (*bhartuḥ* in the text is in the genitive) in the opening stanza, can and ought to be taken as referring to Śiva as well, who is the *bhartā,*protector, support and sustainer of the entire universe, in which case the curse would be read as laid on the erring *yakṣa* by the Lord of the Universe. The significance of the violation of the cosmic law which is what it would then be, is enormous in its gravity. And further, the imporatnce that

19. *Op. cit.*, 7.22.

the poem gives to the Mahākāla passage (34-38), which is central to the poem's structure and vision has greater force and significance. This passage is a 'visionary moment' where the cloud, *megha*, is apotheosised to fit it even better to fulfil the important role it is given; to effect the restoration of *dharma* in the lives of the individual wrong-doer and the world, both maimed by the violation of *ṛta*.

Secondly, though reverie, dream-vision — *svapnasaṁdarśanam* (106), the speaker of the poem travels evey step of the way with his 'other self', *megha,* home to Alakā and his wife, not physically, but *by word and thought.* He devoutly treads the path of pilgrimage duly performing all the prescribed rituals and gestures verbally. To him the pilgrimage is one of expiation (*prāyaścittam*) for wrongdoing. To the cloud on the other hand, it is totally something else; the cloud is sinless, pure in heart and mind. What it does for the *yakṣa* is an act of kindness, of magnanimity (113) to someone need and miserable. And who is more needy and miserable than our *yakṣa*, cursed, banished, deprived of everything, his will paralysed and unable to act, earth-bound? The cloud is performing a dhārmic act, rending assistance to others without thinking of itself and its own interests. It is also following *sva-dharma,* its prescribed *dharma* in the world by following the path laid out by *ṛta* right at the Beginning. The rain cloud in following a natural law, its annual recurrent cycle with unfailing regularity (as it was intended to do and as it did before man started meddling with the universe), is carrying out an all-important function in the economy of the universe, sustaining life on earth at all levels. Before making his urgent plea, the speaker begins with the proper phases of addressing a lofty and noble personage. He panegyrises the rain cloud as nobly-descended, born of a lofty lineage, the lineage no less than that of the celebrated *puṣkarāvartaka* clouds; and as the 'minister' (*prakṛti-puruṣa* of Indra, god of thunder, lightning and torrential rains; as the instrument that brings the divine fertilising force, the sap of life to earth. He offers it flowers — *puṣpāñjali.*

जातं वंशे भुवनविदिते पुष्करावर्तकानां।
जानामि त्वां प्रकृतिपुरुषं मघोनः।।

jātam vaṁśe bhuvana-vidite puṣkarāvartakānām ।
jānāmi tvam prakṛti-puruṣam maghonaḥ

— *Megh*.6

Born in the world-renowned lineage of Puṣkarāvartaka clouds,
I know you to be minister to the fod of thunder, assuming what shape
you will . . .

These celebrated (*bhuvana-vidite*) clouds are described in the Purāṇas as 'possessing deep resonant voices and the power to change shapes at will'; as 'brimful of water, raining down beneficial rains' on earth; and most important of all, as being agents of destruction at the dissolution of the universe — *pralaya*. They are, thus, envisaged as playing a participatory role in the creativre-destructive cycle of the cosmic process, *sṛṣṭi-saṁhāram;* creation-dissolution (the surging forth and withdrawal), a process that is cyclic and recurrent. Through the magic of poetry and the subtle use of language the poem elevates *megha* to a cosmic plane on par with other elemental powers that create and sustain, as well as dissolve and destroy Creation. *Megha*'s status then as the poem creates an appropriate persona for it is higher than that of the speaker, celestial though he is.

Another technique by which the poet elevates *megha* to equip it for its important role in the world of the poem ought to be noted. By various comparisons with divinities in the pantheon, Skanda, Viṣṇu, Kṛṣṇa, Balarāma, and by its close association with the Supreme, Śiva, the rain cloud is touched by the light of divinity. It is further divinised as it nears the holy shrine of Mahākāla; it wears a sacral aura:

> Watched with awe by the Lord's attendants
> because your hue is the colour of His throat; (35)

then it is given a participatory role in the Lord's Cosmic Dance about to begin:

> . . . the exalted office of the temple-drum
> in the evening-rituals offered to the Spear-Armed Lord (36)

Hindu thought and praxis offers three ways of performing religious rituals, prayers and worship (*pūjā*), and of going on pilgrimages: physically, in person; verbally, with words; mentally, in mind and heart — *kāyena-vācā-manasā* — as the religious prescription says. One should 'go in thought' to holy places and pilgrimage spots that are inaccessible, says the *Mahābhārata*. On account of the curse, the *yakṣa* is virtually crippled. All the sacred places that the cloud and we, the readers pass by, see and pause over/at and worship during the long pilgrimage from Rāmagiri, the appointed place of punishment and expiation for the Yakṣa, to the holy lake of Mānasa near Kailāsa, the final dèstination, are inaccessible to the *yakṣa* in his fallen, crippled state. He can, therefore, 'go only in thought' (*manasā*) and offer worship with words (*vācā*). Further he has to go on his pilgrimage by proxy, an option offered in Hindu praxis in cases of extreme disability. *Megha*, travels the path of pilgrimage on behalf of the wrong-doer, because it is not only pure and sinless itself, but also *ṛtāvan,* meaning regular as well as righteous, and *ṛtāyant,* meaning one who observes sacred order, following the divine law, *ṛta*.

Apart form a small 'detour' the route charted by the speaker in the poem is the ancient path of the monsoon clouds that was ordained by *ṛta* to bring plenitude and prosperity to the vast stretch of land that *megha* and all monsoon clouds have always traversed. Says the *yakṣa*:

As your course points due north to Alakā,
the way to Ujjayinī is a detour no doubt,
but do not therefore turn away . . . (29)

because, Ujjayinī is where the holy srine of Mahākāla is situated.

Before *megha* can undertake the pilgrimage for the *yakṣa*, two objectives that the poem has set for itself has to be accomplished: to make *megha*, the *alter ego* of the protagonist, and to elevate *megha* in status to the cosmic plane transforming the cloud into an elemental power.

To accomplish the first of these objectives, the poem creates a perosnality for the rain cloud and then invests it with the virtues and qualities enumerated in treatises on poetics as pertainig to the characterisation of a noble, high-souled hero (protagonist) of a poem or play, the *dhīrodātta nāyaka*.

Megha is an elemental form of being, 'blended of mists and light, winds and water' (5); but by judicious use of epithets — *jala-da, jala-dhara, jīmūta* (giver of water, bearer of water, one who is filled with the precious liquid that sustains life, respectivley), a basic outline of personification is first sketched out for the cloud. Next, the personality of *megha* is filled out investing it with the qualities and virtues of the noble hero: splendour and grace of form, courage and steadfastness of purpose, compassion and magnanimity, poise, courtesy and gently speech, high birth and breeding, loftiness of mind and ringhteousness of conduct. These are qualities and virtues that the *yakṣa* as the nominal hero of the poem is expected to have but does not obviously. *Megha* is created to be the hero, as a foil to the erring *yakṣa*, but more importantly as the ideal, a dhārmic ideal held up for the world to observe and emulate. *Megha* is the dhārmic hero of the poem; the *dhīrodātta nāyaka*.

The onset of the rains is that magical time in a sub-tropical land when the first monsoon clouds are massed in the sky gathering, ready to break the punishing drought and green the parched and thirsty earth. All nature celebrates the arrival of our *megha* coming 'like a king' 'in towering majesty' (*RS*, 2.1), and 'riding high on the path of the kind' (8), welcoming it, grateful for the countless blessings it *showers* on earth and all life.

The speaker as he communes within himself watching this miracle, meditates on the many ways, great and small in which *megha* exercises its beneficial powers; quenching forest fires, cooling scorched earth and shrivelled-up flora with fresh raindrops; brimming the thin trickles of rivers and streams with life-giving water; causing new life to spring up everywhere. These are the outward effects of the inherent nature of rain clouds; the expression of their inherent properties, *svadharma*. As already noted earlier, *svadharma* is the inherent property of a thing or person, and the duty as well, dependent on the station, function and responsibilities and rights of that particular entity in the scheme of things. *Megha* is acting according to its *svadharma*. But the *yakṣa* perceives them as acts of kindness, of service to the needy and helpless flowing out of the nobility, magnanimity and compassion of *megha*'s dhārmic nature; as the outward form of the nature and conduct of a dhārmic hero. The speaker of the poem internalises the dhārmic acts of the rain cloud making them a part of his own imaginative life of thoughts and emotions; and then he voices them rehearsing the various acts of help and kindness in detail over several stanzas, chiefly stanzas 17-28. As the ideal created for the rain cloud by the poem becomes an integral part of the speaker's inner being, we assume that he is learning the ways of his errors and gains some measure of self-knowledge and understanding of an ordered universe.

In addition to the role of a dhārmic hero, the poem is presenting the rain cloud as a *guru*-figure to lead the nominal hero of the poem on the path of *dharma* that he has violated and instruct him in *nīti,* living wisely and well, according to the law.

> Without a sound you offer *cātaka*s[20]
> the water they crave to drink; the answer
> noble ones make is to do the thing wished for. (113)
>
> The riches of the great are best employed
> to ease the miseries of the distressed. (55)
>
> The tenderness of true feeling in the great
> bears fruit in no time . . . (17)

The rain cloud is presented as a *guru* not simply for the benefit of one single erring *yakṣa* (who needless to add is representative in the world of the poem of all humanity), but to the millions who live and work in the land over which monsoon clouds make and have always made their annual, recurrent journey, sustaining the land and its peoples. Humanity is prone to take the blessings it receives from the world in which it lives exploiting the resources of that world for granted, causally, unthinkingly. Like the *yakṣa* lost in *heedlessness* it tends not to value, not to appreciate what it has what it has been given until it is gone. The poem, *Meghadūtam,* The Cloud Messenger, speaks across the centuries to successive generations of readers, as all Kālidāsa's works do in differnt ways.

The course of the monsoon cloud follows physical laws, the laws of nature. The poem gives it a moral dimension. Thus, in the persona of *megha*, the physical and moral aspects of *ṛta,* the law that governs and regulates the entire universe, as noted at the beginning of this essay, are exemplified. Even as the cloud follows its 'natural' course, it is directed to swerve from its accustomed route (29), not into

---

20. The crested cuckoo believed to be so finicky that it will only drink raindrops.

error like the speaker of the poem, the *yakṣa*, but into the path of *dharma* and *bhakti;* the path of righteousness and devotion. It is asked to make a detour west to Ujjayinī to the shrine of Mahākāla, perform there the due rituals of adoration of the Supreme, Śiva who dwells there as Time itself, whom the *yakṣa* in some way has offended; and then, and only then continue on its accustomed route 'ever keeping to north' (16), straight to its final destination.

At Mahākāla, where time and the timeless intersect, the poem pauses for a moment; a moment that stretches into eternity. It is 'a visionary moment'. This is the time and the place where the dance is. Against the blood-red glow of sunset reflected on its dark blue form, blue as Śiva's throat, *megha* thundering its devotion to the divine presence plays the drum for the cosmic dance about to begin. In this passage (see Appendix) the word used, *sandhyā* (meeting point), signifies both sunset and dawn; the two twilights, the two points where day and night meet and part. The poem is, therefore, looking 'before and after', to the beginning and to the end of Time (*kāla*) when the supreme, the creative power as Mahākāla (Great Time), dances the universe into being and then dances it into dissolution, taking it back into itself.

The vision of the cosmic dance is a revelation granted by Śiva in the form of Naṭarāja, Lord of the Dance, to special devotees; sages who have worn themselves out performing the austerest penances, yearning to see the Absolute on earth, manifest in the blazing splendour of its Cosmic Form. This is part of the mystical tradition in India; for instance, Śiva came down to earth to fulfil the boon he had granted to two devotees, and danced in the golden hall of the great temple at Tillai (Chidambaram); Kṛṣṇa revealed himself in his universal form to Arjuna in the *Bhagavad Gitā*, and so on. The vision in Kālidāsa's poem *Meghadūtam* ought to be placed in this long and hoary tradition. It is clear that the poem is saying something significant at this point. As the dance begins (see Appendix for the text and translation of this particular passage in the poem), *megha* the rain cloud encircles Mahākāla dancing the universe into being while the goddess, Śakti, appropriately named Bhavānī here watches with approving gaze. The *yakṣa* sees this vision; experiences it. He witnesses the rain cloud becoming part of this vision. We have to assume that the speaker is found fit to be granted the boon of seeing the vision of the cosmic dance of Śiva Mahākāla. Has he found favour in the eyes of the Supreme whom he seems somehow to have offended and alientated? He still has to continue on the pilgimage 'in thought' as the rain cloud goes on, onward, continuing its journey; contiuning its pilgrimage on his behalf and on behalf of the millions whom it serves distinterestedly. This appears to be the sub-text in the poem.

Within the circle (*maṇḍala*) formed by *megha* at Mahākāla is the sacred space of the dance, the most perfect form of Order, shaping the ordered universe — *ṛtāvarī rodasī;* outside the circle is the boundless infinitude, Aditi; unordered space, *tucchya,* as the Vedas name it. Is iconography, the circle is the *prabhā-maṇḍala,* the flaming circle enclosing the space where the dance is. In the Vedas the circle is *ṛta* itself envisioned by the seers in the form of a wheel, eternal, ever-revolving; the wheel of Time.

> द्वादशारं नहि तज्जराय
> वर्वर्ति चक्रं परि द्यामृतस्य
>
> *dvādaśāram nahi tat jarāya*
> *varvarti cakram pari dyām ṛtasya*
> — *ṚV*, 1.164.11
>
> Twelve-spoked never-ageing revolves
> *Ṛta*'s wheel in luminous space.
>
> पञ्चारे चक्रे परिवर्तमाने
> तस्मिन्ना तस्थुः भुवनानि विश्वा।
>
> *pañcāre cakre parivartamāne*
> *tasmin ā tasthuḥ bhuvanāni viśvā*
> — *ṚV*, 1.164.13
>
> On this wheel five-spoked continuously turning
> are dependent all these worlds.

And we have come full circle, back to the point where we started; at the Beginning, having thought much and learnt a little, the sound message of the rain cloud, *megha* still sounding in our ears. *Megha, ṛtāvan,* righteous and regular, *ṛtāyant,* observing sacred Order, following *ṛta,* continues on its never-ending, ongoing pilgrimage for India's millions, sustaining them, bringing prosperity and plenitude. *Meghadūtam* The Cloud Messenger, Kālidāsa's remarkable poem still carries the same message, still relevant to succeeding generations of readers:

> Whosoever violates *ṛta* does so at his peril.

References

Abbrevations used:

AV — AtharvaVeda. *ṚV — Ṛgveda.* *Megh — Meghadūtam* of Kālīdāsa.

KS — Kumarasmbhavam of Kālīdāsa. *RS — Ṛtusamhāram* of Kālīdāsa.

The translations from the Vedas are by, Chandra Rajan.

The translation of stanzas and the passages in the Appendix are from *Kālīdāsa: The Loom of Time,* Chandra Rajan, Penguin Classics 1989.

Ṛgveda Saṁhitā, edition of the *Ṛgveda* by Max Muller, Chowkhamba, 1965.

Atharvaveda Saṁhitā, ed. S.D. Satvalekar, Gurukul Pardi.

Meghadūtam, Bengal Recension, ed. J.B. Chaudhuri.

Appendix
मेघदूतम

दीर्घीकुर्वन् पटु मदकलं कूजितं सारसानां
प्रत्यूषेषु स्फुटितकमलामोदमैत्रीकषायः।
यत्र स्त्रीणां हरति सुरतग्लानिमङ्गानुकूलः
शिप्रावातः प्रियतम इव प्रार्थनाचाटुकारः ।।३३।।

जालोद्गीर्णैरुपचितवपुः केशसंस्कारधूपै–
र्बन्धुप्रीत्या भवनशिखिभिर्दत्तनृत्तोपहारः।
हर्म्येष्वस्याः कुसुमसुरभिष्वध्वखेदं नयेथा
लक्ष्मीं पश्यंल्ललितवनितापादरागाङ्कितेषु।।३४।।

भर्तुः कण्ठच्छविरिति गणैः सादरं वीक्ष्यमाणः
पुण्यं यायास्त्रिभुवनगुरोर्धाम चण्डीश्वरस्य।
धूतोद्यानं कुवलयरजोगन्धिभिर्गन्धवत्या–
स्तोयक्रीडानिरतयुवतिस्नानतिक्तैर्मरुद्भिः।।३५।।

अप्यन्यस्मिञ्जलधर! महाकालमासाद्य काले
स्थातव्यं ते नयनविषयं यावदत्येति भानुः।
कुर्वन् संध्याबलिपटहतां शूलिनः श्लाघनीया–
मामन्द्राणां फलमविकलं लप्स्यसे गर्जितानाम्।।३६।।

पादन्यासैः क्वणितरशनास्तत्र लीलावधूतै
रत्नच्छायाखचितबलिभिश्चामरैः क्लान्तहस्ताः।
वेश्यास्त्वत्तो नखपदसुखान् प्राप्य वर्षाग्रबिन्दू–
नामोक्ष्यन्ते त्वयि मधुकरश्रेणिदीर्घान् कटाक्षान्।।३७।।

पश्चादुच्चैर्भुजतरुवनं मण्डलेनाभिलीनः
सान्ध्यं तेजः प्रतिनवजपापुष्परक्तं दधानः।
नृत्यारम्भे हर पशुपतेरार्द्रनागाजिनेच्छां
शान्तोद्वेगस्तिमितनयनं दृष्टभक्तिर्भवान्या।।३८।

गच्छन्तीनां रमणवसतिं योषितां तत्र नक्तं
रुद्धालोके नरपतिपथे सूचिभेद्यैस्तमोभिः।
सौदामन्या कनकनिकषस्निग्धया दर्शयोर्वीं
तोयोत्सर्गस्तनितमुखरो मा स्म भूर्विक्लवास्ताः।।३७।।

तां कस्यांचिद् भवनवलभौ सुप्तपारावतायां
नीत्वा रात्रिं चिरविलसनात् खिन्नविद्युत्कलत्रः।
दृष्टे सूर्ये पुनरपि भवान् वाहयेदध्वशेषं
मन्दायन्ते न खलु सुहृदामभ्युपेतार्थकृत्याः।।३८।।

Meghadūtam
(Translation)

33

prolonging the piercing cries of love-maddened sāras-carnes.
Refreshing to the tired limbs of women
after passion's ecstatic play, it removes
their langour like an artful lover
plying his love with amorous entreaties.

34 & 35

Smoke drifting through lattice-screens
from aromatic gums that perfume women's hair
enhances your beautiful form;
Palace-peacocks out of fellow-feeling
present you their gift-offering of dance;
worn out with travel, having passed the night
in her flower-fragrant mansions marked with red lac
from the feet of lovely ladies, approach
the holy shrine of Caṇḍeśvara. Preceptor of the Triple-World,
watched with awe by the Lord's attendants,
because your hue is the blue of His throat.
Its garden are stirred by Gandhavatī's breezes
scented with the pollen of blue-loutes
and fragrances wafted from unguents
used by young women sporting in her waters.

36

If you chance you reach Mahākāla at a time other than sunset,
stay on till the sun disappears from sight;
by performing the exalted office of the temple-drum
in the evening-rituals offered to the spear-armed Lord
you will enjoy the full fruit, O Rain-Bearer,
of the deep-throated rumblings of your thunder.

37

With jewelled bells tinkling as they move with measured steps,
temple-dancers whose hands tire, gracefully waving
chowries with glittering gem-studded handles,
will taste from the first rain-drops you shed,
pleasure as from a lover's nail-marks and shower on you
sidelong glances streaming like a line of honey-bees

38

Then bathed in evening's glow red as fresh china rose flowers
when the Lord of Beings commences His Cosmic Dance,
encircling, merging into the forest of His uplifted arms,
dispel His desire to wear the blood-moist elephant-hide,
your devotion observed by Bhavānī
with steady eyes, her terror now calmed.

22

Levels of Existence

Keshav Malik

As I apply my mind to the subject in hand, namely, Order and Chaos, can I — far as myself am concerned — do any better than become a little more sharply aware of the stimuli in my immediate neighbourhood? I hear the loud blasts of a klaxon, the shrieking and shouting of several dozens of pavement hawkers, the beating of a carpet, a fly attempts to settle on my writing hand even as I constantly attempt to fight it off. As contrasted against these and other negating irritants is the balmy feel of Delhi's winter sun on my back, the soothing play of a gentle breeze among the neem-tree leaves, the sight of a pariah kite taking the thermal in the sky. There is a parallel inward story of fears and expectations in my psyche. Thus, pluses and minuses are among which our lifetime is set. And what is certain is that one is invariably trying to court the pluses and to flee from discordant sounds, sights and smells, or else from situations in which our state of well-being is disturbed unless, that is, we are obliged to put up with them.

From the above, one may also arrive at the conclusion that when things or events are so irritating or worrying one would like to enforce a corrective whereby the said irritants are removed and the state of well-being or rightness prevails. Such rightness may well be spoken of as Order and, its absence, anarchy or Chaos, a state where a free for all obtains; that is, where accidents are endemic, where chance or fate or obliviousness play a major role in the running of the house of human reality.

The observed sequences in natural events, like the rising or setting of the sun or the moon, the cycle of birth and death, etc., may too be called Order, or when deaprting from the norm, Chaos. But even though, on the purely day-to-day plane of conducting human life, those natural events play a vital, it largely invisible role (as backdrop), the human world within the purview of man's own actions looms disproportionately large. The two worlds, of natural events, and that other stemming from the human universe of will and wish, need or greed, are *in tandem* but we are far more aware of the action or non-action, of mankind itself upon its own collective fortunes.

To our conciousness Order or anarchy would seem to inform this world far more fatefully than to the world of evolving or collapsing galaxies and stars.

The universe of humankind is itself a prime universe, built as it is on untold, and contrary potentialities. And accordingly, collectively, the actions of mankind in bulk and in balance make for anarchy or for the Order that is tantamount to peace.

Mankind's life operates on several psychic levels; and those levels of being can clash, else come to terms, that is, be in fruitful co-operation. When fruitful to the generality of mankind, we call it the obtaining of Order, when in conflict with its surroundings, physical or human, it is to be termed anarchy.

Perhaps physical nature knows no Chaos, only laws. But mankind is fatefully burdened, or else gifted with consciousness, cognitive consciousness; and consciousness it is which experiences what may be called Chaos, or Order.

Equipped with memory, with the power of reflection on an ongoing inner and outer reality, mankind becomes maker of models, and its per force yoked life is guided by ideals of rightness or excellence. But those models and ideals, or blue prints, may well be defective, not keeping in harmony with the overall laws of the bigger world. It is then, and that despite good intentions, that Chaos is likely to supervene.

Man is a social as well a reasoning animal but above all he is one who fantasises or imagines without let. Minus imagination, or the dream of possibility, his existence on earth is humdrum; but also when that dream is all contrary to the known laws of nature or else to the norms of common human existence mankind comes to grief via the ensuing anarchy. In ohter words, the full maturation of all the human faculties or the deep interaction between the same, is the prerequisite of human Order, the Order that is life giving, open-ended, inclusive not exclusive.

It is commonplace that mankind labours under the restrictive laws of nature as well it profits when in harmony with them. But as already said above, most of his life's joys and woes come of the given state of human consciousness or else the condition of the human heart, of course, humanly speaking not medically. That is where the maximum order or disorder is experienced. But even when an individual human hear may be in Order, the compulsions of the surrounding social forces may make it a party to anarchy. There is no guarantee that the heart in order receives total pardon. On the personal plane yes, on the universal a question mark remains. The exact position is too complicated in this sphere. And, nevertheless, on occasion, certain individuals receive full repreive from the whole of humanity, that is if they have cut across the earth's fault lines, if they have fulfilled the laws of the human heart, laws ordained in dreams and issuing out of deeply inward being. One does not have to cite examples, those are self-evident. Some of the saints are also our greatest heroes. It is these who propagate the order of the human heart not the

Order of the twentieth-century's totalitarian ideologies — a moment of so-called Order when the very expression order becames a sinister word for those who suffered under its rigours. The order of punctual trains is not bad *per se*, but being so partial, insane.

The greatest disorder or disharmony or Chaos are caused by those of the human emotions which may be called the worst diseases of the ego — envy, jealousy, spite. These demons of the dark have been noted for a long while in the world's scriptures, but it had not always been noted that man could be moral and society or State under which he lived immoral, being beyond the law of the humane. One learnt this most clearly during this present century.

A great virtue of mankind is that it can band itself together, but doing so it can willy-nilly also be the cause of the greatest evil. Hamamkind may be its own worse enemy, and the perpetrator of troubles which fall under the head of Chaos. Chaos, or disorder, does not deal with abstract or mathematical categories alone but with entities suffering pain, capable of exaltation. The Order or Chaos between inanimate objects, or between propositions can be computed without that much difficulty, between human realities it has to be felt by live receptors. There is no way out of this obligation. The formlessness in human motivations, actions, feelings, goals, has to be personally felt, and not only thought out by the human receptor. For, if you do not feel emphathically all is neutral, a bald fact, and of only cerebral notice, not as the stimulator of conscience.

The feel of anarchy of Chaos become pronounced as and when the human instrument is finely honed. A human heart, say Christ's has at its base largeness of vision. This it is which informs the heart and makes it bleed, but not sit in judgement. This heart, inadvertently, is the harbinger of a new Order which is more pliable, more flexible, more forgiving. Of course, in time, the Order is a travesty of itself. Then the fresh need for a new informed heart, nothing less.

It is far easier to determine Order or anarchy in the arts. But even then it is hard to determine the true value of works of arts. Here only a subtly mix of ethics and aesthetic will avail. Vision is what may come out of the mix. And it may be, that, that art is the highest wherein mankind is helped to stand disinterestedly but in suspense before the majesty of the cosmos.

Physical nature knows no real Chaos only implicit laws; man alone knows Chaos, being conversant with his own inner world in a state of health or sickness. Man is a great self-reflector and such reflection is his glory as cause for suffering. Via consciousness troubles mount and so you have per force to constantly search for new humane orders.

Disorder is lack of pattern and form though not lack of logic. The greater the expression of Order in life or works of art or nature, the greater the suffering viewing the surrounding human disorder or squalor. The ideal world that the saints and artists postulate, makes the feel of Chaos, disorder, or meanness, sharper, not less. There is no escape from such an ironical poradox — except via the pang of tragic joy. That alone is assured.

23

Order and Chaos in Indian Music

Prem Lata Sharma

Ṛtam is paired with *satyam* in the famous passage of *Ṛgveda* (X.190.1) which says that *ṛtam* and *satyam* were born of kindled *tapas*. This relates to the primary analysis of the process of certain where Reality is seen in two forms, viz., *ṛtam,* the kinetic aspect of order and *satyam,* the potential aspect of Truth. Thus, *ṛtam* is the framework in which the process of creation, sustenance and dissolution operates. The *sva-bhāva* (own nature) of *ātman* is two-fold in the form of *satyam* and *ṛtam*. Reality speaking, that which is *satyam* in the form of *vastu* (substance), is *ṛtam* in the form of *gati* (movement). This movement is not that of our imagination. We can ask two questions about any entity — one, as to what it is in essence and two, how really is *vṛtti* (movement) taking place in the same. The answers to these two questions are different according to the difference of levels in our knowledge, i.e., in ordinary knowledge the answer would be of one kind, in the scientist's knowledge it would be another kind and in the lnowledge born of *yoga,* it would be still of another kind. The knowledge born *yoga* has also many levels and grounds, hence, the question remains as to what is the absolute form, attribute and *vṛtti* (nature of movement) of a given substance. We proceed in a gradual series of steps of knowledge and total *prajñāna* comes about at the ultimate step. That is the primary meaning of the word *veda*. The vision of essence that is attained when one reaches the level of total *prajñā* makes us realise *what is satyam* and what is *ṛtam.*

There is no limitation of direction, space and time in the *brahman* that is *satyarūpa* because they pertain to movement. Hence, the distinction of light and darkness does not come about until two-fold manifestation in the form of *satyam* and *ṛtam* takes place. The manifestation of *ṛtam* and *satyam* could be viewed in the following equations:

ṛtam	=	*satyam*
rātri (darkness)	=	*prakāśa* (light)
vāyu (air)	=	*vyoma* (ether)

gati (movement)	=	*jñāna* (knowledge)
ākāśa (space)	=	*prakāśa* (light)
samudra (sea)	=	*arṇava* (ocean)
pratyaya (suffix)	=	*prakṛti* (root)

Satyam cannot be limited to *vyoma* (either) or *vāyu* (air), but when it gets paird with *ṛtam* then there is no constraint in its being reflected as *vyoma* or *vāyu* or other elements.

Tapas occupies an important position in the *mantra* cited in the very beginning of this paper and it needs some explantaion. *Tejas* becomes *tapas* when it gets kindled. The letter *pa* in *tapas* is labial. The lips have a two-fold movement — one of opening up and the other of closing in. It represents the 'cosmic value' that discharges the function of *saṁkoca* (contraction) and *prasāra* (expansion). Hence, the basic movement of creation is embodied in the letter *pa*. The letter *ta* in *tapas* is dental. That which is cut or split by the tooth is either covered in the form of *rātri* (darkness), or illumined in the form of *āviḥ* (light). When the process of division begins in creation from the state of the undivided whole, then it proceeds in a movement analogous to the lips or tortoise (*kūrma*). This movement of tortoise can be visible at any point in creation in the form of contraction and expansion. This process of manifestation from the unmanifest gets gradually merged in the unmanifest.

The last letter of *tapas* is *s* which is also dental. This also takes the form of *visarga* and signifies that the act of cutting or splitting is not only a possibility but has really happened and is happening.

Whatever is contained in the undivided or unmanifest is like all the *saṁskāras* or impressions that lie latent in us during deep sleep (*suṣupti*). The content of the unmanifest gets arrayed in the universe after its components get separated in the process of manifestation just as it happens in the case of our impressions when we come back from deep sleep to a state of awakening. The letter *s* and its transformation into *visarga* represents this state of separation and diffusion. Thus, the three letters of *tapas* represent the inside picture of cosmic emergence.

Tapas is the basic effort and form of the manifestation of Existence, Cognition and Bliss from the basic Cause. The vision of cosmicity in acosmicity is made polssible by *tapas*. The undivided bliss that is at the root of the universe as its seed and has been described in the *Taittirīya Upaniṣad* as the source of the Beginning, Sustenance and Dissolution of all beings, is the same as *tapas*. Thus, *tapas* is the determination, strength and effort of the basic substance for manifestation. The basic cause itself is *tapas* in the form of determination, strength and effort.

Words like *tapas, ṛtam* and *styam* are not arbitrary symbols of substances or processes. Each one of them is a specific '*prāṇika* function'. Each one of them does not only have a specific connotation but has also 'a dynamic creative import and impetus', just as each one of the formulae and equations in mathematics and science has an index or sign of operation.

Ṛtam in Indian music

The discovery or establishment of *ṛtam* in music runs into the following channels — (i) intervals, (ii) melodic organisation, (iii) temporal element, (iv) compositional and improvisational forms, (v) conventions of performance, and (iv) emotive content, basic approach and criteria of excellence.

(i) *Intervals*: This has been given primary importance. The *svara, śruti, grāma, mūrchana, tāna* (by omission and permutation, i.e., change of order or sequence), *melā, thāṭa*, etc.

(ii) *Melodic organisation: jāti, rāga* (*grāma-rāga, bhāṣā-vibhāṣā — antarabhāṣā, deśīrāga, rāgāṅa — bhāṣāṅga-kriyāṅga-upāṅga, rāga-rāgiṇī*, etc.).

(iii) *Temporal element: tāla*, cyclic and linear view, *lāya, mārga*, etc.

(iv) *Compositional and improvisational forms: gītaka, dhruvā, prabandha, upohana, ālapti,* etc.

(v) *Conventions:* Varying according to time and space.

(vi) *Rasa-bhāva,* referential and non-referential streams of music, *gāndharva-gāna, mārga, deśī, dṛṣṭa-adṛṣṭa-phala, guṇa-doṣa*, etc.

Conclusion

The long process of foumulation of *ṛtam* in music in the above channels had a close link with the Vedic and Tāntrika world-view in the formative stage. This feature was very vibrant till at least the eleventh century, the time of Abhinavagupta.

In spite of all the formulations of *ṛtam* in music indicated above, the role of *pratibhā* or intuitive flash has always been given supreme importance. The rules are framed not to bind creativity, but to guide the play of the creative impulse. Freedom in creativity operates within *ṛtam* and we may refer to it as 'Chaos' if we want to do so, but really speaking, this freedom is also a part of *ṛtam.*

24

Ṛta-Saṁgīta

R. Sathyanarayana

ṚGVEDA, the earliest record of Hindu culture, views the oneness of the macrocosm from the lattice of the microcosm through several luminous cosmic concepts. One such concept is *ṛta.* This polysemantic word is used some 350 times in this Veda in nearly all its declensions and inflexions, spread over some twenty major conceptual streams. These may be briefly summarised thus:

Ṛta is the cosmic law or cosmic order which pervades and transcends the cosmos in both its macro- and micro-manifestations. It is the spatio-tepmoral substratum for all existence. The various forces and processes which define or describe the universe abide in it and are regulated, ordered and harmonised by it. It is the attractive and cohesive force which holds the cosmos together. It is the principle of continuous, directed flow, appearing in all its tidal rhythms. It is at one non-temporal, incomparable, unique, constant and immutable amidst the ceaseless flux of referential change. It is light emerging from darkness, order from choas, system from randomness. It is the rhythms and melody of creation. It is the equilibrium of individual variaton with the universal law, or individual creativity with the formly established matrix of objective canons.

Ṛta is the power which unifies the many forms of beauty in the macrocosmos as well as in the microcosmos. This *ṛta* is called *rasa* in the human quest for bliss through beauty. *Rasa,* which is *ānanda*, has a thousand streams, too:

रसो वै सः। रसं ह्येवायं लब्ध्वाऽऽनन्दी भवति। (*TaiU* 2.7)

The *Ṛgveda* employs *anṛta,* (untruth, falsity), *vṛjina* (sinful conduct and action) and *dvaya* (equivocation and hypocrisy) as antonyms of *ṛta. Ṛta* is, thus, the universeal moral law. Varuṇa and other gods not only set themselves and models of conduct by strictly obeying *ṛta,* but enforce it by positively conferring boons on those who obey it and by strictly punishing the immoral. Therefore, the individual qualifies for participating in the bliss of cosmic creation and crativity only by subordinating to, and harmonising with, the cosmic law through his own conduct. This is true of his own creative endeavour and quest for beauty.

Conceptual cognates

MYTH AND LEGEND

Ṛta is so fundamental to human thinking and feeling that it appears in many analogous forms in many disciplines in many cultures. It emerges from darkness (*tamas*) in the Vedas and from *pralaya* (deluge, chaos) in the Purāṇas (cf the legend of Manu and the Tāṇḍava dance of Śiva). In Greek mythology too, World Order was created out of Chaos (which originally connoted vacant, unfathomable space). Chaos is the father of Erebus (Darkness); he fathered, by his own sister Nyx (Lat. Nox=night), Aethr (Clear Air) and Hermes (Day). Nyx is the mother of Hypnos (Sleep) and Thanatos (Death). Thermis, 'daughter of Uranus and Gaia is the antithesis of Chaos, and signifies the Order of law and justice. According to the olympian myth, Gaia emerged from Chaos and was the mother of all things. According to the Pelasgian myth of creation, Eurynome rose from Chaos and created all things. Adrasteia, originally a Trojan Phrygian mountain divinity is the guardian of righteousness and is the avenger of wrongdoings. Eunomia is the greek divinity of heavnly order. Dike is the Greek personification of righeousness and virtue.

Anbay is a pre-Islamic divinity of South Arabia, probably cognate with the Mesopotamian Nabu and is an Oracle and the lord of justice (*dharma*). Forseti, probably the equivalent of the Friesian god Fosite, metes out *dharma* to mortals and gods alike, and presides in the shining hall Glitnir. The Sumarian god Hendursanga (corresponding to the Akkadian god of the same name) presides over the laws of the people. The ancient Egyptian god Maat is the personification of World Order, embodying the concepts of justice, truth and lawfulness. She is the daughter of Re, the creator of the world, refnut is the old Egyptian goddess of World Order. Perkunas, the Lithuanian God of thunder, rain and fertility (cf the Vedic god Indra) is the protector of Law and Justice. Răsnŭ (cf *Rājñā* Skt) is the ancient Iranian personification of righteousness and weighs the good and evil acts of people. Samaš is the Babylonian sun god and the divinity of righteousness; Yéloje (also called Pugu) is the ancient Siberian deity of the Yukagir pople and watches over the behaviour of people.

Eventually, the word Chaos came to mean in mythology a great confusion, or randomness of matter out of which the Supreme Being created all life; it is the state of things in which chance reigns supreme, nature that is subject to no law; the entirely confused, unorganised state of primordial matter which existed before the creation of distinct and orderly forms; Chaos is thus the contrast of the word cosmos.

NEGATIVE ENTROPY

Chaos is called entropy in physics and cognate disciplines. Originally arising from the second law of Thermodynamics, it refers to the degree of randomness of the molecular system, i.e., the quantity of heat energy available for doing useful work; the greater the entropy, the less useful the available energy and vice versa. It now signifies more generally the degree of disorder or randomness in a system bearing energy or information. Decreasing entropy, therefore, means more organisation and order, and, therefore, indicates life forces and processes where increasing entropy means death and disorder. All available energy streams from a system which is degenerating from a more ordered and organised state to a lesser one.

In statistical mechanics, entropy cannotes a factor or quantity which is a function of the physical state of a mechanical system and is equal to the logarithm of the proability for the occurrence of the particular molecular arrangement in that state. In communication theory, entropy is a measure of the efficiency of a system (a code or a language) in transmitting information, being equal to the logarithm of the number of different messages that can be selectively transmitted from the same set of symbols; it thus indicates the degree of initial uncertainty that can be resolved by any one message. In cosmology, it signifies the final state reached in the degradation of the matter and energy of the universe, a state of inert uniformity of component elements. It means the absence of form, pattern, hierarchy or differentiation. In culture, entropy is countracted by diversity and heterogeneity.

Thus, *ṛta* which is cosmic order, cosmic law and cosmic interconnectedness is a deterministic process, i.e., negative entropy. From a philosophic viewpoint, it is *Brahman* of the Hindu, *Dharmakāya* of the Buddhist and Tao and Chi of the Chinese.

ORDER, MUTUAL CONSISTENCY AND INTERCONNECTEDNESS

It has been mentioned above that the *ṛta*-view regards both the microcosm and macrocosm as subordinated to a cosmic law of harmony and as constituted of well-interconnected and well-ordered components. This selfsame conclusion seems being arrived at in the latest trends of such diverse disciplines as physics, biology, sociology and psychology.

At the microcosmic, subatomic level, the S-matrix theory, proposed by Geoffrey Chew some three decades ago explains the strong interactions among the subatomic particles in an attempt to bring together quantum mechanical and relativity theories. The S-matrix theory is founded on a non-reductionistic approach which is called the bootstrap philosophy according to which nature cannot be reduced to ultimate, fundamental, building units but should be viewed as a single whole in which all the component parts are mutually self-consistent forming an inter-connected web of relations and events. Nothing — particle, constant, equation, law — is regarded here as fundamental, but the property or behaviour of one component follows from those of others, near and far. The structure of the whole is wholly derived from the overall consistency of the relations among the components themselves. Thus, order, as pervading the totality of interconnectedness is now held to be the very essence of this theory, which may be stated as "Every (subatomic) particle consists of all other paricles". This is remarkabley like Abhinavagupta's explanation of the energy of consciousness in the *Parātrisikā Vivaraṇa* in the *Pratabhijñā* philosophy, *sarvam savātmakam* or the Upaniṣadic *sarvam khalv idam brahma* (*chaU* 3.14.1).

The concept of Order and its ramifications are now perceived as central to all scientific method of observation and as essential to all rational approaches to reality. This is again seen in the central role accorded to order and explicit role assumed by consciousness in the somewhat tentative but visionary theory of the Wholes and Implicate. Order proposed by David Bhom in 1980. The theory seems to explore the Order which the cosmic web of deep, non-manifest relations inhers manifestly. This latent order (the seed of *ṛta*, is called implicate or enfolded. This theory views reality structured as such that the whole is enfolded in each of its parts, again strongly reminiscent of the priniciple *sarvam sarvātmakam.* Consciousness is an essential, explicit requirement in this theory to understand the Implicate Order. Both the S-matrix theory and the Implicant Order theory regard the Universe as a dynamic web of relationships, in which order plays a key role.

Similarly, in the area of psychology, Jung has postulated that psychological patterns are mutually connected both by causal and acausal relationships. He has designated the acausal relationships between symbolic image of the mind and the events of the referential world as synchronicity. Such synchronic relations are perceived as particular instances of acausal orderedness in both mind and matter. Patterns of the mind and patterns of matter are being now thought of as reflections of each other.

Man is now being increasingly recognised in the new systems approach to psychology as an integrated whole in which the physical and psychological patterns depend on each other. The bootstrap approach is being applied more and more to the human psyche in recent deveolpments.This is yet another manifestation of *ṛta* in the mind-matter complex.

Ṛta is rhythm in a spatio-temporal continuum, cyclic when considered merely as periodic recurrence of spiral when viewed against a time co-ordinate. Such rhythms are evident in the areas of sociology and culture. Sorokin, in a detailed and momentous investigation into the history of human culture, argues that all cultural manifestations may be traced ultimately to three value systems, viz., sensate, ideational and idealist. Among these, the sensate value system is remarkably anticipated in the Cārvāka *darśana* in regarding matter as the ultimate reality, sensory perception as the only source of truth and knowledge, and all ethical laws being only relative. On the other hand, the ideational value system holds that reality transcends matter into the spirit, the source of knowledge is spiritual experience, ethical values are absolute and that justice, truth and beauty are superhuman in standard. The third value system, viz., Idealist is synthesised by the cyclical rhythms of interplay between, and harmonious blending of, the other two. Thus, reality partakes of both sensate and ideational values, integrated into a single whole; it gives rise to the highest and most sublimate balanced and integrated formulations and expressions of both and aesthetic fulfilment in art, science, technology and philosophy. Sorokin has convincingly demonstrated the rhythmic recurrences and patterns in the oscillations of these three value systems in many occidental cultures. They apply in large measure to the Hindu culture also. This is a clear manifestation of *saṇskṛit ṛta cakra.*

Saṁgīta

IN THE VEDA

The Vedic seer envisioned *ṛta* as having three inseparable aspects: *ṛta* is *satyam;* as the universal Moral Law, *ṛta* is *śivam.* It is also *sundaram*, being firmly established in splendourous beauty, manifold in its beauteous forms:

ऋतस्य दृळ्हा धरुणानि सन्ति पुरूणि चन्द्रा वपुषे वपूंषि।
ऋतेन दीर्घमिषणन्त पृक्ष ऋतेन गाव ऋतमा विवेशुः।।
—*ṚV*, 4.23.9

The Veda explicitly regards music and dance as two forms of beauty manifested by *ṛta*: *ṛta* which is the cosmic way, is identified as the high and expansive path of *gāndharva*:

अग्निर्गान्धर्वी पथ्यामृतस्याऽनेर्गव्यूतिर्घृत आ निषत्ता।
—*ṚV*, 10.80.6

It is poetic, metrical and musical:

यद्गायत्रे अधि गायत्रमाहितं त्रैष्टुभाद् वा त्रैष्टुभं निरतक्षत।
यद्वा जगज्जगत्याहितं पदं य इत्तद् विदुस्ते अमृतत्वमानशुः।।
—*ṚV*, 1. 164.23

Gāyatrī means to sing, to speak:

गायत्रेण प्रति मिमीते अर्कमर्केण साम त्रैष्टुभेन वाकम्।
वाकेन वाकं द्विपदा चतुष्पदाऽक्षरेण मिमते सप्त वाणीः।।
—*ṚV*, 1. 164.24; *AV*, 9.10.2

गायन्ति त्वा गायत्रिणो . . . —*ṚV*, 1.10.1; *SV*, 342, 134-4

The gods who are the pluralised cosmic power and are bearers of *ṛta* proclaim *yajña* which is of the nature of *ṛta,* in *sāman*s and in *chandas*;

ऋतावानावृतमा घोषतो बृहत्। — *ṚV*, 8.25.4

They sing the *sāman* of *ṛta:*

ऋतस्य सामन् रणयन्त देवाः — *ṚV*, 1.147.1

The celestial path of Uṣas is *ṛta* (*ṚV*, 1.123.91; 4.51.8; 5.80.1.4); she dances her way, baring her bosom:

आधि पेशांसि वपते नतरिवा पोर्णते वक्ष ग्येत

NOTIONS

The following notions are relevant to the discussion of *ṛta* in relation to *saṁgīta*:

1. In *saṁgītaśāstra sampradāya*, *saṁgīta* means the trilogy of *gīta* (song) *vādya* (musical instruments) and *nṛtta* (dance).

2. In the *śruti*, *ṛta* means (a) continuity of flow, (b) rhythm of periodic recurrence, (c) the substrate of all spatio-temporal manifestations, (d) harmonious coexistence of variability (at the microcosmic level of individual creativity) with conformability and subordinantion to *ṛta* (at the macrocosmic level as the universal law), (e) integrater of all forms of beauty through the principles of Truth and Auspiciousness, (f) It is the opposite of Chaos or entropy and is synonymous with Order, organisation, pattern, design, purposiveness, etc.

It may be useful in this context to recall the various meanings of design (as *rta*) in its general sense as well as with reference to art, especially music and dance; it means

(a) to plan or have in mind as a purpose

(b) to devise or propose for a specific function

(c) to create, plan or calculate for serving a predetermined end

(d) to outline or sketch in proportion for creating work of art ot to serve a pattern in the practical arts.

(e) to plan and plot out the shape and disposition of the parts and the structural components thereof

(f) to create, fashion, execute or construct according to plan

(g) to fashion a work of art

(h) deliberate, purposive planning

(i) to fashion a decorative figure or pattern

(j) the arrangement of the elements that make up a work of art; the process of selecting the means and cotriving the elements; steps and procedures for producing what will adequately stisfy some (aesthetic) need. This last menaing is especially relevant to *ṛta* in its manifestation as forms of beauty.

MUSIC ELEMENTS ANDṚTA

Music is the art of purposeive organisation of tones into patterns which are beautiful. Its appeal is twofold: in the sensuousness of the tones and rhythms and in the relational values between the patterns; in other words in their inter-dependence and conformity which is the *ṛta* principle. These values are derived through socio-cultural conditoning of a people. The response to music depends on such conditioning of the collective consciousness of the people. At the same time, it varies from person to person within such a goup because of differences in mental resources, prepardeness, taste and temperament. Such response may occur at different levels — sensuous, behavioural intellectual and aesthetic.

The principal components of music are melody and rhythm; both of these are manifestations of *ṛta* in the sense of continuous flow and of formal beauty. These function in the matrix of objective parameters such as consonance, timbre, texture, tempo, dynamics, etc., while individual expression is variable in confomity and sbordination to these. Melody is a succession of tones perceived as an entity or pattern. It may be regarded as a moving locus, within the co-ordinates of musical space and musical time. (*Ṛta* is the spatio-temporal substrate of all manifestation and is the firm integrator of all manifestataions of formal beauty). Melody patterns into phrases (*varṇālaṅkāras*) each leading to the next such that there is contiuity and structural unity, the relational values adding up to a consistent dynamic whole (*tāna, mūrchanā, krama, ṭhāya, jāti, rāga*). Intra-structural and interstructural continuity is maintained by *gamaka* (aethetically pleasing displacement of *svara* from its notmal position) which also confers contextual personality and flow on the *svara*. In a limited way, *gamaka* is the bootstrapper of the *rāga* in Indian music. The individual character of the melodic form is developed through the objective sonant parameters, viz., *vādi*, *smvādi*, *anuvādi* and *vivādi* each taking individual values and relationships for a given *rāga*.

The melodic form derives its structural unity through the principles of recurrence and variation in different ways at different levels. Differernt parts of it have their own affective correlates which build-up aesthetic tension, expectation, their resolution into surprise, restfulness, etc. The aesthetic locus builds-up various levels of tension as it moves and is finally resolved to rest.

Rhythm is *ṛta* in the sense of (a) orderly movement (b) cyclic or spiral recurrence (c) the principle of organisation and design which regulates the durations of tones, body movements, colours, shade, motifs, balance, groupings and symmetrical proportions in the various arts. It is inhered in the principle of creation and creativity and is, therefore, a cosmic law. This is reflected in the microcosm as biocycles and biorhythms as well as cycles of desire and fulfilment, in fact, of life and death themselves. It is illustrated in every movement of every subatomic paracycle, the atoms, molecules and macromolecules. It is reflected in the macrocosm as movements of the sun and the stars, the earth, moon and the other planets, the tides and the seasons, etc. Rhythm renders time dynamic and we organise our preception of time by means of rhythm. In music, it pervades words, *svaras*, *tāla* and *laya*. *Tāla* is the organisation of musical time into fixed quantity, fixed order and disposition of accents, etc. Individuation is accomplished through as bring individual values to these and through *laya* (tempo). Rhythmic organisation in Indian music proceeds in terms of measure of musical time (*tāla āvartta*) organisation of time values within this measure (*aṅga*) speed of the measures (*laya* and *kalā*), relative speed (*kalā, mārga*), grouping (*jati, jāti, gati*) and corresponance to actual time (*kāla*). Among these, *laya* stimulates of simulates mood, tension, restfulness, agitation, vigour, gaiety, etc., depending on its speed and structure. Thus, it indicates not only the gait of music but also its character to some extent. Musical time is much more elastic than physical time. It seems to be rooted in inner time and is thus amenable to subjective variation and individual creativity. Timbre is an aural analogue of colour. It is a characteristic of frequency, its experience in aural and visual perceptions have cognate relations. Timbre helps in focusing our musical experience. Here again classification of instrumental sound and of singing voice are based on objective criteria and provide for individual variation. Dynamics, like tempo, also stimulates or simulates mood, tension, restfulness, agitation, vigour, gaiety, etc. It is determined by the caste, understanding and iterpretation of the performer and by the limitations of the medium. Both tempo and dynamics contribute considerably to the expressiveness of music.

MUSICAL FORM

As Arnold Schoënberg says, musical form is the organisation of a piece which helps the listener to keep the idea in mind to follow its develpment, its growth, its elaboration, its fate. Śārṅgadeva declared, *prabandha* (musical form) is a dynamic organisation — *prabandha puruṣa* — endowed by the composer with eyes, hands and feet. A good musical form aims at a balance between opposites; unity and diversity, symmetry and asymmetry, movement and pause, activity and rest, Recurrence and variation is basic to musical form. Repetition caters to our need for security and stability of the familiar and fixes the material in our mind as point of reference. Variation helps sustain interest and caters to our need for change. The interaction between these confers distinctiveness on a music form. This is true of all art forms. Melody, rhythm, tempo, texture, timbre and dynamics and other elements confluence in musical forms realise their interrelations and collectively give a feeling of unity, direction and distination. It is only then that the form becomes satisfying and covincing. Each of these elements takes on a particular mould or mode and is woven in a specific way into a dynamic and self-consistent web of interactions and interrelations, which is unique to each form, even like the features which are assembled into a distinct face and to which each conforms and is subordinated.

All form is governed by an important principle of design, viz., unity in variety. Too much rigidity in unity leads to monotony and too much variety, to Chaos. This principle is realised through coherence which is conditioned by perceptual grasp, and through interest which is conditioned by pleasure. Pleasure in turn is — at least partly — conditioned by intelligibility. Unity (in variety) is served by other principles such as the dominance (of a small number of themes to which other themes are hierarchically related), mutual consistency (of such themes) and balance, i.e., appropriate proportion between the parts and restfulness). On the other hand, variety (in unity) is served by the principles of thematic variation (*saṅgati* in Karnataka music), contrast (introduction of a new or different theme as a foil) and rhythm.

A musical form or archetypal composition may be regarded as a generic strucutral pattern in which the criteria of formal design are satisfactorily fulfilled. It consists of one or more segments (or movements) each being built-up of a motif which is enlarged into a theme by developmental methods. Many individual compositions of the same musical system are patterned after this.

The sung word is ubiquitous in Indian music. It dominates all vocal music except *rāgālāpana* and *tāna*. Here also, nonsensic, carrier syllables have a part to play. Barring a few instances in Hindustani music, nearly all formal repertoire in instrumental music is fashioned after vocal music in India and is recognised in textual tradition also. The sung word plays a significant role for two reasons; vocal or instrumental articulation of melody and rhythm is strongly influenced by the syllabic content. Secondly, the emotional, poetic or lyrical content of the words strongly influences the *gamaka, kāku* and dynamics of the melody. So much so, music becomes subsurvient or subordianate to the purpose and purport of the word in word dominant (*mātupradhāna*) songs. Metrical rhythm plays a similar but less influential part in music composed for words.

STYLE

Closely related to form is style in all expressional modes, aesthetic or otherwise. Style is the characteristic manner of presentation of a musical work. It is the totality of the devices and procedures, peculiarities and proclivities of the composer and of the performer in the matter of melody, ryhthm colour, form and texture. Style also means the characteristic manner of collective presentation of a music of definite, historical era, or epoch representaing the thinking, feeling, attitude, goals and ideals of the period in its total reaction to the aesthetic, ethical, religious, philosophical, social and cultural environment.

In a generic sense, style also refers to type (Hindustani, Karnataka) form (*dhrupad*, *khyāl*, *ṭhumrī*), medium (*sitāra*, *saroda*), function (classical, light classical, folk, jazz), individuals and nation. Such national width gives rise to some ambiguity or overlap. It embraces all the factors which have a bearing on the grammar, syntax, idiom, and rhetoric. Style is an hierarchical expression in the sense of individual variation, functioning in an interconnected, interdependent web of collective expression in the context of beauty.

Musical style is a more or less complex system of sound — rhythm relationships understood and performed by a music community under the following conditions:

(i) Only some sounds or basic sound combinations are possible in the system.

(ii) Such sounds may have multiple contextual values within defined limits.

(iii) Combinations of phrases of such sounds may be made only in certain ways.

(iv) The above three conditions involve probabilistic relationships which prevail within the given musical system.

(v) Such probabilistic relationships are functions of the context within a musical form in particular, as well as within the style system in general.

PROBABILITY-DETERMINISM

Musical experience oscillates between probability and determinism. The psychostylistic conditions mentioned above (iv, v) emphasise the role of probability in the musical process. Early in this presentation, entropy (and, hence, *ṛta* by contrast) has been interpreted in terms of satistical mechanics and information theory. Musical progression (melodic or harmonic) is a stochastic process (a process involving a random variable, i.e., a system in which a sequence of elements (e.g., tone and rhythms), is generated according to certain probabilities). Uncertainty is major factor in musical communication; the nature of musical style is probabilistic, music progression is a Markoff chain or process (a stochastic process in which the probabilities depend on the previous elements). These are echoes of information theory in music. As the progression (sequence of tones and rhythms) become longer, i.e., as the music unfolds more and more, the probability of a particular conclusion (*nyāsa* and its subvarieties) increases, i.e., the uncertainty (which is systemic in music) decreases. Since music is an artificial, i.e., man-made system, the tendency towards maximum certainty is overocome with designed uncertainty, introduced by the composer or performer in the form of deviation, delay or ambiguity (*anuvādi*) and tension (*vivādi*), as the pattern moves towards completion.

However, as music moves through such a haze of probabilities, it also establishes, besides expressing sensuousness and affect, certain norms through the interrelations, and interdependences (obtaining among its units or unitary combination) which are characteristic of its nature, grammar, idiom and syntax. Even amidst the prevalence of probability, the meaning of any term or series of terms (tone-rhythm or its series) depends on its relationships with all other terms possible within the sytle system.

Principles of pattern perception in music are embodied in general or universal laws (*saṁgīta ṛta*) such as the laws of good continuation of melody and rhythm, the law of Präganz (as a consequence of which memory supplies the ellipses in irregularity, incompleteness , asymmetry, etc., in the whole work or in its parts), laws of melodic and rhythmic completion and closure, of melodic progression, of structural gaps, of saturation, of return, etc. In Indian music, the laws of melody are embodied topographically through the ten tonal nuclei called *rāgadaśaprāṇa*s. Similarly, the laws of rhythm are embodied through the ten temporal modalities called *tala daśaprāṇa*s. Such laws are more or less common to all evolved systems of music and are only particular manifestations of *ṛta* — the law of cosmic harmony and rhythm.

Art is a language of symbols, a language of emotions transcending the constraints of reason. Let me, therefore, cease to speak of ratiocination through the Sciences but instead, make this presentation a statement of my credo: *ṛta* is cosmic music and cosmic dance because like these arts, it manifests harmony, order, balance, symmetry and law emerging out of Chaos. My distinguished and learned colleagues have generated many seminal concepts of *ṛta* in their illuminating discourses. Let me now try to show how Indian music and dance enshrine these concepts besides being modes of *upāsanā*, of *sādhanā*. For, the ultimate goal of these arts as well as of *ṛta* is *ānanda*. This is achieved at the level of *brahmāṇḍa* (macrocosm) as that *rasa*: रसो वै सः. It is achieved at the level of microcosm (*piṇḍāṇḍa*) when this selfsame *rasa* proliferates on earth into a thousand streams in which man bathes and emerges pure: तस्मिन्त्सहस्रशाखे। नि भगाहं त्वयि मृजे। (*TaiU* 1.4) Music and dance are two major streams among them. The individuated *rasa* manifests in many foms of beauty in the individual: पुरूणि चन्द्रा वपुषे वपूंषि (*ṚV*, 4.23.9) according to his/her *saṁskāra*. However, it always culminates into *viśrāntī* (repose); then this *rasa* becomes that *rasa*. In music, *ānanda* is of the form of cosmic sentient energy (*caitanya*) and is called *nādabrahman*:

चैतन्यं सर्वभूतानां विवृत्तं जगदात्मना।
नादब्रह्म तदानन्दमद्वितीयमुपास्महे ।।
— सङ्गीतरत्नाकरः, 1.3.1

In dance, *ānanda* is the eternal manifestation of the king of Dancers — Naṭarāja — during his *ānandatāṇḍava*.

In the context of the Physical Sciences, *ṛta* emerges as the dynamics of configuration, as the joining of configuration to configuration. Such dynamism is movement. This is *ṛta*. Music is the process of *varṇa* or *gānakriyā*, i.e., melodic kinesis. Configurations of sound and rhythm occurring in the four *varṇālaṁkāra*, viz., *sthāyī, ārohī, avarohī* and *sañcārī* are progressively and consistently joined to catch other to generate larger and more complex melodic configurations called *sthāyas*. These are further joined and ordered into segments called *svasthānas*, being articulated by the law of melodic activity and of pause and patterned by rhythms. They are further governed by the principles of balance, harmony or sonance and symmetry. They are then organised into a whole by the law of melodic kinesis which is implicit in the ten vital elements of *rāga* called *daśaprāṇa*. Both the configurations and their joining occur at different structured levels, viz., the three registers. The final result is an interconnected, interdependent, dynamic and vibrant whole. It is a configuration of configurations, a relationship of relationships, the meaning of a series of individual meanings. This is the mathematical meaning of *ṛta*. In Indian music, this is called *rāga* in melody and *tāla* in rhythm; their combined organisation into a finite predetermined form is called *prabandha*.

Corresponding to this, dance is the movement of the body beautiful: चन्द्रा वपुषे. Activity and pause occur in *cārī* and *sthānaka* repectively. Dynamic configurations of head, glances, lips, shoulders, torso, arms, elbows, hands, fingers, waist, hips, thighs, knees, legs, feet and toes, operating in the kinematics of *cārī*, *bhramarī* and *maṇḍala* are joined to each other to generate complex configurations of *karaṇa*s; these are joined to give further configurations of *aṅgahāra*s in many different spatio-temporal designs. Interconnected, interdepedent, dynamic and articulated in movement and stillness, the lower configurations are joined to yield higher configurartions, according to the principles of harmony, balance, symmetry, recurrence and variation. These are organised according to the law of unities and culminate into meaning of meanings which, here, is *rasa*.

The *bhramarī* and *maṇḍala* of the dancer sysmbolise the journey of the *jīva* in the expanse of existence, gyrating and revolving in the cycles of birth and death, in the centrifugal and centripetal forces of *māyā* round the *ātman*: एष पुरुषो माया परिभ्रामितः। *Saṁkara Bhagavat pāda*, *Dakṣiṇāmūrti-stotram*. The *bhramarī* and *maṇḍala* are analogous repectively to the axial spin of the electron and of the planets and to the circular or elliptical orbitals of the electron and the planets in the atom or star systems in the microcosm and macrocosm respectively.

Ṛta manifests in the physical world as the law of octaves in the behaviour of the chemical elements and to the homology of the compounds of carbon and silicon. This amounts to regeneration at a higher level — vertical recurrence — with a constant increment of amplitude. Spiritual ascent of the *jīva* to divinity in terms of incarnation and reincarnation through cycles of birth is similar to this. Music symbolises this not only in the law of octaves but also in the cycles of the fifths, fourths and even of the third. The locus of the individual soul in its ascent is marked with vertical recurrences (*ūrdhvasparśa*), progressive donation of experiential residue (*saṁskāra*) to the next birth (*saṁskārapradāna*) and progressive shedding of earlier phases (*niṣkāsa*).

Abhinavagupta has shown an amazing parallel to this in the locus of the moving *śruti* in which maturity to *svaratva* is realised at several levels of cyclicity (or spirality) resulting in both the diversity and identity of *svaratva*. The vertical journey of the *svara* is marked with such recurrent diversity and unity in both quality and quantity. This leads to the realisation of the *rāga* when the moving *svara* incarnates by contrived order as *vādi*, *saṁvādī* and *anuvādī* and by contrived chaos as *vivādī*. In dance, vertical recurrence is symbolised by *utplutibhrāmarī*.

Ṛta appears in mathematics as beauty of numbers in simple ratios. This is realised in music as *svara* relationships in the scales revealing such ratios, e.g., pythogorean scale and the *vīṇā* keyboards obtained by Rāmāmātya, Paṇḍarīka Viṭṭahala, Hṛdayanārāyaṇa, Locana and Ahobala as well the *śuddhasvara* scale (theoretical standard) expounded by Bharata and others in India.

Ṛta is cosmic rhythm. It is the cosmogenic force which emanated from the drum of *Naṭarāja* when he concluded his cosmic dance. Musical sound organised into patterns by the rhythm became word-sound and from this emerged all creation:

नृत्तावसाने नटराजराजो ननाद ढक्कां नवपञ्चवारम्।
उद्धर्तुकामः सनकादिसिद्धान् एतद्विवमर्शे शिवसूत्रजालम्।।
— *माहेश्वरसूत्राणि, नन्दिकेश्वरकारिका*

These patterns were cosmogenic, aphoristic, auspicious formulae: *Śivasūtras*. All rhythm is comprehended and systematised by *tāla* which is both definitive and distinctive only to Indian music and dance. It is so-called because it establishes a common temporal substrate, i.e., *tāla* for existence and is function of melodic and dance events. Through simultaneity and successivity these may be located and measured exactly in time. All the aspects of sound and movement in these arts are summarised into ten vital elements called *prāṇa*s (as in *rāga*), *laya* (rhythm) is foremost among these. Temporal rhythm, which appears as the cyclicity (or spirality) of the compression and expansion of the universe is essence of the *catur-yuga* concept in India.

Because *ṛta* is the principle of cosmic creation, it is *yajña*. This is clucidated in the *puruṣa-sūkta* of the *Ṛgveda*. Both music and dance are intimately connected with *yajña* in the Veda and are, indeed, called Veda itself. Singing/dancing/acting is the *yajña-kriyā*, its performer the *kartṛ* and *rasa* the *yajñaphala*. The *dakṣiṇā* given to the *sahṛdaya* is both guaranteed (*niyatāpti*) and regulated (*niyantritāpti*). It is both direct and immediate in the form of *rasa*. It cleanses both performer and connoisseur by catharsis because it transforms by depersonalisation and universalisation (*sādhāraṇīkaraṇa*). Dance is a peaceful, visual *yajña*: शान्तं क्रतुं चाक्षुषम् (कालिदासः *मालविकाग्निमित्राम्*, 1.4); music is *nādayajña*. The sentient offers both himself/herself and the insentient in order to ascend to divinity: स्वर्गकामो यजेत. In turn, both receive the fruit in the form of the rhythm of life which is expressed as beauty in various forms.

Man in sentient. He has to some extent the free will to shape his own destiny. He is bracketted between the insentience of microcosm of the electron and the insentience of the macrocosm of the expanding universe. Through insentient, both are governed by the sentient *ṛta* through order and harmony. Their obedience to *ṛta* has a message to man whose sentience is enveloped by insentience — he needs a universal language for communication and discourse. In these days, when the bogie of literacy is predominant, nothing less than a message which would embrace even the pre-language cultures of the tribes and aborigines would suffice. The immedicacy of its appeal should spring from intimate familiarity and universal beauty. Such a message can radiate from what better sources than music and dance? For, they are ubiquitious, i.e., *uddhura jagadgītaṁ* (*सङ्गीतरत्नाकरः*, I.1) and auspicious, i.e., *śaṁkaram* (*ibid.*). They are *śaṁkaram* because they enable man to fulfil his moral duty (*dharma*), which is enjoined on him by the Moral Law which is *ṛta*. Both music and dance are more than mere panderers to sensuous pleasure: they are time-honoured and tested instruments for practising the Moral Law. For, is not whole of India — east, west, north or south — the only country in which all her saints were singers and all her greatest singers were saints?

This is so because the very first issue of the Moral Law is that of ownership and of sharing. Music and dance are the cultural property of the collective consciousness of a people both may be freely shared by all the individuals without greed or conflict, bridging the gulf between the haves and the have notes; they are perhaps the best sources of pleasure and joy which are shared by giver or receiver alike with enthusiasm and without reservation.They are, therefore, excellent social integrators.

Integration and collectivity are grandly symbolised on a cosmic scale in yet another way in the context of *ṛta*. Astrophysics has shown that the entity matter-energy of the galaxies has a tendency to collectivity, i.e., patterned distribution and concentration in space. This is known as CAF, and is the consequence of cosmic rhythm. It corresponds amazingly to the figure of the dancing Naṭarāja, as indeed shown by Fritjof Capra in his Tao of Physics. Is this a coincidence?

Order is the perception of a pattern among the Chaos of sense data. This consitutes meaning. All existence, all life, all beauty, all art — in fact, *ṛta* is an oscillation: oscillation between creation and chaos, between involution and evolution, between referential and non-referential consicousness, between intuitive insight of creativity and its grammatical articualtion in *śāstra*, between the *asti-bhāti-priyam* of the *jīva* and the *sat-cit-ānanda* of *brahman.*

Man oscillates through the music and dance of the electron and of the galaxies. *Ṛta* teaches him his place therein and teaches how to live.

THE SONG

Music is the symbolic song of *ṛta*; its form embraces process; the interrelations are derived from interactions, which build together a mutually consistent, harmonious, vibrant whole. It inifies polar opposites by oscillation. Its meaning and purpose are not reducible to fundamental units, but may be understood only through the mutual relevance and interdependence of its parts. The whole song is a gestalt. Not only its tones but also the overtones contribute to the appeal — sensuous and sublime. Its rhythms are manifested in the microcosms and macrocosms of both the sentient and the non-sentient. Its continuous flow bridges the infinitesimal and the eternal in time. This song of *ṛta* glimpses the Infinite through the lattice of the Finite.

A song of the saint Tyāgaraja becomes specially relevent to us.

शोभिल्लु सप्तस्वरसुन्दरूल भजिंपवे मनसा। प।
नाभिहृत्कंठरसनानासादुलयंदु। अ.प.।

धरऋक्सामादुललो। वरगायत्रिहृदयमुन।
सुरभूसुरमानसमुन – शुभत्यागराजुनीयेड़।। च।

Let us contemplate the vision of the Vedic seer:

त्रतस्य हृळहा धरुणानि सन्ति पुरुणि चन्द्रा वपुषे वपूंषि ।

All human endeavour is summarised by the Hindu into *dharma*, *artha*, *kāma* and *mokṣa*. *Ṛta* is universal *dharma; artha* and *kāma* could conform to and to subordinated to *dharma*. Universal *dharma* is the *ṛta* of the subatomic particles and molecules of the referential world, of his own biological world and of the galacteal comments of the macrocosm. Thus, the *ṛta* of the sentient *piṇḍāṇḍa* breacketted and embraced on both sides by the *ṛta* of the microcosmic and macrocosmic *brahmāṇḍa*. Emancipation and Enlightenment result on man accomplishing *dharma, artha* and *kāma* when his spirit oscillates between, and unifies, the two *ṛtas*.

References

Barton, Owen, *Worlds Apart*, Wesleyan University Press, Connecticut, 1963.

Bohm, David, *Wholeness and Implicate Order*, Routledge & Kegan Paul, London, 1980.

Bohm, Dravid & Hailey, B., on the Intuitive Understanding of Nonlocality as Implied by Quantum Theory: *Foundations of Physics*, Vol. 5, 1975; pp. 93-109.

Chew, G.F., 'Bookstrap': A Scientific Idea?: *Science*, vol. 61, pp. 762-5, May 23, 1968.

———, "Hadron Bootstrap :Triumph of Frustration?" *Physics Today*, Vol. 123, pp. 23-8, Oct. 1970.

Copra, Fritjof, *The Tao of Physics*, Bentam Books, New York, London, 1984.

Idem, *The turning Point*, Flamingo Edition, Fontana Peperbacks, London, 1990.

Delbruck, Max, *Mind From Matter*? Blackwell Sciencetific Publications, Oxford, 1984.

Heisenberg, W. *Physics and Beyond*, Herper & Row, New York, 1971.

———, *Physics and Philosophy*, Harper and Torchbooks, New York, 1958.

Matnaga, *Brihaddeśī*, ed. Premlatha Sherma, *Kalamulasastra Series*, Vols 8, 10, Indira Gandhi National Centre for the Arts & Motilal Banarasidass, New Dehi, 1992, 1994.

Needham, J., *Science and Civilization in China*, Cambridge University Press, Cambridge, England, 1956.

Sarngadeva, *Sangitaratnākara*, Adyar edn. by S. Subrahmanya Sastri, Adyar

Sathyanarayana, R., *Nihsankahṛdaya*, comm. on Sarngadeva, *op. cit.*, Prasaranga, Mysore University, Mysore, 1967.

Sorokin, Pitirim, A., *Social and Cultural Dynamics*, 4 vols, American Book Co., New York, 1937-41.

The Contributors

Chaturvedi, Badrinath : Formerly a member of the Indian Administrative Service (IAS). Was a Homi-Bhabha-Fellow during 1971-3 and a visiting Prof. at the Centre for Policy Research (CPR), New Delhi 1990-2. Publication: *Dharma, India and World Order*. Andrew's Press, Edinburgh, 1993. During 1985-6 he was invited by a Swiss Intercultural Foundation to spend a year in Europe to work on the history of the Western encounter with India.

Chakrabarti, Arindam : Ph.D. Philosophy, University of Oxford. Currently, Professor of Philosophy, East-West Centre, University of Hawai, USA.

Chandra, Lokesh : Scholar of languages and culture of South-East Asia and Far East. Publications: *The Esoteric Iconography of Japanese Mandals; A New Tibeto-Mongol Pantheon; Sanskrit Texts from the Imperial Palace at Peking and Buddha in Chinese Woodcuts.*

Chung, Tan: Formerly Prof. in the Centre for East Asian Languages, Jawaharlal Nehru University, New Delhi. Taught *Imperialism in China* at the University of Delhi. Author of *China and the Brave New World;* and *A Study of the Opium Wars*. Currently a consultant at IGNCA, New Delhi.

Desai, Devangana : Art Historian, specialises in the study of Temple Art and Ancient Indian Terracottas. She is the author of *Erotic Sculpture of India, A Socio-Cultural Study* and *Khajuraho Temples: Religion and Images.* Visiting Professor of the Ananthacharya Indological Research Institute, Bombay and Chairman of the Museum Society of Bombay.

Jitatmananda (Swami) : B.Sc. M.A.; Head of Ramakrishna Mission School of Foreign and Indian Languages, Hyderabad; Lectures delivered on Vedanta Philosophy and Modern Science and Message of Swami Vivekananda. Publication: *Swami Vivekananda. Prophet and Pathfinder* (1985).

Joshi, M.C. : Specialisation in early historical archaeology and Indian art including Indo-Islamic architecture. Carried out archaeological investigations in major parts of north India and excavated some historical sites including Mathura, New Delhi, Patna. Contributed number of original research papers on Indian archaeology, Indian art including Indo-Islamic architecture, Indian Culture, etc. Publications: *A Monograph on the Monuments at Dig; Sakta Tantras in the Context* *of History* (in Hindi); *King Chandra of Mehrauli*; *Taj Mahal* (with Amina Okada). He has been former Member-Secretary IGNCA, New Delhi.

Khanna, Madhu : Ph.D. in Sanskrit Studies with a specialisation in Tantra from the University of Oxford (1986). She has been a Homi-Bhabha-Fellow-in-residence at the IGNCA, New Delhi from 1991-3. Her publications include: *The Tantric Way* (co-author); *Yantra*: *The Tantric Symbol of Cosmic Unity and The Sricakra as Goddess Tripurasundari*, *A Psychocosmic Paradigm of Self Awareness* (in Press). At present, Associate Professor, IGNCA, New Delhi.

Malik, Aditya : M.A. in Ancient Histroy, Culture and Archaeology, Pune University. Ph.D. University of Heidelberg, Germany. Publication: *Das Puskara Mahatmya* 1993, New Delhi, 1993. Currently teaches in Dept. of Philosophy & Religious Studies at University of Canterbury, Christchurch, Newzealand.

Malik, Keshev : Poet and critic, former editor *Indian Literature* monthly, and literary editor *Thought*, a weekly. His latest volume of verse (1986) was entitled, *Shapes in Feeling Plaster*. At present art critic for the *Times of India*, New Delhi. Has published eight volumes of poetry, one of prose and edited five anthologies of poetry in translation from Indian languages.

Malik, S.C. : Formerly at the M.S. University of Baroda and at I.I.A.S. Shimla, he is a U.G.C. Research Scientist and Professor of Anthropology. Apart from several papers in international journals, his works are: *Understanding Indian Civilisation — A Framework of Enquiry*; *Indian Civilisation: The Formative Period — A Study of Archaeology as Anthropology and Others*. His recent book is *Modern Civilisation: A Crisis of Fragmentation*.

Malville, John McKim: Professor of Astrophysics, University of Colorado. Author of books: *A Feather for Daedalus: Explorations of Science and Mythology*, *The Fermenting Universe: Myths of Eternal Change*, *Prehistoric Astronomy of the Southwest* and some sixty publications in astrophysics.

Misra, Vidya Niwas : Sanskrit scholar, Linguist and hermeneutist and a creative writer. His works on Panini and Mahabharata have been highly commended. He is at present preparing a glossary of key terms in Indian art and a Vedic Source book of Arts for IGNCA and working on Panini's metalanguage and its application on computation.

Mukhopadhyaya, Satkari : Specialises in Sanskrit learning. Studies Shastras. Formerly Chief Editor for research publications in the Chowkhamba Sanskrit Series, Varanasi. Served as the Librarian in the US Library of Congress Office in New Delhi (1976-85). Formerly worked as a coordinator (Kala-Kosha Division) in IGNCA, New Delhi.

Rahman, A. : Graduated from the Aligarh Muslim University, Aligarh. Degree in Biochemistry from the Indian Institute of Science, Bangalore. Founder-Director of the National Institute of Science, Technology and Development Studies (CSIR); President of the International Council for Science Policy Studies of ICSU. His Publications include: six books, ten monographs and over a hundred special papers, many of which have been translated in Polish, Russian, Rumanian, French, German and Chinese.

Rajan, Chandra : M.A. English Literature, St. Stephen's College, Delhi University. Taught at University of Western Ontario, Canada. Currently teaching at the Lady Sri Ram College, Delhi University. Author of books: *Winged Words*, an anthology of English Poetry 1967; *Kalidasa*, The Loom of Time, 1989. *The Panchtantra of Vishnu Sharma* 1993 and the *Vetala Panchavinsatika of Sivadasa* 1995.

Ravindra, Ravi : Professor and Chair of Comparative Religion. Professor of International Development Studies and Adjunt Professor of Physics at Dalhousie University, Halifax Canada, 1977. Member Institute of Advance Studies in Princeton, 1978, Member of Institute of Advanced Studies, Shimla. Recipient of several awards and grants. Author of more than a hundred papers on Physics, Philosophy and Religion.

Sahni, Varun : Assistant Professor, Inter-University Centre for Astronomy and Astrophysics (IUCAA) Pune, (1987-90), Postdoctoral fellow at the Canadian Institute of Astrophysics (CITA) and the Department of Physics, University of Toronto, Canada 1985-7, Research Associate with Professor P.C.W. Davies at the University of New Castle-upon Tyne, U.K. (1988-9), Visiting Fellow, Institute of Astronomy, Cambridge, U.K. Authored and co-authored more than a dozen articles and conference proceedings.

Saraswati, Baidyanath : M.A., Ph.D.: Formerly Prof. Department of Archaeology, North Eastern Hill University, Shillong, Meghalaya; Publications: *Contributions to the Understanding of Indian Civilisation; Kasi: Myth and Reality of a Classical Cultural Tradition: Brahmanic Ritual Tradition in the Crucible of Time*. Former UNESCO Professor and Head of Janpada Sampada Division at the IGNCA.

Satyanarayan, R. : M.Sc. (Chemistry), Ph.D. D. Litt. Exponent of the theory and practice of Shree Vidya Tantra. Noted public speaker on Indian Philosophy, Yoga, Tantra, Mantra, Advaita, Veda, Upanishad and related subjects. Published more than fifty research papers on various aspects of music and dance.

Sharma, Prem Lata : M.A. (Hindi, Sanskrit), Ph.D. *Sangeetalankara*; Vice Chancellor, Indira Kala Sangeet Vishvavidyalaya, Khairagarh, M.P.; Member, Music Audition Board of AIR; Chairman, M.P. Sangeet Natak Academy.

Publications: Critical edition of *Rasavilasa*, *Sangeet Raja*; Editor: *Chitrakavya Kautukam*, *Japasutram* (translation), *Ekalingamahatmayam*.

Singh, Ramjee : Director, Gandhian Institute of Studies, Varanasi, 1992-4; Vice-Chancellor, Jain Vishwa Bharti Institute 1980-92, Head, Department of Gandhian Thought, Bhagalpur University. Author of twenty-five books, two hundred papers and three hundred articles the world over on philosophy of religion and Gandhian thought.

Talwar, G.P. : Professor of Eminence, is the Founder Director of the National Institute of Immunology, New Delhi. He has made outstanding contribution in the field of Reproductive Immunology and in the Immunology of Leprosy. As Head of the ICMR, WHO Research and Training Centre in Immunology, he has organised a number of Training Workshops on Laboratory Method. Publications: *Immunology of Contraceptions; Text Book of Bio-Chemistry and Human Biology*; *Recent Advances in Reproduction and Regulation of Fertility, Regulation and Growth of differentiated Function in Eukaryote Cell.*

Tripathi, Gaya Charan : M.A. (Sanskrit), Agra 1959; Ph.D. on Vedic Deities, Agra 1962; D.Phil. on Vaishnava legends in the Puranas, Freiburg (Germany) 1966; D.Litt. on Vaishnava Temple ritual of Orissa, Allahabad 1986. Taught at the Universities of Aligarh, Udaipur, Freiburg, Heidelberg, Tübingen, Berlin, Leipzig and British Columbia (Vancouver). Principal, G.N. Jha Central Sanskrit Research Insitute, Allahabad 1977-2001. Published more than 20 books (mostly edited Sanskrit texts) and over 80 Research papers. At present, Prof. and Head, Kala Kosha Division, IGNCA, New Delhi.

Tripathi, K.D. : M.A. Sanskrit, Allahabad University. Formerly, Director, Kalidas Academy, Ujjain. Ex-Professor and Head Department of Dharma-Agama, Faculty of Sanskrit Learning and Theology, Banaras Hindu University.

Vatsyayan, Kapila : M.A. University of Delhi, University of Michigan; Ph.D. Banaras Hindu University: D.Litt. Rabindra Bharati University, Mount Holyoke College and University of Manipur; Padam Sri — 1990. Formerly Additional Secretary, Dept. of Culture: Secretary, Dept. of Arts, Ministry of Human Resource Development, and Member Secretary and Academic Director of the IGNCA. Books: *Classical Indian Dance in Literature and the Arts; Ramayana and the Arts of Asia; Dance in Indian Painting; The Square and the Circle of Indian Arts;* and the *Gita Govinda* (six volumes) among others.

Index